P9-DIZ-957

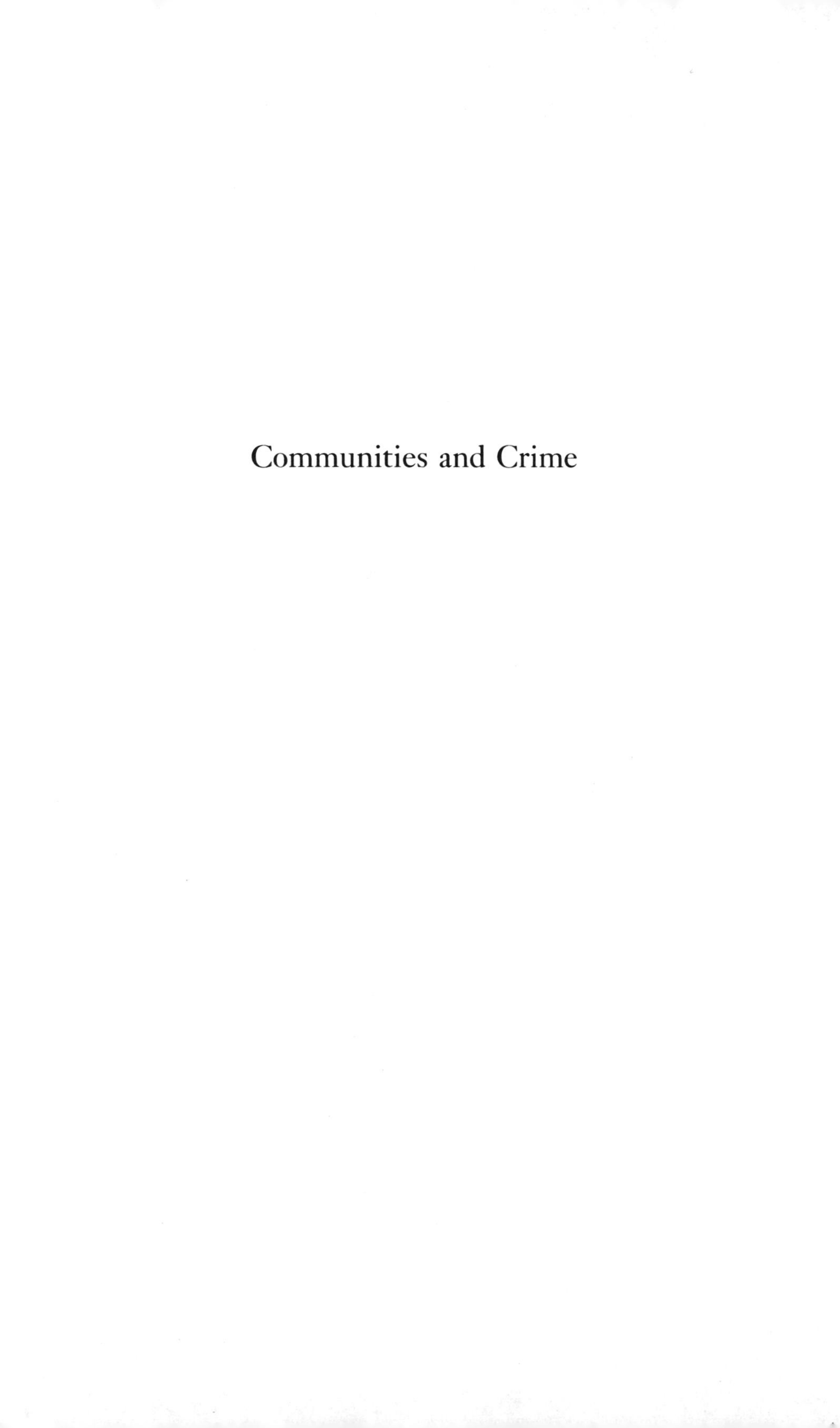

Communities and Crime

# Communities and Crime

*Edited by*
*Albert J. Reiss, Jr., and Michael Tonry*

Crime and Justice
*A Review of Research*
*Edited by Michael Tonry and Norval Morris*
*with the Support of The National Institute of Justice*

VOLUME 8

*The University of Chicago Press, Chicago and London*

This volume was prepared under Grant Number 84-IJ-CX-0011 awarded to the Castine Research Corporation by the National Institute of Justice, U.S. Department of Justice, under the Omnibus Crime Control and Safe Streets Act of 1968 as amended. Points of view or opinions expressed in this volume are those of the editors or authors and do not necessarily represent the official position or policies of the U.S. Department of Justice.

The University of Chicago Press, Chicago 60637
The University of Chicago Press, Ltd., London


Printed in the United States of America
91 90 89 88 87 86 5 4 3 2 1

ISSN: 0192-3234
ISBN: 0-226-80802-5

LCN: 80-642217



The paper used in this publication meets the minimum requirements of American National Standard for Information Sciences—Permanence of Paper for Printed Library Materials, ANSI Z39.48-1984.

# Contents

# Preface

From 1920 to 1940, a group of Chicago sociologists spearheaded one of criminology's most influential intellectual movements by drawing attention to the roles of communities in explaining crime. The pioneering figures were E. W. Burgess, Clifford R. Shaw, and Henry D. McKay. Shaw and McKay devoted their careers to documenting how crime and delinquency rates vary among communities and to speculating about ways in which the structure and organization of communities are linked to variation in crime rates. Employed by the State of Illinois in the Institute for Juvenile Research, Shaw and McKay went to considerable effort to test their theory by intervening to reorganize communities. Community organizations, epitomized by the Chicago Area Projects, became their social laboratory.

What came to be called the ecological approach to understanding crime continued into the 1940s. However, it soon gave way to research and theory that focused more on individual behavior and less on communities and that shifted attention to the roles that cultural and social structure play in shaping delinquent and criminal behavior. Still, that theory and research were grounded in understanding why communities varied so substantially in their crime rates.

For reasons that are not altogether clear, from the 1950s to the late 1970s, theory and research in criminology focused principally on trying to explain why some persons become law-breakers while others are law-abiding. Much of that research focused on "correlates" of crime, that is, factors that differentiated criminals from noncriminals.

Yet the Chicago tradition of criminology, while dormant, was not dead. The tradition was kept alive by a small cadre of Chicago-trained sociologists and researchers who had been co-workers of Shaw and McKay. And, more recently, others rediscovered the viability of that tradition quite independently. Of particular interest to one of the editors who conceived this volume was the idea that the notion of "criminal careers" of communities could enhance our understanding of crime and its causes. On exploring recent work relevant to that concept, it quickly became apparent that considerable work is again under way on communities and crime and that much of this work is not yet widely known.

Thus was the idea born to commission the volume *Communities and Crime* as part of the *Crime and Justice* series. The idea was met with enthusiasm by the editorial board of *Crime and Justice* and by the contributors to this volume. The volume itself has a history. It began with outlines for each contribution and a close working relationship between editors and contributors. Midway, when first drafts were ready, a two-day conference was held at which all the contributors and some additional researchers and practitioners were present. Each contributor presented and defended his own work and acted as reviewer of the other drafts. Following the conference, the editors drew these commentaries together to aid in final revisions of the essays that are presented in this volume.

This volume, like all the others in the *Crime and Justice* series, has been generously supported by the National Institute of Justice and its director, James K. Stewart. We appreciate that support and the recognition underlying it that first-rate scholarship is demanding—in time, money, and effort.

This is the first in a series of *Crime and Justice* volumes dedicated to specific bodies of research. Others are now in process, each with National Institute of Justice support, on family violence, prediction and classification, and drugs and crime.

Like the larger series of which they are a part, these "thematic" volumes constitute an effort to transcend disciplinary boundaries and to pull together the best of modern scholarship. Whether we succeed in these immodest efforts, our readers must judge. We hope that our readers will agree that the contributions in this volume are testimony to the vision of the early Chicago criminologists and to the vitality of the tradition that they represent.

Albert J. Reiss, Jr.
Michael Tonry

*Albert J. Reiss, Jr.*

# Why Are Communities Important in Understanding Crime?

People commit crimes. And people are crime's victims, directly in crimes of violence, indirectly when their property is taken or destroyed, more indirectly still when the property taken or destroyed belongs to their community or government or organization. Much modern criminological theory and research have accordingly attempted to understand individual patterns of criminality and victimization. What social, psychological, economic, cultural, and biological factors cause individuals to commit crimes? Why some and not others? What are the patterns of individual criminality, of individual "criminal careers"? When and why do people become criminally active? When and why do they desist? How many crimes do they commit, of what types? How can we identify high-rate offenders? How can the state, individuals, or organizations intervene in individuals' lives to prevent or curtail or deter or incapacitate involvement in crime? Why and where and when do individuals become victims of crime? Who become crime victims?

Just as many of the questions researchers and theorists ask about crime focus on individual behavior, so do the major data sources. The official statistics, victimization surveys, and self-report studies all produce information mostly, though not exclusively, about individual criminals and individual victims.

Nonetheless, our sense of personal safety and potential victimization by crime is shaped less by knowledge of specific criminals than it is by knowledge of dangerous and safe places and communities. Dangerous

Albert J. Reiss, Jr., is William Graham Sumner Professor of Sociology at Yale University.


0-226-80802-5/86/0008-0001$01.00

places sometimes identify themselves by the visible signs of crime environments such as broken windows, graffiti, vandalized property, and drawn iron gates. Still, the common way to think about safe and dangerous communities is to think of them as aggregations of law-abiding and criminal persons.

Beginning more than sixty years ago, some sociologists were puzzled by the simplicity of this argument. They called attention to the persistence of high crime rates in some communities despite substantial changes over time in the social and cultural characteristics of their residents. On documenting those changes, they turned their attention to speculating about what it was about the structure of those communities that led successive generations to turn to criminality. Although this ecological approach to investigating crime waned, and the numbers of its adherents declined for a time, it has recently been reinvigorated. The work of long-time scholars of communities has received renewed attention, and new traditions and approaches have emerged.

More recently, scholars have been puzzled by the way that the crime rates of communities change substantially over time—that is, communities like individuals can have careers in crime. Today's safe environment can become tomorrow's dangerous one. Analysts also wonder whether it is possible to reduce crime rates by changing communities rather than by trying to change people who are called criminals. These competing and complementary foci—individuals and their communities—form the basis of much contemporary theory and research about crime.

The aim of this essay is to foster the convergence of individual- and community-centered theories and research. Section I introduces two modern criminological research traditions that focus respectively on individuals as victims and offenders and on variability in community crime rates; it then demonstrates how these traditions can be linked. Section II summarizes evidence on the concentration of offenders and victims of common crimes in lower-status neighborhoods and among persons from low-status backgrounds. It also offers hypotheses to explain that concentration. Section III discusses social changes and corresponding changes in community crime rates and comments on both internal and external sources of changes. Section IV considers policy implications of current knowledge about these processes. Section V, the conclusion, argues that individual and community-centered approaches must be merged, explains why existing data sources are not adequate for research with a community focus, and outlines research strategies for effecting that merger.

## I. Competing and Complementary Theories about Crime

A crime is an event or sequence of events in time and space that violates a criminal statute. Phenomenologically, crimes are social constructions of harms; those causing them are defined as offenders who must be penalized for the injuries inflicted on others regarded as victims. There may be other parties such as witnesses. As a rule, theories about crime explain only properties of crimes and the behavior of victims and offenders. Third parties, such as witnesses, are not covered.

There are two major theoretical traditions in theory and research about crime phenomena. One tradition focuses on explaining the behavior of individuals as victims and offenders. Most commonly, these theories direct attention to only one of the parties. There are theories, for example, about what causes only some persons to behave as delinquent rather than about what causes delinquency. Others explain why some people become victims instead of what causes victimization by crime. The other major tradition centers on explaining crimes and their variation in time and space. A few theories link these two traditions by explaining either how changes in individual behavior affect variation in crime or how changes in the aggregate properties of crime affect individual behavior.

### A. *Explaining Victim and Offender Behavior*

A focal point of behavioral theories of offender behavior is the "criminal career." The key dimensions of criminal careers are their *participation*, or *prevalence* rate, that is, whether one enters a population of offenders, the *frequency* of a participant's offending, the *mix* of different crimes committed, and the *duration*, or length, of the career.

The range of crimes covered varies among different theories as do the properties of events used to test them. Some theories are more concerned with explaining participation in a delinquent or criminal career. Others explain variation in the dimensions of individual careers, for example, why some persons have higher rates of offending than others, why some careers are short and others long, or how social selection processes result in some persons being characterized as offenders and others not. These theories usually explain only why some persons commit crimes and others do not, failing to explain why the offender prevalence rates of communities and societies vary over time or among them. To the degree that these theories account for changes in aggregate offending rates over time and territory, the causes are found in changes in individual criminal career dimensions, such as changes in individual rates of offending or entry rates into criminal careers.

Attention has been drawn to biases in measurement and implementation of concepts in behavioral theories of crime. Examples are a bias toward person, rather than organizational, offender and victim measures of crime (Reiss 1982*a*, pp. 549–50), a predilection for persons as actors in common crimes, scanting organizations as actors in organizational crime (Vaughan 1983, p. xiii), and a selective emphasis on major crimes of trespass to the neglect of violations of trust (Shapiro 1984, p. 8).

Theories about victim behavior usually explain only why some persons become victims and others do not or how behavior changes because of experiences as a victim. Among the major consequences of criminal victimization attended to are fear and precautionary steps taken following victimization. Notably neglected is the relationship between victims and offenders. Victims and offenders are not distinct populations but overlap considerably; offenders frequently have high rates of multiple victimization (Singer 1981, p. 779). Just as for offender-based theories, so the primary models of victim precipitation, facilitation, vulnerability, opportunity, attractiveness, and impunity (Sparks 1981, pp. 772–77) explain only the differences in individual rates of victimization and not variation in rates of victimization in time and territory. This restriction follows in part from the person-centered bias of victim sample surveys (Reiss 1981, p. 709).

### *B. Explaining Community Variability in Crime Rates*

The second major tradition of theory and research on crime phenomena takes as its major point of departure observations about variation in crime in time and territory. Of special interest are explanations of variation among communities at one time and among communities and societies over time.

Theories about temporal changes in crime rates account for their rise and fall independent of changes in individual offending and participation rates. The causes of temporal variation generally are sought in antecedent social changes such as changes in the size, composition, and movement of a population—for example, changes in the birth rate—or changes in structure and organization—for example, changes in opportunities to commit offenses, in employment, or in the apprehension and sanctioning of violators.

Theoretical interest in temporal variation in crime rates has concentrated in recent years on *community crime careers.* Models have been developed to explain why communities experience rising crime rates at some times and falling rates at others. Somewhat analogous to models of individual criminal careers, models about community crime careers attempt to explain changes for particular communities rather than secular changes in crime rates. Early theories held that the dynamic structures of territorially organized populations accounted for changes in community crime rates. A classic example is E. W. Burgess's theory of how city growth leads to changes in the structure and composition of its local communities (Burgess 1925, pp. 47–52; McKenzie 1925, pp. 63–79). Burgess emphasized that rapid growth and population redistribution affect crime rates because they undermine local institutions and their controls; social disorganization results from the metabolic processes of growth (Burgess 1925, pp. 53–54).

Theories about the territorial distribution of crime explain variation in criminal offending and victimization among societies and communities or its subdivisions such as neighborhoods. Much of the early research on variation in community crime rates took as its point of departure that in the short run the crime rates of a community remain relatively stable despite changes in the composition of its population (Shaw and McKay 1942, pp. 146–58), even though in the long run there is considerable variation in the structure and composition of local communities in an urban area that is associated with differential rates of crime and delinquency (Shaw and McKay 1942, pp. 22–27). Much of the work of Shaw and McKay (1931, 1942) and their associates (Shaw et al. 1929) attempted to explain this seeming contradiction in terms of the social structure and organization of urban communities. They observed, for example, that there was much temporal variation in race, nativity, and nationality group delinquency rates but that these diverse groups displayed relatively similar rates of delinquency in similar social areas and that each group displayed the effect of disproportionate concentration in its respective areas at a given time. They concluded that these observations failed to sustain any contention that group characteristics cause delinquency and, consequently, that its causes must be found in their respective patterns of territorial distribution in the city (Shaw and McKay 1942, p. 156). High crime rates, they inferred, are associated with the diminished capacity of local institutions and organizations to control the behavior of residents—a condition often termed "social disorganization."

Whyte (1943) subsequently challenged this view of social disorganization by observing that lower-status neighborhoods are highly organized and that the differences among communities lie in part in the ways they organize around law-violating as well as law-abiding activity. At about the same time, Sutherland (1942) drew attention to differential social organization of communities as an explanation for differences in their crime rates: "Differential group organization . . . should explain the crime rate, while differential association should explain the criminal behavior of a person. The two explanations must be consistent with each other" (1942, p. 21).

Offenders and their victims live in relatively close proximity and are concentrated in high-crime-rate areas. This observation is consistent with others that show that offenders, on average, also have high rates of victimization (Singer 1981, pp. 781–86) and that crime rates are lower where the residential density of offenders is low. Models to account for these patterns are based on both ecological and information search and processing decision theories. The ecological models posit that offenders minimize time and distance costs in searching for victims; beginning with their residence, the search ends at the first available opportunity to commit the crime (Brantingham and Brantingham 1978). Information search and processing theories emphasize either how offenders rationally select and process information in deciding to commit a particular crime (Clarke and Cornish 1985) or how environmental and situational cues selectively affect and interpret the choice of a particular victim or criminal opportunity (Taylor and Gottfredson, in this volume). These models lack empirical testing since little research has been done on how offenders select victims or targets of their offenses (Clarke and Cornish 1985). These explanations vary in the extent to which they focus on community and organizational, as contrasted with individual, determinants in selecting criminal opportunities (Taylor and Gottfredson, in this volume). It seems doubtful, however, that individual offender decisions largely account for differences in the concentration of crime in space, given the ubiquity of criminal opportunities.

Recent research likewise demonstrates that communities may vary considerably in their structural stability over time and in the temporal stability of their crime rates. These observations raise questions of whether there are patterned changes in urban communities that explain community crime careers (Kobrin and Schuerman 1981; Bottoms and Wiles, in this volume; Bursik, in this volume; McDonald, in this volume; Schuerman and Kobrin, in this volume) and of how changes inside and outside of local communities affect the stability of their crime rates

(Bursik and Webb 1982; Bursik, in this volume; McDonald, in this volume).

What seems common to many of these explanations is that, while there are clear differences in social structure and social control among areas that vary in their crime rates, outside social and, therefore, historical changes explain how communities come to have a particular structure that creates the conditions in which crime is endemic. Just how much of that structure is a consequence of some orderly rate and pattern of change is unclear. Ecological theories generally emphasize that processes of change are orderly and incremental and that they are introduced by naturally occurring social changes, thereby scanting the role of planned social interventions.

### *C. Linking the Major Traditions*

The two major traditions on crime focus, respectively, on individual behavior and on ecological and organizational stability and change in accounting for crime. One way these traditions are linked is in explaining differences in victimization rates of individuals. The risk of victimization by crime varies among communities (Bureau of Justice Statistics 1985*a*, p. 3; Bureau of Justice Statistics 1985*b*) and even within them by place of occurrence (Bureau of Justice Statistics 1985*a*, p. 6), the clock (Bureau of Justice Statistics 1985*a*, p. 6; Hindelang, Gottfredson, and Garofalo 1978, pp. 40, 77), and the calendar. Likewise, the social location and life-style of persons affects their probability of victimization by crime. Hindelang et al. (1978, pp. 241–66) have developed a life-style-exposure model that links these sources of variation in victimization rates by demonstrating that people's risk of victimization by crime varies considerably in the course of their daily rounds. These changes in risk vary with a person's life-style and social position. Exposure to victimization changes with daily movements because aggregate risks of victimization vary by time and location. Many daily movements are not a matter of deliberate choice since there are organized routines of work and residence. Indeed individuals may be unaware of how often their risk of victimization changes during a particular day as they move from home to school or work and for leisure activities.

This linking of aggregate with individual risk explains variation in individual rates of victimization as a consequence of both aggregate risk and perceptions of aggregate risk. Perceptions of crime induce structural and compositional changes in communities that in turn affect their aggregate crime rates. Perceptions of the crime rates of communities, for example, lead law-abiding individuals to move from high- to low-crime-rate areas, often increasing the density of offenders and thereby the risk of in-movers and those who remain (Reiss 1977, p. ii; Skogan 1981, pp. 34–35; Taub, Taylor, and Dunham 1981).

Aggregate patterns of crime in communities have consequences for individual and corporate behavior in yet other ways. The dynamic processes associated with the aging and development of communities (Alschuler 1965; Taub et al. 1981; Wilson and Kelling 1982; Reiss 1983) may feed back negative images about the quality of life in an area, leading to selective changes in its population size and composition that increase its crime rate. Patterns of criminal activity likewise have considerable consequence for the quality of life in a community. Crimes often regarded as less serious, such as vandalism, littering, loitering, pandering, and prostitution, have consequences for both the actual and the perceived quality of life in an area.

The destruction of property, often by juvenile vandalism and graffiti, affects public and private space alike. Not only do public recreation, housing, school, and transportation facilities (as well as private businesses, organizations, and residences) bear the visible signs of littering, graffiti, and vandalism (Wilson and Kelling 1982), but defacement and destruction often render them useless to the community (Reiss 1982*b*, pp. 575–80).

Soft crimes such as harassment, panhandling, chronic loitering, and offensive and threatening behavior, moreover, must be dealt with in going about in public. Perhaps even more than street crime, soft crimes lead to the depopulation of organizations as well as people from central city and other business districts, particularly as they contribute substantially to fears of victimization by crime (Reiss 1985*a*, pp. 6–8).

Traditional theories generally neglect the relation of collective or corporate actions to the crime patterns in communities. Yet some clear links have been shown.

### *D. Crime Drives Resource Allocation*

A resource-dependent theory of organizations holds that organizational survival depends on an organization's capacity to mobilize resources (Pfeffer and Salancik 1978, pp. 258–62). Typically, organizations control relatively few of the resources essential to their survival. To survive they must interact with those who control those resources. For many organizations, especially communities where crime is endemic, the control of resources to cope with crime becomes a major factor in their physical and social survival. It becomes so not only because crime makes it necessary for each organization to allocate some resources to crime losses and crime prevention but also because organizations' own resources often are inadequate to deal with the costs of crime that threaten their survival.[1] Consequently, they must depend on other organizations to provide them, such as law enforcement agencies, insurance companies, and anticrime organizations.

The organizations and residents of neighborhoods and communities within large cities are especially resource dependent in dealing with crime and its consequences. Crime can determine resource allocations for their victims. Although many victims are persons, the rate of victimization is higher for corporate than for individual actors, and the mean loss for corporate actors is substantially higher (Reiss 1982*b*, pp. 549–50). In any case, corporate community losses from crime are substantial when the losses from crimes against all its property, such as schools, and recreational, transportation, and other government property, are taken into account. These losses are not spread evenly across the local communities of the municipal corporation, so compensation for such losses varies considerably among them. What is clear is that any individual or organization must allocate some of its resources to replace or compensate for losses from crime. A sizable portion of the total resources of any municipality with a high crime rate must be allocated to crime losses and crime control.

Theoretically, some crimes of theft may be regarded as transfers of ownership, with replacement costs being borne by the victim who loses the property. That victim must allocate resources to replacement or to compensate for the loss whether by insurance coverage or by direct appropriation from assets. When property is destroyed, as is often the case with community property, the community suffers an aggregate loss of value. Additionally, repair of damaged or replacement of destroyed property requires either the acquisition of additional resources or a reallocation of resources intended for other purposes. Money for teachers and learning resources, for example, may have to give way to replacing broken school windows, park benches, or public lavatories. When offenders destroy public property the victim is the public and its treasury.

Destruction of public property, then, is a collective victimization; its

[1] Set aside are the symbiotic and conflict relationships between organizations that profit from criminal activity and their host or environing communities.

consequences fall disproportionately on municipal corporations and local communities with high crime rates. Within municipalities, some communities bear disproportionately the consequences of loss and replacement. Public facilities may be unavailable for considerable periods while they are being repaired or while funds are being found for replacement. Lags in repair and replacement are visible and, by increasing fear and selective flight, may escalate crime rates.

Within any corporate community, its constituent neighborhoods or urban villages (Gans 1962) depend largely on the central taxing authority for resources to deal with crime. Constituent communities are denied the power to tax and ordinarily to allocate public resources, such as law enforcement and regulatory inspections, that may reduce the level of criminal activity or ameliorate its consequences. Some local organizations may be able to afford limited protection by spending their own resources to protect property, employees, or customers physically, but in lower-status communities most cannot since there are limits to how much of these costs can be passed on to inhabitants. Indeed large chain organizations—which could spread such costs across a large number of units located in low- as well as high-crime-rate communities—deliberately avoid doing business in high-rate communities or move out early in the cycle of rising crime. Some independent entrepreneurs that remain have limited resources for crime control. Many turn to forms of self-protection that include arming with weapons.

The only collective resource often available to the inhabitants of these high-crime-rate communities are those associated with vigilantism and organization. In its more benign mode, these take the form of local "Crime Watch" groups that mobilize public law enforcement or of local clubs that provide alternative opportunities for their young people. In its more virulent mode, self-help may take the form of armed patrol or political organization and violence against those perceived as threatening community stability and responsible for crime (Rieder 1985, pp. 57–94), although these are relatively rare in our modern cities. On the whole, a community's civic resources of self-protection appear to be limited resources in what is depicted as "the war on crime."

## II. Territorial Organization and Crime

Considerable controversy surrounds the question whether there are class or status differences in delinquency and crime. The consistency of findings on the territorial and social status concentration of crimes, victims, and offenders from offending and victimization surveys, police statistics on crime rates, the statistical portrait of the social status of victims and their offenders, and the propinquity of offenders to their victims all point to a higher concentration of offenders and victims of common crimes in the lower social strata and in low-status neighborhoods (Reiss 1976, p. 68). Moreover, the social status and delinquency rate of a neighborhood has an effect on one's chances of becoming a delinquent independent of one's social status. Reiss and Rhodes (1961, p. 729) concluded that low-status male youths are more likely than are those from the middle or upper strata to be delinquent in each kind of status neighborhood, but a boy living in a high-crime-rate area was far more likely to be delinquent than the same status boy in a low-crime neighborhood. Moreover, the neighborhood effect is greatest for low-status youths, suggesting that these neighborhoods are organized in ways that engender delinquency. Just what causes these neighborhood effects is not altogether apparent.

Attention to high-delinquency areas once centered on the delinquent gang, a territorially organized, age-graded peer group with a well-defined leadership and membership that recruited and socialized new members into delinquent behavior as a major cause of delinquency. These gangs were thought to be endemic in lower-status areas with high delinquency rates. Although some of these territorially based groups could be regarded as conflict or violent gangs that defined a neighborhood segment as their "turf" to be defended against outsiders (Yablonsky 1962; Miller 1975), most youths who engage in delinquency are not members of such highly structured groups (Klein and Crawford 1967; Morash 1983, p. 329). Rather, most delinquent youths are joined in networks (Sarnecki 1982, pp. 144–51; Sarnecki 1986) made up of loose clusters of youths linked together in co-offending (Klein and Crawford 1967; Sarnecki 1982, p. 151; Sarnecki 1986). These networks are based primarily in neighborhoods or communities. Co-offending emerges when parental and community controls over youths are weak, giving rise to a peer-control system that supports co-offending and to networks that simplify the search for accomplices. The greater the density of delinquents in a community network, the easier it is to search for accomplices. Individual offenders, consequently, often have a large number of different co-offenders in even a relatively short period of time.

There is reason to conclude that youth networks exist in most communities but that their organization differs with the social status of the community. Commonly in working-, middle-, and upper-status communities, peer networks are organized around an adolescent value culture, especially the value climates of schools and their conventional activities such as dating and athletics (Coleman 1961, pp. 173–219). By contrast, in lower-status communities male youths organize around local street-corner groups (Whyte 1943; Suttles 1968, pp. 155–56) that define both a personal and a collective identity (Suttles 1968, p. 173). Some, such as Suttles (1968, pp. 13–35) and Rieder (1985, pp. 26–44) posit an ordered segmentation of antagonistic, or oppositional, groups based on common ethnic identity and mutual responsibility for safety since threats to personal safety are common in the high-crime neighborhoods of lower-status families. Moreover, if Suttles is correct, it is unlikely they will join others outside their immediate neighborhood, as they are perceived as threats to their safety. There is, as well, an ecological basis for this territorially ordered segmentation and corporate unity (Suttles 1968, pp. 35–38; Rieder 1985, pp. 13–26) since the territory usually is physically as well as socially bounded. Territorial bounding facilitates social bonding and communication for mutual protection of personal safety. Wilson and Herrnstein (1985, pp. 301–2) speculate that lower-status youths are most constrained by neighborhood boundaries to their physical movement and social communication. Consequently, they are most vulnerable to local peer values and controls.

Despite the theoretical consistency of these views, there is very little empirical research to support their causal inferences. Just how neighborhood effects operate independent of status—and perhaps other unmeasured effects—requires further theoretical and empirical work.

### A. *Complex Integration of High-Crime Communities*

William Whyte (1943), in challenging the view that lower-status neighborhoods were socially disorganized, first drew attention to their complex integration around conventional and law-abiding, as well as illicit and lawbreaking, behavior, institutions, and organization. The urban slum and lower-status communities, he concluded, operated under a set of norms and social controls that produced an ordered way of life supporting both conventional and illegal behavior.

Extensions of this perspective link individual aspirations and behavior to culturally defined goals and means (Merton 1957), holding that, when legitimate means to social mobility are scarce (as they are generally for lower-status persons), people will use illegitimate means such as criminal activity to get ahead (Merton 1957, pp. 145–46; Cloward 1959, pp. 164–76). This framework has been elaborated by Cloward and Ohlin (1960), who see delinquent youth developing special modes of adaptation because they have unequal access to conventional means to get ahead in the larger society. Faced with a common problem, they evolve subcultures that provide alternative means of getting ahead (Cloward and Ohlin 1960, p. 107). These alternative subcultures substitute illegitimate means such as criminal activity for legitimate means to success. Cloward and Ohlin (1960, pp. 107, 144) describe three distinctive delinquent subcultures—criminal, conflict, and retreatist—as collective adaptations to these pressures. The criminal and conflict subcultures are based on illegitimate means of getting ahead, whereas the drug subculture is a retreatist adaptation (1960, pp. 152–60).

Subcultural solutions, they contend, will vary from one neighborhood to another, "according to the articulation of these structures in the neighborhood" (1960, p. 161). The more stable slum neighborhood, where criminal activity is organized to provide opportunities for upward mobility, produces a criminal delinquent subculture (1960, p. 166). Those characterized by high transiency and weak social controls create a conflict subculture because the social disorganization of the community leads to struggles for power over limited opportunities (1960, pp. 171–78). These two distinct adaptations are a consequence of differences in neighborhood opportunity structures and neighborhood integration. Cloward and Ohlin suggest that youths who fail to succeed in either a criminal or a conflict opportunity system—the former providing material success and the latter the prestige of reputation—regard themselves as a "double failure" (as failing in both conventional and nonconventional opportunity systems) and retreat into the use of drugs or other withdrawal behavior (1960, p. 186). Spergel (1964), by comparing three different slum neighborhoods, concludes that youths produce different subcultures, depending on the distinctive characteristics of a neighborhood and its integration as well as on its opportunity structure.

Although this theoretical development links individual motivation that is socially structured by the larger society to neighborhood opportunity systems and social structure, it does not explain how these communities come to have these different opportunity systems. Why, for example, does one neighborhood have a highly developed racketeering system, another is organized around the sale and consumption of drugs, and yet another has no organized illegitimate opportunities system?

Perhaps part of the puzzle may be solved by examining how crime is organized in society and, in particular, how it is organized in neighborhoods and local communities. An examination of organized criminal activity discloses differences in the way that conventional and white-collar crimes are organized, especially in the way they are organized within communities and through local organizations and institutions.

Illegitimate opportunity systems organized around white-collar lawbreaking occur in conjunction with legitimate activity—in the interstices, so to speak, of legitimate organized behavior. Price-fixing and bid rigging, for example, are special ways of organizing competitive market behavior. The laundering and investment of illegal gain links two types of organization—that of syndicated crime and that of conventional capital organizations such as banks, real estate firms, and investment houses. Note that activities such as these do not have visible community locations. They exist only as secret and clandestine transactions that are cloaked as legitimate, not criminal, transactions.

By contrast, organized criminal activity must have visibility even when the organization itself is largely invisible. The syndicate hierarchy may be invisible, but the organized criminal activity that is the source of its income is not. And it is precisely the nature of much syndicated criminal activity that it locates, and is visible, in largely lower-status slum neighborhoods. The sale of numbers, pimping and prostitution, gambling, and other forms of vice have their visible place in lower-status neighborhoods. The particular locus of such activities can vary considerably—the public street for pimping and prostitution; the alley, doorway, abandoned building, or the more conventional front of the smoke shop for the sale of drugs; and the newsstand and the bar for the numbers racket. These illegal markets must be localized to facilitate transactions as they need not be for white-collar lawbreaking. Lower-status neighborhoods are commonly their host. Yet this symbiotic relationship does not necessarily imply widespread neighborhood support for illegal activity. The work of Bottoms and Xanthos (1981), Bottoms and Wiles (in this volume), and others suggests that a community may be sharply divided, albeit often acquiescent, over the presence of illegal activity. All members of a neighborhood in which such activities are located, however, must take them into account to some degree in carrying out their daily life; this is not the case for organized white-collar lawbreaking. We must await further research to understand more fully why only some lower-status neighborhoods are host to such organized criminal activity.

*B. Community Structure and Crime Rates*

Communities vary considerably in their demographic and organizational structures and explanations of variation in community crime rates often are linked to variation in social structure. Yet such concomitant variation does not necessarily imply that variations in structural and situational conditions of communities cause their crime rates.

One causal hypothesis linking community social structure and delinquent or criminal behavior holds that deviance or criminality result both from the failure of personal controls to deter deviant conduct and from the failure of formal and informal social controls to induce and reinforce conformity (Reiss 1951, pp. 201–3; Hirschi 1969). The basic causal argument is that certain kinds of community structure either weaken forms of social control that induce conformity to law-abiding norms or generate controls that inhibit conformity.

Families and, in adolescence, peer groups are the primary developmental and control organizations influencing young people's conduct. Antisocial behavior is often said to result when families cannot, or for some reason fail to, exercise conforming control over the behavior of their children. This failure is enhanced in adolescence when peer groups support antisocial behavior.

Delinquency theories identify two major structural sources of weak family control. One is the weakened control of parents that results from a conflict of generational cultures such as that between immigrants who settle in low-status communities and their native-born offspring. Youths are drawn into conflict with their parents over the divergent cultural expectations of parents and peers. Parental authority and control is replaced by that of peers. The other structural source is a broken family structure. This is held to be especially consequential for male youths who lack the disciplinary authority and identification with a father as principal disciplinarian, so they take to the company of male adolescent peers. In either case the effect of weakened family control is heightened when a strong peer-control system forms an antisocial subculture.

Just how communities have an incremental effect on delinquency rates is not altogether clear, but the major outline of the argument for an incremental effect can be illustrated using the example of a broken family structure. High-delinquency communities have a disproportionate concentration of female-headed households with dependent children because, on average, these households have incomes at or below the poverty line so that these women are forced to seek residence in low-cost, often poor-quality, housing (Smith, in this volume).[2] That kind of housing is disproportionately available in slum communities, and it becomes available in large supply either through the eligibility of female-headed households for low-cost public housing (Rainwater 1970) or when vacancy rates are substantial because of the exodus of residents. The weakened parental control of these households—often exacerbated by the fact that the mother must work and leave adolescents largely unattended—means that their children, especially their male children, take to the streets and playgrounds, where they come into contact with similarly situated youths. In low-status communities the resulting density of similarly situated peers gives rise to a peer-control system with a subculture that often forms around antisocial conduct.

High-crime communities also harbor large numbers of other single persons—the single aged person and the unattached young—so that the community lacks a larger network of parental or family control. In low-status communities the unattached may also include persons with nonconforming or antisocial life-styles. Among them may be adult career offenders, alcoholics, pimps and prostitutes, and organized-crime members. Together they constitute an organized under-life of the community and represent its opportunities to get ahead. They serve as role models for the young male delinquents who may become linked into these adult networks either by casual employment or by communication. The foregoing illustration is one plausible, albeit incomplete, explanation for the findings that the crime rate of a neighborhood affects the chances of a boy's becoming delinquent independent of his status and that low-status boys are at greatest risk in low-status, high-crime-rate neighborhoods.

The neighborhood effect on crime thus operates in several related ways in low-status communities. A neighborhood's structure and organization disproportionately select households and unrelated individuals who form networks that create and support delinquency and adult crime. Correlatively, there is a selective out-migration of the kinds of families and businesses that sustain conformity. The density of settle-

[2] The concentration of female-headed households and children in a high-crime-rate community is illustrated by Rainwater (1970, pp. 13–14) in his statistical portrait of Pruitt-Igoe, a large-scale public housing project in St. Louis. The project is described as a black ghetto with 9,952 persons, of whom 6,895 (69 percent) were minors. There were two and a half times as many adult women as men living in the project. Female-headed households with children made up 63 percent of the households in Pruitt-Igoe.

ment of high-risk males in the neighborhood has an incremental effect because it creates strong peer networks and a subculture that supports delinquency as a solution to their common status problem. The extensive peer network increases the prevalence rate through recruitment into delinquency, and the ready availability of co-offenders in these networks increases individual rates of offending. Moreover, since offenders generally move only short distances to their victims (Suttles 1968, p. 207) and select their victims either from within their own or from adjacent neighborhoods, the density of offenders affects substantially the crime rate of their own neighborhood. Territorial concentration of both victims and offenders in neighborhoods, then, is associated with high crime rates.

## III. Social Change and Changes in Community Crime Rates

The work of Clifford Shaw and Henry McKay drew attention to variation in the crime rates of both individuals and communities. Shaw (1930, 1931, 1938) and McKay (1967) explored the dimensions of criminal careers from onset to desistance. Their explanations were more concerned with career delinquents and criminals than with variation among delinquent and criminal careers since they presented and dissected only the careers of long-duration, high-rate offenders.

By contrast, although Shaw and McKay (1931, 1942) and Shaw et al. (1929) described and explained variation in crime among communities, they did not arrive at a parallel conception of community crime careers. This failure to explain variation in the crime rates of communities over time stemmed from several separate but related conclusions. One conclusion was that, as cities grow, community growth and change follow a natural order of differentiation and configuration (1942, pp. 18–22). A related conclusion was that, while one type of community structure may replace another as the city grows (1942, pp. 24–27), its configuration remains stable. Moreover, Shaw and McKay observed that community crime rates varied according to the physical configuration of the city and with the economic and social composition of its communities, such that crime rates were highest in the zone of transition adjacent to the central business district and lowest in upper- and middle-income areas farthest removed from the city's center. Of even greater significance to them was that, when the demographic composition of a community changed, its rate of delinquency remained relatively stable. This led them to seek an explanation for why delinquency rates, although varying from community to community, remained relatively stable in each community despite changes in their demographic composition (1942, pp. 42, 142–83). Their conclusion was that differences in community social values and organization accounted for the differences in their rates of delinquency. They inferred from this pattern that, no matter what population moved into a community, its constant social and economic organization would produce the same crime rate. Their explanation:

> It is assumed that the differentiation of areas and the segregation of population within the city have resulted in wide variation in opportunities in the struggle for position within our social order. The groups in the areas of lowest economic status find themselves at a disadvantage in the struggle to achieve the goals idealized in our civilization. These differences are translated into conduct through the general struggle for those economic symbols which signify a desirable position in the larger social order. Those persons who occupy a disadvantageous position are involved in a conflict between the goals assumed to be attainable in a free society and those actually attainable for a large proportion of the population. It is understandable, then, that the economic position of persons living in the areas of least opportunity should be translated at times into unconventional conduct, in an effort to reconcile the idealized status and their practical prospects of attaining this status. Since in our culture, status is determined largely in economic terms, the differences between contrasted areas in terms of economic status become the most important differences. Similarly, as might be expected, crimes against property are most numerous. [1942, pp. 180–81]

They went on to point out that, where communities are characterized by divergent value systems (McKay 1949, p. 34), their delinquency rates are enhanced because the divergence weakens conventional control.

Although Shaw and McKay had observed that communities radically change their community structure over time and hence, by inference from their theory, would have changed their delinquency rates, their attention focused on explaining differences among communities with stable delinquency rates. Their answer lay, as noted, in differential community organization and control (1942, pp. 177–83).

### A. *Internal and External Sources of Community Change*

Recent work on communities and crime has turned to the observation that Shaw and McKay neglected: not only do communities change their structures over time but so often do their crime rates (Kobrin and Schuerman 1981; Bursik and Webb 1982; Bursik, in this volume; McDonald, in this volume; Schuerman and Kobrin, in this volume; Skogan, in this volume), a recognition that communities as well as individuals have crime careers. Perhaps not surprisingly, they draw on the same dynamic processes of urban change that underlie the work of Burgess and of Shaw and McKay on urban growth. The main difference is that these same factors are used to explain change rather than configuration.

The two major sources of change in a community's crime rate are the dynamic shifts in the population of a city that can lead to changes in the social and organizational structure of a community and the aging and the evolution of a city's community configuration. Additionally, some theorists contend that crime itself is a source of community change since population shifts may be engendered or accelerated by responses to changes in its crime rate. These theories were originally grounded in the observation that not all the communities Shaw and McKay observed still exhibit stability in crime rates. Of special interest is the movement of central city communities from low to high crime rates (Bursik, in this volume; Schuerman and Kobrin, in this volume). Likewise there is interest in communities moving from high to lower crime rates, for example, as the result of upward shifts in their socioeconomic structure—a shift popularly referred to as gentrification (Bottoms and Wiles, in this volume; McDonald, in this volume).

Yet these two approaches to explaining variation in community crime rates may not be as antipodal as they seem. Reiss (1976, pp. 81–82) concluded that they appear inconsistent primarily because the politically organized, or governmental, community rather than the metropolitan community is used to test these theories. For what now characterizes urban growth and agglomeration in U.S. society is its configuration beyond central city boundaries: U.S. cities have experienced rapid growth since 1950; population growth more than doubled the number of suburban and satellite communities in the metropolitan configuration. Were the forces producing that configuration to have remained constant, the number of high-delinquency communities would have more than doubled in the central city given the lower density of housing units in the areas available for lower-status-family settlement. Thus the differentiation among urban communities and their configuration observed by Shaw and McKay remains, with low-crime-rate and the more middle class communities at the periphery and with high-crime rate communities at the core. What must be understood, therefore, is that the rate of population growth itself affects the rate at which the number of any kind of differentiated community multiplies. That multiplication results in many central city communities showing shifts from lower to higher crime rates (Schuerman and Kobrin, in this volume). There can also be internal shifts from high to lower crime rates such as occur in some communities with gentrification (McDonald, in this volume).

### *B. Changes in Law and Its Enforcement*

The causes of urban growth and community change just considered are primarily demographic and socioeconomic causes. Other kinds of social change likewise may cause changes in community structure that affect their crime rates. One that seems to have played an increasing role in changing the urban landscape and the structure of communities is changes in law and its enforcement, especially changes in law and its public administration. A few examples may illustrate how such changes may affect crime rates in urban communities.

Federal legislation, the administration of federal programs, and appellate court decisions have had some marked effects on the physical, moral, and social order of communities. These changes often are incremental, and their cumulative effects can ultimately destroy the integrity of communities as viable collectivities to control the behavior of their inhabitants. Rainwater (1970) first drew attention to the way in which federally owned and subsidized public housing policies undermine local institutions and living arrangements so that crime becomes endemic among young persons in large-scale public housing enclaves. Bottoms and Wiles (in this volume) also draw attention to ways that national and local policies and programs for private as well as public housing affect the crime careers of communities. Federal programs may also destroy the physical integrity of communities. The creation of a national freeway system in the United States destroyed the physical integrity of many low-income ethnic communities in the central cities, forcing their residents to relocate. Since these were generally low-income or working-class areas, their residents placed pressure on other areas of central cities, thereby changing their composition (Alschuler

1965). Other laws and appellate decisions eroded the capacity of local communities to use zoning to control what residents regarded as crime nuisances such as the adult peep-show parlor and dirty bookstore, the discotheque, the public bath, or simply the nightlife strip. Such businesses largely attract outsiders and often the local and nonlocal criminals who prey on them. Some of the decisions of appellate courts that constrained police procedures of search, seizure, and arrest have also been viewed as restricting the capacity of local authorities to control street life, especially to contain within particular bounds pimping and prostitution, drug sales, loitering, and public behavior that residents regard as threatening. In our largest cities, where corruption of law enforcement and regulation is not uncommon, communities often deteriorate physically for lack of enforcement of housing and sanitation codes and for a general neglect of urban amenities.

Beginning in the 1940s, federal intervention also took the form of urban planning and massive infusions of resources to curb physical deterioration of communities, urban poverty, and other local conditions thought to be crime inducing. There is little agreement on just how effective such programs were in dealing with these specific conditions of urban blight and the plight of their residents. Yet there have been many doubts about whether these resources created viable communities able to control their own destinies (Jacobs 1961). Gans (1962, pp. 281–335) concluded that the redevelopment process in Boston's west end destroyed its urban village because it destroyed "a functioning social system." Much of the argument about the malign effect of intentional intervention may ignore that dynamic growth can produce similar results. But in any case, both positions lead to the conclusion that communities have a delicate balance of moral and social integration that rarely survives rapid change. They both presume that among the consequences of disruption are weakened community control and, at least in the short run, an increased amount of crime and disorder.

## IV. Policy Implications of Variation in Community Crime Rates

Behavioral theories about crimes are constructed around persons or organizations as their basic unit of observation and explain how they become victims or offenders and why individual rates of victimization or offending vary. Complementary theories take crimes and their constituent elements as the basic units and explain why their rates vary among organized aggregates such as groups, communities, or societies.

Crime policies ordinarily differ substantially, depending on whether the policy analyst bases a policy on explanations of the effect of crime on the behavior of persons and organizations or on their collectivities such as groups, networks, neighborhoods, communities, or societies.

Policies based on variation in individual behavior typically opt for direct intervention in the lives of persons—such as victims and offenders—or for indirect intervention to change the behavior of whatever is held directly to cause variation in their criminal behavior. Interventions into the lives of victims and offenders are generally of three kinds.

One set of interventions seeks to prevent the behavior from occurring by altering its causes. These may include, for example, teaching parenting skills to forestall antisocial behavior in children or therapeutic intervention in the lives of "predelinquents" whose future offending is predicted. Similarly, there may be policies and programs for imparting skills to victims to prevent their victimization.

Once delinquent or criminal behavior has occurred, that is, one is an offender or victim, interventions may try to change the behavior of that person so that the behavior will not be repeated. There are many examples of policies and programs based on this change perspective, most of which can be subsumed under the rubric of either punishment or rehabilitation. It is assumed, for example, that punishing persons by deprivation of property or liberty will result in desistance from offending or that rehabilitation technologies such as drug treatment or group therapy will change an offender into a conforming person. For victims, punishment may take the form of disincentives such as higher insurance rates and rehabilitation may provide assistance in altering victim proneness.

Yet there is a third course where criminal behavior can be neither prevented nor altered. The consequences of crime for victims can be prevented by restricting opportunities for repeated criminal behavior. Incapacitating offenders in jails and prisons, for example, restricts their victimization to their co-residents, and even that can be prevented with solitary confinement. Similarly, the premises of victims may be secured against criminal intrusion even to the point where they become prisoners of their secure space.

Policies based on theories about what causes a person to behave as a delinquent or criminal person lead, then, to creation or adoption of interventions that will prevent unwanted behavior by disrupting a causal sequence that leads to it, for example, by changing the offender into a conforming person or by controlling his opportunities to offend. The intervention may be directly into the life of the person, as in a drug treatment program, or it may be indirect, by manipulating structures or situations believed to cause conforming rather than deviant conduct. For example, a program may be designed to create legitimate employment opportunities for offenders on the presumption that such opportunities will change offenders by giving them legitimate means to get ahead. Similarly, if one concludes that the rate of law enforcement (Smith, in this volume) or of sanctioning offenders (Sampson, in this volume) in a community has an indirect effect on offending behavior, one may choose to reduce crime rates by altering policing (Sherman, in this volume) or sanctioning strategies in communities. Likewise, if there is good reason to conclude that the availability of opportunities to commit crime has an effect on the crime rate, those opportunities may be manipulated. Thus when it was found that locking devices on cars had a substantial effect on automobile theft rates, changes in locking hoods, doors, and, in some countries, even wheels, were mandated by law or agreement.

Policies based on theories that explain variation in the crime rates of collectivities, by contrast, lead to the creation or adoption of interventions that alter the cultural or social structure of collectivities or the social controls that cause this variation.

Theories that explain community variation in delinquency and crime rates as a consequence of variation in their moral and social integration lead to interventions controlling conditions that destabilize communities. If, for example, it is concluded that female-headed households per se are not conducive to sons becoming delinquent but rather that the concentration of low-status, female-headed households in a community gives rise to a strong peer-control system that creates a delinquent subculture, then intervention might take the form of controlling the density of their settlement in a community. Or, if it is found that housing policies contribute to the concentration of adult offenders (Bottoms and Xanthos 1981; Bottoms and Wiles, in this volume), then one may elect to alter those policies so as to reduce those concentrations.

Similarly, when there is reason to conclude that the mobilization of a community to control conduct affects its crime rate, then one may want to intervene in whatever causes a diminished capacity. Where public programs or laws destabilize a local population and hence its capacity to control conduct locally, one may question the soundness of such policies. It is somewhat anomalous that an environmental impact review is required before the physical environment of a community can be altered but that none is required when profound changes are deliberately introduced into its collective life. Where such changes might affect the kind and level of law enforcement required of the collectivity, no approval that such resources will be available is required (Reiss 1982*a*, p. 144). Moreover, no impact review ordinarily is required when a superhighway is proposed that will intrude into the territory of a community or a business, even though its placement there is widely regarded as inimical to the community's collective welfare.

Just when, how, and where one should intervene to reduce crime, as, for example, whether to intervene at the individual, neighborhood, or societal level, is perplexing when causal models predict effects of intervention at each level. Consider employment interventions, for example. Jobs may be given to offenders to reduce their offending, neighborhood labor markets can be developed to provide an employment structure with a graded set of opportunities for advancement, or one can stimulate general economic growth in the society on the presumption that it eventually creates more job opportunities for the unemployed who are at greatest risk of offending. McGahey (in this volume) concludes that general job training and employment programs aimed at offenders and stimulation of general economic growth generally show no effect on crime rates. He suggests that this null effect stems from the fact that these interventions do not take into account the roles of local neighborhood labor markets and community organizations as critical, necessary links in employment. For many lower-status persons, the primary opportunity system is the local community and the opportunities it presents for employment and social mobility.

The empirical foundation of policies and programs calling for community interventions to reduce crime is that the structure and organization of communities affect the crime rate independent of the individual characteristics of residents and offenders or of the culture and organization of the society. Offender characteristics contribute to predictions of recidivism, and so does the density of offenders in a community and its social organization. Each of these factors has an effect on recidivism independent of the others. Thus a crime-reduction program for delinquent recidivists may require intervention into the lives of delinquents, their families, and communities. Offenders and their families, for example, might be moved from high- to low-density-offender communities. Yet, unless one altered the community structure and organization of low-status neighborhoods, it would continue to affect the crime rate unless offenders and their density of residence in a community are solely responsible for the crime rate.

Given reasons to conclude that there are individual, local community, and societal effects on the crime rate, interventions solely at one of these levels may be expected to produce, at most, a limited effect. Correlatively, if we assume that there are feedback and interaction effects among these units, as, for example, that the density of offenders in a neighborhood affects the prevalence of offenders in a community, their individual crime rates, and the selective in- and out-migration of families from the community, then interventions to reduce the density of offending in a community, or to reduce its causes, may have a substantial effect on a community's crime rate.

Little is known about just what kinds of intervention to reduce crime can be undertaken in local communities under a democratic system of government or of their cost relative to programs for intervening in the lives of individuals. Some community interventions—such as neighborhood redevelopment and public housing—may actually contribute indirectly to an increase in the crime rate by reducing local social control. Many interventions to change the behavior of individual offenders likewise fail to show substantial effects, and some may also increase an individual's risk of offending. Despite the failure of interventions directly into offenders' lives, there remains a strong presumption that intervening directly in the lives of individuals is less costly and more effective. Moreover, there seems to be a presumption that it is unlikely one can intervene directly to alter neighborhood structures to produce changes that reduce crime despite the evidence from deliberate massive social changes—such as urban redevelopment and public housing—that such changes are at least possible. Coupled with these presumptions is yet another that accepts dynamic demographic and community growth and change as a natural process in democratic societies and therefore one that cannot be controlled. Perhaps these conclusions about intervention are in part a consequence of the fact that societal intelligence, including that of social science research, is organized to know much more about individual behavior than about collective life and that what we know about collective life is largely gained by aggregating information about individuals and organizations for collectivities.

## V. What We Need to Know about Communities and Crime and How We May Know It

The intelligence that a society gathers about crime and its causes structures and limits its capacity to understand and to control crime. Lacking measures on many theoretically significant variables, it cannot properly test most theories, nor can systematic observation lead to the development of new theories without appropriate concepts and their measures. Moreover, a society's policies and programs will be shaped by the concepts and measures of information that is collected.

Two facts about crime that societies have known for a long time are that participation and offending rates vary considerably among individuals and communities. Governmental intelligence on crime and offending is gained largely by collecting information on crime and its victims and offenders for administrative territories. What we know about such administrative territories is gained by censusing and record keeping for individuals and organizations. Governments, however, collect very little information on the collective properties of administrative units for which they routinely report information. Even more unfortunate, these administrative units do not coincide with symbolic organized territories that are theoretically significant, such as local communities.

Generally speaking, governmental agencies collect far more information on crime rates and criminals than on their causes. Moreover, whenever information on crime phenomena is aggregated for administrative units, little causal information is available for those same units. Administrative agencies rarely are obliged to collect information on the organizational properties of their reporting units or on factors that might explain variation in crime rates. Additionally, information on victims is rarely provided by local governmental units even though law enforcement and criminal justice agencies routinely collect such information. Consequently, our primary sources of information on victims are local and national victimization surveys. These surveys provide considerable information on victimizations, less on victim characteristics, and relatively little on what might explain variations, for example, victims' life-styles, or on the situations, places, and communities where victimizations occur.

Governmental data-collection deficiencies aside, there likewise are very real limits to the utility of social science data for developing and testing theory or for developing and implementing social policies. Social science research on crime draws either on governmental statistics and records or on designs that collect information from individuals. The primary way of doing this is to question or test individuals about their offending and their victimization by crime and about their personal, affiliation, and situational characteristics that might explain that behavior. Rarely is information collected about the communities in which they live independent of what an individual supplies as "background information." Ordinarily, information about individuals cannot be aggregated to communities with unique identities. The main exception to this conventional science is community ethnography, where information is gathered not only on crime and individual behavior but also on its contexts—how people behave together, influence one another, and are organized to constitute a community (Whyte 1943; Liebow 1967; Suttles 1968; Merry 1981; Rieder 1985).

Generally speaking, then, although social science investigations collect information on victim and offending behavior and their presumed causes, they fail to collect information that can be linked to explain community variation in crime rates. Even ethnographers of communities, like most investigators of the causes of crime, fail to gather information on the behavior of most individuals in a community that can then be linked to their rich information on community organization and behavior. Major studies of peer delinquency and co-offending also are disappointing in this respect since they focus primarily on linking individuals to peer-group organizations and processes, thereby scanting the rich community context of ethnographers (e.g., Short and Strodtbeck 1965; Klein and Crawford 1967). Ethnographies have an additional shortcoming. They provide only limited tests of theories or policies by focusing on a single community or, at most, on a cluster of neighborhoods where one cannot vary community properties.

If our understanding of crime and criminal behavior and its control is to advance, governmental data collection and scholarly research must be designed to collect individual, organizational, and community-level information. This is necessary to determine whether, in what way, and how much the organizations to which one belongs and the community in which one lives have an independent effect on crime.

This will require some radical rethinking about internal and external validity of research designs. When designing surveys, all too much attention has been given to whether the information for individuals is valid and to what population of individuals the findings can be generalized. Increasingly, the external validity of surveys is presumed to obligate investigators to select national samples so that findings can be generalized to a society. This ordinarily means that even in large sample surveys, such as the National Crime Survey, with a cluster sample design, information is usable for too few individuals to link them to community-level variables (were that information to be collected, which it is not). Moreover, the sample-selection procedure does not yield a random selection of individuals from an identifiable community. Indeed in a national sample survey the investigation of community variability is traded off for societal level generalization. Additionally, national probability sample surveys of households and their members preclude collecting information on social networks (e.g., sociometric ties), organizations, and social processes. All this information is essential to disentangle individual from group and community effects on crime.

To collect information on social processes and community change draws attention to another shortcoming of most survey research designs. The typical sample survey that is used to investigate crime causation and control is a cross section of time. Yet the understanding of both individual and community behavior requires repeated observations over time. Longitudinal designs are very expensive, and to repeat them for a sample of communities is to multiply their cost. Nevertheless, big science is not low cost.

Communities as well as individuals, then, must constitute the units of observation for understanding both individual and community crime rates. Yet just as individuals are part of an organized order, so are communities. Variation in their crime rates must be understood in terms of the behavior of their residents and their structural properties but also in terms of their place in an organized or symbiotic order. To understand those relationships also has design implications. Data collected for a probability sample of communities will provide insufficient information on their exchanges or their place in a dynamically organized and changing system of communities. We may learn much more by studying the variability among communities in relation to one another—such as by investigating variability among the communities of Chicago (Bursik, in this volume) or of Los Angeles (Schuerman and Kobrin, in this volume) or, preferably, among their metropolitan areas—than from a national sample of such local communities for all U.S. cities. To be sure, Chicago and Los Angeles are each a single case of a central city or metropolitan community, and more than a few cases are required for external validity.

Finally, to understand variation in community crime rates, communities must be observed over time. This requires longitudinal research designs so that information can be collected as communities change. To detect change requires repeating observations at relatively short intervals of time. Retrospective designs have less utility for detecting change for a number of reasons but particularly so if one is collecting information on communities and their organizations where "recall" is limited to the contents of its records and the memories of its surviving members. In any case, retrospective designs ordinarily are restricted to the information that organizations routinely collect. Although government organizations may retain continuous records on crime rates and offenders, they either do not collect information on what may cause variation in these rates or it is collected at such infrequent intervals that it cannot be systematically linked to variation in crime rates.

The foregoing discussion of the research designs required to enhance our understanding of communities and crime leads to the conclusion that their execution requires big science. Such research will require teams of scientists who can be organized to design, collect, and analyze information over decades of data collection. And such designs will be costly.

An equally compelling conclusion of this essay's linking of the several traditions of theory and research is that more is to be gained by linking those traditions than by their continued separate development and testing. Longitudinal designs that follow not only changes in the structure, composition, and organization of communities but also the individuals who reside there will permit us to partition the variation attributable to individuals and to communities. Yet such complex designs will present additional problems that arise because communities are dynamic units (Reiss 1985*b*, pp. 169–72). The resident population of any community will change considerably over time owing to the dynamic processes of any population—births, deaths, and migration. Similarly, its population of organizations will change considerably. And, over time, the boundaries as well as the structures of communities change. The problems presented by such dynamic changes are formidable, but they must be regarded as challenges to design and analysis rather than as grounds for despair and for continuing the practice of doing research on crime using either individuals or communities as units for observations.

## REFERENCES

Alschuler, A. A. 1965. *The City Planning Process*. Ithaca, N.Y.: Cornell University Press.

Bottoms, A. E., and P. Wiles. In this volume. "Housing Tenure and Residential Community Crime Careers in Britain."

Bottoms, A. E., and P. Xanthos. 1981. "Housing Policy and Crime in the Public Sector." In *Environmental Criminology*, edited by P. J. Brantingham and P. L. Brantingham. Beverly Hills, Calif.: Sage.

Brantingham, P. J., and P. L. Brantingham. 1978. "A Theoretical Model of Crime Site Selection." In *Crime, Law, and Sanctions*, edited by M. D. Khron and R. L. Akers. Beverly Hills, Calif.: Sage.

Bureau of Justice Statistics. 1985*a*. *Criminal Victimization in the United States, 1983*. National Crime Survey Report. U. S. Department of Justice, Bureau of Justice Statistics. Washington, D.C.: U.S. Government Printing Office.

———. 1985*b*. *Locating City, Suburban, and Rural Crime*. Bureau of Justice Statistics Special Report. Washington, D.C.: U.S. Department of Justice, Bureau of Justice Statistics.

Burgess, E. W. 1925. "The Growth of the City: An Introduction to a Research Project." In *The City*, edited by R. E. Park, E. W. Burgess, and R. D. McKenzie. Chicago: University of Chicago Press.

Bursik, R. J., Jr. In this volume. "Ecological Stability and the Dynamics of Delinquency."

Bursik, R. J., Jr., and J. Webb. 1982. "Community Change and Patterns of Delinquency," *American Journal of Sociology* 88:24–42.

Clarke, R. V., and D. B. Cornish. 1985. "Modeling Offenders' Decisions: A Framework for Research and Policy." In *Crime and Justice: An Annual Review of Research*, vol. 6, edited by Michael Tonry and Norval Morris. Chicago: University of Chicago Press.

Cloward, R. A. 1959. "Illegitimate Means, Anomie, and Deviant Behavior." *American Sociological Review* 24:164–76.

Cloward, R. A., and Lloyd Ohlin. 1960. *Delinquency and Opportunity: A Theory of Delinquent Gangs*. Glencoe, Ill.: Free Press.

Coleman, J. S. 1961. *Adolescent Society*. Glencoe, Ill.: Free Press.

Gans, H. J. 1962. *The Urban Villagers*. Glencoe, Ill.: Free Press.

Hindelang, M. J., M. R. Gottfredson, and J. Garofalo. 1978. *Victims of Personal Crime: An Empirical Foundation for a Theory of Personal Victimization*. Cambridge, Mass.: Ballinger.

Hirschi, T. 1969. *Causes of Delinquency*. Berkeley: University of California Press.

Jacobs, J. 1961. *The Life and Death of Great American Cities*. New York: Vintage.

Klein, M. W., and L. Y. Crawford. 1967. "Groups, Gangs, and Cohesiveness." *Journal of Research in Crime and Delinquency* 4:142–65.

Kobrin, S., and L. Schuerman. 1981. *Interaction between Neighborhood Change and Criminal Activity: An Interim Report*. Los Angeles: University of Southern California, Social Science Research Institute.

Liebow, E. 1967. *Tally's Corner: A Study of Negro Street Corner Men*. Boston: Little, Brown.

McDonald, S. C. In this volume. "Does Gentrification Affect Crime Rates?"

McGahey, R. M. In this volume. "Economic Conditions, Neighborhood Organization, and Urban Crime."

McKay, H. D. 1949. "The Neighborhood and Child Conduct." *The Annals.* 261:32–41.

———. 1967. "Report on the Criminal Careers of Male Delinquents in Chicago." *Task Force Report: Juvenile Delinquency and Youth Crime.* President's Commission on Law Enforcement and Administration of Justice. Washington, D.C.: U.S. Government Printing Office.

McKenzie, R. D. 1925. "The Ecological Approach to the Study of the Human Community." In *The City*, edited by R. E. Park, E. W. Burgess, and R. D. McKenzie. Chicago: University of Chicago Press.

Merry, S. E. 1981. *Urban Danger: Life in a Neighborhood of Strangers.* Philadelphia: Temple University Press.

Merton, R. K. 1957. *Social Theory and Social Structure.* Glencoe, Ill.: Free Press.

Miller, W. B. 1975. *Violence by Youth Gangs and Youth Groups as a Crime Problem in Major American Cities.* Washington, D.C.: U.S. Government Printing Office.

Morash, M. 1983. "Gangs, Groups, and Delinquency." *British Journal of Criminology* 23:309–31.

Pfeffer, J., and G. R. Salancik. 1978. *The External Control of Organizations: A Resource Dependence Perspective.* New York: Harper & Row.

Rainwater, L. 1970. *Behind Ghetto Walls: Black Families in a Federal Slum.* Chicago: Aldine.

Reiss, A. J., Jr. 1951. "Delinquency as the Failure of Personal and Social Controls." *American Sociological Review* 16:196–208.

———. 1976. "Settling the Frontiers of a Pioneer in American Criminology: Henry McKay." In *Delinquency, Crime, and Society*, edited by J. F. Short, Jr. Chicago: University of Chicago Press.

———. 1977. "Analytical Studies in Victimization by Crime." Report no. 5, Law Enforcement Assistance and Administration grant no. 75-SS-99-6013. New Haven, Conn.: Yale University, Institution for Social and Policy Studies.

———. 1981. "Towards a Revitalization of Theory and Research on Victimization by Crime." *Journal of Criminal Law and Criminology* 72:704–13.

———. 1982*a*. "Forecasting the Role of the Police and the Role of the Police in Social Forecasting." In *The Maintenance of Order in Society*, edited by R. Donelan. Ottawa: Canadian Police College, RCMP and Minister of Supply and Services, Canada.

———. 1982*b*. "How Serious Is Serious Crime?" *Vanderbilt Law Review* 35:541–85.

———. 1983. "Crime Control and the Quality of Life." *American Behavioral Scientist* 27:43–58.

———. 1985*a*. *Policing a City's Central District: The Oakland Story.* Washington, D.C.: U.S. Government Printing Office.

———. 1985*b*. "Some Failures in Designing Data Collection That Distort Results." In *Collecting Evaluation Data: Problems and Solutions*, edited by L. Burstein, H. E. Freeman, and P. Rossi. Beverly Hills, Calif.: Sage.

Reiss, A. J., Jr., and L. E. Rhodes. 1961. "The Distribution of Juvenile Delinquency in the Social Class Structure." *American Sociological Review* 26:720–32.

Rieder, J. 1985. *Carnarsie: The Jews and Italians of Brooklyn against Liberalism.* Cambridge, Mass.: Harvard University Press.

Sampson, R. J. In this volume. "Crime in Cities: The Effects of Formal and Informal Social Control."

Sarnecki, J. 1982. *Brottslighet och Kamratrelationer: Studie av ungbrottsligheten i en svansk kommun.* Stockholm: Brottsforebyggnde Radet (National Council for Crime Prevention). Portions translated by Denise Galarraga as *Criminality and Friend Relations: A Study of Juvenile Criminality in a Swedish Community.* Washington, D.C.: National Institute of Justice, National Criminal Justice Reference Service, April 1984.

———. 1986. *Delinquent Networks.* Stockholm: National Council for Crime Prevention.

Schuerman, L., and S. Kobrin. In this volume. "Community Careers in Crime."

Shapiro, S. P. 1984. *Wayward Capitalists: Target of the Securities and Exchange Commission.* New Haven, Conn.: Yale University Press.

Shaw, C. R. 1930. *The Jack-Roller.* Chicago: University of Chicago Press.

———. 1931. *The Natural History of a Delinquent Career.* Chicago: University of Chicago Press.

———. 1938. *Brothers in Crime.* Chicago: University of Chicago Press.

Shaw, C. R., and H. D. McKay. 1931. *Social Factors in Juvenile Delinquency.* Vol. 2, no. 13. Washington D.C.: U.S. Government Printing Office.

———. 1942. *Juvenile Delinquency and Urban Areas.* Chicago: University of Chicago Press.

Shaw, C. R., F. M. Zorbough, H. D. McKay, and L. S. Cottrell. 1929. *Delinquency Areas.* Chicago: University of Chicago Press.

Sherman, L. W. In this volume. "Policing Communities: What Works?"

Short, H. F., Jr., and F. L. Strodtbeck. 1965. *Group Process and Gang Delinquency.* Chicago: University of Chicago Press.

Singer, S. I. 1981. "Homogeneous Victim-Offender Populations: A Review and Some Research Implications." *Journal of Criminal Law and Criminology* 72:779–88.

Skogan, W. G. 1981. "Impacts of Crime on Attitudes and Behavior." In *Reactions to Crime,* edited by D. A. Lewis. Beverly Hills, Calif.: Sage.

———. In this volume. "Fear of Crime and Neighborhood Change."

Smith, D. A. In this volume. "The Neighborhood Context of Police Behavior."

Sparks, R. F. 1981. "Multiple Victimization: Evidence, Theory, and Future Research." *Journal of Criminal Law and Criminology* 72:762–78.

Spergel, I. 1964. *Racketville, Slumtown, Haulburg.* Chicago: University of Chicago Press.

Sutherland, E. H. 1942. "Development of the Theory." In *The Sutherland Papers,* edited by A. Cohen, A. Lindesmith, and K. Schuessler. Bloomington: Indiana University Press.

Suttles, G. D. 1968. *The Social Order of the Slum: Ethnicity and Territory in the Inner City.* Chicago: University of Chicago Press.

Taub, R. P., D. G. Taylor, and J. D. Dunham. 1981. "Neighborhoods and Safety." In *Reactions to Crime*, edited by D. A. Lewis. Beverly Hills, Calif.: Sage.

Taylor, R. B., and S. Gottfredson. In this volume. "Environmental Design, Crime, and Prevention: An Examination of Community Dynamics."

Vaughan, D. 1983. *Controlling Unlawful Organizational Behavior: Social Structure and Corporate Misconduct*. Chicago: University of Chicago Press.

Whyte, W. F. 1943. *Street Corner Society*. Chicago: University of Chicago Press.

Wilson, J. Q., and G. Kelling. 1982. "Broken Windows: The Police and Neighborhood Safety." *Atlantic* (March), pp. 29–38.

Wilson, J. Q., and R. J. Herrnstein. 1985. *Crime and Human Nature*. New York: Simon & Schuster.

Xanthos, P. 1981. "Crime, the Housing Market and Reputation: A Study of Some Local Authority Estates in Sheffield." Ph.D. dissertation, University of Sheffield.

Yablonsky, L. 1962. *The Violent Gang*. New York: Macmillan.

*Robert J. Bursik, Jr.*

# Ecological Stability and the Dynamics of Delinquency

ABSTRACT

Shaw and McKay's ecological approach to social disorganization and delinquency was developed under the assumption that Chicago was characterized by a stable set of ecological dynamics. This enabled them to interpret the relative stability of the location of high delinquency areas in the city. This essay examines the degree to which stability has characterized Chicago since 1930 and the extent to which social disorganization remains a viable approach to the explanation of delinquency. Since World War I, due to an acceleration in processes of suburbanization, Chicago underwent very dramatic ecological changes. In areas characterized by the most rapid changes, there were dramatic increases in delinquency, which is consistent with the social disorganization perspective. An examination of areas whose development differed substantially from the pattern predicted from the general social disorganization model suggests that ecological theories would benefit from a consideration of dynamics external to local communities and must be careful in the ways in which local communities are defined.

When the second edition of *Juvenile Delinquency and Urban Areas* appeared in 1969, Terrence Morris (1970) hailed its republication by noting that "in the study of the sociology of crime, there can be few whose contribution has been more influential than that of Clifford Shaw and Henry McKay." Scarcely fifteen years later, the ecological

Robert J. Bursik, Jr., is an Assistant Professor of Sociology at the University of Oklahoma. This research was supported in part by grant 84-IJ-CX-0071, awarded by the National Institute of Justice. The author would like to express his appreciation to Harold Grasmick, Janet Heitgerd, Yoko Baba, Jean Wood, and James Lynch for their helpful comments and suggestions. In addition, I would like to thank Michael Tonry, Albert J. Reiss, Jr., and the reviewers of this volume, whose insights were extremely valuable.


0-226-80802-5/86/0008-0002$01.00

work of Shaw and McKay is considered by many to be little more than an interesting footnote in the history of community-related research. Some criminologists have concluded that ecological research is primarily an atheoretical exercise in the mapping of criminal phenomena (Baldwin 1979; Davidson 1981; Nettler 1984).

Recently, however, the ecological framework has experienced a quiet, but significant, revival. One reason has been the "rediscovery" that the urban processes related to crime can only be appreciated as they unfold over time (Bursik and Webb 1982; Shannon 1982; Bursik 1984; Schuerman and Kobrin 1983, in this volume). Thus the "new" ecology of crime and delinquency has moved away from the analysis of static relationships to the study of changes in these relationships in the context of urban dynamics. Such an orientation is far from new, for it formed the core of the Shaw and McKay research (Shaw et al. 1929; Shaw and McKay 1942, 1969). Unfortunately, the processual aspects of this perspective gradually disappeared in much of the subsequent ecological research.

As Schuerman and Kobrin have noted (1983), the spatial model of Shaw and McKay was built upon the assumption of a stable ecological process in which a city's local communities have ongoing, relatively permanent roles in the process of economic-related, geographic mobility. Yet, while such an assumption may have been valid for the historic period in which Shaw and McKay wrote, its pertinence for current research must be carefully reevaluated in light of the important changes that have occurred in recent decades, such as the open housing decisions and the rise of urban planning (Janowitz 1967).

This essay examines the changing ecological roles of Chicago's local community areas between the years 1930 and 1970 and the effect of such changes on patterns of delinquency within those areas. Contrary to Shaw and McKay's assumption of stability, the ecological structure of Chicago has been in a period of reformulation for several decades. Of primary interest, however, is the degree to which these new dynamics are reflected in the delinquency rates of local communities. Shaw and McKay's concept of social disorganization would predict that neighborhoods characterized by rapid ecological redefinition will also be likely to experience significant increases in their delinquency rates. If this is not the case, then the notion of social disorganization may have been peculiar to a specific historical context and of no current value in theoretical models of crime and delinquency.

Before describing the data and analyses, I provide background information on the Shaw and McKay model in Section I and on their underlying assumption of ecological stability in Section II. Methods of measuring change in ecological models of crime and delinquency are described in Section III. A brief description of the Chicago data used in this study is provided in Section IV. The data consisted of male juvenile referral rates and measures of ecological change in local community areas. Results of the analyses are presented decennially (1930–70) in Section V. Some local communities may be characterized by significantly different processes of change from those of other local areas. The role of these communities in ecological models is examined in Section VI. In Section VII, conclusions about the relationships between ecological processes and delinquency are offered. Section VIII assesses the value of ecological approaches to the study of crime.

## I. Shaw and McKay's Model of Ecological Process

Shaw and McKay's work was firmly grounded in the Park and Burgess (1924) ecological model of urban structure. Park and Burgess stated that "the problems of community organization are for the most part problems of accommodation, or articulation, of groups within the community and of the adjustment of the life of the local community to the life of the wider community of which it is a part" (1924, p. 720). This articulation and accommodation were felt to reflect the "moral order" of human society, which organized the interrelationships between people and provided the arena for the struggle for status.

The moral order was considered to be interdependent with a biotic level (i.e., noncultural) of organization that reflected the "natural" dynamics of the competitive market system and resulted in the existing pattern of land usage and the spatial location of population groups. Local community areas of a city were assumed to develop primarily as a result of this process and not as a consequence of any conscious interaction between social groups. This assumption is reflected in the references to "natural areas" found throughout the work of Park and Burgess.

The key component of these natural dynamics was considered by Burgess to be mobility within the city (1925). Although he recognized that both economic and cultural dynamics were responsible for the spatial differentiation that resulted from this movement, Burgess argued that the most sensitive single indicator of these processes was the distribution of land values. Thus, although Park and Burgess noted the importance of the moral order to the structure of human society, they implied that the primary concern of human ecology was with the biotic level of organization.

This emphasis is reflected in Burgess's concentric zone theory of urban structure. Neighborhoods located in the zone of transition surrounding the central business district were the least attractive in the city, thereby functioning as the typical initial area of residence for immigrant ethnic groups due to the availability of inexpensive housing. When fuller assimilation into the economic structure permitted, these groups were assumed to relocate to better residential neighborhoods farther removed from the central business district, to be replaced in this zone by newer waves of immigrants. This ongoing process gave rise to the familiar pattern in which the socioeconomic composition of neighborhoods increased with distance from the central business district.

Shaw and McKay detected a similar (although inverse) relationship between delinquency rates and distance from the central business district. More important, however, their data indicated that there was a general stability in these rates over a forty-year period. That is, certain areas of the city continued to be characterized by high rates of delinquency regardless of the population groups residing in them. Although they were aware that these patterns were far from perfect and that certain noneconomic processes were reflected in the spatial distributions (as in the case of nonwhites), they concluded that the pattern of delinquency rates was generally related to the same ecological processes that gave rise to the socioeconomic structure of urban areas.

Although economic mobility was at the heart of this process, Shaw and McKay did not posit a direct relationship between economic factors and rates of delinquency, as pointed out by Kornhauser (1978) and Tittle (1983). Rather, areas characterized by economic deprivation and physical deterioration tended to have high rates of population turnover (since they were abandoned by the residents as soon as it was economically feasible) and population heterogeneity (since the rapid changes in composition made it difficult for populations in these areas to make a concerted resistance against the influx of new groups). These factors were assumed to determine the extent to which a community structure was able to realize the common goals of its residents and solve common problems (Kornhauser 1978, p. 63; Shoemaker 1984, p. 72). Thus Shaw and McKay's central thesis was that high rates of delinquency reflected the inability of a community to engage in self-regulation (i.e., social disorganization) and not its economic structure per se.

The emphasis on internal stability and self-regulation clearly makes the Shaw and McKay model a variant of what Berry and Kasarda have defined (1977, pp. 72–75) as the systemic model of community structure, which focuses on the degree of interdependence and the density of networks within a community. As their research has shown (pp. 59–71), the development of primary associations that result in informal structures of social control is less likely when these local networks are in a continual state of flux. Similarly, Bursik and Webb (1982, pp. 39–40) have argued that, during periods of rapid internal change, formal community structures of control may disappear or may be extremely resistant to the inclusion of new residents. Thus, the construct of social disorganization is directly related to the dynamics of change that may disrupt these two basic sources of internal control.

## II. The Assumption of Ecological Stability

Shaw and McKay concluded that the local community areas of a city maintained an ongoing, consistent role in the dynamics of the urban system. Thus, a strong assumption of stability also underlies their ecological model. As they note (1969, p. 42), "areas within Chicago have been differentiated in such a way that they can be distinguished from one another by their physical or economic characteristics or, at any given moment, by the composition of the population." That is, while the racial and ethnic composition of the neighborhoods may be historically specific, the economic characteristics that increase the likelihood of social disorganization remain relatively stable over time. Such a statement can be traced directly to Park and Burgess's emphasis on the "natural," or biotic, dynamics of the competitive market system that resulted in the existing pattern of land usage. Therefore, communities were assumed to maintain their dynamic characteristics over time, thereby maintaining a stable overall ecological pattern. This aspect of their ecological model enabled Shaw and McKay to interpret easily what may have been the primary finding of their research—the relative stability of local community delinquency rates over time regardless of racial and ethnic changes in the composition of those areas.

Schuerman and Kobrin have argued that the notion of ecological stability assumed by Shaw and McKay disappeared after World War II, when an acceleration in the rate of urban decentralization occurred that significantly altered the character of the invasion and succession processes (Schuerman and Kobrin 1983, in this volume). Their analysis indicates that neighborhoods are playing new roles in the overall urban structure and, to a large extent, these roles are still being defined. It must be noted that the Schuerman and Kobrin research was conducted in Los Angeles, and it is not clear whether or to what extent such findings apply to Chicago, where Shaw and McKay conducted their work. Bursik and Webb (1982) and Bursik (1984), however, have presented evidence that similar processes of redefinition occurred in Chicago, especially after World War II.

Bursik and Webb note (p. 40), for example, that during the period studied by Shaw and McKay, there were traditional nonstable areas in the zone of transition with high rates of delinquency that served as conduits for incoming white immigrant groups. At the same time, the Black Belt of Chicago provided a similar function for incoming black residents. After 1950, entirely new neighborhoods began to serve such functions for the black population, and the velocity of change involved in the invasion and succession process changed markedly. This does not imply that Shaw and McKay's stability assumption was misplaced. Rather, Shaw and McKay were only able to reach their conclusions concerning stability after considering the patterns of delinquency rates over a forty-year period and interpreting them within the context of current sociological thinking concerning urban dynamics. It can be argued that Shaw and McKay were as influenced by theories of urban dynamics as they were by theories of criminal etiology.

Unfortunately, much of the recent ecological crime research can be criticized for not being sensitive to developments in urban sociology. As Berry and Kasarda detail (1977), as early as the 1930s there was a growing skepticism concerning the approach to human ecology that underlied Shaw and McKay's work. While the ecological approach received an enormous boost with the publication of Amos Hawley's *Human Ecology* in 1950, which posed the central problem of ecology as the analysis of community adaptation to change, the findings have rarely been incorporated into ecological models of crime. Rather, such models, at least implicitly, continue to include the assumption of ecological stability.

There are two possible reasons for this. First, and most obvious, Shaw and McKay had access to a unique data set that spanned a forty-year period of juvenile court referrals. With the exception of Schmid's work (1960*a*, 1960*b*), this has not been true of widely cited subsequent work, such as Lander (1954), Bordua (1958–59), Chilton (1964), Rosen and Turner (1967), Gordon (1967), and Chilton and Dussich (1974). Thus, due to data restrictions, the analytic approaches of these important studies were cross-sectional and could not investigate the dynamics of change in the ecological structures related to crime and delinquency.

However, the enduring assumption of stability was not entirely due to these limitations. A second reason can be traced to the publication of Lander's (1954) ecological study of Baltimore. Shaw and McKay's work often did not clearly differentiate between social disorganization and the presumed outcome of that disorganization (i.e., increased rates of delinquency). This led Lander (p. 10) to conclude that the value of the social disorganization construct "is dubious in view of the fact that social disorganization itself has to be defined as a complex of a group of factors in which juvenile delinquency, crime, broken homes . . . and other socio-pathological factors are included." Thus, Lander defined delinquency *as* social disorganization and focused his research efforts on determining the other community characteristics that should be included in this general complex. This interpretation moved ecological models away from the dynamic causal processes of Shaw and McKay to a concern with simple, cross-sectional associations.

Lander's work might not have had such a strong impact on future ecological research had it not presented findings that apparently indicated that "anomic" rather than economic factors were correlated with delinquency rates. This was an important contradiction of the Shaw and McKay model, which was built entirely on the assumption of a strong zero-order relationship between the socioeconomic composition of an area and its delinquency rate. Lander's research led to the important series of replications cited above that confirmed the existence of the economic status and delinquency relationship. However, even after the issue was resolved, most subsequent studies continued to ignore the full dynamic implications of Shaw and McKay's model and remained associational rather than processual formulations.

Such a limitation presents no problems if the ecological structure of an urban system is in a state of equilibrium. However, as noted above, such an assumption is extremely questionable. For example, as Rosen and Turner (1967) observe, the structure of the 1960 ecological data from Indianapolis analyzed in Chilton's dissertation (1962) is much more congruent with Lander's 1948–52 Baltimore data than with the structure of the 1949–50 data analyzed by Chilton in 1964. This suggests that the ecological dynamics associated with delinquency in Indianapolis may have changed during that ten-year period. Bursik's (1984) analysis also illustrates the dangers of inferring a state of equilibrium from a single wave of ecological data. The associational structure of Chicago during 1950 was significantly different from what preceded it and could only be interpreted in the context of historical changes in residential patterns of settlement that occurred in Chicago then. Any attempt to infer a stable ecological structure on the basis of the 1950 data would have been highly misleading.

In sum, much of the ecological work that has appeared in the Shaw and McKay tradition has been limited by the assumption of ecological stability. However, even in the more recent work that is sensitive to this issue, the full effects of the changing ecological roles of local communities have not been rigorously examined. For example, Schuerman and Kobrin examine only the ten highest crime areas of Los Angeles during 1970; while they are able to document important shifts in the structures of these neighborhoods over twenty years, they do not do so in light of overall changes in the ecological structure of Los Angeles. Likewise, Bursik and Webb's analysis (1982) does not attempt to decompose the relative effects of the components of ecological change on changes in delinquency rates. For the ecological perspective to regain its position as a viable theoretical approach to the study of local community dynamics related to delinquency, such analyses are essential.

## III. The Study of Ecological Change in Models of Crime and Delinquency

The examination of ecological change is not as straightforward as it may appear. One approach that immediately suggests itself is the use of "gain scores" (i.e., the proportional increase or decrease in the level of a variable in two successive periods of time). Such a method was used in Hunter's (1974) analysis of ecological stability in which he factor-analyzed the differences between various measures of areal composition for each ten-year period between 1930 and 1960 in Chicago. However, there are several serious problems with such an approach. In particular, as Bohrnstedt (1969, p. 116) illustrates, such gain scores are correlated with the initial level of that variable; due to the regression toward the mean phenomenon, that correlation tends to be negative.

The confounding of a gain score with its prior level is especially troublesome in the analysis of ecological change. A measure is needed to differentiate between compositional change due to the stable ecological role of a community and change reflecting a redefinition of that role. Although it may initially seem to be counterintuitive to assert that change is possible in a stable structure, recall that certain neighborhoods were assumed by Shaw and McKay to be continually characterized by change. Therefore, change that is associated with this ongoing role needs to be separated from change that is, in a sense, unexpected.

In addition, it is desirable to standardize these change scores in terms of the dynamics of the entire urban system. For example, if the economic base of a city changes dramatically over time, certain changes in the overall ecological system might be expected as a result. A prime example was the recruitment of black labor from the South by northern cities when the flow of white immigration began to disappear. The recruitment had a major effect on the racial composition of such cities. A measure of compositional change that cannot take such dynamics into account may incorrectly infer that a community is playing a new economic role in the urban system when, in fact, the entire system has changed and the relative ecological position of the area has remained identical.

An ideal measure incorporating both considerations is the residual change score suggested by Bohrnstedt (1969) and used in criminological work by Elliott and Voss (1974) and Bursik and Webb (1982). To create such a measure, one regresses the level of a variable at time $t$ on its level at time $t-1$. The residual for each community is the measure of change. Since this score represents the difference between the level of a variable at time $t$ and the level that was predicted on the basis of time $t-1$, the measure is automatically corrected for ongoing patterns that characterize the area; that is, it represents change that was unexpected given the prior ecological position of the community. In addition, since all of the communities in the urban system are used to compute the regression equation, general trends that have characterized that system are also controlled. In this essay, the residual change score has been used to specify change in all of the variables under consideration.

A second consideration in the analysis of change is the "natural" development of ecological areas. It may be that the ecological redefinitional process unfolds gradually over time. Yet, since 1950, there has been a great resurgence in planning activities. As Suttles has noted (1972, p. 41), the expanded role of such programs led to the emergence of "artificial neighborhoods" that reflected not only the economic processes considered by Shaw and McKay but also "politics and some cultural image of what the city ought to be like." As a result, many neighborhoods have undergone dramatic changes that are almost completely unrelated to past developmental patterns. Therefore, it is important to investigate the possibility that some neighborhoods are exceptions, "outliers" from the overall pattern of urban change. For example, changes noted by Bursik and Webb (1982) in Chicago may not have represented the city as a whole but only one or more neighborhoods whose patterns of change were so dramatic that they affected the shape of the entire relationship.

An equally important consideration is that the examination of outliers may suggest new theoretical formulations of the general ecological model of crime. As Lazarsfeld pointed out (see Kendall and Wolf 1949), these "deviant cases" should not be a source of embarrassment to an investigator. Rather, the analyst may discover evidence of additional factors that operate at the ecological level or may refine the measurement of the variables already used in the analysis. Thus, the examination of outliers can play a significant role in the development of ecological models.

The existence of such communities was investigated in the analyses reported here through the use of the DFFITS statistic developed by Belsley, Kuh, and Welsch (1980); DFFITS reflects the degree to which each observation affects the fitting of the regression equation by comparing the predicted values that are derived when an observation is included and then excluded from the model. In order to derive this measure, the residual change score for delinquency rates was regressed on all of the other change scores in the analysis. Cook and Weisberg note (1982, p. 345) that there is no absolute level at which one can determine whether an observation is influential. However, they argue that scores with an absolute value of one or more should be considered to be suspect since they reflect a shift of over 50 percent in the multivariate confidence interval of the beta weights when that observation is included in the model. This guideline has been used in the following analysis.

## IV. The Data

The delinquency change scores used in the analysis are based on the rates of male referrals to the Cook County, Illinois, juvenile court (computed per 1,000 male juveniles ages ten to seventeen) for the years 1930, 1940, 1950, 1960, and 1970 in each of Chicago's officially recognized local community areas. As in prior analyses of these data, the center-city Loop area (community area 32) was eliminated from all analyses due to its very small number of male juveniles. This limitation leaves seventy-four communities available for each of the periods of observation. A complete description of these data can be found in Bursik and Webb (1982) or Bursik (1984). It should be noted, however, that the early series of delinquency rates are based on the original Shaw and McKay data and that the 1970 series was collected by McKay while he was still at the Institute for Juvenile Research in Chicago. Thus, it is possible to reexamine the Shaw and McKay thesis with the same set of data that they used in their original analysis.

Measures of five aspects of compositional change have been drawn from census materials and are used to reflect ecological change: the residual change scores in the percentage nonwhite, the percentage foreign born, the percentage of males that are unemployed, the percentage of owner-occupied dwelling units, and the percentage of households with more than one person per room.[1] These indicators were selected on the basis of two considerations. First, all were consistently available in the census materials for the years under examination. Second, they closely approximate (within the limits of data availability) the economic and compositional variables used in the analysis of Shaw and McKay.

It is important to point out that there are no direct measures of Shaw and McKay's construct of social disorganization. Although such indicators appear to be valid reflections of the processes of change assumed by Shaw and McKay to affect the ability of a community to regulate itself, direct measures of this ability are not available in this data set (nor, for that matter, in most traditional data sets used in ecological analyses). Therefore, one must be very cautious in drawing causal inferences from this analysis. Whether or not the findings are consistent with the social disorganization perspective, they do not provide a definitive test of the causal mechanisms that are involved.

## V. Ecological Change and Delinquency in Chicago

Results of the analysis are reported in this section for decennial periods beginning in 1930 and ending in 1970. The relationships between delinquency rates and compositional variables are described in each subsection and are compared with the earlier findings of Shaw and McKay.

### *A. 1930–40*

The search for outliers indicated that only one local community (Ashburn, community area 70, with a DFFIT statistic of −2.58) may have been characterized by a significantly different process of change from that of the other local areas of Chicago during this decade. While

[1] The density measure for 1930 reflects the average number of persons per room and is drawn from a special census of Chicago conducted in 1934. See Burchard and Arvin (1935).

such outliers are discussed in a later section, it is worth noting that in every other period of change examined in this paper, DFFIT detected several outlying communities. The existence of a single area with a unique relationship between ecological change and changes in delinquency rates suggests that the assumption of an ongoing ecological process may be warranted for this ten-year period.

The correlation matrix for the remaining areas is presented in the Appendix. As our initial model, we hypothesized a two-dimensional structure of ecological change, one dimension reflecting the household status of the communities (household density, the percentage of owner-occupied dwelling units, and the unemployment rate) and the other reflecting their racial and ethnic composition. However, as shown in table 1, a single process of ecological change, density, was found to underlie both sets of dynamics.[2]

Neither the owner-occupied indicator nor the nonwhite composition significantly loads on the factor. Given the correlated error between owner-occupied and household density, there is some indication that a common, unmeasured component of change underlies both of these indicators. However, there is no evidence that a second factor is necessary to reproduce adequately the correlation between them. In general, this indicates that changes in the percentage of dwelling units that are owner occupied in a community were generally independent of the other ecological dynamics under consideration.

Likewise, changes in the nonwhite composition are also randomly associated with the other indicators of change. This finding reflects the historic development of racially related settlement patterns in Chicago. Chicago has always been a very segregated city. For example, in the ten cities analyzed by Lieberson (1963, p. 122), Chicago ranked first in the spatial segregation of blacks from foreign-born whites in 1910, 1920, and 1930 and first in their segregation from native whites, except during 1930 when Chicago was second only to Syracuse. Prior to World War II, blacks were generally forced to live in one of the local communities composing the traditional Black Belt. Although there was some settlement in previously all-white areas, this movement was very gradual, sporadic, and typically met with violent opposition.

[2] The decision as to the number of factors that should be fit to each correlation matrix was guided by the procedure developed by Jöreskog (1971). The chi-square statistic indicated that the 1930–40 and the 1950–60 matrices were generated by a single factor (9.31, $p$ = .097, and 11.47, $p$ = .043, respectively; for each test, df = 5). However, one factor did not provide a satisfactory fit to 1940–50 or 1960–70 (84.81, $p$ = .0001, and 31.57, $p$ = .001, respectively).

TABLE 1

The Ecological Structure of Change, 1930–40

| Indicator | Dimensions of Ecological Change | |
|---|---|---|
| | Factor Loadings | Unique Variance |
| Density | .836 (.171) | .301 |
| Owner-occupied | .255* (.179) | .935 |
| Unemployed | .536 (.140) | .712 |
| Nonwhite | −.074* (.129) | .995 |
| Foreign born | −.362 (.132) | .869 |

NOTE.—$N$ = 73. Standard errors are reported in parentheses. All effects not greater than twice their standard error are marked with an *. All effects with a magnitude of zero have been preset to these values. Correlated measurement errors: density, owner-occupied = −.307 (.138). Standard regression weight of delinquency on the factor = .396 (.133). $R^2$ = .157. $\chi^2$ = 11.00, with 8 df ($p$ = .202).

In addition, the 1930–40 period was characterized by a significant decrease in the rate of black in-migration from the South. As Hirsch (1983, p. 4) documents, this led to a reduction of the pressure to expand the Black Belt and resulted in a period of neighborhood consolidation rather than transition. Therefore, as shown by the measure of unique variance in table 1, changes in the nonwhite composition of Chicago's communities at this time were generally random and not associated with any broad pattern of ecological redefinition. (In a principal factor model, the unique variance can be interpreted as the proportion of an indicator's variation that cannot be "explained" by variation in the underlying dimensions of ecological change.)

Some evidence in table 1 suggests that a degree of such redefinition did occur involving the foreign-born composition, household density, and rate of unemployment. However, with the exception of household density, the bulk of these changes were also randomly associated, as shown by the magnitude of the unique variances. Thus, it does not appear that a great deal of systematic change in the ecological structure of Chicago occurred during this period, and Shaw and McKay's assumption concerning stability at this time is generally warranted.

Given this finding, one would not expect a major redefinition of the distribution of delinquency rates in Chicago during this period. As shown in table 1, there *is* a significant increase in delinquency rates associated with positive changes in the construct, and, contrary to Shaw and McKay's thesis, an unexpected increase in the foreign-born population is associated with a decrease in these rates. However, the relationship is weak, with an $R^2$-statistic of only .157. Therefore, it may be concluded that at this stage in Chicago's history, Shaw and McKay's conclusions concerning the existence of ongoing areas of social disorganization and high delinquency regardless of compositional change are generally upheld.

*B. 1940–50*

The importance of outliers is well illustrated in the second period of change. An examination of DFFITS indicates that three local communities had a significant influence on the form of the regression equation relating changes in the delinquency rate to the other indicators of change: Washington Park (community area 40 with a DFFIT of 1.69), Burnside (community area 47 with a DFFIT of 7.52), and West Pullman (community area 53 with a DFFIT of −2.09).

Bursik and Webb (1982) concluded that changes in the delinquency rates of Chicago's neighborhoods were unrelated to concurrent ecological changes between 1940 and 1950. However, they did not examine the possibility that this result may have occurred due to the effects of one or more communities characterized by atypical processes. The Bursik and Webb analysis used a slightly different set of variables from those used in this paper. However, despite these differences, findings very similar to theirs are produced when outliers are not eliminated from the analysis: only 8.7 percent of the variation in the changes in the delinquency rate is associated with variation in the indicators of ecological change. This suggests that Chicago maintained its ecological stability through 1950. However, the existence of three outliers, including one with an enormous value of DFFIT, suggests that such a conclusion may have been premature.

The findings presented in table 2 represent the structure of change when these communities are excluded from the analysis. As is apparent, the elimination of these areas had a major effect on the fit of the model in that the percentage of variation in delinquency that can be explained has increased dramatically to 40 percent (from 8.7 percent when these communities are included).

The reasons for this change from the 1930–40 period can best be

TABLE 2

The Ecological Structure of Change, 1940–50

| Indicator | Dimensions of Ecological Change | | |
|---|---|---|---|
| | Factor 1 Loadings | Factor 2 Loadings | Unique Variance |
| Density | .863 (.101) | 0 | .255 |
| Owner-occupied | −.378 (.113) | 0 | .857 |
| Unemployed | .868 (.100) | 0 | .247 |
| Nonwhite | .700 (.080) | −.605 (.083) | .034 |
| Foreign born | 0 | 1.004 (.137) | .050 |

NOTE.—$N$ = 71. Standard errors are reported in parentheses. All effects not greater than twice their standard error are marked with an *. All effects with a magnitude of zero have been preset to these values. Correlated measurement errors: density, foreign born = −.294 (.075). Correlation between Factors 1 and 2 = −.129* (.135). Standard regression weight of delinquency on Factor 1 = .391 (.113). Standard regression weight of delinquency on Factor 2 = −.449 (.102). $R^2$ = .400. $\chi^2$ = 9.64, with 5 df ($p$ = .086).

understood through an examination of the measurement model of the exogenous change variables. Two important differences from the stable structure of the preceding decade can be noted. First, the role of nonwhite compositional change has changed significantly. Not only does it clearly load on a racial/ethnic factor, but the dynamics of this process are also associated with changes in the housing status characteristics of these communities.

As Holt and Pacyga have argued (1979, p. 11), poorer blacks often financed resettlement into previously all-white areas by overcrowding into the dwelling units. Thus, table 2 indicates that unexpected increases in the nonwhite composition were related to similar increases in the density of households and a decrease in the percentage owner-occupied. Likewise, given their economic position, such changes were also related to increases in the percentage of unemployed males.

The second difference from the 1930–40 structure is that these changes were far from random, indicating that important processes of ecological redefinition were occurring. Again, with the exception of the owner-occupancy indicator, at least three-fourths of the variation in each of these indicators is related to the two dimensions of change.

Therefore, the assumption of a stable ecological system is untenable given the new roles being played by these communities.

These findings reflect the important changes that characterized Chicago after World War II. Previously, Bursik and Webb (1982) suggested that such neighborhood transitions were an outcome of the Supreme Court open housing decisions of 1948 that made restrictive covenants illegal. However, Hirsch (1983, p. 16) has argued that those decisions simply dealt a "final blow" to a practice that had not been effective in the protection of white homogeneity for many years. Rather, he attributes the rapid racial change during this period to the beginning of the white suburbanization process that followed World War II, which provided a new source of available housing in the central city. Due to the economic gains made by blacks during the war years, they could compete with the white population for this housing. This trend of movement out of the Black Belt was accelerated by the extreme shortage of housing in that area and a resurgence of migration from the South that increased the size of the black population in Chicago by 77 percent during this period.

Hirsch's argument is supported by the existence of two independent dimensions of ecological change. As Holt and Pacyga note (1979, p. 11), white residents, spurred on by real estate speculators, viewed the incoming blacks as a single economic group and perceived the arrival of any blacks as "tantamount to the imminent transformation of the area into a slum ghetto" and subsequently fled. Yet, prior to the white movement to the suburbs, blacks of all economic classes had been forced to live in the Black Belt. When more housing became available, members of the black middle class were able to purchase new residences in formerly all-white areas. I feel, therefore, that the first dimension of change represents the areal dynamics associated with the influx of poor nonwhites, while the second reflects racial change regardless of associated economic dynamics.

The significant effect of the first dimension on changes in the delinquency rate is understandable in terms of the Shaw and McKay model, since it represents the transformation of new neighborhoods into areas of relative instability, such as traditionally were found in the zone of transition during earlier periods of Chicago's history. However, the effect of the second dimension is a direct contradiction of Shaw and McKay's thesis that changes in delinquency are unrelated to compositional changes. Nevertheless, when their notion of social disorganization is considered in the context of Berry and Kasarda's systemic approach to community structure, this finding is understandable. The formal and informal networks necessary to the effective self-regulation of the community are extremely hard to maintain during periods of rapid compositional change. Thus, it is not surprising that areas with very large unexpected increases in their composition would also be characterized by concurrent increases in the delinquency rate (for a more detailed discussion of this phenomenon, see Bursik and Webb [1982] or Bursik [1984]).

*C. 1950–60*

While the Bursik and Webb analysis (1982) failed to detect the ecological changes occurring between 1940 and 1950, one would expect that the shape of the relational trend that they detected between 1940 and 1970 would be fairly robust despite the inclusion of outliers in their model. As they show (1982, table 3), 75 percent of the racially related compositional change that occurred in Chicago between 1940 and 1950 was of the foothold variety, in which nonwhites remained in the minority in an area although their composition increased by at least 10 percent. However, between 1950 and 1960, the dominant form of change (64 percent) was rapid neighborhood turnover, with nonwhites moving from a minority to majority status in the ten-year period. Since these areas were changing much more rapidly during this decade, the association between delinquency and ecological change should be much stronger than between 1940 and 1950 due to the presumed more rapid disruption of local networks and the growing entrenchment of the new socially disorganized areas.

As shown in table 3, the elimination of three outliers from the analysis (Near North Side, community area 8 with a DFFIT of 1.17; Burnside, again with a DFFIT of −1.19; and Englewood, community area 68 with a DFFIT of −1.2) does not destroy this important pattern. The $R^2$-statistic increases by more than 35 percent over the 1940–50 period to .542. That is, over half of the variation in changes in local delinquency rates can be explained by the processes of ecological redefinition during this period. The structure of ecological redefinition related to delinquency has again changed significantly. While the degree of variation that the exogenous variables share in common is over 50 percent for all of the indicators except the percentage of owner-occupied dwelling units, the unique variances are significantly higher than they were in the preceding decade for all but percentage nonwhite. Thus, while redefinition is continuing to occur, it is somewhat

TABLE 3

The Ecological Structure of Change, 1950–60

| Indicator | Dimensions of Ecological Change: Factor Loadings | Unique Variance |
|---|---|---|
| Density | .745<br>(.105) | .445 |
| Owner-occupied | −.168*<br>(.123) | .972 |
| Unemployed | .715<br>(.106) | .489 |
| Nonwhite | .951<br>(.093) | .096 |
| Foreign born | −.797<br>(.102) | .364 |

NOTE.—$N$ = 71. Standard errors are reported in parentheses. All effects not greater than twice their standard error are marked with an *. All effects with a magnitude of zero have been preset to these values. Correlated measurement errors: density, foreign born = −.133 (.063). Standard regression weight of delinquency on the factor = .736 (.105). $R^2$ = .542. $\chi^2$ = 9.98, with 8 df ($p$ = .266).

less systematic than in the preceding period. In addition, the two dynamics related to nonwhite movement are no longer in operation. Rather, during this period, no systematic patterns of change appear that are unrelated to changes in household status.

To some extent, then, the dynamics of ecological change in Chicago had returned to a pattern similar to that found between 1930 and 1940 with two major differences. First, nonwhite movement became an integral component of ecological redefinition. Second, these dynamics were much more systematic than those found between 1930 and 1940, significantly redefining the ecological role of many of these neighborhoods. This changed role was accompanied by increases in the delinquency rate due to rapid internal changes. Since these changes tended to be much more rapid than those of 1940–50, the association of changes in delinquency rates to these patterns increased.

### *D. 1960–70*

During this final period of analysis, Bursik and Webb (1982) argued that the magnitude of the relationship between changes in the delinquency rate and ecological redefinition should decrease from the level observed in 1950–60 due to a deceleration in the neighborhood turnover process. Between 1960 and 1970, 41 percent of the changes in racial composition were again of the foothold variety, while only 32 percent represented a rapid turnover. In addition, many of the areas characterized by rapid racial changes in the past now began the process of entrenchment as the nonwhites strengthened their position as the dominant group.

Despite the elimination of two outliers from the analysis (Oakland, community area 36 with a DFFIT of −1.25, and South Shore, community area 43 with a DFFIT of 1.20), the pattern is verified: the $R^2$-statistic has fallen from .542 during the previous decade to only .316. Thus, the relationship of ecological change to changes in the delinquency character of Chicago's local areas began to weaken at this time.

One might expect that the ecological structure of Chicago was beginning to stabilize at this point. However, as shown in table 4, this is not entirely the case. A two-factor solution very similar to that derived for 1940–50 appears to underlie these dynamics. There are some important differences that must be noted. First, changes in nonwhite composition are no longer a part of the household composition dimension of change. Second, the two factors are no longer orthogonal: although they represent distinct processes of ecological change, they tend to occur mutually during this period. Nevertheless, as a comparison of the unique variances presented in tables 2, 3, and 4 indicates, the ecological changes are more systematic than those for 1950–60 and nearly as systematic as those for 1940–50.

A reason for this resurgence of ecological redefinition has been offered by Berry and Kasarda (1977, pp. 23–31). During this decade, a large housing surplus arose in Chicago due to an increase in construction accompanied by the growing movement to the suburbs that began after World War II. At the same time, "downward pressure was exerted on the prices of older housing units . . . and discriminatory pricing was eliminated" (p. 24). As a result, "many families improved their housing conditions dramatically" (p. 24). Thus, in a manner similar to the effects of the initial suburbanization that followed World War II, these developments in the real estate market opened up new areas of settlement previously unavailable to nonwhite families and significant degrees of racial change occurred.

Since these ecological changes were more systematic than those occurring between 1950 and 1960, the question arises why the association of these dynamics with changes in delinquency is not as strong during this final period. The answer is that, while the redefinition process was more systematic than in the preceding decade, the general rate of this

TABLE 4

The Ecological Structure of Change, 1960–70

| Indicator | Dimensions of Ecological Change | | |
|---|---|---|---|
| | Factor 1 Loadings | Factor 2 Loadings | Unique Variance |
| Density | .802<br>(.116) | 0 | .357 |
| Owner-occupied | −.194*<br>(.129) | 0 | .962 |
| Unemployed | .831<br>(.116) | 0 | .309 |
| Nonwhite | 0 | .974<br>(.124) | .051 |
| Foreign born | 0 | −.666<br>(.121) | .556 |

NOTE.—$N$ = 72. Standard errors are reported in parentheses. All effects not greater than twice their standard error are marked with an *. All effects with a magnitude of zero have been preset to these values. Correlated measurement errors: none. Correlation between Factors 1 and 2 = .578 (.109). Standard regression weight of delinquency on Factor 1 = .312 (.154). Standard regression weight of delinquency on Factor 2 = .321 (.148). $R^2$ = .316. $\chi^2$ = 8.91, with 7 df ($p$ = .259).

process was not as rapid. Therefore, the processes of increased instability assumed to be related to increased social disorganization were not as pronounced.

## VI. The Role of Outliers in Ecological Models

The preceding analysis indicates that the ecological structure of Chicago has undergone significant changes since 1940. This ecological redefinition resulted in significant changes in the delinquency rates of Chicago's local communities as new areas became characterized by the instability related to social disorganization. The degree of such changes in delinquency depended on the rate at which these dynamics of resettlement occurred.

While these findings characterize Chicago as a whole, an examination of residuals suggested that, during each period of analysis, one or more communities may have existed that experienced significantly different processes of change. In one case, this evidence was spurious, since the anomaly arose due to a very unstable delinquency rate. In 1930, as Hunter has shown (1974, p. 55), Ashburn was a newly developed area that was "little more than prairie"; its population of 733 residents was the smallest in the city.

Of that population, only fifty-six were male juveniles between the ages of ten and seventeen, who were involved in two court referrals. This resulted in a very large delinquency rate of 35.7 per 1,000 boys. In 1940, this rate fell to zero, apparently representing a dramatic drop in the residual change score. Since the difference between two and zero referrals in a population of this size can legitimately be assumed to reflect random fluctuation, we certainly cannot infer the existence of a different set of ecological dynamics for Ashburn during this period.

This is not the case for the other outliers, whose residual change scores are based on much larger population bases. Unfortunately, we do not have the historical materials at hand for some of these areas that would enable us to examine each of these cases in sufficient detail. Luckily, the dynamics of one of these areas (South Shore) has recently been the subject of a book by Taub, Taylor, and Dunham (1984).

The focus here is on two areas whose dynamics have especially important implications for the development of ecological theories of crime and delinquency. The first of these is Burnside, an area that emerged as an outlier in both 1940–50 and 1950–60. Between 1940 and 1950, Burnside was characterized by the largest change in delinquency rates in the city. Yet, during that time, the area maintained its status as a small, extremely stable blue-collar area with a large concentration of foreign-born whites, owner-occupied homes, and essentially no non-white residents. Therefore, its change during this period is totally unexpected given the processes characterizing the other areas of Chicago. Bursik (1984) has suggested that, contrary to the traditional ecological focus on the internal dynamics of communities that are related to crime and delinquency,[3] this increase may have reflected a protective response to rapid racial changes that were occurring in nearby areas in a manner analogous to Suttles's (1972) notion of the defended community. In this regard, Berry and Kasarda have noted that the defensive reactions of most communities to date have primarily involved a response to the potential influx of groups with a perceived lower status, which has historically taken the form of white, ethnic efforts to defend their neighborhoods from black resettlement.

In an initial examination of the generalizability of this process, Heitgerd and Bursik (1984) present evidence that such compositional

[3] I want to emphasize that, while this is the case for ecological work in the Shaw and McKay tradition, there has been research in criminology that has focused on adjacency effects and crime. See, e.g., Boggs (1966).

dynamics external to the local community can play a significant role in the production of delinquency rates. Such a finding is wholly consistent with Hawley's (1950) reformulation of the ecological perspective as the analysis of linkages that exist between communities. In a more recent article (1981, p. 9), he argues more forcefully that the problem of community organization is a problem of adjustment to an environment that includes "the influences that emanate from other organized populations in the same or other areas. In certain circumstances, [this] acquires a more critical importance. . . ." However, such orientations are extremely rare in ecological models of crime. The identification of Burnside as an outlier in this analysis emphasizes the need to incorporate such external factors into our models if we wish to make them sensitive to current urban dynamics.

A second outlier poses a problem that has received considerable attention from criminologists and urban sociologists: the definition of the local community in ecological studies. As the setting for Zorbaugh's (1929) *The Gold Coast and the Slum*, the Near North Side of Chicago will be familiar to many readers.[4] Between 1950 and 1960, it too was characterized by a large increase in its delinquency rate, changing from 14.97 to 45.13 referrals per 1,000 during that period. One might expect that this was due to the expansion of the Cabrini Green Housing Project in 1958, a large, high-rise complex of great internal instability. Yet, Hunter (1974, p. 45) has called this area an "anomaly" in that the increasing influx of poor blacks into this housing project was accompanied by a significant increase in the socioeconomic status of the overall community. In the data analyzed here, for example, the rate of change for the unemployment rate was two standard deviations *below* the mean for the city as a whole.

This contradictory pattern reflects the extreme economic heterogeneity that has persisted in this area since the publication of Zorbaugh's book. The lakefront section of the Near North Side, spurred on by urban renewal, continues to be a fashionable high-income area of the city; the western section remains one of the poorest. Thus, it is extremely questionable whether the Near North Side can be considered to form a single community in any sense of the word.

Many criminological ecologists (see Shannon 1982; Schuerman and Kobrin 1983, in this volume) have taken great pains to identify the true

[4] It is interesting that Shaw and McKay also detected the outlying characteristics of the Near North Side (1969, p. 55).

ecological units in the cities they have examined. As the findings for the Near North Side indicate, the acceptance of predetermined geographic boundaries can confound the various subprocesses in these areas and result in findings that are extremely misleading. In many cases, such as ours, the examination of such internal differentiation is not possible due to the limitations of the data.

Yet such considerations are very important in terms of the full model of social disorganization developed by Shaw and McKay. Earlier in this essay, it was cautioned that this analysis does not provide a full test of the model in that no direct measures of the local community networks that are assumed to intervene between rapid change and delinquency were available. It is likely that some of the communities used in the analysis are characterized by several sets of such networks with varying capabilities for self-regulation. Therefore, a researcher must be extremely cautious in the use of such data.

This examination of outliers should have three major benefits. First, and most important, our prior failure to do so masked the important changes that occurred in Chicago between 1940 and 1950. Although three areas were eliminated during this period, the differences between the two models primarily reflects the role of Burnside, which had an extremely high value of DFFIT. Thus, even the elimination of a single observation can greatly alter the inferences to be made.

Second, it has been suggested that the traditional emphasis on the internal dynamics of local communities has ignored a component of urban dynamics that has important implications for the development of ecological theories of crime and delinquency. That is, in certain contexts, delinquency may represent an organized response to perceived external threats. Finally, the acceptance of politically defined boundaries without a careful examination of the differentiation within those boundaries may seriously confound several different ecological processes located in those areas.

## VII. Conclusions

The preceding analysis has an important implication for ecological theories of crime and delinquency. As Schuerman and Kobrin (1983) noted for Los Angeles, the assumption of ecological stability has not been warranted in Chicago since the 1940–50 period. To illustrate the inferential dangers that may arise when these dynamics are ignored, a traditional static analysis on the 1970 data was performed, regressing the delinquency rate in 1970 on the measure of nonwhite for that same

TABLE 5

Regression of the 1970 Delinquency Rate on the 1970 Static NONWHITE Indicator

| | Standard Beta | Metric Beta | Standard Error | $t$-Value | $p$-Value |
|---|---|---|---|---|---|
| Intercept | .000 | 8.561 | 1.106 | 7.743 | .0001 |
| Nonwhite 1970 | .742 | .209 | .023 | 9.258 | .0001 |

NOTE.—$R^2$ = .550. $F(1,70)$ = 85.703.

year. Table 5 presents the results of a standard regression analysis. As can be seen, the findings are typical of patterns found with cross-sectional data. However, while a researcher would most likely conclude that something about nonwhite communities makes high rates of delinquency more likely, it is impossible to determine the extent to which this pattern is ongoing or a temporary reflection of a changing urban structure.

A dynamic approach provides important additional insights into these processes. The 1970 nonwhite composition indicator was decomposed into two components: its value during 1960 and, through the residual change score, the level of the 1970 rate that could not be predicted on the basis of 1960. Thus, the 1970 data have been partitioned into the elements of stability and change. Such a decomposition retains all of the information found in the static model; this can be seen in a comparison of the $R^2$-values in tables 5 and 6. However, it is now in a form that is able to differentiate between the association related to ongoing patterns of nonwhite composition and that pertaining to unexpected disruptions of that composition.

The findings of table 6 provide a much more informative picture of the ecological dynamics associated with the static delinquency rate of 1970. While the ongoing pattern of nonwhite composition does have a significant relationship with the level of delinquency in these areas, the magnitude of that association has noticeably decreased. Rather, as can be seen, a large proportion of the race-related static association reflects unexpected increases in the nonwhite population. These increases should be related to the increased inability of a community to regulate itself during periods of great instability. By decomposing the static association in this manner, therefore, it can be seen that a significant part of the cross-sectional relationship reflects the effects of the ecolog-

TABLE 6

Regression of the 1970 Delinquency Rate on the 1960 Static NONWHITE Indicator and Its 1970 Residual Change Score

| | Standard Beta | Metric Beta | Standard Error | *t*-Value | *p*-Value |
|---|---|---|---|---|---|
| Intercept | .000 | 11.058 | 1.005 | 11.002 | .0001 |
| Nonwhite 1960 | .639 | .208 | .026 | 7.918 | .0001 |
| Nonwhite 1970 (Residual) | .362 | .199 | .044 | 4.484 | .0001 |

NOTE.—$R^2$ = .551. $F(2,69)$ = 42.325.

ical redefinition of areas and not any factor specific to nonwhite composition per se.

A similar analysis of the 1930–40 data (not presented) indicates that, if an ecological system is characterized by a general, ongoing stability, such considerations are not necessary. The inclusion into the equation of the change in nonwhite composition during this period does not provide any significant explanatory power over the nonwhite composition in 1930. That is, cross-sectional inferences based on that period would not have confounded the effects of ecological redefinition with the effects of ongoing community dynamics. Only if an urban system is characterized by ecological equilibrium can one make robust inferences concerning the underlying causes of community rates of delinquency with cross-sectional data. Without testing the assumption of stability, ecological models will not only have a limited degree of theoretical power, but they will have an interpretive framework that is generally unrelated to the dynamics of modern urban areas.

## VIII. Discussion

As noted above, Shaw and McKay assumed that the spatial distribution of delinquency rates reflected the underlying dynamics of a stable ecological system. Evidence has been presented that, since World War II, Chicago has undergone a significant process of ecological redefinition, primarily as a result of the processes of suburbanization that began at this time. Reiss (1976, p. 81) has observed that the resulting changes in delinquency rates such as those documented in this essay may be natural outcomes of the dynamics of city growth since "given their movement to areas of lower housing density . . . the lower classes will occupy proportionately more territorial area." Combined with the "growing evidence that official rates of delinquency and crime are increasing in areas outside of central cities" (p. 81), Reiss's observations suggest that studies (such as this one) that restrict themselves to the delineation of the ecological system as defined by the political boundaries of the central city may be ignoring a significant portion of the actual system.

Because an important part of the ecological perspective concerns the symbiotic relationships between different parts of the system, a reliance on the central city alone may result in an incomplete understanding of the urban dynamics that are involved in delinquency. Such a position is supported by the work of Berry and Kasarda (1977, chap. 10), who present evidence that the expansion of the suburban ring is associated with changes in the occupational and industrial organization of the central city.

Two implications for the development of ecological theories of crime and delinquency are indicated by the investigation of symbiotic relationships in the urban environment:

1. What may appear to be exogenous shocks to an ecological system (e.g., the construction of a large industrial plant in a suburb with a low rate of tax assessment) may in fact be integral, endogenous developments within the system itself. By using central city boundaries to determine the scope of the ecological system, it would not be possible to examine the general effects this had on the ecology of the area as a whole and the effects it subsequently had on local social disorganization and delinquency rates.

2. Given such considerations and the processes of city growth on which they are based, central city–based ecological studies of crime and delinquency may be observing the gradual transformation of the central city into an area similar to Burgess's zone of transition. Such analyses can certainly provide important insights into the community and delinquency relationship. Yet it must be recognized that, if the "real" ecological system continues to expand, these studies will become more analogous to Zorbaugh's work in the Near North Side of Chicago (which examined in detail a small part of the system) than to Shaw and McKay's focus on the entire ecological structure.

I recognize, of course, that there are recent significant social trends, such as gentrification (see McDonald, in this volume), that are already having an effect on the modification of this process. Nevertheless, it is important to consider whether increasing instability and delinquency rates within the central city are a necessary outcome of urban growth.

The social disorganization approach of Shaw and McKay has at times been criticized as "conservative" because of its argument that the internal dynamics of communities are an outcome of "natural" market mechanisms. Snodgrass (1976, p. 10), for example, argues that their focus might have "turned outward to show political, economic and historical forces at work . . . the interpretation left business and industry essentially immune from analysis . . . in the causes of delinquency." To some extent, this is a caricature of their position (see, e.g., their discussion of the invasion and succession of industrial and commercial enterprises). However, it is true that this aspect of their work was largely undeveloped, and it is easy to get the impression that the distribution of delinquency is the natural outcome of economic competition for desirable space.

Likewise, in this analysis, the processes of suburbanization and the resulting effects on the stability of the local communities of the central city may appear to be solely the result of the housing shortages characterizing Chicago in the early 1940s. However, it is also true that much of the instability in these changing neighborhoods was induced by nonmarket mechanisms (for a very detailed discussion of the interaction between these two forces, see Hirsch [1983], chap. 1).

What new construction that did occur shortly after World War II was of a type and in a location not suited to easy black resettlement; Hirsch's argument strongly suggests that this was a conscious effort on the part of the housing and lending industries. Taking advantage of this and the large increases in the black population, landlords within the Black Belt tended to subdivide existing apartments into much smaller "kitchenettes," many of which lacked bathroom facilities. Such efforts resulted in strong "push" factors that encouraged many residents to leave the community even before it was economically feasible.

Thus, the "natural" aspects of instability due to market mechanisms were greatly accelerated by efforts to reap quick profits at the expense of the residents. Therefore, to some extent, the social disorganization reflected concerted efforts at market manipulation. If instability can be fostered by such efforts, then it must be logically possible also consciously to create situations conducive to stability. McKay notes (1967, p. 115) that in some areas of Chicago once characterized by instability (except those "close to the heart of the city where rapid change is a permanent characteristic"), stability has gradually developed and delinquency rates have declined. If programs were developed to foster (or accelerate) these stabilizing patterns, then a decreasing rate of delinquency should result.

It is interesting that such a proposition has its roots in the work of Shaw and McKay. Shaw in particular considered himself to be a social reformer as well as sociologist. Based in part on the findings of his ecological work, he created an umbrella organization (the Chicago Area Project) that attempted to support neighborhood efforts at developing local informal and institutional networks of control. The correspondence of such an approach to the notion of social disorganization is apparent. Although the success of the CAP has been debated (see Schlossman and Sedlak 1983), the important point is that such nonmarket-related processes may be able to alter the nature of ecological dynamics.

Unfortunately, one of the reasons that ecological approaches are considered to be inherently conservative is that they tend to be grounded in very early formulations of urban process. An important theme of more recent work concerns the dynamics of political decision-making processes that can significantly alter the character (and ecological structure) of the city. A fuller consideration of these recent developments than has been considered by urban sociologists is necessary if the ecological approach is to remain a viable approach in the future.

## TABLE A1

### Correlations for Each Period of Change

| Variable | DENSITY | OWNERSHIP | UNEMPLOYMENT | NONWHITE | FOREIGN BORN |
|---|---|---|---|---|---|
| Correlations for 1930–40 change: | | | | | |
| Delinquency | .307 | .138 | .232 | .127 | −.242 |
| Density | | −.094 | .488 | −.047 | −.261 |
| Ownership | | | .042 | −.052 | −.216 |
| Unemployment | | | | −.216 | −.109 |
| Nonwhite | | | | | −.098 |
| Correlations for 1940–50 change: | | | | | |
| Delinquency | .384 | −.064 | .407 | .617 | −.497 |
| Density | | −.179 | .777 | −.655 | −.381 |
| Ownership | | | −.253 | −.174 | −.204 |
| Unemployment | | | | .707 | −.180 |
| Nonwhite | | | | | −.679 |
| Correlations for 1950–60 change: | | | | | |
| Delinquency | .557 | −.252 | .540 | .696 | −.581 |
| Density | | −.297 | .516 | .706 | −.727 |
| Ownership | | | −.114 | −.120 | .134 |
| Unemployment | | | | .684 | −.542 |
| Nonwhite | | | | | −.763 |
| Correlations for 1960–70 change: | | | | | |
| Delinquency | .351 | −.010 | .460 | .484 | −.403 |
| Density | | −.136 | .664 | −.505 | −.268 |
| Ownership | | | −.206 | −.068 | −.085 |
| Unemployment | | | | .433 | −.259 |
| Nonwhite | | | | | −.649 |

## REFERENCES

Baldwin, John. 1979. "Ecological and Areal Studies in Great Britain and the United States." In *Crime and Justice: An Annual Review of Research*, vol. 1, edited by Norval Morris and Michael Tonry. Chicago: University of Chicago Press.

Belsley, David A., Edwin Kuh, and Roy E. Welsch. 1980. *Regression Diagnostics*. New York: Wiley.

Berry, Brian J. L., and John D. Kasarda. 1977. *Contemporary Urban Ecology*. New York: Macmillan.

Boggs, Sarah. 1966. "Urban Crime Patterns." *American Sociological Review* 30:899–908.

Bohrnstedt, George W. 1969. "Observations on the Measurement of Change." In *Sociological Methodology, 1969*, edited by E. F. Borgatta. San Francisco: Jossey-Bass.

Bordua, David J. 1958–59. "Juvenile Delinquency and 'Anomie': An Attempt at Replication." *Social Problems* 6:230–38.

Burchard, Edwin L., and Martin J. Arvin. 1935. *District Fact Book for Seventy-five Chicago Local Communities*. Chicago: Chicago Board of Education.

Burgess, Ernest W. 1925. "The Growth of the City." In *The City*, edited by R. E. Park, E. W. Burgess, and R. D. McKenzie. Chicago: University of Chicago Press.

Bursik, Robert J., Jr. 1984. "Urban Dynamics and Ecological Studies of Delinquency." *Social Forces* 63:393–413.

Bursik, Robert J., Jr., and Jim Webb. 1982. "Community Change and Patterns of Delinquency." *American Journal of Sociology* 88:24–42.

Chilton, Roland J. 1962. "Social Factors and the Residential Distribution of Official Delinquents, Indianapolis, Indiana." Ph.D. dissertation, Indiana University.

———. 1964. "Continuities in Delinquency Area Research: A Comparison of Studies for Baltimore, Detroit and Indianapolis." *American Sociological Review* 29:71–83.

Chilton, Roland J., and John P. J. Dussich. 1974. "Methodological Issues in Delinquency Research: Some Alternative Analyses of Geographically Distributed Data." *Social Forces* 53:73–80.

Cook, R. Dennis, and Sanford Weisberg. 1982. "Criticism and Influence Analysis in Regression." In *Sociological Methodology, 1982*, edited by S. Leinhardt. San Francisco: Jossey-Bass.

Davidson, R. Norman. 1981. *Crime and Environment*. New York: St. Martin's.

Elliott, Delbert S., and Harwin L. Voss. 1974. *Delinquency and Dropout*. Lexington, Mass.: Heath.

Gordon, Robert A. 1967. "Issues in the Ecological Study of Delinquency." *American Sociological Review* 32:927–44.

Hawley, Amos. 1950. *Human Ecology*. New York: Ronald.

———. 1981. *Urban Society: An Ecological Approach*. 2d ed. New York: Wiley.

Heitgerd, Janet L., and Robert J. Bursik, Jr. 1984. "The Defended Community and Patterns of Spatial Autocorrelation." Paper presented at the annual meeting of the American Society of Criminology, Cincinnati.

Hirsch, Arnold R. 1983. *Making the Second Ghetto.* Cambridge: Cambridge University Press.

Holt, Glen E., and Dominic A. Pacyga. 1979. *Chicago: A Historical Guide to the Neighborhoods. The Loop and South Side.* Chicago: Chicago Historical Society.

Hunter, Albert. 1974. *Symbolic Communities.* Chicago: University of Chicago Press.

Janowitz, Morris. 1967. "Introduction." In *The City*, edited by R. E. Park, E. W. Burgess, and R. D. McKenzie. Chicago: University of Chicago Press.

Jöreskog, Karl G. 1971. "Simultaneous Factor Analysis in Several Populations." *Psychometrika* 36:409–26.

Kendall, Patricia L., and Katherine M. Wolf. 1949. "The Analysis of Deviant Cases in Communication Research." In *Communications Research 1948–49*, edited by P. L. Lazarsfeld and F. Stanton. New York: Holt & Co.

Kornhauser, Ruth R. 1978. *Social Sources of Delinquency.* Chicago: University of Chicago Press.

Lander, Bernard. 1954. *Toward an Understanding of Juvenile Delinquency.* New York: Columbia University Press.

Lieberson, Stanley. 1963. *Ethnic Patterns in American Cities.* Glencoe: Free Press.

McDonald, Scott C. In this volume. "Does Gentrification Affect Crime Rates?"

McKay, Henry D. 1967. "A Note on Trends in Rates of Delinquency in Certain Areas of Chicago." In *Task Force Report: Juvenile Delinquency and Youth Crime.* President's Commission on Law Enforcement and Administration of Justice. Washington, D.C.: U.S. Government Printing Office.

Morris, Terrence. 1970. "Book Review: *Juvenile Delinquency and Urban Areas*, 2d ed." *British Journal of Criminology* 10:194–96.

Nettler, Gwynn. 1984. *Explaining Crime.* 3d ed. New York: McGraw-Hill.

Park, Robert E., and Ernest W. Burgess. 1924. *Introduction to the Science of Sociology.* 2d ed. Chicago: University of Chicago Press.

Reiss, Albert J., Jr. 1976. "Settling the Frontiers of a Pioneer in American Criminology." In *Delinquency, Crime and Society*, edited by J. F. Short, Jr. Chicago: University of Chicago Press.

Rosen, Lawrence, and Stanley H. Turner. 1967. "An Evaluation of the Lander Approach to Ecology of Delinquency." *Social Problems* 15:189–200.

Schlossman, Steven, and Michael Sedlak. 1983. *The Chicago Area Project Revisited.* Santa Monica, Calif.: Rand.

Schmid, Calvin F. 1960*a*. "Urban Areas: Part I." *American Sociological Review* 25:527–42.

———. 1960*b*. "Urban Areas: Part II." *American Sociological Review* 25:655–78.

Schuerman, Leo A., and Solomon Kobrin. 1983. "Crime and Urban Ecological Processes: Implications for Public Policy." Paper presented at the annual meeting of the American Society of Criminology, Denver.

———. In this volume. "Community Careers in Crime."

Shannon, Lyle W. 1982. "The Relationship of Juvenile Delinquency and Adult

Crime to the Changing Ecological Structure of the City." Executive report submitted to the National Institute of Justice, Washington, D.C.

Shaw, Clifford R., and Henry D. McKay. 1942. *Juvenile Delinquency and Urban Areas*. Chicago: University of Chicago Press.

———. 1969. *Juvenile Delinquency and Urban Areas*. 2d ed. Chicago: University of Chicago.

Shaw, Clifford R., Frederick M. Zorbaugh, Henry D. McKay, and Leonard S. Cottrell. 1929. *Delinquency Areas*. Chicago: University of Chicago Press.

Shoemaker, Donald J. 1984. *Theories of Delinquency*. New York: Oxford University Press.

Snodgrass, Jon. 1976. "Clifford R. Shaw and Henry D. McKay: Chicago Criminologists." *British Journal of Criminology* 16:1–19.

Suttles, Gerald D. 1972. *The Social Construction of Communities*. Chicago: University of Chicago Press.

Taub, Richard P., D. Garth Taylor, and Jan D. Dunham. 1984. *Paths of Neighborhood Change: Race and Crime in Urban American*. Chicago: University of Chicago Press.

Tittle, Charles R. 1983. "Social Class and Criminal Behavior: A Critique of the Theoretical Perspective." *Social Forces* 62:334–58.

Zorbaugh, Harvey W. 1929. *The Gold Coast and the Slum*. Chicago: University of Chicago Press.

*Leo Schuerman and Solomon Kobrin*

# Community Careers in Crime

ABSTRACT

Urban ecologists have documented the stages through which residential communities in American metropolitan areas move as they undergo physical and social deterioration. Criminologists have documented the roles of deteriorated urban neighborhoods as areas of high rates of crime and delinquency. Less is known about how neighborhoods evolve into high-crime areas. Using a developmental model, this research investigated the twenty-year histories of Los Angeles County's highest-crime-rate neighborhoods in 1970. Three distinct stages were identified: emerging, transitional, and enduring. Use of cross-sectional and time-series analyses revealed that neighborhood deterioration precedes rising crime early in the cycle but that, as neighborhoods move into the later enduring stage, rising crime rates precede further neighborhood deterioration. Among the changes signaling neighborhood deterioration and rising crime rates were a shift from single- to multiple-family dwellings, a rise in residential mobility, unrelated individuals and broken families, the ratio of children to adults, minority group populations, females in the labor force, and nonwhite and Spanish surname population with advanced education. Early in the cycle, the speed of change in neighborhood characteristics exceeds the rate of increase in crime, while later, the accelerating crime rise outstrips the velocity of neighborhood change. Efforts to prevent the development of new high-crime areas must focus on neighborhoods in the emerging stage of the deterioration cycle.

Leo Schuerman and Solomon Kobrin are Professors at the University of Southern California, Social Science Research Institute. This essay was prepared with partial support from grant 78-NI-AX-0127 from the National Institute of Justice. Data files were graciously provided by the Los Angeles County Department of Probation, the Los Angeles County Assessor's office, and the U.S. Bureau of Census's decennial population and housing censuses. Points of view expressed herein are those of the authors and do not necessarily represent the official position of the Justice Department and Los Angeles County agencies.


0-226-80802-5/86/0008-0003$01.00

Urban ecologists have documented the stages through which residential communities in American metropolitan areas move as they change from desirable residential environments into high-crime and delinquency areas. Two loosely joined research literatures attempt to explain this historical transformation.

First, scholars have provided an account of the cycle of urban land use through multiple stages. These start with initial residential settlement by single-family dwellings, followed by stages of increased density of residential settlement, and downgrading for commercial and industrial uses, giving way to abandonment and demolition, and moving finally into the stage of urban renewal (Hoover and Vernon 1962). An earlier account focused on patterns of urban growth, seen as inducing an invasion of industrial and commercial land uses into contiguous residential areas, resulting in their deterioration (Burgess 1926). These were known as ecologically based theories.

Second, criminologists using the ecological perspective have shown that there is a general relation between severely declining urban neighborhoods and rates of crime and delinquency. For example, Shaw and McKay (1942) in Chicago, Morris (1958), and Schmid (1960) in Seattle have demonstrated that deteriorated residential areas have consistently been characterized by the city's highest rates of crime and delinquency. The specific stages through which these areas moved in their progress toward a condition of high criminality have not been adequately explored. Nor did the earlier theories account for the consequent transformations in socioeconomic and subculture characteristics of high-crime areas.

In this study, we used a "developmental" model, based on longitudinal data spanning a twenty-year history of Los Angeles County's highest-crime areas, to ascertain how and where neighborhoods evolve into high-crime areas. The analyses showed three definable stages in the development of high-crime areas: emerging, transitional, and enduring.

Early in the process, neighborhood structural deterioration precedes rising crime. As the neighborhood moves into the later enduring stage, rising crime rates precede accelerated rates of neighborhood deterioration. Thus neighborhood structural components become not causes but consequences, and crime emerges as the dominant force in neighborhood change.

Early in the process, the speed of change in neighborhood characteristics exceeds the rate of increase in crime. By the time an area reaches the enduring stage, the speed of change in neighborhood characteristics is outstripped by an accelerating crime rate that becomes the single driving condition of the crime area.

Taken as a whole, high-crime areas in the contemporary metropolis appear to be an inevitable, or "natural," product of ecological, economic, social, and political forces. However, these areas do not come into existence all at once but over a span of time, whose length is probably a reflection of the growth rate of any given metropolis. The question arises whether there is any point in the developmental sequence at which intervention may reduce the likelihood that a neighborhood will evolve into a high-crime area.

## I. Problems of Measurement and Analysis

The neglect of research into the etiology of community careers in crime has resulted from lack of adequate time-series data and the unavailability of appropriate analytical techniques for assessing the interaction between neighborhood deterioration and crime.

Researchers have not had access to time-series crime data at an adequate level of detail or geocoded to units of urban space for which a similar time series of social data is available. Such analysis requires longitudinal data on crime classified by type of offense and keyed to spatial subareas, such as census tracts, for which measures of social characteristics are available.

Data meeting these requirements are available in the County of Los Angeles. These data consist of all petitions to the juvenile court for criminal offenses prosecutable if committed by an adult and for status offenses. Each petition is assigned to a subareal unit of residence. There are 1,142 subareas similar to U.S. Bureau of Census census tracts except that the physical boundaries are comparable over time for the total County of Los Angeles. Thus they represent a spatial "idealized" set of census tracts for the census years 1950, 1960, and 1970. Data on the number of juvenile offenders by census tract of residence were used as a surrogate measure of all crime because crime report data at the neighborhood level were not available for all of these census years. The appropriateness of use of the number of juvenile offenders as a surrogate measure of crime is shown by the very high correlation between their spatial distributions. For example, in five data sets in Chicago over the three-decade period, 1900–1927, the correlation ranged between .84 and .89 (Shaw et al. 1929). Similarly, in Los Angeles County in 1970, zero-order correlations between spatial distributions of adult con-

TABLE 1

Zero-Order Correlations between Juvenile and Adult Offenses, by Type of Offense, Los Angeles County, 1970

| | Adult Conviction Offenses† | | |
|---|---|---|---|
| Juvenile Offenses* | Felony | Property | Person |
| All prosecutable offenses:‡ | | | |
| Density per square mile | .83 | .64 | .12 |
| Rate | .45 | .34 | −.01 |
| Juvenile offenses: | | | |
| Property: | | | |
| Density per square mile | .80 | .72 | .09 |
| Rate | .53 | .45 | −.01 |
| Person: | | | |
| Density per square mile | .71 | .72 | .07 |
| Rate | .68 | .64 | −.02 |
| Status: | | | |
| Density per square mile | .74 | .45 | .17 |
| Rate | .30 | .15 | .00 |

* Population ten to seventeen years of age.
† Population eighteen to thirty years of age.
‡ Felony and misdemeanor offenses (excluding traffic violations).

victions for felony offenses and for three measures of the distribution of juvenile offenders ranged from .71 to .80 (table 1).

A second problem was to find an analytical method capable of grouping together contiguous census tracts into clusters, or "neighborhoods," whose homogeneity was empirically defined by similarity in their crime measures and in measures of their land use, demographic, socioeconomic, and subcultural features. A modified form of the Geary Contiguity Measure (Geary 1954) provided a suitable means of establishing subareal clusters based on the number of juvenile offender crimes per square mile petitioned to the court for felony and misdemeanor offenses and for status offenses (the "subareal density measure"). The use of subareal density was the more appropriate measure, because it represents an index of *concentration* of officially identified offenders within census tracts; and it is, therefore, more relevant to the issue of neighborhood deterioration. Residents are likely to perceive the crime level of their neighborhoods in terms of the frequency with which criminal behaviors come to their attention, and this is keyed most directly to residents' perceptions of neighborhood change.

The clustering algorithm used selects the subarea with the highest magnitude of the given feature—in this case, crime density—and searches for inclusion in the cluster only those contiguous subareas found to be statistically homogeneous. An ever-widening cluster is obtained until all contiguous subareas are statistically homogeneous, and all surrounding subareas outside the cluster are statistically different, say, at the .05 level of significance. By selecting the next-highest value outside the defined area as the new starting point for the construction of the next cluster, the process may be repeated until no additional starting points are available. In the current study, 1,142 subareal crime density measures, when subjected to the statistical spatial clustering process, yielded 192 clusters that were both spatially and statistically homogeneous with respect to their crime levels. From these, the "highest" crime clusters in 1970 were identified. There were ten such clusters, and they included a total of 214 subareas.

Finally, a method for characterizing and measuring community structure had to be developed. From the human ecology and urban studies literature, we distilled four basic social structural components or dimensions: land use, population composition, socioeconomic status, and subculture. Each was defined in terms of measures available from the U.S. Census and from other sources in 1950, 1960, and 1970. *Land use* measures included, among others, concentration ("density") and distribution ("rates") of single- and multiple-family dwellings, industrial and commercial parcels, and traffic-generating establishments (such as offices, restaurants, and shopping centers). The *population composition* component included the size and density of neighborhood populations, residential mobility, household composition, median age, and the youth dependency ratio (the ratio of the number of persons under age eighteen to those aged eighteen to sixty-five). Among the *socioeconomic status* variables were occupation, unemployment, education, and housing conditions.

The fourth social structural component, *subculture*, is difficult to define but is nevertheless crucial for understanding the relation between a community's character and formal and informal social controls. Developing a measure of subculture is especially difficult when data must be drawn from secondary sources like the U.S. Census and other administrative records. The variables included such correlates of weakened social control as the ethnic composition of local populations, features of family organization related to child neglect, and the kind of normative heterogeneity indicated by the presence of a population

TABLE 2

Percentage of Census Tracts in 1950 and 1960 High-Crime Clusters Reappearing in 1970 High-Crime Clusters, by Levels of Persistence

| 1970 Cluster Number | Number of Census Tracts, 1970 | Rate of Prosecutable Offenses, 1970 | 1960 Tracts in 1970 | 1950 Tracts in 1970 |
|---|---|---|---|---|
| High (enduring): | | | | |
| 1 | 48 | 5.19 | 95.8 | 97.9 |
| 2 | 13 | 2.39 | 76.9 | 76.9 |
| 9 | 15 | 2.50 | 80.0 | 80.0 |
| Medium (transitional): | | | | |
| 4 | 32 | 4.24 | 100.0 | 18.8 |
| 5 | 10 | 4.33 | 100.0 | 40.0 |
| 6 | 27 | 3.91 | 70.4 | 29.6 |
| 10 | 43 | 2.35 | 76.7 | 25.6 |
| Low (emerging): | | | | |
| 3 | 10 | 3.09 | 90.0 | .0 |
| 7 | 7 | 2.37 | 100.0 | .0 |
| 8 | 9 | 3.21 | 44.4 | .0 |

highly diverse in educational level. Variables indexing local subculture were drawn directly from these features.

## II. Stages in the Development of High-Crime Areas

After the highest 1970 crime density census tract clusters, or "neighborhoods," were identified, the same clustering procedure was used to identify the highest crime density clusters in 1960 and 1950. For these years only seven high-crime clusters emerged. It was, however, feasible to determine which census tracts in the 1970 high-crime clusters were present in the 1960 and the 1950 high-crime clusters. There is substantial variation among the top ten 1970 clusters in their overlap with the top seven in 1960 and 1950. However, it should be noted that once a neighborhood reached a high-crime area status in 1950 or 1960 it always remained among the highest cluster subareas through 1970. Table 2 classifies the 1970 clusters according to their inclusion of tracts falling into the high-crime clusters in 1960 and 1950. Three types of 1970 high-crime areas become apparent: three clusters containing a high proportion (77–98 percent) of tracts that were in the 1950 high-crime clusters, four clusters that include from 19–40 percent of such 1950 tracts, and three clusters that contain no tracts that were among the 1950 high-crime areas.

TABLE 3

Weighted Mean Rate of Juvenile Prosecutable Offenses, by Stages of Development as High-Crime Areas, Los Angeles County

| | Emerging | Transitional | Enduring |
|---|---|---|---|
| 1970 | 2.94 | 3.44 | 4.18 |
| 1960 | .71 | .92 | 1.24 |
| 1950 | .36 | .50 | 1.08 |

The first three clusters, those that had persisted as the county's high-crime areas from 1950 to 1970, reflected a substantial duration in which criminal activity had become a stable or *enduring* feature and represented the final stage in the developmental cycle. The second group of clusters was labeled *transitional*. These clusters appear to be at an intermediate stage of development where the proportion of census tracts in the 1970 high-crime clusters moved from a moderately high level in 1950 to an even higher level in 1960. The group that contained no overlap between 1950 and 1970, but increased to moderate levels in 1960, was called *emerging*. These clusters were relatively new arrivals as high-crime areas; they may be thought of as being in the early stage of development. Crime levels for 1950, 1960, and 1970 for each group are shown in table 3.

## III. Trends in Social Characteristics

Rapid changes throughout the county over the two-decade period considered, during which its population approximately doubled, meant that changes in the highest crime areas required some form of standardization in order to pinpoint real changes across time. To do this a unit share measure was used. This measures each subarea's proportional share of the total unit of analysis (e.g., the County of Los Angeles). Thus it provides a way of highlighting a local subarea's percentage of any prevailing characteristic in the total area, and it reflects any social trends that may exist relative to a given time. For example, table 4 shows that approximately 18 percent of countywide owner-occupied housing in 1950 was located in the ten highest 1970 crime areas. By comparing this 1950 unit share standardized to the county total value, it can be seen that there is a real decline to only 13.5 percent by 1970.

TABLE 4

Twenty-Year Trend in Unit Share of Land Use Variables, Ten Highest Crime Census Tracts, 1970, Los Angeles County

| Variable | 1950 | 1960 | 1970 | % Change, 1950–70 |
|---|---|---|---|---|
| Owner housing | 18.15 | 14.88 | 13.46 | −25.8 |
| Rental housing | 22.88 | 19.55 | 16.86 | −26.3 |
| Single-family dwellings | 16.79 | 14.27 | 14.07 | −16.2 |
| Multiplex dwellings | 21.93 | 26.16 | 17.32 | −18.2 |
| Apartment dwellings | 11.73 | 9.66 | 7.21 | −38.5 |
| Commercial units | 19.35 | 17.70 | 16.56 | −14.4 |
| Industrial units | 25.13 | 21.53 | 20.35 | −19.9 |
| Traffic generators | 19.98 | 16.89 | 13.66 | −15.5 |

*A. Land Use Variables*

Table 4 also evidences declines in commercial and industrial land use in the ten high-crime areas as a group, suggesting a general trend toward abandonment. The deterioration of these areas for traditional residential use between 1950 and 1970 was also evident, as the average square mile density of owner-occupied housing declined from 1,742 to 1,513, and the average density of renter-occupied units increased from 2,081 to 2,810. As table 5 shows, the trend in decline and abandonment was most prominent in the enduring high-crime areas, less in transitional areas, and least in the emerging areas.

*B. Demographic Variables*

This component of neighborhood social structure includes population size and measures of unrelated individuals, the widowed and divorced, residential mobility and stability, youth and aged-dependency ratios, and median age. Unit share measures for only the first five of these variables were feasible for all three census years. The most striking twenty-year trends were a 24 percent mean unit share decline in population (table 6), varying from 44 percent in the enduring high-crime areas to 21 percent in the emerging areas (table 7); a threefold mean unit share increase in residential mobility, greatest in the transitional and emerging areas and least in the enduring areas; and a twenty-year percentage increase in the youth dependency ratio that was greatest in the enduring high-crime areas and least in the emerging areas.

TABLE 5

Twenty-Year Trend in Unit Share of Land Use Variables, Ten Highest Crime Census Tract Clusters, by Stages of Development as High-Crime Areas, Los Angeles County

| Stage and Variable | 1950 | 1960 | 1970 | % Change, 1950–70 |
|---|---|---|---|---|
| Emerging: | | | | |
| Owner housing | 2.50 | 2.00 | 1.75 | −30.0 |
| Rental housing | 2.68 | 2.94 | 2.90 | 8.2 |
| Apartment dwellings | 1.31 | 1.28 | 1.40 | 6.9 |
| Commercial units | 2.68 | 2.46 | 2.66 | −.7 |
| Industrial units | 2.91 | 2.45 | 2.08 | −28.5 |
| Transitional: | | | | |
| Owner housing | 10.07 | 9.47 | 9.25 | −8.1 |
| Rental housing | 11.40 | 9.99 | 8.97 | −21.3 |
| Apartment dwellings | 8.15 | 7.04 | 5.11 | −37.7 |
| Commercial units | 10.76 | 9.74 | 9.07 | −15.7 |
| Industrial units | 6.62 | 5.96 | 6.62 | . . . |
| Enduring: | | | | |
| Owner housing | 5.52 | 3.41 | 2.74 | −50.4 |
| Rental housing | 8.80 | 6.67 | 4.99 | −43.3 |
| Apartment dwellings | 2.27 | 1.34 | .80 | −64.8 |
| Commercial units | 5.91 | 5.50 | 5.18 | −12.4 |
| Industrial units | 15.60 | 13.12 | 11.65 | −25.5 |

*C. Socioeconomic (SES) Variables*

Among occupation, employment, education, and housing variables used to measure SES, the most unexpected finding was the declining trend from 1950 to 1970 in the unit share of those in the semi- and unskilled occupations (table 8). Percentage reductions in the professional and skilled occupations, and in population with advanced education, were expected. The declining trend in unemployment is misleading since these data are based on those answering affirmatively the census question whether they are seeking employment. The reduction over this period in unit share of housing lacking plumbing probably reflects the addition of public housing over the two-decade period in the ten 1970 high-crime areas. Distinct differences in unit share trends for socioeconomic variables are evident for the three clusters (table 9). The emerging high-crime areas are distinguished by their unit share loss of the professional and skilled occupational groups and of population with

TABLE 6

Twenty-Year Trend in Unit Share of Demographic Variables, Ten Highest Crime Density Census Tract Clusters, 1970, Los Angeles County

| Variable | 1950 | 1960 | 1970 | % Change, 1950–70 |
|---|---|---|---|---|
| Total population | 21.71 | 17.90 | 16.57 | −23.7 |
| Unrelated individual | 19.67 | 29.12 | 14.59 | −25.8 |
| Widowed and divorced | 22.13 | 18.63 | 16.24 | −26.6 |
| Residential stability | 22.53 | 17.45 | 16.43 | −27.1 |
| Residential mobility | 4.87 | 18.02 | 16.99 | 248.8 |

TABLE 7

Percentage Change in Mean Unit Share, 1950–70, Selected Demographic Variables by Stages of Development as High-Crime Areas, Los Angeles County

| | Stage | | |
|---|---|---|---|
| | Emerging | Transitional | Enduring |
| Total population | −21.3 | 1.5 | −43.7 |
| Unrelated individuals | 34.4 | −17.6 | −49.0 |
| Widowed and divorced | 4.1 | −15.1 | −41.7 |
| Residential stability | −27.1 | −4.1 | −44.3 |
| Residential mobility | 240.3 | 268.3 | 110.7 |

TABLE 8

Twenty-Year Trend in Unit Share of Selected Socioeconomic Variables, Ten Highest Crime Density Census Tract Clusters, 1970, Los Angeles County

| Variable | 1950 | 1960 | 1970 | % Change, 1950–70 |
|---|---|---|---|---|
| Professional occupations | 15.33 | 9.97 | 9.09 | −40.7 |
| Skilled occupations | 20.91 | 14.86 | 13.26 | −36.6 |
| Semi- and unskilled | 27.45 | 24.04 | 20.58 | −25.0 |
| Unemployment | 25.77 | 23.71 | 19.47 | −24.4 |
| Population with advanced education | 13.50 | 9.20 | 7.78 | −42.4 |
| Housing lacking plumbing | 23.91 | 14.18 | 17.18 | −28.1 |
| Housing overcrowded | 26.43 | 27.19 | 26.94 | 2.0 |
| Housing turnover* | ... | 15.71 | 19.41 | 23.5 |

* Data for 1950 were not available.

TABLE 9

Percentage Change in Weighted Mean Unit Share, 1950–70, Selected Socioeconomic Variables, by Stages in Development as High-Crime Areas, Los Angeles County

| | Stage | | |
|---|---|---|---|
| | Emerging | Transitional | Enduring |
| Professional occupations | −25.2 | −24.7 | −71.0 |
| Skilled occupations | −23.2 | −20.0 | −64.3 |
| Semi- and unskilled | 4.0 | 9.6 | −58.3 |
| Unemployment | 6.0 | 11.8 | −51.1 |
| Population with advanced education | −15.1 | −32.6 | −76.0 |
| Housing lacking plumbing | 15.0 | −8.8 | −53.3 |
| Housing overcrowded | 12.5 | 37.3 | −26.3 |
| Housing turnover* | −3.7 | 32.9 | 38.4 |

* Trend for 1960–70. Data for 1950 were not available.

advanced education, and an increase in share of unskilled laborers and unemployed persons, combined with a rising share of the county's overcrowded and deteriorated housing.

*D. Subculture Variables*

Subculture variables included ethnicity, female participation in the labor force, the educational status of ethnic subgroups, and juvenile status offenses. These variables were selected as representing the normative elements in behavior patterns that reflect both historic and contemporary group experience. They are notable for their high associations with levels of cross-generational social control. The main two-decade trends were stability in the very large unit share measures of black population in the high-crime areas, the contrasting decline in Spanish surname population, and the relatively high and stable proportion of nonwhite female labor force participation (table 10). For the last, their unit share was highest in 1950 (63 percent) and in 1970 (52 percent). Thus, of the nonwhite female participants in the labor force, over half resided in 1970 in the 214 census tracts encompassed by the ten highest crime density clusters. When unit share trends are disaggregated by cluster groups at different stages, those at the emerging stage differ sharply from the other two on virtually each of the subculture variables (table 11). The percentage increase in unit share of the

TABLE 10

Twenty-Year Trend in Unit Share of Subculture Variables, Ten Highest Crime Density Census Tract Clusters, 1970, Los Angeles County

| | 1950 | 1960 | 1970 | % Change, 1950–70 |
|---|---|---|---|---|
| Black population | 64.74 | 72.49 | 67.03 | 3.5 |
| Spanish surname population | 43.83 | 31.59 | 23.07 | −47.4 |
| Anglo population | 17.53 | 16.45 | 8.23 | −54.1 |
| Nonwhite female labor force | 63.47 | 62.43 | 51.73 | −18.5 |
| Spanish surname female labor force | 49.49 | 32.49 | 22.38 | −54.8 |
| Anglo female labor force | 18.34 | 10.02 | 7.81 | −57.4 |
| Nonwhite advanced education | 63.66 | 48.00 | 28.17 | −55.7 |
| Spanish surname advanced education | 43.78 | 13.95 | 14.57 | −66.7 |
| Anglo advanced education | 11.97 | 6.73 | 5.42 | −54.7 |
| Mexican foreign born | 44.16 | 19.31 | 31.85 | −27.9 |
| Status offenses | 25.97 | 28.40 | 26.35 | 1.5 |

black and Spanish surname population far exceeded that of clusters in the transitional stage and contrasted with unit share declines of both in the enduring high-crime areas. The emerging areas also experienced a dramatic rise in their share of nonwhite and Spanish surname females in the labor force. Equally striking was the sharp upward trend in the emerging areas in unit share of the nonwhite and Spanish surname population with advanced education. These components of minority groups may thus constitute a "leading edge" of movement into emerging high-crime areas. Finally, the largest percentage increase in status offenses (66 percent) occurred in the emerging areas.

## IV. Targeted Findings of the Relationship between Changing Neighborhoods and the Development of High-Crime Areas

Trends in neighborhood social conditions and in crime have thus far been examined descriptively. How these trends are related to one another constitutes the significant problem for inquiry, particularly the relations between change and development in neighborhood structural features and changes in local area crime levels.

### A. *Structural Dimensions and Crime*

The aim in the following sections is to transform the multiple mea-

TABLE 11

Percentage Change in Weighted Mean Unit Share, 1950–70, Selected Subculture Variables, by Stages in Development as High-Crime Areas, Los Angeles County

| | Stage | | |
|---|---|---|---|
| | Emerging | Transitional | Enduring |
| Black population | 540.0 | 164.3 | −59.1 |
| Spanish surname population | 426.6 | 14.8 | −64.5 |
| Anglo population | −41.1 | −35.0 | −81.5 |
| Nonwhite females in labor force | 733.9 | 84.7 | −74.1 |
| Spanish surname females in labor force | 482.8 | −12.6 | −69.7 |
| Anglo females in labor force | −31.0 | −43.0 | −89.1 |
| Nonwhite advanced education | 2,268.4 | −35.6 | −90.0 |
| Spanish surname advanced education | 1,581.5 | −58.5 | −85.4 |
| Anglo advanced education | −29.3 | −46.2 | −89.9 |
| Mexican foreign born | 163.9 | −8.5 | −41.1 |
| Status offenses | 66.2 | 26.1 | −22.2 |

sures of each component of neighborhood social structure and of crime into a single composite indicator score. The composite indicators provide a summary measure of each of the independent structural variables and of the dependent crime variables. While this procedure sacrifices detail, the composite indicator values produce a substantial gain in the clarity of these relationships. For example, with respect to the relationship between neighborhood socioeconomic status and crime, the fundamental concern should be to derive a measure of the concept of socioeconomic status itself and not with the individual operational expressions of the concept.

Each of the components of neighborhood structure and offense type was measured by many variables, or indicators. In the interest of both economy and clarity, the multiple measures of each component were summarized through a factor analytic procedure to derive a single score representing the value of that component for any given spatial unit. The relevant units were census tract clusters or sets of clusters defined by a range of crime measures or stage of development as a high-crime area.

Since the factors to be extracted are predetermined, the method of choice is one-factor analysis (see Schuessler [1971, pp. 47–60] for implementation of this model). In summary, the use of a one-factor analysis is the most defensible approach because the variables already described were a priori developed as indirect measures to express a conceptually relevant element of social structure. As such, the unique measures can be applied to a one-factor model of factor analysis in order to confirm mathematically the variables' relative contribution to the designated conceptual factor. The output of the procedure was a set of composite indicator score values of structural components and crime expressed as a proportion of the variance explained in each indicator in 1950, 1960, and 1970.

Whether the one-factor model is the preferred method for deriving composite indicator scores was tested by conducting a traditional factor analysis that examines all variables at once and not separately. The usual purpose under this procedure is to reduce the large number of variables to a small number of underlying "hidden" factors that are both interpretable and theoretically relevant. No meaningful factors emerged or could be identified by any degree of orthogonality (i.e., factors are uncorrelated to each other in a ninety-degree mathematical space). This finding was perhaps predictable, given the ecological context of the variables employed. Processes of neighborhood segregation and specialization have the effect of clustering urban space attributes within delimited units whose measures are highly and uniformly intercorrelated. In statistical terms, the degrees of freedom are undefinable. They are restricted because of the bias introduced by the segregation of the variables within spatial ecology. Hence, the variables are constrained to cluster mathematically through factor analytic techniques because of the spatial clustering and not necessarily because of an underlying factoral dimension. For example, census tract clusters with high densities of multiple-family dwellings are also likely to contain high proportions of unrelated individuals, high youth dependency ratios, high concentration measures of the labor force in unskilled occupations, and high concentration measures of ethnic minority groups. The test consequently confirmed the appropriateness of the one-factor model for purposes of estimating composite indicator scores.

In developing the one-factor model for each neighborhood structural component, each variable within the composite was constructed to provide consistent values reflecting low to high scores for crime or neighborhood structural deterioration. Thus, the final values are meaningfully translatable for a range of low to high composite indicator scores.

### B. Lead-Lag Relations: Neighborhood Conditions and Crime

For many urban dwellers, the sequential relation between neighborhood deterioration and crime may seem either obvious or irrelevant. Those who have escaped to less endangered areas may see the rising crime of the neighborhoods they have left as a manifestation of their deterioration. Other emerging changes that have overtaken these neighborhoods tend to be seen as having developed simultaneously with their now exacerbated crime problems.

Those who must deal with urban problems from a policy and planning standpoint must, however, concern themselves with the spread of neighborhood decay and crime. It is important to understand the kinds of changes that result from rapid deterioration and those that result from slow increases in crime.

The trends depicted earlier indicate that in the emerging high-crime areas all four types of neighborhood conditions indexing deterioration increased between 1950 and 1970. The evidence presented was far from conclusive, however. The time sequences between the types of change were pictured rather than subjected to a detailed measurement analysis. To address the time-order issue, five questions might be asked of the data.

1. Does neighborhood change occur prior to crime change?
2. What is the degree to which crime for a subsequent period can be accounted for by particular neighborhood conditions in a prior time period, and at what stage of neighborhood transformation does each condition most account for later crime patterns?
3. What is the comparative amount of change over time between specific neighborhood conditions and crime?
4. Do neighborhoods deteriorate at a faster rate than crime increases, or does crime increase at the higher velocity?
5. Are the relative change velocities the same at all stages of neighborhood transformation?

Cross-lagged correlational analysis (Pelz and Andrews 1964) addresses the problem of causality in a time-series context. With an independent and dependent variable measured at successive time points, the size and direction of the correlation between the independent variable at Time 1 and the dependent variable at Time 2 can be compared with the size and direction of the relationship between the dependent variable at Time 1 and the independent variable at Time 2. Only if the former is larger than the latter can the inference be drawn that, being

TABLE 12

Cross-lagged Correlations, Structural Component Composite Indicator Scores, and Crime, 1950–60 and 1960–70, Los Angeles County

| | 1950–60 | | 1960–70 | |
|---|---|---|---|---|
| | Structural $T_1$, Crime $T_2$ | Crime $T_1$, Structural $T_2$ | Structural $T_1$, Crime $T_2$ | Crime $T_1$, Structural $T_2$ |
| Land use | .30 | .27 | .17 | .21 |
| Demographics | .47 | .27 | .18 | .46 |
| SES | .57 | .42 | .62 | .50 |
| Subculture | .35 | .38 | .65 | .24 |

temporally prior, the independent variable is causally related to the dependent variable. The inference is valid only if three assumptions are met.

1. The change rate in the independent variable between Time 1 and Time 2 is constant.
2. The causal effect of the independent variable on the dependent variable does not occur instantaneously.
3. Both the independent and the dependent variables change at a comparable and stable velocity. For example, the Time 2 cross-sectional correlation cannot be larger than the cross-lagged correlation obtained by regressing the Time 1 independent on the Time 2 dependent variable.

It is important that these assumptions be met in time-series analyses that are sharply focused on determining causal priorities among a small set of candidate independent variables. In the most general case, shifts in lead-lag relation are most discernible when the entire county is treated as the unit of analysis. The data presented in table 12 suggest two reasonably distinguishable processes in the production of high-crime neighborhoods: *acceleration* and *transformation*. The distinction provides an identifying marker for determining an urban neighborhood's stage at a given time, and its likely direction of subsequent movement.

The cross-lagged correlations in table 12 suggest that, in the initial stage of neighborhood change, land use and population composition are precursors of impending change in neighborhood crime levels. The evidence for this is found in the comparative size of cross-lagged correlations between the variables of structure and crime.

Thus, the correlation of 1950 land use composite indicator score with 1960 prosecutable offense score (.30) is greater than the correlation between crime at Time 1 and land use at Time 2 (.27). Similarly, the correlation of demographic characteristics at Time 1 with crime at Time 2 (.47) exceeds that between demographic at Time 2 and crime at Time 1 (.27). While land use change was exerting a moderate effect in driving up crime (e.g., shifts from single to multiple dwellings and rising numbers of commercial parcels), change in population composition and even more emphatically in SES was exercising a stronger effect. As was suggested earlier, the latter changes included a shift in population density together with increases in unrelated individuals, broken family units, and a reduced mean age of the population. With these changes instituted and undergoing gradual acceleration during the early period, the stage is set for neighborhood transformation into a high-crime area.

In summary, ecological change proceeds at an increasing rate to a point at which the social and cultural character of a neighborhood is qualitatively altered. The evidence that these structural changes are causally prior to changes in neighborhood crime levels is found in the comparative correlation magnitudes for socioeconomic and subcultural composite indicators with crime during the earlier (1950–60) and later (1960–70) periods. During the earlier period, there is an almost uniform time priority of all structural composite indicators with the exception of subculture. The exception may indicate simply that rising crime in 1950 and beyond began to introduce changes in the course of the decade in the affected neighborhoods so that by 1960 they produced the first signs of their transformation. The 1960–70 decade presents a quite different picture. The ecological processes of land use and demographic change no longer exhibit a similar time priority. That effect is now taken over by the SES and subculture composite indicators, with substantial disparities in the cross-lagged correlations. Both SES and subculture in the 1960–70 decade show higher correlations for 1970 crime with 1960 SES (.62) and subculture (.65) than does 1970 SES (.50) and subculture (.24) with 1960 crime. Determinants of the crime measure thus appear to shift over time from ecological to social and cultural forces, with the latter in turn inducing further neighborhood transformation.

TABLE 13

Cross-lagged Correlations, Structural Component Composite Indicator Scores, and Crime, Ten 1970 Highest Crime Census Tract Clusters, Los Angeles County

| | 1950–60 | | 1960–70 | |
|---|---|---|---|---|
| | Structural $T_1$, Crime $T_2$ | Crime $T_1$, Structural $T_2$ | Structural $T_1$, Crime $T_2$ | Crime $T_1$, Structural $T_2$ |
| Land use | .27 | .31 | .37 | .28 |
| Demographics | .28 | .25 | .33 | .44 |
| SES | .47 | .48 | .52 | .24 |
| Subculture | .21 | .21 | .51 | .07 |

It can be deduced that a prominent feature of the transformation is the placement of neighborhood populations in the status order of the metropolitan region, with implications for changes in crucial social control institutions. Of these, the two most relevant to crime are the family and the neighborhood as an associational network. Both institutional complexes come to be characterized by instability and normative ambiguity. The routinization of adaptive practices constituting a local subculture is also indicative of institutional transformation. An important element of such local cultures is the historical experience of ethnic groups and its effect on orientations to the legitimacy of political authority. Such institutional and cultural transformations of neighborhoods may have the effect of accepting a high level of crime as an inevitable if unwanted outcome.

With some differences due to combining clusters at different stages of development as high-crime areas, the ten 1970 high-crime areas also show a basic shift in causal priority from land use and demographic characteristics to those of SES and subculture (table 13). During the 1950–60 period, only the 1950 demographics/1960 crime correlation exceeds that of the 1950 crime/1960 demographics. However, in the later 1960–70 decade there occurs a distinct shift to a predominance of SES and subculture priority, although land use appears by that decade also to exert a causal effect (.37 versus .28). But unlike the situation in the 1950–60 period, when the two correlations for both SES and subculture were virtually identical, during the 1960–70 decade the 1960 SES/1970 crime cross-lagged correlation was much larger than the obverse (.52 versus .24). The same was true of subculture (.51 versus .07).

TABLE 14

Cross-lagged Correlations, Structural Component Composite Indicator Scores, and Crime, 1950–60 and 1960–70, Emerging, Transitional, and Enduring High-Crime Areas, Los Angeles County

| | 1950–60 | | 1960–70 | |
|---|---|---|---|---|
| | Structural $T_1$, Crime $T_2$ | Crime $T_1$, Structural $T_2$ | Structural $T_1$, Crime $T_2$ | Crime $T_1$, Structural $T_2$ |
| Emerging: | | | | |
| Land use | .46 | .26 | .42 | .50 |
| Demographics | .36 | .26 | .33 | .55 |
| SES | .74 | .36 | .74 | .51 |
| Subculture | .56 | −.13 | .60 | .70 |
| Transitional: | | | | |
| Land use | .38 | .61 | .49 | .35 |
| Demographics | .43 | .57 | .61 | .43 |
| SES | .46 | .62 | .77 | .46 |
| Subculture | .39 | .52 | .65 | .06 |
| Enduring: | | | | |
| Land use | .06 | .15 | .34 | .35 |
| Demographics | .16 | .12 | .16 | .47 |
| SES | .22 | .25 | .25 | .04 |
| Subculture | −.11 | .00 | .44 | −.22 |

In brief, when the ten high-crime areas are combined, lead-lag relations between crime and structural factors during the earlier 1950–60 period appear to show, with the exception of demographic features, that structural factors in 1960 drive the 1970 crime measures. This is most evident with respect to SES and subculture.

Similar relationships are apparent in table 14 when the ten 1970 high-crime clusters are disaggregated with reference to their crime status in the developmental process. In those census tract clusters that were emerging as high-crime areas in 1970, the early 1950–60 decade exhibits uniform temporal priority for all of the structural composite indicators. However, in the following decade, with the exception of the SES indicator, further changes in structural components appear to have been driven by rising crime levels. In this respect, the emerging areas in the 1960–70 decade resembled the next stage, transitional high-crime areas, during the earlier 1950–60 decade. There, also, rising crime appeared to be temporally prior to changes in their structural composite indicator measures. It is of interest to note, further, that in the 1970 transitional high-crime areas the earlier 1950–60 effects of rising crime would seem to have so transformed their structural components as to once again accord them temporal priority in relation to their crime level changes in the 1960–70 decade. Notably, the SES and subculture composite indicators come into prominence as precursors of rising crime. Finally, in the enduring high-crime areas, the general shift through time from the temporal priority of the land use and demographic composite indicators to the temporal priority of SES and subculture is complete. During the earlier 1950–60 decade neither structural nor crime variables exhibit strong temporal priority. By the later 1960–70 decade, it becomes apparent that, while their high crime levels have effected further changes in their demographic characteristics, both the SES and subcultural composite indicators have become the important temporal forces in sustaining their high crime levels.

In summary, the cross-lagged correlations suggest a general developmental trend. The earlier temporal priority of land use and demographic variables shifts later to the temporal priority of socioeconomic and subcultural factors. What is suggested, then, is that in the formation of urban high-crime neighborhoods changes in ecological character, introduced by accretions in changed land use and in the composition of their populations, set the stage for their transformation through qualitative changes in social organization and subculture that sustain their continuing status as high-crime areas.

### C. *Cross-lagged Regression Analysis*

In this analysis, standardized regression coefficients are derived expressing the relationship between composite structural scores as the independent variables at Time 1 and the composite crime indicator as the dependent variable at Time 2. For purposes of assessing change over the 1950–70 period, each of the two decades was analyzed separately. For the 1950–60 decade, the 1960 crime measure was regressed on the 1950 structural measures. For the 1960–70 decade, the 1970 crime measure was regressed on the 1960 structural measure. The proportion of variance explained ($R^2$) in the Time 2 crime measure was calculated for each decade.

Findings from this analysis support the results from the cross-lagged correlation analysis. As neighborhoods move from a low to a high crime state, there occurs an earlier change in the ecological factors of land use and population characteristics followed later by a predominance of change in their socioeconomic and subcultural character. This is partially confirmed by the data in table 15, in which cross-lagged

TABLE 15

Cross-lagged Regression Coefficients, Crime Regressed on Composite Structural Scores, Ten Highest 1970 Crime Clusters, Two Decades, Los Angeles County

| | 1950–60 | 1960–70 |
|---|---|---|
| Land use | .06 | .46 |
| Demographics | .90 | −.42 |
| SES | −.21 | .17 |
| Subculture | −.14 | .42 |
| $R^2$ | .30 | .38 |

coefficients are presented for the ten 1970 high-crime clusters. Although the expectation of a larger positive coefficient for 1950–60 than for the 1960–70 cross-lag with respect to land use is not realized, possibly due to its relatively slower pace of change, it is met by the early and late comparative coefficients for the demographic component cross-lags. The high beta (.90) in the 1950–60 period is followed by a moderately high (−.42) beta in the 1960–70 period. The effect on crime of early demographic change subsides sharply during the later period as the change stabilizes. This sequence is then sharply reversed in the case of SES and of subculture. While the earlier period cross-lag coefficient for SES is moderately low (−.21), in the later 1960–70 period it shifts to .17. Even more striking is a similar shift across time in the case of the subcultural component: from a cross-lag of −.14 for 1950–60 to the moderately high .42 for the 1960–70 cross-lag. Except for land use, the data thus offer substantial confirmation of the proposition that earlier ecological and later sociocultural structure is an effective influence in the development of an advancing community career in crime.

In table 16, a further test of the robustness of these findings is shown by differences among cross-lagged coefficients among the 1970 high-crime clusters. The size of the regression coefficient for 1950 land use/1960 crime declines from the emerging through the transitional to the enduring stage clusters. A similar reduction in the size of the same coefficient is evident for the demographic composite indicator, with the contrast sharpest between the emerging and the enduring stages (.98 vs. .67). While a shift from ecological to socioeconomic and subcultural predominance is not apparent in moving from the early to late stage of

TABLE 16

Cross-lagged Regression Coefficients, Crime Regressed on Composite Structural Scores, Two Decades, Ten 1970 Highest Crime Clusters, by Stage of Development, Los Angeles County

| | 1950–60 | 1960–70 |
|---|---|---|
| Emerging: | | |
| Land use | .45 | −.25 |
| Demographic | .98 | ... |
| SES | −.49 | .82 |
| Subculture | .29 | .26 |
| $R^2$ | .60 | .58 |
| Transitional: | | |
| Land use | .23 | −.77 |
| Demographic | 1.48 | .67 |
| SES | −.67 | .94 |
| Subculture | .17 | −.11 |
| $R^2$ | .31 | .69 |
| Enduring: | | |
| Land use | −.08 | .87 |
| Demographic | .67 | −.97 |
| SES | −.12 | .18 |
| Subculture | −.22 | .53 |
| $R^2$ | .12 | .48 |

development during the 1950–60 period, it is quite evident within each stage across the two decades. In the emerging stage clusters, the coefficient for land use 1950/crime 1960 declines from .45 to −.25 for land use 1960/crime 1970. Similarly, the high .98 coefficient for the 1950–60 demographic-crime cross-lag disappears entirely during the 1960–70 decade (a partly artifactual effect of the stepwise procedure employed). Their effect is replaced in the emerging stage clusters by a notable increase across the two decades in the SES cross-lagged coefficients from −.49 in 1950–60 to .82 in 1960–70. The effect of subculture remains virtually unchanged across the two decades. This seemingly is an indication that, as an emerging high crime area in 1970, not enough time had passed for the development of a local subculture in which crime has become entrenched. Much the same pattern of shift from earlier ecological effects to later SES effects is also seen in the transitional high-crime areas. The cross-lagged regression coefficient for land use 1950/crime 1960 of .23 is reduced to −.77 for the land use 1960/crime 1970. The same shift across the two decades is true as well for the composite demographic indicator—from 1.48 in 1950–60 to .67 in 1960–70. Again, their effect on the crime measure is replaced by SES. This moves from a cross-lagged regression coefficient of −.67 in the 1950–60 decade to a high coefficient of .94 in the 1960–70 decade.

In the enduring stage high-crime clusters, it is the cross-lagged coefficient of demographics 1950/crime 1960 that exhibits a sharp "disappearing" effect when compared with that for the 1960–70 period from .67 to −.97. For reasons that are yet obscure, the same effect is not evident with respect to land use. We can only speculate that, given the delayed effect of land use change on crime, it is not until a high-crime area reaches its maximum development, as in the case of the enduring high-crime clusters, that the physical transformation of the area becomes fully established. In any event, the notable feature respecting the temporal shift from ecological to sociocultural forces in the creation of high-crime areas is seen in the differences between the SES and the subcultural cross-lagged regression coefficients in the enduring stage clusters. Most striking of these is the rise in prominence of subculture effects across the two decades. While the 1950–60 SES-crime cross-lagged coefficient moves from a modest −.12 to a modest .18 for the 1960–70 decade, the change for subculture is from −.22 in 1950–60 to .53 in 1960–70. It would appear that, as neighborhoods "mature" further into high-crime areas, the most significant sustaining structural component becomes a set of adaptive practices, sufficiently collectively shared to support a relatively high level of law violation.

The cross-lagged regression analysis using composite indicator scores illuminates the structural dynamics involved in the creation of urban high-crime areas. The transformation of urban neighborhoods from a crime-free to a crime-ridden state proceeds from its initial physical change to change in population composition to change in its socioeconomic character to change in prevailing normative controls.

### *D. Deviational Correlation Analysis*

Extending the well-supported sociological observation of an inverse relationship between social change and social control, it may be postulated that the rate at which social control declines in an urban subarea, operationally defined by rising crime measures, is a function of the velocity of social change. The testable prediction that follows is that the greater the velocity of prior structural change in a neighborhood, the more precipitous will be the rise in its subsequent crime measure. Correspondingly, as structural change decelerates, so will the rise in the crime measure.

A deviational change correlation measure is particularly useful here because it is a precise measure of relative change velocity (Duncan, Cuzzard, and Duncan 1961; Myers 1964). Deviational change correlation assesses the comparative speed of change in dependent and independent variables. This comparative speed over time can be mathematically expressed by regressing interannually a given variable onto itself. Here the measure is the same but the independent variable is a time point prior to the dependent variable (its independent status). For example, this might be 1950 crime density distributions regressed on 1960 crime density distributions. The differences between the actual values and those predicted by the interannual regressions for the variable (i.e., the residuals or outliers) represent a way of accurately measuring relative deviations in normal change. Furthermore, interannual correlation of the residuals for the independent and the dependent variable then expresses their comparative degree of change velocities and direction of the change. In the analysis presented here, we employ the composite indicator score values for each structural component in order to derive their interannual velocity change measures. Composite indicator score values for both the independent structural variables and the dependent crime variable provide more informative summary measures because they appropriately weight the contributions of the individual indexes in each structural component.

Two separate deviational correlation analyses are performed. The first is a multiple deviational regression/correlational procedure that compares the residual composite scores of change in crime with the residual composite scores for the four structural components. The residual values are obtained by performing an interannual statistical regression for 1950 and 1960 as the independent variables with 1970 as the dependent variable for each respective set of composite scores. The residual output values from the interannual regressions are then treated as the independent and dependent values of a multiple regression process. In addition to obtaining the degree of relation as expressed in the multiple correlation, the resultant beta values are especially useful as indicators of deviational change of the neighborhood structural components with the change in crime over the 1950–70 period. Here the sign and size of the standard regression coefficients express the direction and degree of change in velocity that each neighborhood structural component experiences. As an expression of change over time, we can concurrently measure the influences on the rapidity of change in neighborhood crime.

The second form of deviational correlation analysis focuses on change in the crime composite score during the 1960–70 decade in relation to change in the structural composite scores during the preceding 1950–60 decade. This "cross-lagged" deviational change analysis is designed to detect those temporally prior structural components whose earlier rate of change affected the later rate of change in crime for census tract clusters at the several stages of development.

Comparative change velocities in composite structural components and crime over the 1950–70 period are shown in the data of table 17. Change velocities in three of the four structural components exceeded those for crime principally in clusters at the emerging stage. The exception is provided by subculture at all three stages of development, whose change velocity was outstripped by that of crime. The largest coefficients indicating higher change velocities for the structural components are those for demographics (.69) and for high SES (−.58). With the exception of a higher rate of change in demographics than in crime, clusters in both later stages of development exhibit small but uniform indications of a more rapid change in crime than in structural components. As indicated earlier, this again suggests that in the course of their "maturation" the initial significant development in urban high-crime areas is a relatively greater change velocity in their land use and demographic characteristics. The relation is reversed in the later stages of the cycle, with the rate of change in crime overtaking the rate of change in the other structural features of these neighborhoods, again with the exception of the demographic component.

The information provided by this analysis simply compared the velocity of change in the structural features of high-crime areas over the twenty-year period with the velocity of change in their crime measure during the same period. More to the point is the extent to which the velocity of change in the components of neighborhood structure during the first decade of the twenty-year period affected the velocity of change in crime during the second decade. The question was assessed in a cross-lagged multiple deviational correlation analysis presented in table 18.

The findings of this analysis provide the best test of the prediction from social change theory, namely, that it is the speed of structural

## TABLE 17

Standardized Regression Coefficients and Adjusted $R^2$, Multiple Deviational Correlations of Crime, 1950–70, and Structural Components, 1950–70, by 1970 High-Crime Census Tract Clusters, Los Angeles County

| | | | Stage of Development | | |
|---|---|---|---|---|---|
| Structural Component | County | Ten 1970 Highest-Crime Clusters | Emerging | Transitional | Enduring |
| Land use | −.09 | −.20 | .30 | −.17 | −.51 |
| Demographics | .52 | .37 | .69 | .24 | .38 |
| High SES* | −.10 | −.04 | −.58 | −.15 | −.07 |
| Low SES† | −.10 | ... | −.18 | −.12 | −.05 |
| Subculture | −.09 | −.15 | −.39 | −.04 | −.06 |
| $R^2$ | .08 | .12 | .48 | .04 | .30 |

* Professional and managerial occupations; skilled occupations; sixteen years or more of education; average income; average home value; average rent; average education.

† Semi- and unskilled occupations; unemployment; housing lacking plumbing; overcrowded housing.

## TABLE 18

Standardized Regression Coefficients and Adjusted $R^2$, Multiple Deviational Correlations of Crime, 1960–70, and Structural Variables, 1950–60, by 1970 High-Crime Census Tract Clusters, Los Angeles County

| | | | Stage of Development | | |
|---|---|---|---|---|---|
| Structural Component | County | Ten 1970 Highest-Crime Clusters | Emerging | Transitional | Enduring |
| Land use | .14 | .31 | −.58 | .31 | .49 |
| Demographics | −.17 | −.19 | −.12 | −.09 | −.41 |
| High SES | −.07 | −.15 | −.19 | −.41 | −.23 |
| Low SES | .14 | .04 | .96 | .09 | −.11 |
| Subculture | .23 | .18 | .22 | .24 | .13 |
| $R^2$ | .14 | .14 | .66 | .33 | .17 |

change rather than solely the fact of such change that initiates the transition of city neighborhoods from a low- to a high-crime state. However, the prediction is silent respecting the specific structural components whose earlier change velocities might be most highly related to the velocity of later change in the crime measure. The earlier cross-lagged correlation and cross-lagged regression analyses both suggested an initial precedence of change in the ecological factors of land use and demographics. Those analyses did not, however, deal with the velocity of change. The present analysis does and provides empirical grounding for a more discriminating view of the dynamics of neighborhood transformation with respect to crime.

Given that the velocity of land use change is constrained by cost problems of substantial magnitude, it is perhaps not surprising that in the emerging areas there was a strong inverse relationship between the change velocities of land use and crime. That is, there was a likely contrast between a low velocity of land use change and a high velocity of change in the crime measure, as indicated by the −.58 coefficient. However, the effect of a slow acceleration in land use change may be seen in the transitional and enduring high-crime area areas by .31 and .49, respectively. Similarly, change velocity in demographics during the 1950–60 decade cannot be seen as "driving" the velocity of crime change in the 1960–70 decade: crime increased at a faster rate in the later period than did the demographics in the earlier period. Thus, for the emerging stage areas, earlier decade change velocity in neither of the ecological factors of land use and demographics exceeded the crime change velocity in the later decade. However, for the transitional and enduring stage areas, early decade land use change velocity does exhibit a "driving" force in relation to their later decade crime change rates.

By contrast, earlier change velocity in both the socioeconomic and subcultural components had substantial and sustained effect on later decade crime change velocity. The effect was most evident in the case of SES with respect to the emerging stage areas, as indicated by a coefficient of .96. Areas in the later two stages of development were less influenced by the 1950–60 velocity of SES change in relation to crime change velocity during 1960–70. Thus, in all likelihood SES velocity change for these areas had already occurred prior to 1950, with the relationship to their subsequent crime change velocity stabilized by the 1960–70 decade. As to the subcultural component, change rates in the earlier decade exceeded those for crime in the later decade in areas at all three stages of development, with ultimate reduction in change velocity (.22, .24, and .13, respectively) as a persisting force in inducing the later rise in their crime measures.

Finally, the total effect of earlier change velocity in the components of neighborhood structure on later change rates in crime may be seen in the measures of explained variance ($R^2$). These consistently declined in magnitude from the emerging to the transitional to the enduring stage areas, with values from .66 to .33 to .17, respectively. The emerging areas, however, demonstrate the most striking relation. In these areas, rapid change in neighborhood structure in the previous decade explains much of the variance in the subsequent decades of accelerated transformation into high-crime areas. As the emerging areas are transformed over time to become permanently established high-crime areas, earlier patterns of change in their structural features, having already had their effect, become less important. It may be, then, that once neighborhoods become established as high-crime areas, they no longer respond to partial alterations in structural features. This is illustrated by the frequently unrealized hope that improved housing alone will reduce crime.

## V. Summary and Conclusions

The transformation of urban communities from low- to high-crime areas was investigated by relating changes in the social features of neighborhoods to changes in their crime measures. This was accomplished with several forms of time-series analysis. The study focused on census tract spatial clusters with the highest crime measures in Los Angeles County in 1970. The clusters were delineated using a modified form of the Geary Contiguity Measure (Geary 1954). Crime measures and their land use, demographic, socioeconomic, and subcultural characteristics in 1950, 1960, and 1970 were examined retrospectively. Comparative twenty-year change trends in the variables constituting each of the four dimensions of neighborhood social structure and of crime were examined. This was followed by an analysis of lead-lag relations between change in the crime measure and change in measures of neighborhood conditions and of lead-lag relations in their velocities of change. For this analysis the multiple variables of each dimension of neighborhood structure were reduced to a single composite score.

An examination of the 1970 highest-crime areas, relative to 1950 and 1960 high-crime clusters, revealed that neighborhoods were in three distinct stages of development: (1) Emerging—relatively new crime areas that were virtually crime free in 1950, then demonstrated moderate to high levels of crime in 1960, and attained high-crime status in 1970; (2) Transitional—crime areas that showed in 1950 moderately high criminal activity and continued to demonstrate an upward movement throughout the two decades; and (3) Enduring—crime-impacted neighborhoods with high-crime densities throughout the twenty-year period. The principal land use changes associated with a rise in neighborhood crime measures were a shift from owner- to renter-occupied housing and from single- to multiple-dwelling units, as well as a decline in unit share of dwellings of all types and of commercial and industrial parcels. The county's enduring high-crime areas appeared to be undergoing a slow process of abandonment.

Demographic changes included a reduction in unit share of population, together with a rise in residential mobility and broken families. An increase in unrelated individuals and in the youth dependency ratio was particularly prominent in the emerging high-crime areas.

The most striking socioeconomic change was the reduction in unit share of semi- and unskilled occupations. The loss was most marked in the enduring high-crime areas, suggesting the persistence there of a growing residue of "discouraged" workers no longer counted among those seeking employment. Housing indicators highlight the onset of physical deterioration in the emerging high-crime areas, with twenty-year rises in their share of overcrowded dwellings. Density measures of the SES variables of occupational distribution and educational attainment show the emerging high-crime areas as most heterogeneous and the enduring areas as least.

Stability in their unit share of black population and of nonwhite female labor force participation were the notable twenty-year trends in subculture variables in the county's ten highest crime census tract clusters. However, differences in trends were evident for clusters at the several stages of development as high-crime areas. Density and rate increases of the two minority population groups occurred in the emerging but not in the enduring high-crime areas. Similarly, increases in the density and rate of status offenses and of nonwhites with advanced education characterized only the emerging high-crime areas.

With transformation of the multiple variables of each structural component to a composite indicator score, distinctions in causal sequences between changes in structural dimensions and changes in crime levels were investigated. In the emerging stage areas, changes in land use and in population composition appear as important precursors of change in neighborhood crime levels. Neither of these components preceded crime change in neighborhoods at the later stages of development. The precursors of crime change in the latter areas were, instead, socioeconomic status and subculture. It appears, then, that the prior structural changes early in the neighborhood transformation process are ecological in character, shifting in the later stages to prior change in sociocultural factors.

Findings based on cross-lagged correlation analysis were substantially confirmed by cross-lagged multivariate regression analysis, which revealed more conclusively the effects of sequential change in neighborhood conditions on changes in crime measures. When a neighborhood moves from a low- to a high-crime state, there occurs an earlier change in the ecological factors of land use and population composition and a later predominance of prior change in their socioeconomic and subcultural character. As neighborhood deterioration advances and crime rises, the sequence of change in the components of neighborhood social structure begins with shifts in land use. These involve principally an increase in multiplex dwellings and in renter-occupied housing. Changes in population composition then occur, marked by rising proportions in the minority ethnic groups, of single-parent families, and of unattached individuals. The structural component that then moves into prominence is that of socioeconomic status, to be replaced finally by subcultural change. Thus, initial limited changes in land use induce a larger number of demographic changes, in turn fostering a still larger number of changes in the socioeconomic features of the resident population. As the capstone, they proliferate in ethnic, occupational, and educational patterns representing shared adaptations to the set of background conditioning factors.

The final and perhaps most crucial set of measures focused on the relationship between change velocities in neighborhood structure and the velocity of change in the crime measure. The most definitive of these measures examined the effect of neighborhood change velocity in the first decade of the twenty-year period on the crime change velocity in the second decade. Only the composite scores for structural components and for crime were used. The principal general finding was that it is the speed of structural change rather than solely the fact of such change that initiates the transition of city neighborhoods from a low- to a high-crime status. Specifically, while initial changes had been found to involve the ecological factors of land use and population composition, velocity changes in neither of these components during the first decade spurred the change rate in crime during the second decade. Instead, it was the high velocity of first-decade change primarily in socioeconomic status and secondarily in subculture that were highly related to the second-decade acceleration in the crime measure. These relationships in the emerging high-crime areas contrasted with those found in the enduring high-crime areas representing neighborhoods in the terminal stage of transformation. In those latter areas, it was only the first-decade velocity in land use change and in subculture change that bore a high relationship to the rate of crime change in the second decade. By the terminal stage, the effects of change velocities in socioeconomic status and population composition on the rate of crime change appear already to have taken place.

## VI. Implications for Intervention

A number of implications for crime control policy are suggested by these findings. The point of intervention of probable maximum payoff for crime control is in the emerging high-crime areas, with effort devoted to the deceleration of demographic and socioeconomic change. Any neighborhood that has had a high level of crime over a period of several decades may be considered "lost" territory for purposes of effective crime reduction. These are the urban areas that absorb a disproportionate share of police resources, necessarily devoted to keeping an already precarious order from further deterioration. Even those neighborhoods identified as transitional high-crime areas may already be destined to become crime-ridden enclaves. Only a strenuous effort of containment by the police offers hope that the pace of neighborhood transformation may be slowed.

It remains clear, then, that only the currently emerging high-crime neighborhoods may offer some opportunity to reverse their eventual establishment as persisting high-crime areas. The indicators by which emerging high-crime areas may be identified are reasonably clear.

First, they are likely to be located in the "middle-aged" rather than in the oldest residential areas. In Los Angeles County, these were areas in which both single- and multiple-dwelling units were built before 1940 but in which no commercial or industrial land use had occurred by 1970. Second, their demographics are characterized by sharply rising measures of single-parent families and unrelated individuals and an escalation of residential mobility during the preceding decade. Third, one of the notable land use changes during the preceding decade had been a shift from predominantly owner-occupied to renter-occupied housing. Fourth, the socioeconomic composition of their populations is highly heterogeneous with a mix of residents in both higher- and lower-income occupations. Fifth, with respect to subcultural characteristics, there is a trend in the prior decade toward a high increase in the density and a substantial and steady increase in the rate of ethnic minorities, with a striking increase within these groups of those with advanced education. Additional subcultural features include a rising rate of non-white females in the labor force and a rising rate of juvenile status offenses. The emerging high-crime areas represent communities of unsorted mix at the point just preceding the onset of the ecological processes of segregation and residential specialization.

Whether policy initiatives can be suggested capable of inhibiting or reversing what has proven to be a predictable course of development depends on the existence of countervailing "natural" social forces. A number of these may be indicated, although they are likely to be relatively weak in relation to those of residential segregation and specialization. First, both home owners and renters may initially be reluctant to cut the ties of sentiment to their neighborhoods. Second, residence in the close-in older urban city areas is likely to rise in value in the future in part as an effect of the "gentrification" movement and in part because of rising costs of commuting from the suburbs and hinterlands. Recent research on neighborhood change and crime in Chicago also suggests that the preservation of the city's older areas can be reinforced by institutional and corporate investment in these areas (Taub, Taylor, and Dunham 1984). Third, there is evidence that earlier patterns of middle-class "white flight" from the older urban areas has declined, with a consequent small but steady increase in the number of racially mixed, stable, middle-class urban communities.

Based on these factors, policies designed to interrupt the impending deterioration of the emerging high-crime areas would in the first instance attempt to control their advancing cross-class mix. This can be accomplished only by vigorous local political control of zoning, planning, and building code requirements. There may be some possibility of designing these specifically for the endangered areas in such a way as to establish a ratio of lower- to middle-class residents irrespective of racial composition that sustains the orderliness of public space. Moreover, such changes would have to be supplemented by a set of social and educational services to help lower-class families and their children, even if small in number, cope with their social and economic problems. Finally, because the emerging high-crime areas are frequently within easy access from the enduring high-crime areas, and therefore highly vulnerable to predatory invasion, a crucial element of policy would concern law enforcement. It is likely that the emerging areas would have to be established as special police administrative districts with a higher than average ratio of police to population and with an emphasis on foot patrolling.

There is little reason to assume that these policy initiatives can be readily implemented. There is even less reason to assume that, if implemented, they might have substantial payoff in crime reduction since they leave untouched the major sources of metropolitan crime in the enduring high-crime neighborhoods. However, policy moves in the direction indicated are warranted despite the obstacles they are bound to face. They might slow the spread of serious crime problems to hitherto low-crime neighborhoods, with the effect ultimately of stemming the current trend toward a gradual enlargement of the city area affected.

## REFERENCES

Burgess, Ernest W. 1926. "The Natural Area as the Unit for Social Work in the Large City." Cited in *Delinquency Areas* by Clifford R. Shaw, Frederick M. Zorbaugh, Henry McKay, and Leonard S. Cottrell. Chicago: University of Chicago Press, 1929.

Duncan, Otis, Ray P. Cuzzard, and Beverly Duncan. 1961. *Statistical Geography: Problems in Analyzing Area Data.* Glencoe, Ill.: Free Press.

Geary, R. C. 1954. "The Contiguity Ratio and Statistical Mapping." *Incorporated Statistician* 5:115–45.

Hoover, Edgar, and Raymond Vernon. 1962. *Anatomy of a Metropolis.* Garden City, N.Y.: Anchor.

Morris, Terrence. 1958. *The Criminal Area.* London: Kegan Paul.

Myers, George C. 1964. "Variations in Urban Population Structure." *Demography* 1:156–63.

Pelz, Donald C., and Frank Andrews. 1964. "Detecting Causal Priorities in Panel Study Data." *American Sociological Review* 29:836–48.

Schmid, Calvin. 1960. "Urban Crime Areas: Part I." *American Sociological Review* 25:527–42.

Schuessler, Karl. 1971. *Analyzing Social Data: A Statistical Orientation.* Boston: Houghton Mifflin.

Shaw, Clifford R., and Henry D. McKay. 1942. *Juvenile Delinquency and Urban Areas.* Chicago: University of Chicago Press.

Shaw, Clifford R., Frederick M. Zorbaugh, Henry McKay, and Leonard S. Cottrell. 1929. *Delinquency Areas.* Chicago: University of Chicago Press.

Taub, Richard, D. Garth Taylor, and Jan D. Dunham. 1984. *Paths of Neighborhood Change.* Chicago: University of Chicago Press.

*Anthony E. Bottoms and Paul Wiles*

# Housing Tenure and Residential Community Crime Careers in Britain

ABSTRACT

The notion of a "criminal career," though generally used in reference to individuals, can be applied also to residential communities. The key to understanding community criminal careers in Britain lies within the operation of the housing market. The urban geography of most large British cities has resulted from historical developments unique to housing tenure in Britain. The tenure picture is unlike that portrayed in the Chicago model of concentric ring development, and the distribution of British offender rates therefore does not correspond to expectations of the Chicago model. Bureaucratic mechanisms for allocating housing in the public rental sector have profound direct and indirect effects on offender distributions and community crime careers. These mechanisms may help to maintain the stability of offender rates in particular communities, exacerbate the rate, or reduce the rate by changing practices in a given public authority housing area. Private rental, although severely diminished in importance during the twentieth century, offers an alternative form of tenure to the more common owner occupation and public housing. Its location in decaying areas around city centers and its attraction to a transient clientele often result in high offender rates. Changes in the social composition of the area that were initiated by government changes in housing policy have made some areas into more desirable residential districts without causing dramatic declines in offender rates. The future of the main tenure forms—owner occupation and public

Anthony E. Bottoms is Wolfson Professor of Criminology and Director of the Institute of Criminology, Cambridge University. He was formerly Professor of Criminology at the University of Sheffield, from 1976 to 1984. Paul Wiles is Director of the Centre for Criminological and Socio-Legal Studies at the University of Sheffield.


0-226-80802-5/86/0008-0004$01.00

housing—remains uncertain and complicated, so it is difficult to predict how offender rates will change. The decline of private rental areas will undoubtedly continue. Changes in the criminal career of one area will probably affect careers in other areas.

From its earliest days criminology has shown an interest in the geography of crime. The work of, for example, Guerry in France and Mayhew in England in the nineteenth century or of the Chicago School in America in the interwar years is well-known and has exercised a powerful influence (for a review, see Morris [1957]). The subject has recently been revived and revivified in the wake of C. R. Jeffrey's (1971) *Crime Prevention through Environmental Design* and Oscar Newman's (1972) *Defensible Space* (see, generally, Brantingham and Brantingham 1981, introduction).

There is, however, a very interesting and insufficiently remarked on difference between the work of Shaw and McKay (1942) at the time of the Chicago school and modern so-called environmental criminology. Shaw and McKay studied primarily the "delinquency rates" of Chicago and other cities, that is, the areas where juvenile offenders lived. Modern environmental criminology, we are told in the first paragraph of a recent book on the subject, is the study of "the place in time and space where (law, offender, and target) come together"—in other words, it is about places where offenses are committed (Brantingham and Brantingham 1981, p. 7).[1] Yet it is now quite clear from many analyses (going back at least to Morris [1957], pp. 20–21, 119–30) that these two indices—area offender rates and area offense rates—can have very different geographical distributions. For example, in Britain offense rates in most cities are particularly high in the city center, but offender rates show a much less concentric pattern (see, e.g., Baldwin and Bottoms 1976, maps 2–4, pp. 58, 75–76). Technical aspects of the offender rate/offense rate distinction are elaborated in the Appendix; as can be seen, the distinction between the two may still be made whether one is using

[1] The reasons for this shift of criminological attention from explaining the areal distribution of offender rates to explaining the areal distribution of offense rates would repay detailed study. Speculatively, we would suggest that they include (1) a heightened pessimism about crime prevention efforts based on changing offenders' behavior patterns and a belief (justified or otherwise) that preventing offenses through, e.g., reduction in offense opportunities is the more promising policy option and (2) the ready availability, especially in the United States, of data sets comprising offense data in contrast to a relative dearth of offender data sets.

official (police-recorded) offense and offender data or, alternatively, survey-based data (victimization and self-report studies).

In this essay we are concerned with *community crime careers*. But what does this concept mean? The idea of a "career" in everyday speech refers to processes of change and development through life, often in an occupational context; a career in this sense is shaped partly by individual choice and partly by a variety of external pressures and/or opportunities. In a similar way, we can and do talk in criminology of individual "crime careers"—for example, one person heavily involved in crime as a teenager might become law-abiding after an early marriage, while another whose adolescent crime consisted only of occasional petty thefts might in his twenties become attached to a professional criminal group and commit multiple armed robberies. In much the same manner, whole communities can in the course of time change from "respectable" to "deviant," or vice versa, and thus by analogy we can speak of a "community crime career." "Community," of course, can refer to any group of people in a designated social space who interact to produce a culture that then affects their life-style and life chances—we can talk, for example, of the community of the workplace, or of the church, or of the school. Geographical areas are one possible locus of "community": although for individual residents the area may not be the most important community to which they belong, it will be a rare district indeed that has no community life whatsoever. The community crime careers of *residential communities* is therefore a legitimate subject of criminological attention.

In principle, "residential community crime careers" could refer either to changing patterns of offense victimization in an area over time, or to the changing criminal activity of the residents, or to both of these. The former would be measured by *offense* or victimization rates, the latter by *offender rates* (see App.). In this essay our primary interest is in the second of these two possibilities, that is, in offending by residents and the ways in which this changes over time in different residential communities.

The central argument of this essay is that, at least in Britain, the key to an understanding of (offender-based) residential community crime careers lies in the operations of the housing market. This argument cannot be understood without some grasp of the way in which housing and offender rates are generally related in Britain. Table 1, derived from early research work in Sheffield, an industrial city in the north of

TABLE 1

Distribution of Census Enumeration Districts and Mean Offender Rates by Dominant Tenure Type in Sheffield, 1966

| Dominant Tenure Type in Enumeration District* | Number of Enumeration Districts | Offender Rate for Young Males Ages 10–19 | Offender Rate for Adult Males Ages 20 and Over |
|---|---|---|---|
| Owner occupied | 72 | 6.6 | 1.1 |
| Rented from private landlord | 47 | 15.3 | 3.8 |
| Rented from local authority (public housing) | 64 | 14.4 | 3.1 |
| Mixed | 21 | 12.4 | 1.8 |
| Total | 204 | | |

SOURCE.—Baldwin and Bottoms (1976, pp. 108, 129).

NOTE.—Offender rates computed per 1,000 of relevant population per annum.

* A tenure is classified as dominant within the enumeration district if more than 50 percent of the households in the enumeration district hold their residence by that tenure type.

England, shows male offender rates by the main housing tenure types.[2] The city (population approximately 500,000) was divided for the purposes of the 1966 10 percent census into some 200 enumeration districts with a population around 2,500. In seventy-two of these districts, the main housing tenure type was owner occupation; in sixty-four, renting from the local authority (public housing); in forty-seven, renting from a private landlord; while in the remaining districts no one tenure type was dominant. Taking the three main tenure-type areas, it can be seen that the mean offender rates across all local authority and all privately rented areas are broadly similar, while the mean offender rate in owner-occupied districts was much lower.[3] More detailed analyses at the time

[2] The concentration on Sheffield here and throughout the paper obviously reflects our own research activities and university affiliation over the last decade. It should not be assumed that in all respects Sheffield is necessarily typical of Britain as a whole. But since (as we show later) there are differences in housing tenure distribution and in housing policies in different local areas in Britain, there is some advantage in a primary concentration on one city when giving examples, for the different aspects of housing and crime in the city can then be more coherently understood as a whole.

[3] Herbert (1982, p. 87) replicated this analysis using data for Cardiff (Wales) in 1966 and 1971 but restricting the study to offenders under twenty years old. He found the highest offender rates in the private rental sector, though this sector was small (14 out of 119 enumeration districts); rates for local authority areas were relatively high and those for owner-occupied districts low.

failed to find any owner-occupied district that was also a high-offender-rate area. However, more detailed analyses of the other two housing sectors showed enormous variation of offender rates within each sector; that is, some privately rented districts had high rates, and some had low rates; some local authority areas had high rates, and some had low rates. Moreover, the research found some interesting differences in the population composition and in the statistical associations with the offender rates in, respectively, the local authority and the privately rented sectors taken as a whole (e.g., the privately rented sector had more recent migrants to the city, while the local authority sector had larger households and fewer one- or two-person households). Also, in some instances, there was little difference between certain high- and low-offender-rate areas within these sectors in terms of key social variables such as social class, even though such variables did generally discriminate between high- and low-offender-rate districts in the city (see, generally, Baldwin and Bottoms 1976; Mawby 1979).

Taken together, all this suggests that if we are interested in residential areas with high offender rates in the British context we should concentrate very strongly on the privately rented and the local authority housing sectors; that within these sectors there is sometimes considerable variation in criminal activity in apparently socially similar areas; and that the two sectors themselves differ somewhat taken as a whole. The case for looking closely at aspects of the housing market when considering residential offending patterns looks strong.

When the focus is (as it is here) on residential community crime careers, the case looks even stronger. This is so for two reasons. First, and to anticipate later sections of this essay, research into the changing crime careers of particular residential communities has shown conclusively that certain changes in area careers can be understood only if some aspects of the housing market and of housing policy are taken into account. Second, housing policy and housing tenure distributions have themselves been subject to rapid change in postwar Britain, and it can be shown empirically that these changes have had important effects on the spatial distribution of offenders within British cities generally, as well as on criminal activity in particular local areas that have been subject to tenure change or to change resulting from alterations in national or local housing policy or practice. These broader social changes in housing policy and in housing tenure distributions therefore require some explanation if residential community crime careers in Britain are to be understood adequately. This is particularly necessary when writing for non-British readers since there are important differences between the British housing market and those of every other industrialized society (Kemeny 1981; Donnison and Ungerson 1982). This unique housing market has produced a very particular urban geography and some very particular urban-offender-rate patterns and residential community crime careers.

This essay consists of four sections. Section I discusses forms of housing tenure in Britain and how their distribution has changed historically; the social effects of these tenure patterns and tenure changes in terms of urban and regional geography, social class and status, and politics; and the possible relations between housing tenure allocation mechanisms and residential community crime careers. Section II discusses variations in residential community crime careers in the local authority housing sector in Britain; social processes, including housing policy, related to these variations; and recent attempts to reduce the crime and offender rates in public sector housing by positive social programs. Section III discusses residential community crime careers in privately rented housing areas in Britain, both examining the consequences of the rapid historical decline of this tenure form and considering the crime patterns and social effects in the relatively few privately rented areas still remaining. Section IV, the conclusion, reemphasizes the centrality of access to housing, and its direct and indirect effects, in shaping residential communities and their community crime careers and speculates about likely future tenure changes in Britain and their possible effects on residential community crime careers.

Two important technical points should be made, and both are related to our primary focus on the offender rate as a key index for residential community crime careers. First, it should not be assumed that offender rates and offense rates in residential areas are unconnected. Rather it is known from a study of police-recorded notifiable offenses in Sheffield that, when the city center and other similar "offense-attracting" areas are excluded, there is a strong, though not perfect, correlation between the offender rate and the offense rate in the remaining (residential) districts (Baldwin and Bottoms 1976, pp. 97–98; Mawby 1979, chap. 2).[4] More recently, Herbert and Hyde's (1984, p. 69) study of residen-

[4] "Notifiable offenses" is now the standard term used in England and Wales for those crimes in respect of which the police are obliged to make annual statistical returns to the Home Office of "offenses known to the police" as well as of persons prosecuted. (In respect of other offenses usually, though not necessarily, less serious, they have to make returns only in respect of persons prosecuted.) The category of "notifiable offenses" is

tial burglary in Swansea—after considering empirically a number of hypotheses concerning the determination of the geographical distribution of that offense—concluded in similar vein that "[w]hilst not seeking to divert attention and resources from the study and focus upon individual households which are victims of crime, the area hypotheses suggest that the more general concept of a *vulnerable area* is valid and worthy of consideration in both research and policy terms. Of the area hypotheses, *offender-residence comes the closest to a general explanation* (of offense rates), but the others are useful in association, or as major strands in explaining the vulnerability of particular types of area" (emphasis added).

The second technical point concerns the validity of areal offender rates as indices. Areal offender rates are almost always derived initially from police-recorded data. How do we know that these are not an artifact of, for example, differential police surveillance or of differential public reporting in different areas? This question has been very carefully considered in the course of research in Sheffield by making detailed analyses of the way in which officially recorded crimes, and detected offenders, came to police attention in seven different residential areas with contrasting official offender and offense rates, by conducting a victim survey in these same areas, and by some participant observation work in four of the areas. The results suggest that a good deal of confidence can be placed on the assumption that within a city the residents of small areas that have high official (police-recorded) offender rates usually do actually commit more offenses than do the residents of areas with low police-recorded offender rates (Mawby 1979; Xanthos 1981; Bottoms et al. 1986).[5] In what follows, we shall assume this to be the case. We must, however, enter the important reservations that, in making this assumption, we are first confining ourselves to the usual kinds of notifiable offenses, such as thefts, bur-

broadly similar to the old category of "indictable offenses." It includes violence against the person, sexual offenses, burglary, robbery, theft and handling stolen goods, fraud and forgery, criminal damage, and a few other offenses.

[5] Strictly speaking, a self-report study of residents in the seven areas was also required to test police-recorded offender rates; one was attempted, but in the opinion of the researchers there were reasons for believing its results to be not fully valid (see Bottoms et al. 1986). For the record, the comparative results it produced were broadly in line with all other findings. However, since in these seven residential areas official offender and offense rates covary (see text), household victimization survey data, which are believed to be more valid, offer an adequate substitute for a self-report study, provided that offenses against residents within the area and outside it are carefully distinguished (see also the App.).

glaries, taking cars, and assaults, and are saying nothing about, for example, white-collar or corporate crime and its distribution[6] and, second, that the assumption we have made would almost certainly be true only when considering comparative small-area offender rates within a city covered by a single police force, rather than areas in different cities, because of possible differences in recording methods in different police forces.[7]

## I. Housing Tenure, Policy, and Allocation in Britain

In this section, we discuss housing tenure and housing policy in Britain as essential background to later sections. We conclude the section by outlining a number of possible ways in which housing allocation is linked to the development of residential community crime careers.

### A. *The Political Economy of Britain*

The political economy of postwar Britain needs to be understood in considering housing policy in the last forty years since it constitutes the framework within which housing policy was determined and house building and demolition took place. This is not, of course, the place for an extended discussion of British political economy (for which, see Middlemas [1980]), but it is necessary to make a few brief points. The politics of postwar Britain have been dominated by the problems of economic decline and by successive attempts to manage economic development within a corporatist framework of cooperation between government and representatives of capital and labor. This can most clearly be seen in the "postwar settlement," as part of which the involvement of labor in economic planning was achieved by government accepting responsibility for providing the social wage. Thus was created the British "welfare state," which, for most of the postwar period, has enjoyed all-party support. Central to this settlement was a commitment

[6] For American readers we should add that "the usual kinds of notifiable offenses" do not, in most parts of Britain, include offenses such as homicide, robbery, or rape, which all exist but by American standards are very rare. Also there is in most British cities a marked absence of organized or professional crime.

[7] For a penetrating study of large-area notifiable offense rate differences in three counties served by different police forces, see Farrington and Dowds (1985). The results showed considerable rate distortion due to different police interview tactics and recording practices in one of the areas. Interestingly, as in the Sheffield small-area study, there were no discernible area differences in the public reporting of crime.

to maintaining full employment and providing new and better housing, partly through a much-expanded public housing sector. These various policies were characterized by a spirit of idealism that believed inter alia that a reduction in crime would follow from improved social conditions.

Corporatism and the welfare state, however, failed to halt either economic decline or crime, and early postwar idealism gradually withered away. Especially from 1979 onward, the British state has turned to alternative strategies. Much of our essay is concerned with the effects of the housing policies of the postwar settlement on residential community crime careers. The more recent changes in the economy and the state since 1979 have only just begun to have a measurable effect on housing. Their effect will undoubtedly be to change residential community crime careers, but in precisely what ways is still somewhat unclear. We do, however, offer some speculative comments at the end of this essay.

### *B. Housing Tenure in Britain*

In nineteenth-century Britain, houses were either owned or, for the vast majority of people, rented from private landlords. However, since then the situation has changed significantly, especially since the Second World War as can be seen from table 2.

TABLE 2

Housing Tenure in Great Britain, 1945–83

| Year | Owner Occupied | Privately Rented* | Local Authority (Public Housing) |
|---|---|---|---|
| 1945 | 26 | 62 | 12 |
| 1951 | 29 | 53 | 18 |
| 1961 | 43 | 31 | 27 |
| 1969 | 49 | 21 | 30 |
| 1971 | 53 | 16 | 31 |
| 1979 | 55 | 13 | 32 |
| 1983 | 57 | 11 | 32 |

SOURCES.—1945–79: Malpass and Murie (1982, p. 54, table 3.3); 1983: United Kingdom (1985, p. 125, table 8.5).

NOTE.—Data are percentages of all households.

* Includes housing associations.

By the late twentieth century in Britain, private landlords have almost become an extinct species. Two main developments have been responsible for this decline: the development of the building societies that expanded owner occupation and the rise of local public authorities as landlords. These changes have had profound social and geographical consequences, but before discussing these we must examine how these changes have occurred and what their effect on tenure patterns has been.

1. *The Building Society Movement.* Historically, capital for house building other than for housing built for the workers of some great productive enterprise was provided mainly locally. This was usually lent to landlords who repaid the interest on their loans and took their own profit out of rents. This remained the main source of house-building capital in Britain until the First World War. However, from the late eighteenth century onward, a new form of capital provision for house building—the "building society"—began to develop, which was radically to alter this pattern.

The earliest building societies consisted of groups of artisans who banded together to help each other fund and build houses for themselves. Building societies then changed significantly in the mid-nineteenth century, when they began to borrow money for building from different people from those to whom they lent money to build houses. They became investment and financing institutions but with the unique attributes that they only lend money for property, are not in themselves profit making, and are legally owned by their investors.

Building societies became and have remained a popular form of investment because they provide a safe return. Their attractiveness was enhanced after the First World War when government began to offer tax concessions to building-society investors. This effectively discriminated against private landlords and favored owner-occupiers in the housing capital market. The discrimination was further widened when government also granted tax relief to house purchasers of private houses (mostly, borrowers from building societies) on their mortgage interest repayments. This became increasingly important from the 1950s onward as income tax increased.

The invention of the building society therefore created an easy way of providing long-term capital for individual house purchases. The result was a huge growth in owner occupation until it is now the main type of tenure in Britain. As can be seen from table 2, owner occupation was the tenure type for only 26 percent of households in 1945, but by 1983 this had increased to 57 percent. Governments, through tax concessions and, lately, political encouragement, have done much to encourage this growth of owner occupation. However, they have done so by mechanisms that have simply adjusted the market and so have denied themselves any significant role in physical planning in this tenure sector.

2. *Local Authority Housing.* Public housing in Britain has its origins in the nineteenth-century concern with the health dangers of overcrowded slums, leading to local sanitary and poor-law authorities becoming involved in housing standards and sometimes management or even building. Nevertheless, the provision of housing by local authorities prior to the First World War was fitful and very localized (see, generally, Merrett 1979). As already explained, private rental was still the main form of tenure at this time. The war economy, however, so disrupted building that a major housing problem resulted. The only way to solve this problem was by an increased public building program funded by both central and local government finance. This was partly because the private market could not respond quickly enough, especially for the poorer tenants returning from the war, but also because the experience of a state-run economy during the war had fostered a general belief in government planning (see, particularly, Johnson 1968; see also Middlemas 1980). This belief and indeed the postwar housing program soon collapsed—but local authorities were now irrevocably involved in the provision of housing. In the 1930s public health concerns reemerged, and local authority house building focused on slum clearance—a problem that the market, left to itself, could not solve. Once again, after the Second World War, the country faced a huge housing crisis because of a lack of building during the war and as the result of enemy action. The building of public housing was to be the immediate solution not only because of the ease of planning in this sector but also because such provision chimed in with the welfare state philosophy of reconstruction. The vision of the welfare state included a large public housing sector as the alternative to private rental and not just as a residual tenure for the poor. A massive program of public house building was started, therefore, on the basis of government controls of the economy that were continued from the war. Gradually, however, these wartime controls on the economy and therefore the building industry were relaxed, and as a result private house building began to expand. For a while the provision of public housing once more took on a more restricted role with the very large slum-clearance pro-

grams of the 1960s. Subsequently, government was again forced to adopt a more general role in housing provision, mainly because of demographic changes that meant that households in Britain increased much faster than did the population. Finally, from 1979 onward public housing has begun to return to a residual role. This is a result of central government policy to sell public housing to sitting tenants at advantageous prices and the curtailment of public expenditure restricting new building. However, both of these policies have been resisted by some local authorities.

In spite of these variations in policy, which largely reflect the changing fortunes of the economy, the general result has been a great increase in the provision of public housing. Rented property in Britain has increasingly come to mean publicly built and managed housing. Public housing stock increased from 2.5 million dwellings in 1951 to almost 7 million in 1979 and then declined by almost 0.5 million by 1983 as tenants bought their rented homes under government schemes (United Kingdom 1985). As can be seen from table 2, the percentage of households in local authority housing increased from 12 percent in 1945 to 32 percent in 1979. Since then, the decline in local authority housing stock due to the Conservative government's policies has halted this increase, and, if these policies continue, they will almost certainly produce a further decline in the future.

3. *The Decline of Private Rentals.* Privately owned and rented property has declined from being the dominant tenure in the nineteenth century to a position in 1983 where it represented little more than 10 percent of all households. Private landlords have not received the public subsidies of owner-occupiers (tax relief) or of local authority tenants (central and local government subsidies). At some periods private landlords have been more overtly constrained, especially by Labour governments; landlords, after all, are the traditional bêtes noires of socialism. However, although measures such as rent control legislation are often cited as the cause of the decline of the private rental sector, the relative disadvantage of private landlords in the capital market has been much more important.

Not only has the private rental sector shrunk, but its nature has also changed. As a recent commentator put it, "The single most important change in type of housing (in Britain) has been in the relative sizes of the unfurnished and furnished rental sectors. It is clear that the decline in the size of the rental sector has occurred entirely in the unfurnished sub-sector, with the furnished sub-sector actually increasing by one percentage point between 1958 and 1975, and the ratio of furnished to unfurnished dwellings rising from 1:17.5 to 1:3 in the same period" (Kemeny 1981, p. 133). This change in the nature of privately rented accommodation has meant that this has increasingly become a transitional tenure, providing a home for households until they can find their way into one of the two dominant tenures. This is hardly surprising since furnished private rentals offer some of the poorest accommodation in Britain (see United Kingdom 1985, p. 125, table 8.6).

The investing of private capital into new housing for rental is now very rare in Britain with the exception of some atypical areas such as central London. Notwithstanding the present government's general desire to "privatize" the economy, this situation is not likely to change. The main change in tenure in the near future will undoubtedly be an increase in the owner-occupied sector, both because of more new building in this sector and because of the sale of local authority houses. The privately rented sector will almost certainly decline further. Given these major changes in tenure patterns and given likely future trends, it is now time to examine the main social effects.

### C. *The Social Effects of Tenure Patterns*

The twin effect of the work of building societies and the housing programs of local authorities has been to create a highly successful post-1945 housing program in Britain: no other country has demolished and rebuilt so much slum housing, and space per family is among the best in the world (on this and housing policy generally, see Donnison and Ungerson [1982]). Much more important than these considerations, however, are the social consequences of having housing so sharply divided into two main tenures.

Basically, tenure has reflected and reinforced, in bricks and mortar, class divisions in Britain. As the two dominant tenures emerged, especially after the Second World War, they gave a new shape and meaning to class patterns. However, housing tenure does not simply mirror class. Although tenure is clearly class related, within tenure types other aspects of housing provision have subtly reworked social relations. Without wishing to imply a crude physical determinism, housing provision has historically been closely related to the geography and nature of several aspects of social behavior and attitudes, including crime, in contemporary Britain.

1. *Tenure and Urban Geography.* In any country where housing and income are related, there will be an effect on urban geography: there

will be rich and poor areas of the city, desirable and undesirable places to live. In Britain, urban geography has been especially influenced by the history of the emergence of the two dominant tenure types.

The provision of public, local authority housing has been mainly within major public programs either to create postwar housing or to effect slum clearance. Such large-scale programs have produced similarly scaled solutions: large public housing areas, or, as they are known colloquially, "council estates." The means of funding and building this housing has meant that it was created as part of a general local government planning process, whereas the mechanism for government subsidy of private housing did not create the same planning opportunities. British planners working on these large public programs were animated by the spirit of postwar reconstruction and the welfare state accords. They were building the "new Jerusalem," in which decent housing would be the basis for creating a fairer, more just society. The cramped back-to-back, small terraced houses of industrial Britain, with their damp walls, inadequate sanitary facilities, and small paved backyards, would be replaced by spacious, well-built family dwellings with gardens. Housing would not be subservient to industrial needs: the new houses would not, like their predecessors, huddle around the factory. Among other things, there was a strong belief that the criminality of residents would decrease as they were moved from the slums to these better dwellings. This was part of the unbridled faith in planning. Whole new communities could be created and planned from the town hall—and, to give them the maximum chance, many of the estates were built in pleasant "green-field" sites on city edges.

The optimistic belief in the planners' abilities was, of course, to some extent misplaced. The new estates were often inconveniently far away from the city center or from places of employment in separately planned industrial zones. The commercial life of the estates rarely consisted of much more than the planners' provision of a few corner shops and a pub. The "new Jerusalems" were all too often isolated, and isolating, dormitories. The form of government subsidy for public housing meant that such large-scale planning was possible, but, since subsidies were not channeled through tenants, this meant they had little say in the form and nature of housing. Ironically, the quality of housing in the public sector is often better than in the private sector, but it offers less variety and variation. The management of the estates could be equally paternalistic—unresponsive to tenants' needs and stifling of tenant initiatives. Moreover, crime did not decrease; various research studies "demonstrated quite clearly that new council estates, though structurally superior to slum residences, have had no profound effect on overall levels of officially recorded delinquency, and, in some cases, perhaps even a slight adverse effect" (Baldwin 1975, p. 12). When the later slum-clearance programs of the 1960s were carried out, economic constraints and the new cheaper technology of industrialized building methods led to the creation of high-rise apartments on city-center sites that were made available by earlier clearance. They were geographically less isolated, but their design meant that they were frequently socially anomic. In any case, the apartments ran counter to a powerful cultural preference in Britain for houses with gardens, and they soon became the most undesired tenancies. Sometimes they have become so hated that they cannot be let and have had to be demolished.

The result of these various processes is that most large British cities have a very particular urban geography. An archetypal city will have a central business and shopping district. This will be surrounded by areas of high-rise local authority housing, the remains of much older property that either provides the main private rental sector or has recently been recolonized for owner occupation, and perhaps some light industry. Beyond this will be newer housing divided into distinct areas of large local authority estates or owner-occupied developments. Industrial development in this region will be separately zoned but near to the local authority housing or the bottom end of the owner-occupier market. Finally, in the surrounding countryside will be homes for the more affluent owner-occupiers.

Tenure type, then, has created the geography of the modern British city. While tenure may be closely related to wealth, it is not quite the same thing. Certainly, the importance of local authority housing in Britain has meant that urban geography is not simply the result of the market as traditionally conceived. One important consequence when making comparisons with the United States is that British cities do not fit the Chicago model of concentric-ring development. Therefore, the distribution of offender rates in British cities does not fit the Chicago model. Instead it is related to the geography of the British tenure patterns (see, e.g., the maps in Baldwin and Bottoms [1976], pp. 75–76; Herbert [1982], chap. 5).

2. *Tenure and Regional Variations.* When considering the tenure patterns and therefore the offender distributions of British cities, we must remember that there are significant regional variations. For example, in

1979, 63 percent of tenures in the southwest region of England were owner occupied, but in Scotland only 35 percent were. Conversely, 54 percent of tenures in Scotland were local authority rentals compared with only 22 percent in the southwest (United Kingdom 1981, table 6.7). What explains these differences is that economic decline and regional poverty in parts of Britain have curtailed the growth of owner occupation and have necessitated a proportionately greater provision of local authority housing.

These regional variations do not mean, of course, that regional offender rates will simply vary according to tenure proportions. However, they do mean that offender rates within tenure types will vary according to tenure proportions. A city with a large public housing sector, for example, will be likely to have a greater offender rate variation within that sector than will one with a small public housing sector. We return to this matter below.

3. *Tenure and Social Class.* The most obvious aspect of the development in Britain of two main tenure types is that this is a class division. Whether one uses household income as the measure of social class (United Kingdom 1985, p. 126, table 8.8) or the socioeconomic group of the head of the household as defined by the registrar-general (United Kingdom 1983, p. 115, table 8.7), there is a direct correlation between tenure and social class. The greater the household income, or the higher the socioeconomic status of the head of the household, the more likely it is that the head of the household will be an owner-occupier with a mortgage. The lower are these two measures, the more likely the household will be to live in local authority housing. That this is a true class effect and not just a matter of income can be seen from the fact that owner occupation is higher among nonmanual groups than among manual ones even if income is held constant (United Kingdom 1985, p. 126).[8] In the contemporary Britain of high unemployment levels, this class division is further reinforced. In 1979–80, the latest period for which figures are available, of those heads of households who were employed, 60 percent were owner-occupiers, and only 28 percent lived in local authority housing. Of those heads of households who were available for work but were unemployed, 56 percent lived in local

[8] In the case of those who own their houses outright, the correlation with socioeconomic status still holds but not that with household income. However, this is simply because such households consist mainly of those who have paid off their mortgages and are now living on retirement pensions, and therefore the finding does not invalidate the general relation between social class and tenure type.

authority housing, and 30 percent were owner-occupiers (United Kingdom 1982, p. 150, table 8.11). Unemployment has increased since then, and these divisions almost certainly will have widened as a result (see United Kingdom 1984, p. 122, fig. 8.10).

Crudely, then, the two main tenure types in Britain reflect social class: the middle class comprises mainly owner-occupiers, and the working class mainly tenants of the local authorities. However, one must remember that the increase in owner-occupied tenures means and will continue to mean that, nationally speaking, an increasing number of working-class families will live in such tenures. One must also remember that there will be significant regional variations in the speed of this development.

4. *Tenure and Politics.* This relation between social class, tenure, and relative regional wealth has also had political consequences. Not only do tenure data demonstrate a correlation with social class, but that relation is part of everyday British social consciousness. To become an owner-occupier is not simply to cross a legal property distinction but is symbolically to cross a class divide—it is *the* indication of upward social mobility. Conversely, to live on a council estate is in many towns the ultimate working-class signifier. Naturally, those who make such a symbolic journey are likely to change their social persona in other ways. Owner occupation has been used as the basis for a political philosophy by the Conservative party in Britain, epitomized in the slogan, "a property-owning democracy." When in government, the party's policies have been to encourage owner occupation and to shift tenure types by selling local authority housing to tenants. It is widely assumed that owner-occupiers will support Conservative party policies and vote them into power. If this were indeed true, the growth of owner-occupied tenures would guarantee a permanent majority for the Conservative party. Fortunately for the health of political democracy in Britain, the reality is a little more complex. However, tenure types in Britain have nevertheless become associated both with class and with the politics of class.

5. *Tenure and Social Status.* The relation of tenure type to social class is, as we have already said, a crude one. If we shift our conception of social hierarchy from socioeconomic class to status in the Weberian sense, then we can explore distinctions within class and tenure types. Status, both other- and self-perceived, in Britain is much more subtle than a simple bipartitism, so within tenure types crucial status distinctions exist. For owner occupation, the market and its pricing mecha-

nisms reflect the summation of these distinctions. Physically identical housing, offering the same facilities, can command very different market prices, depending on beliefs about the relative social standing of different areas. For local authority tenure, the picture is more complicated.

Since the end of the First World War, local authorities have been involved in building and managing housing, using both local and central government funds. From 1935 the authorities were allowed to pool all housing income, including subsidies as well as rents, and to set this in common against their costs, including interest repayments. The result is that rents charged to tenants can be equalized across properties regardless of the actual debt costs of particular homes. This has meant that local authorities can fix rents with reference to nonfinancial criteria that they deem socially desirable. Financial balancing of income and costs is achieved for the housing stock as a whole and not for individual properties. In practice, cross-subsidization of rents has taken place in local authority housing. The effect of this is that the market mechanism for allocation in the owner-occupied tenure does not apply to local authority tenures.

A mechanism for allocation is nevertheless still needed for local authority housing, and this has been provided by administrative means (see further below). Within this, lack of a complete pricing mechanism has meant that other criteria for rank ordering local authority property have emerged. Inter alia, the social reputation of different properties and areas, not being reflected in rents, has instead had complex direct and indirect effects on allocation practices and consumer choices. The result is that within the local authority housing sector different areas are perceived as having very different social standing. This may not be reflected either in the physical nature of the accommodation or in the rents charged but may have an absolutely central effect on the social life of an area, including crime.

What then of the third tenure type in Britain, namely, private rental accommodation? One consequence of the decline of this tenure is that very little new housing is built for private rental.[9] As a result, over half (56 percent) of all private rented housing in Britain in 1983 was built before 1919, and 73 percent of it was built before the end of the

[9] An exception to this since about 1970 are the housing associations that in 1980 were responsible for about 9 percent of all newly completed dwellings (Donnison and Ungerson 1982, p. 148). Housing association properties are, however, not truly private rental accommodation: they are discussed briefly in Sec. III.

Second World War (United Kingdom 1985, p. 125, table 8.15). The majority of private rental tenures are older properties, mainly in inner cities. They are marginal properties, and this is yet another reason why this tenure is likely to decline further. However, their marginality as property means that such accommodation may be especially useful for socially marginal tenants. Owner occupation depends on the kind of financial rectitude that is usually associated with industrious and dominant social life-styles; there are few more powerful definers of social normality than the building societies. Local authority housing has been concerned mainly with housing families and old people, although the very decline of the private rental sector is beginning to change this situation. Private rental accommodation, frequently in the decaying areas around the centers of cities, has provided homes for marginal groups as diverse as students, single parents, prostitutes, and newly arrived immigrants. Small as the private rental sector has been in recent years, it has provided homes, often temporary, for groups that the two dominant tenure types have found difficult to accommodate and locations for certain types of deviant behavior. We return to this and to the likely consequences of the further decline of this tenure later.

### *D. Mechanisms of Housing Allocation*

We have said much about tenure patterns in Britain and a little about how this relates to offender rates. Given that offender rates can vary between and within tenures, sometimes for areas of similar social composition, the mechanisms of allocation between and within tenure types must be a critical part of any explanation of offender-rate distribution. Before going on to examine residential community crime careers, it is therefore vital to explore these mechanisms briefly.

It would be perfectly possible to have different housing tenures but only one mechanism for allocation: within a capitalist economy this would be the price mechanism of a market. Within such a system, price would reflect relative demand for a particular property or area, which itself would be the summation of all judgments of social desirability set against the supply. Ability to pay any price would depend not only on income but also on credit worthiness and the rules governing inherited wealth. Whether such a system would encourage ownership, rental, or some other form of tenure would depend on the relative long-term advantages of each form. We have seen in Britain how income-tax incentives for owner-occupiers—which during part of the postwar period crucially reduced real interest rates below the inflation of the capital value of houses—encouraged this tenure. No economically rational actor in postwar Britain who could raise a mortgage would have rented rather than bought a home unless their housing needs were of a very temporary nature. Private rental therefore increasingly tended to become a tenure for the poor and the socially deviant.

Local authority housing on the other hand, at least after 1935, did not use a price mechanism for allocation. Although there are some price differences in rents for different kinds of local authority housing, they are not as large or of the same nature as those that a market price would produce. Certainly, price variations within this tenure sector cannot explain offender-rate variation: a Sheffield study produced a correlation of only −0.17 between offender rate and the average rent on local authority estates (Baldwin and Bottoms 1976, p. 170). What then are the allocative mechanisms within the local authority sector?

Allocation procedures vary from authority to authority, but basically two main procedures have been used: a points system and a date-order system. Points systems score applicants in relation to various criteria of need, such as quality of present accommodation, family size, overcrowding, and length of time already spent on the waiting list for a house. How long a household spends on the waiting list therefore depends on the authority's assessment of its needs. A date-order system allocates simply on the basis of length of time spent on the waiting list. In both cases, length of time on the waiting list is an important aspect. However, these mechanisms are not as straightforward as they might appear. First, most authorities have basic eligibility criteria, and, at least in the past, these have frequently excluded such groups as immigrants from other countries or from other parts of Britain, single households, or those already in owner-occupied tenures. Second, there are usually different criteria for transferring from one house to another within the sector than there are for getting into it in the first place. Basically, it can take a long time to transfer houses within the housing stock of a single local authority, and it is often almost impossible to transfer between authorities. Finally, the systems do not necessarily oblige applicants to accept the first property offered by the authority; for our purposes this is especially important.

Although price does not differentiate the social desirability of different housing areas in the local authority sector, nevertheless such judgments are made. Since tenants are usually allowed to state their preferences at least to some extent as to where they would like to live, these judgments are reflected in the relative lengths of the waiting lists for different properties. This means that a prospective tenant can gain a tenancy much more quickly if he is prepared to live in one of the unpopular estates or apartment blocks. The ability to avoid such unpopular tenancies conversely depends on the ability to wait for housing, especially since many authorities reduce an applicant's place on the waiting list if he or she refuses a given number of offers. In this bureaucratic system of allocation, relative desperation for rehousing replaces the wealth criterion of a price market. Those participating in a price market can, however, enter or leave the market whenever they wish, exchanging homes as often as they want and can afford. The allocative mechanisms operated by the local authorities allow households to enter the system on only limited occasions specified by the rules of the particular system. Prospective tenants are well aware of this and are usually very conscious of the socially critical nature of their ability to withstand the pressures until they gain a desirable allocation.

### E. *Allocation and Residential Community Crime Careers*

The existence of different housing sectors in Britain and their attendant allocative mechanisms can have a number of effects on (offender-based) residential community crime careers. First, there is the immediate effect of allocating different groups in the population within the framework of a given housing market. Second, there are the secondary, or long-term, effects of such allocation. Third, there are the consequences of changes in the market or its mechanisms of allocation.

At any particular time the housing market's allocative mechanisms will distribute groups of the population in specific ways. One key to this will be the policies pursued by each local authority and how these policies affect both the size of the public housing sector and the criteria for access to the sector. These policies may affect the age, social class, ethnic, occupational, or family-type mix of those living in particular areas of public housing. Furthermore, since such policies are largely determined at local levels and in response to local conditions, there will be both local and regional variation in the results. In a similar way, access to the other housing sectors is partly determined by the policies of building societies in granting mortgages and by government policies with regard to private rentals. The effect on community offender rates of patterns of allocation per se will depend on the relative criminogenic potential of different groups and how they are distributed within the housing market. For example, if vandalism is committed especially by children (as some research has suggested), then an allocation process that concentrates families with young children in certain areas will produce high vandalism offender and offense rates in those areas. If this were all that was involved, then we could influence the geographical distribution of offender rates by housing allocation but not the overall crime rate. However, such a model takes no account of the dynamics of social process.

Allocation mechanisms can influence not only the differential distribution of social groups within the housing market but also the mix of groups within an area and the social life they create. The interactive effects within and between groups, the development of particular cultural patterns, or both may be more criminogenically important than any initial propensity to offend. Furthermore, once the population of an area is allocated and its community crime profile established, this will be further influenced by the wider social response to that community. In any case, some of the factors that may influence a community crime pattern as a result of allocation, such as age distribution, are not static. Allocation policies at one time, therefore, have many indirect and longer-term effects. Even though housing areas in postwar Britain have had relatively stable populations, not least in the public housing sector, this does not mean that they will necessarily have stable community crime careers.

Equally important, allocation and housing policies can and have changed over time. Sometimes the effects of such changes are intended, for example, a local authority making its housing more available to disadvantaged groups, or the building societies encouraging owner occupation by lower-paid workers. However, the effects may also be unintended; for example, either of the above changes could alter the relative population stability of a local authority housing estate. The interplay of intended and unintended effects both within a housing sector and between sectors can produce complex long-term consequences for residential community crime careers.

Given the local nature of much housing policy and allocation in Britain and the consequent local and regional variations, the available national data sets are not very useful in studying residential community crime careers. Furthermore, the nature of the indirect and unintended effects of allocation on crime means that such careers can be studied only by detailed examination of highly localized cultures. For these reasons community crime careers in Britain have been analyzed best by local research studies, though these have been limited in number. Nevertheless, evidence is available that clearly illustrates the relation between housing policy and practice and residential community crime careers in the public and the private rental sectors.

## II. The Community Crime Careers of Public Sector Estates

Public sector housing and privately rented housing are the two housing sectors in Britain with the highest offender rates; within both sectors there are considerable variations in offender rates. In Sheffield in 1971, for example, the official offender rate per thousand dwellings averaged 37.6 across the twenty-four largest local authority estates in the city, but the rates for individual estates varied from 3 to 105 per thousand dwellings (Baldwin and Bottoms 1976, p. 165). Clearly, therefore, at any time some local authority estates have virtually no offending that comes to official notice, while others are highly visible as criminal areas. It is unlikely that all public sector estates have a similar residential community crime career, and experience and research confirm this. Often the offender rate for estates tends to be stable over time whether the rate is high or low. However, some estates over a lengthy period have a changing offender rate—an estate that is visibly criminal at one point may not be so later on, while another may trace an opposite progression. In short, there is considerable variation in residential community crime careers in this housing sector.

These variations cannot be understood except within the context of the housing allocation processes. The best way to examine this is through some specific examples.

We begin with estates that have remained stable in their low offending rates. We leave out estates that are, for demographic reasons, unlikely ever to have an offending problem, such as, for example, the considerable number of small developments built in the public sector in the 1960s and 1970s specifically to meet the housing needs of old people. We are interested rather in estates that, in terms of their demographic structure, could reasonably have developed a high offender profile but have not done so.

A good example was found in the Sheffield study in an area that we call "Stonewall." Table 3 shows some of the main social characteristics of Stonewall at the time of a research survey in 1975 and contrasts the estate with "Gardenia," another local authority estate physically adjacent to Stonewall (the two are separated only by a main road containing a suburban shopping area). These two estates were chosen for research analysis because they are so close to each other but vary greatly in

TABLE 3

Social Characteristics of Residents in Gardenia and Stonewall Public Housing Estates, Sheffield, 1975

| | Gardenia | Stonewall |
|---|---|---|
| Social class of head of household:* | | |
| 1, 2 | 3 | 9 |
| 3 | 57 | 53 |
| 4, 5 | 39 | 37 |
| Total | 100 | 100 |
| Sex:† | | |
| Male | 52 | 49 |
| Female | 48 | 51 |
| Total | 100 | 100 |
| Age:† | | |
| Under 10 | 16 | 10 |
| 10–16 | 14 | 12 |
| 17–24 | 14 | 14 |
| 25–54 | 33 | 35 |
| 55 and older | 22 | 28 |
| Total | 100 | 100 |
| Country of origin:‡ | | |
| Great Britain | 97 | 97 |
| Ireland | 1 | 3 |
| New Commonwealth and Pakistan | 0 | 0 |
| Other | 2 | 0 |
| Total | 100 | 100 |
| Length of stay in current dwelling:‡ | | |
| Less than 5 years | 26 | 23 |
| 5–10 years | 14 | 18 |
| 10–15 years | 11 | 9 |
| More than 15 years | 49 | 50 |
| Total | 100 | 100 |
| Age full-time education completed:‡ | | |
| 14, 15, 16 | 95 | 96 |
| Higher age | 5 | 4 |
| Total | 100 | 100 |
| Mean household size from survey results: | | |
| All residents | 3.3 | 3.1 |
| Residents aged 10 or older | 2.7 | 2.8 |

SOURCE.—Bottoms et al. (1986).

* Social class as measured by registrar-general's classification.

† Data are percentages of all residents.

‡ Data are percentages of survey respondents.

TABLE 4

Offending Indices for Gardenia and Stonewall

| | Gardenia | Stonewall |
|---|---|---|
| a) Official offender rate for notifiable offenses (1971) | 9.7 | 3.2 |
| b) Official offense rate for notifiable offenses (1971) | 8.5 | 2.4 |
| c) Victimization survey rate for offenses within area (1975) | 51 | 15 |
| Ratio c:b* | 6:1 | 6:1 |

SOURCE.—Bottoms et al. (1986).
NOTE.—Data are per 100 households per annum.
* Note the different years involved.

criminality and reputation—a point brought out in table 4, which shows that, both on official measures and on victim survey measures of crime, there is roughly a threefold difference between the two estates.[10] Yet the two estates are not very different in social composition. Both are unambiguously working class, of British origin, and have reasonably similar distributions for variables such as age, sex, household size, length of stay in area, and proportion leaving school at the earliest available opportunity (see table 3). The differences in these variables are clearly not sufficient to explain the crime-rate differences between them. Thus, since Gardenia is manifestly a highly criminal estate and since Stonewall has many of the same social characteristics as does Gardenia, it must have been possible for Stonewall also to have become a criminal area.

That it has not done so has, nevertheless, a reasonably simple explanation. This estate was built mainly in the early 1920s under the provisions of the 1919 Housing Act. Most public housing built before 1930 was built to a fairly good level of accommodation (by the standards of the day), and, since at this time rents reflected costs, it tended to be within the reach of only the artisan sector of the working class; there were no "slum-clearance" estates. Stonewall was one of these "artisan" estates and early on acquired a desirable reputation. This it has always retained despite being no longer so clearly artisan. Within the framework of local authority allocation processes, once an estate acquires a good reputation, it tends to be sought by others. But it also develops a

[10] The data in table 4 repeat some information in the table in the App. but are presented separately here for clarity and convenience.

TABLE 5

Application Type of Certain Incoming Tenants in Gardenia and Stonewall, 1973–74*

| Application Type* | Gardenia | Stonewall |
|---|---|---|
| Priority rehousing | 15<br>(29%) | 3<br>(23%) |
| General waiting list | 23<br>(44%) | 2<br>(15%) |
| Transfers from other estates | 14<br>(27%) | 8<br>(62%) |
| Total | 52 | 13 |

SOURCE.—Adapted from Bottoms and Xanthos (1981, p. 211).

* Excluding slum clearance, intraestate transfers, and exchanges. "Slum clearance" is an important category that has priority within the Sheffield allocation system but has been excluded here to show more clearly the relative frequency of the other types of incoming tenants. For the full table, see the original source.

long waiting list, so that those in severe housing need cannot quickly get into that particular estate; the proportion of vacancies filled by transfers from other local authority estates thus tends to be much higher in "good" estates than in those with an undesirable reputation (see table 5 for data on this for Gardenia and Stonewall). These "transfer" cases are overwhelmingly those seeking to improve themselves within the public sector—to obtain a more desirable place within that market.[11] Transfers tend to be sought by persons seeking "respectability" and trying to achieve this by transferring to a different estate, though still within the public sector. If an estate begins as "respectable" and is strongly sought after by others and if nothing occurs to disturb that reputation, then that area is extremely likely to have a stable career as a low-offender-rate community. The essential reason is that the residents of the estate are originally recruited from those whose social norms, though unambiguously working class, are nevertheless definitely not favorable to criminality; these social norms are transmitted to offspring and reinforced in various ways within the life of the community; and the norms are shared by those who are able to enter the estate under the local authority allocation system. Broadly, this is what has

[11] There are, however, some other reasons for transfer of lesser numerical importance—e.g., a move to another estate to be living nearer to one's parents or other family members.

occurred in Stonewall, and a participant observation study of the area in the 1970s confirmed that it had a very different set of social norms from those prevalent in its neighbor, Gardenia (Xanthos 1981).[12]

Just as it is possible for an estate within the public sector to have a stable crime-free career, so it is also possible for it to have a stable "criminal" career. An example of this within Sheffield is another pre-1939 estate called "Blackacre," studied by Baldwin (1974). This had its origins under later legislation from that of Stonewall and Gardenia, and this later legislation was specifically aimed at slum clearance. The city council pulled down a somewhat notorious slum area of the city that contained, among others, several members of gangs who at that time were running extensive protection rackets and illegal betting outlets and were apparently prepared to use violence. The inhabitants of the demolished area, including the gang members, were rehoused en bloc in Blackacre. Not surprisingly, therefore, Blackacre had from its beginning "an extraordinary reputation," and, equally unsurprising, this "has, as far as one can tell, remained virtually unchanged since the time it was originally built" (Baldwin 1975, p. 17). Certainly, up to the time of research done in the late 1960s and early 1970s, Blackacre maintained a position as one of the areas with the highest official rates of criminality of any in Sheffield (although by that time there was no evidence of organized gangs or of protection rackets being run from the estate—the crimes were mostly the common run of notifiable offenses). The adverse offender figures and, more generally, the very negative reputation of Blackacre were widely known within the city—certainly by police, housing department officials, and social workers, but just as clearly by most Sheffield residents, including people living in Blackacre and, more significantly, people who formed the queue for housing within the local authority sector. Although there was no evidence in Sheffield (as opposed to some other local authorities) of the housing department deliberately "dumping" potential tenants whom they regarded as problematic on to an estate such as Blackacre, nevertheless it was an estate avoided by most or all who could do so within the given

[12] However, at the time of research in the 1970s, some residents felt that Stonewall was poised for a decline because of a recent influx of slum-clearance tenants who, under the rules of the Sheffield allocation system, are in a particularly favored position and had thus been able to secure a high proportion of the recent vacancies even on a desirable estate like Stonewall. For details of this situation, see Bottoms and Xanthos (1981), esp. pp. 216–17 and the table on p. 211. In this source, Stonewall is referred to as "CHL" and Gardenia as "CHH."

allocation processes, and, no doubt partly for this reason, a quarter of the new male tenants moving to Blackacre in a particular year studied had a criminal conviction in the previous ten years.[13] Additionally, Blackacre developed an extraordinarily stable residential pattern, with half the households having lived there for more than thirty years at the time of Baldwin's (1974) survey; since some members of this long-resident community were committed to a mild version of a set of criminal norms, it would not be too surprising if these norms were transmitted to others coming into the estate from noncriminal backgrounds. In short, Blackacre is the reverse case of Stonewall. The one begins with a low offender rate and a good reputation, the other with a high offender rate and a bad reputation; both maintain their position steadily over time, and the mechanisms of the bureaucratic allocation system of the local authority allow this to occur.[14]

Not all areas in the public sector with a continuing high offender rate follow Blackacre's pattern. A Sheffield apartment complex, "Skyhigh," offers an interesting contrast. This estate was initially filled in the 1960s, when much postwar building development had already taken place, so it was possible for the housing department to offer tenancies to households who had been on the waiting list very little time. These consisted mainly of young families with small children who came from all over the city and who tended to see Skyhigh as a transitory tenancy. The area soon had the highest residential mobility rate within the Sheffield public sector and never developed into a stable community. Research in the 1960s and 1970s showed it to have a high offender rate and much vandalism; it was the least-desired estate of any in Sheffield and had an exceptionally high rate of tenant dissatisfaction relative to other estates (including most other high-offender-rate estates). Its undesirability meant that it was the most easily accessible of Sheffield's main estates to those desperate for housing, and these families had more than their fair share of family and social problems. Thus, as in Blackacre, the initial allocation of tenants in Skyhigh favored criminogenic poten-

[13] See Baldwin and Bottoms (1976, p. 177)—Blackacre is "Estate III" among the "high rate estates" listed in table 33 on that page. Note, however, that not all high-offender-rate estates have nearly such high proportions of incoming tenants with previous criminal records—see the other data in the table.

[14] For another case study of a prewar public sector estate with a continuously adverse reputation over many years, see Damer (1974), although in this case it appears that the reputation was undeserved in criminal terms since the estate did not have a higher offender rate than that of surrounding estates.

tial (though of a very different sort), but in Skyhigh this did not create a stable criminal subculture. Rather it allowed Skyhigh to become a socially unstable area with many anomic features. In both cases a continuing residential community crime career was the result, though, respectively, with a stable and a more changing population of offenders, reflecting the very different general residential mobility of the two areas.[15]

Some estates within the public sector have had a changing community crime career. Some of these changes simply reflect demographic shifts over time. Particularly in the early postwar period, a prime target for local authority housing provision in many districts was the young married couple with young children. A number of new postwar estates were populated at the outset almost exclusively with such couples who were coming from the general waiting list for public housing and who were glad to be relieved of the necessity of continuing to live with parents or parents-in-law, or in cramped accommodation within the privately rented sector. Given this kind of age concentration, some of these estates acquired a mild reputation as delinquent areas while the tenants' children were in their adolescence; but, being more socially stable than Skyhigh, as the peak age of criminality passed and children left their parents' homes, the offender rate went down. There is, as far as we know, no researched analysis of such an estate in the British criminological literature, but the phenomenon itself was common enough in many towns in postwar Britain and was often commented on by local policemen, probation officers, and the like.

Much more interesting criminologically are estates that have undergone a radical change in criminality. A small estate of this kind on Merseyside was studied by Owen Gill (1977), and, as this research is also notable as a particularly successful attempt to link housing processes with actual behavior on the street, it merits some careful consideration.

Gill began his research with a straightforward attempt to understand the life-styles of a group of boys from a particular street in Merseyside; but he found that this purely appreciative stance was not enough, and,

[15] For a fuller discussion of Skyhigh, see Bottoms and Xanthos (1981). In that paper Skyhigh is referred to as "CFH." It should be noted from the Skyhigh example as from other examples in this section that the distribution of households with family problems within the local authority sector is far from an equalized one, and this sometimes has implications for criminality. Full discussion of this point is, however, beyond the scope of this essay.

to explain the boys' action, a major examination of how Luke Street became what it was and how its identity was sustained was required: "I have been drawn into issues of housing policy, policing, and urban stereotyping" (Gill 1977, p. ix).

In the 1930s a planning decision had been taken to locate all the local authority's housing for large families in one small area. That area was originally a desirable one, and its properties were in considerable demand from potential tenants. However, in the 1950s two things happened: many of the original tenants moved out when their families grew up, and other, physically more "desirable" estates were built elsewhere in the town. Luke Street became less popular, and "better" tenants (as judged by housing visitors' reports) were more likely to be allocated to the new estates.[16] The housing department began sending "less desirable" tenants to Luke Street, provided that they were large families (because of the size of the houses). Less "desirable" large families are often categorized as "problem families"; established residents noticed the difference and complained. As one wrote to the local housing department, "I would like to make application for an exchange of house and district. When I first moved down to this area six years ago I was quite happy with the district and my neighbors, but for the last two years things have gone from bad to worse. My children are coming in using obscene language which they never hear in my house. It is something they have picked up from outside. The class of people who have come here in the past two years have made it impossible to bring up my children decently no matter how I try" (Gill 1977, pp. 30–31). The local housing department decided to formalize the informal processes that had begun. An official decision was taken to rehouse in Luke Street what a housing committee report later referred to as "the town's problem families, social misfits, etc." (Gill 1977, p. 24). The remaining socially aspiring families moved out. The area then acquired a dreadful reputation, and it became exceedingly difficult for the housing department to rent the houses. At the time of Gill's research more than one in ten of the houses was empty. These empty houses were promptly vandalized, lowering the desirability of the area still further. To live in Luke Street was itself highly stigmatic. Everyone, including the police,

[16] Most local authorities employ "housing visitors" to make social assessments of potential local authority tenants and their needs, although the use made of such assessments varies considerably by area—it seems, e.g., to be far more important in the actual process of allocation in the Merseyside district studied by Gill than it is in Sheffield.

regarded Luke Street residents with suspicion; the boys of Luke Street, with cramped accommodation at home (because of large families) and banned from the local youth club, regarded the street as their natural habitat, but even here they felt they were picked on by a hostile police.[17] Police-adolescent encounters on the street are sensitively described by Gill and are related back to the structural condition of Luke Street and its place in the housing market.

Luke Street, then, had become a dead-end, difficult-to-let estate with more than its share of police attention and a much higher than average rate of criminality (forty-one of the sixty-nine families in the street had at least one member with a criminal conviction, many of which had come about only after allocation to Luke Street). Yet it had begun life as a pleasant, desirable estate, presumably with a low offender rate. The processes that effected the change were various. They included generational effects (people wanting to move from large houses after children have grown up); the state of the local public housing stock (people wanting to move to more desirable estates as they were built); and a specific managerial process of "dumping" allegedly undesirable tenants in Luke Street after it began its downward spiral. The dumping process was achieved through housing visitors' assessments of the state of applicants' existing (pre–Luke Street) accommodation, assessments that were not disclosed to the applicants (for data on this, see table 6). The whole process is not unfairly described by Gill as one of "bureaucratic manipulation, stigmatization, and cultural accommodation" (p. 15).

In the Luke Street example we see in strong form the effect of the managerial/bureaucratic processes of the local authority housing department, both in the obvious relevance attached to housing visitors' gradings of applicants and in the decision deliberately to place "problem families, social misfits, etc.," on the estate. These processes of "grading" and dumping applicants are widely reported in local studies of council house allocation in Britain, yet it is important not to overstate them, for they are not the sole determinants of declining reputations. Indeed, in Gill's own study, the type of housing stock in Luke Street and surrounding it are also emphasized as important variables, as is the ability of some potential tenants to refuse offers of accommodation in

[17] It would be a mistake to believe that this is a feature of most "problem" estates in the public sector; rather, it is exceptional since as Burbidge (1984, pp. 136–37) puts it, "[I]t is a commonplace among those who have consulted residents on run-down estates that, despite any alleged 'delinquent' character of the population, they want more and better policing of their communities."

TABLE 6

Housing Department's Categorization of Luke Street Families

| | *N* |
|---|---|
| Conditions of pre–Luke Street dwelling: | |
| Very good | 0 |
| Good | 2 |
| Fair | 5 |
| Poor | 18 |
| Very poor | 17 |
| Total | 42 |
| Condition of applicant's own room in pre–Luke Street dwelling: | |
| Very clean | 0 |
| Clean | 4 |
| Fair | 21 |
| Dirty | 16 |
| Very dirty or verminous | 3 |
| Total | 44 |
| Type of applicant as judged by housing visitor: | |
| Good | 0 |
| Fair | 23 |
| Poor | 6 |
| Requires supervision or is unsuitable | 15 |
| Total | 44 |

SOURCE.—Gill (1977, p. 25).

Luke Street. Niner (1975) correctly emphasized that, apart from the specific allocation procedures of the local authority, other facts are equally important in deciding who moves in or out of an area. These include the relative length and composition of the waiting list for different areas, reflecting their reputations and applicants' social aspirations; the differential ability of applicants to refuse offers of tenancy; and the type and quality of accommodation available for allocation.

This general point is well exemplified by a study of the Gardenia estate in Sheffield, the "criminal" neighbor to Stonewall. The particular interest of Gardenia lies in the combination of three aspects of its history. First, it is now one of the most criminal of the public housing estates in Sheffield, with high official offender rates, a strongly adverse reputation, and a well-settled population, nearly half of whom have lived there for over fifteen years (see table 3). Second, it began life in a completely different fashion, as one of the earliest of Sheffield's estates, built to a deliberately "garden-city" plan for the artisan sector of the working class and regarded as a highly desirable estate for many years (see Gaskell 1976). Finally, in its transition from desirable to undesirable, or from noncriminal to criminal, Gardenia has almost certainly not been assisted by any process of dumping or "adverse grading" by the local authority housing department (see Bottoms and Xanthos 1981). It therefore presents a very important and interesting contrast to Luke Street.

Explaining why Gardenia's community crime career changed is not easy, but what seems to have happened is as follows. Some of the artisan-type housing that was built in the same part of Sheffield a little later than Gardenia had better physical amenities, and this caused some waning of Gardenia's popularity in the interwar period. Sometime during or after the Second World War, it began quite rapidly to acquire a distinctly adverse reputation, with talk of "villains," "fighting in the streets," and so forth. The speed of the acquisition and transmission of this reputation may have been enhanced, first, by the relatively poor physical state of the houses by this time, in comparison with some of the more recently built estates (including Stonewall), and, second, because the area has a very distinctive and rather inappropriate popular name that made it easily identifiable in newspaper crime reports. The Sheffield research was unable to discover in detail the exact origins of the "tipping" process that occurred in the 1940s in Gardenia, but locals tend to attribute it to the chance allocation of a couple of so-called problem families to the estate for reasons that are not clear. This cannot be verified, but it is important to notice that everything else could, given the allocation system, have followed from a chance allocation of this sort. This is because other (self-defined) "respectable" residents could have taken this allocation as evidence of the estate beginning to "go downhill" and so began to move out, while those willing to move in became a progressively restricted group owing to the spiraling situation. In other words, a downward spiral can occur in local authority housing even without the managerial processes of dumping and grading evident in Luke Street, and this seems to have happened in Gardenia.

The effects of this process in Gardenia are worth noting in a little more detail. The first effect is on potential tenants, who tend to avoid the estate where possible. The result is that Gardenia has the shortest waiting list of any housing estate (as opposed to high-rise developments) within the Sheffield allocation system, so that those in the most need of housing—and those who can afford to wait the extra time to avoid an apartment in a high-rise development—tend to put it down as a first choice, albeit reluctantly. These "strong-housing-need applicants" form one of two main groups of those entering Gardenia. The others are those seeking to join other family members (the area has very strong interlocking family networks). The second effect is on families who actually do come to Gardenia. Once a family is housed there, it is not easy to get off quickly—especially on to one of the more desirable estates—because of the complications of the allocation system and the relatively lowly place of "transfer" applications within it. It then seems likely that there is a socialization process into the deviant subcultural norms of the estate, especially among the children, who all go to school together and tend to associate with each other in the public spaces of the estate. If such deviant socialization does occur, it will of course tend to perpetuate Gardenia's reputation as a high-offender-rate area. Participant observation research has shown that there are some families who, having moved to Gardenia because of extreme housing need, then try to avoid the potential socialization effects by living in virtual isolation.

We know, then, that community crime careers in local authority housing can move from noncriminal to criminal. But can the process be reversed, perhaps with special help from those concerned with social policy? This subject has recently received much attention in Britain, particularly as a result of programs of social action developed by the National Association for the Care and Resettlement of Offenders (NACRO) (a crime-focused national nongovernmental agency) and the Department of the Environment (the central government department responsible for housing policy).

The management of local authority estates in Britain has historically been bureaucratic and very paternalistic. If this paternalism is removed or reduced, a different social situation is obviously created, and NACRO in particular has sought to see how far such a change might lead to crime reduction. A NACRO pilot project was developed in Widnes, Cheshire, in the late 1970s and reported in 1980 (Hedges et al. 1980); this project was designed "to test out the theory that only if people have a sense of belonging and responsibility for the place in which they live will they want to look after it and improve it. We set out to see whether people's attitudes might change if improvements were made to the estate and to the services provided by the authorities based on the wishes and priorities of the residents; and, if so, whether there would be less vandalism on the estate" (Hedges et al. 1980, p. 1). The estate chosen for the project was one with serious crime (especially vandalism) problems yet without being so acute that no remedial measures of this kind would stand much chance. Improvements made were partly environmental (including improvement of defective street lighting, provision of a "kickabout" area for youth) and partly social (including appointment of a beat policeman and a part-time community worker). Each improvement in itself perhaps seems trivial or commonsensical. What is important is the way all the improvements were linked by the common theme of having arisen through intensive consultation with tenants. A subsequent formal evaluation suggested that there had been some genuine reduction in burglary on the estate, as measured by a victim survey (although this was not evenly achieved in different parts of the estate); that vandalism to houses and shops had decreased (though there was an increase in vandalism of trees and shrubs); and that many residents believed social conditions on the estate had improved. The results, while not wholly favorable, were sufficiently encouraging to lead NACRO to develop action projects on a range of other high-crime-rate estates. Formal evaluation of the projects is awaited, and available data on crime on the estates are few, but the results are, generally speaking, considered by NACRO to be favorable, though by no means uniform in different estates (for a description of NACRO's work in London, see Bright and Petterson [1984]).

The Department of the Environment's concern is, naturally, rather more specifically focused on housing management: "The starting point . . . was to see how the less popular council housing could be better managed and thereby provide more acceptable living environments. The improvement of tenants' security from crime and vandalism was seen as an indispensable element in this, but it was not the sole focus" (Burbidge 1984, p. 132). The Department of the Environment, in an action project known as the "Priority Estates Project," developed a multipronged strategy for estate improvement. This included certain design and equipment features, such as installation of entry phones in apartment complexes and the strengthening of front doors; manning measures, such as a full caretaker service and night watchmen to guard empty properties during modernization; improved management of estates to reduce the numbers of empty dwellings; the decentralization of management to estate level with increased responsiveness to local tenants' concerns; improved allocation procedures to avoid dumping of undesirable tenants or overhigh child densities;[18] and policing changes of a broadly "community policing" variety. Again, formal evaluation of

[18] A Home Office Research Unit study showed that high child density was strongly associated with vandalism on public sector estates—see Wilson (1980).

these initiatives has yet to be reported, but initial impressions are favorable. The work to 1983 is summarized and reviewed by Burbidge (1984), and what is notable is that, in a number of the local areas studied (though not all), there is apparently reasonably clear evidence of a reduction in general crime, or vandalism, or both as well as an improvement in residents' satisfaction with the estate generally.

It is too early to report definitively from any of these studies about a reversal in an adverse or worsening community crime career, but the results to date are sufficiently interesting to suggest that a permanent reversal of high offender or offense patterns within some local authority housing estates can perhaps be achieved. An apparent lesson of the projects is, however, that this is unlikely to occur except by attention to all aspects of life on the estate since "where crime and vandalism exist they cannot be disentangled entirely from any aspect of estate management" (Burbidge 1984, p. 148).

These attempts at reversing the criminal careers of a community only in part operate on the allocation mechanisms. They concentrate mainly on improving, or halting the decline in, the physical, management, or social quality of the estates. As we have seen, allocation policies are central to the reputation of estates and their offender rates, but the "tipping" of an estate can be triggered by an absolute, or relative, qualitative decline. The aim, therefore, of these programs is to reverse the qualitative decline while preventing allocative policies that could rapidly lead to tipping (such as a large number of inhabitants in the peak crime-age groups). Where such reversal programs will become much more difficult is if the problem estates also move toward mixed tenure patterns, which could occur as a result of the sale of council houses to tenants. We return to this problem below.

## III. The Community Crime Careers of Privately Rented Areas

The historical decline of private rental tenures was caused by disadvantageous treatment of private landlords in the capital market reinforced by legislative and political antipathy and by the counterattractions of alternative tenures. In the postwar period, private rental tenures were either removed under slum-clearance programs or transferred into other tenures by selling either to owner-occupiers (often sitting tenants) or, less often, to local authorities as a preliminary to a redevelopment scheme. Occasional privately rented properties are still to be found scattered throughout areas that are now dominantly owner occupied in nature; quite often the landlords of such houses own only one rental property that they may well have inherited.

Dominantly private rental *areas* are increasingly rare outside of central London. Where they do exist, they commonly consist of large old houses converted to multioccupation. Quite often they are in areas that have suffered from "planning blight," that is, areas where possible future redevelopment has depressed the market value of the properties. Such areas may also have been "redlined" by the building societies, that is, defined as areas where, because of planning blight, the societies are not prepared to lend new money to prospective owner-occupiers. This will prevent the inflow of new mortgaged owner-occupiers to the area and further depress the market values.[19] In such a situation, private rental tenure becomes an alternative proposition. The capital costs of the properties will be relatively low, and multioccupation will maximize rental income. By renting the property as furnished, some rent controls can be avoided, and furnished properties are in any case likely to attract short-term tenants, which ensures that rentals can regularly be increased in line with inflation. In this way, capital returns can be met even within the possibly short life span of properties threatened by a redevelopment scheme provided that redevelopment is not too imminent.

Given that in this limited way the market can still produce private rental areas, who will want to take up tenures in such areas? The answer is any household whose need cannot be met in the two dominant tenure sectors. In a private rental area there will probably be some tenants who are long-term tenants of the areas; they may well be exceptions to this general answer since they might in fact be able to gain a local authority tenure or a mortgage. For the rest there will be a number of disparate groups. In any housing market there will be people who need short-term, probably furnished, accommodation, which, because the other two tenures have been mainly concerned to house families, they may not be able to satisfy. There will be households who cannot afford to become owner-occupiers but, because of the criteria of

[19] There is an alternative source of a mortgage sometimes available in poorer districts, namely, a mortgage from the local authority. However, such finance is usually not made available in areas of planning blight but rather in areas that it is hoped will shift upmarket to owner occupation yet where the building societies have shown some reluctance to lend. In any case, the availability of local authority mortgages is subject to the sometimes rapid vicissitudes of the money available to the authority for such purposes at a particular time.

the particular local authority's allocation procedures, cannot immediately gain access to a local authority tenure. This category includes especially households who, at any rate in the past in many local authority areas, have been regarded as low priorities, such as single parents, single adults, or newcomers to the local authority area. This latter group has been particularly important since most local authorities give priority to long-term residents. For those in local authority tenures, movement to another authority is usually possible only on the basis of direct exchanges—a crude and inefficient barter mechanism that has reduced labor mobility. Newcomers in private rental areas may include such people as well as students and immigrants. In the 1950s and 1960s, external immigrants, especially Afro-Caribbeans and Asians, frequently found their first home in Britain in the private rental sector. Finally, private rental has provided accommodation for those who are deviant tenants, ranging from prostitutes to drug peddlers and some of their clients. Such deviants would more than likely be excluded by the bureaucratic management of local authority housing or run out by pressure from their respectable neighbors in owner-occupier areas. Also private rentals are often in decaying areas near to city centers and so are ideally situated for the supply of illicit services; and the "deviant-area" status that is necessary to market the supply of such services is available only in this tenure type.

The decline of private rental tenures has meant that not all these housing needs can still be satisfied by this housing tenure. To respond to this, local authorities have had to relax their allocation criteria. They have, for example, increasingly housed single-parent and single-adult households and have offered their unwanted and unloved high-rise flats to groups such as students. This response has been reinforced by legislative action, and the Housing (Homeless Persons) Act, 1977, was designed to force local authorities to house those who were homeless even if they were newcomers to their areas. There is evidence, however, that the accommodation offered under this legislation is sometimes deliberately stigmatizing and that housing officers sometimes resent what they see as queue jumping of their allocation mechanisms.

From what has been said it will be obvious that, since tenure types are a legal artifact, houses themselves can undergo changes in tenure. Private rental tenure may not be a permanent legal status for an area; indeed, given the decline of that tenure nationally, it quite likely will not be. This raises the question of what happens to the residential community crime career of an area if it undergoes tenure change wholly or in part.

This issue can be explored by reference to two contrasting, privately rented areas in Sheffield. The first, which we may call "Graybridge," was in 1966 a low-offender-rate, mainly privately rented district with some owner occupation. The subsequent history of the area depended on a decision by the city council that one-half of it should be demolished while the other half should be retained. The section to be retained gradually shifted toward owner-occupier tenure as individual landlords sold the properties in line with the historical trends we have previously outlined. By the time of a population survey in 1975, nearly three-quarters of the households in this part of the area were owner occupied. A victimization survey revealed continued low offense rates for most crimes, and police and probation sources suggested a continued low offender rate. The area thus looked set to become a typical low-crime-rate area at the bottom end of the price range for the owner-occupied sector, with a population mainly composed of households headed by a skilled manual or a low-grade nonmanual worker.

The other half of Graybridge was less stable. The decision in favor of early demolition naturally produced uncertainty and a feeling of dissatisfaction with the area. As houses became vacant, they were often not resold or relet on the private market; either the local authority took them over as temporary public housing, or they were left empty. The latter phenomenon produced a high vandalism level, which seems to have spilled over to occupied dwellings (the 1975 victim survey showed high vandalism rates against respondents' property but low rates of other criminal victimization in this part of Graybridge). The dwellings taken over by the local authority were filled with families especially desperate for accommodation (the waiting list was very short) and included a significantly higher-than-average proportion of families with a history of rent arrears. Although only about one in ten houses in the area was thus taken over by the local authority, the social effect of the advent of these new tenants on the existing residents was adverse, adding to the feelings of neglect created by empty houses nearby and a local housing stock, which it was in no one's interest to improve given its short life expectancy. A research worker noted a strong feeling, "expressed most clearly by 'private residents' (owner-occupied and rented) that the social environment of Graybridge is deteriorating just as the properties physically deteriorate under the blight of clearance." In this circumstance it was perhaps remarkable that crime remained so low in 1975. But, not long afterward, this part of Graybridge was indeed demolished.

The contrasting histories of the two halves of Graybridge sum up very well the changing nature of the privately rented tenure in the postwar period and the two likeliest ultimate destinations: upmarket to owner occupation or eventual submission to the bulldozer. In this particular case both parts retained fairly low offending rates, though obviously this depends in part on particular local conditions, including the previous history of the district and the length of the period of planning uncertainty in the section affected by the clearance threat.

With this as background, we can now turn to examine a rather different area of Sheffield, with a much higher offender rate, which, at different times in its history, has seemed destined first for the bulldozer, then for the alternative destination. As the history of this district is of special interest, we treat it in some detail. The area, known as "Havelock," is located close to the city center and was developed in the period 1851–98 as an area with substantial houses for the merchant class. In the twentieth century this class moved out, and by the 1930s multiple occupation of these houses had become a feature of the area that has continued up to the present. However, the area has never become completely one of rental tenures or of multioccupation: owner occupation of some houses, especially the smaller ones, has always been a feature.

By the late 1960s the area had acquired a distinct geographical and social form. In land area and in population size (around 2,000) it was small. It was bounded on the north by the university and by hospital-owned property, interspersed with some small professional businesses; to the east was a new main inner-city ring road; to the south was a new area of local authority low-rise apartments; and to the west and southwest an area of nineteenth-century housing of greater architectural merit than Havelock itself, legally protected as a conservation area in 1970 and with most of the properties owned by either middle-class owner-occupiers, small professional businesses, or the local polytechnic. These surrounding features have remained basically unchanged to the present day.

In the 1960s and early 1970s, Havelock was under "planning blight" because of possible eventual (but, in contrast to Graybridge, not imminent) slum clearance and had therefore been redlined by the building societies. The only things that distinguished it from many similar decaying inner-city areas were its size and its location: it was not part of a larger decaying area but was instead small, discrete, and surrounded by properties of quite different status. These differences were to play an important part in its subsequent history.

A survey of Havelock conducted by members of the University of Sheffield Town Planning Department in 1975 showed that the area was very mixed socially (Crook et al. 1976).[20] Single and retired people made up more than one-half of the households, but married couples and single parents with children under school age made up one-third. The age structure of the population was younger than that of Sheffield as a whole and had a significantly greater proportion of young people in their late teens and early twenties. Over one-third of the people in the area had lived there for less than two years, and this group contained the youngest heads of households, single parents, students, and young single workers. On the other hand, 45 percent of the sample had lived in the area for more than ten years.

These different groups were not distributed evenly within the area. The longer-stay residents, the older residents, the gainfully employed, and those of higher socioeconomic status were more likely to live in the outer, peripheral parts. The inner core, to which the social reputations we will discuss in a moment particularly attached, had a higher proportion of the young, the unemployed, students, and shorter-stay residents. Finally, previous research showed that this inner-core area had a higher proportion of black immigrants than did any other area of Sheffield (Macrae 1974). The Town Planning Department's survey concluded its review of the housing role of the area as follows.

> What conclusions can be made from this about Havelock's role in the Sheffield housing market? First, the area is attractive to young and single people wanting a furnished place near to their work or place of study. Second, because of its stock of cheap, readily available furnished accommodation Havelock is a place where those who are forced to move and who lack access to other sectors of the market can get something to rent quite readily. . . . Parts of Havelock have very substantial properties which, whilst long ago

[20] Very similar results were also generated by another survey carried out in the same year as part of the Sheffield crime study—see Bottoms et al. (1986). (Note that in that paper Havelock is referred to as "Redlight.") The similarity is important because the response rate in the crime survey was substantially better; but we have quoted from the Town Planning Department survey to facilitate direct comparison with that department's later survey (see table 7).

> [they] housed single families, lend themselves to conversion. This, of course, is far from being a one-way process for many houses have reverted back to single-family use. The telling fact is that, as Macrae showed, 90 percent of dwellings in [the central core of the area] have at some time been in multiple occupation in the last forty years. The area thus has a resource of properties which have, as a result of owners' decisions, flexibly responded to different demands placed on them. Clearly though this is far from the whole story since this report has also looked at the way Havelock meets the needs of a wide range of other groups—immigrants generally, young couples setting up home for the first time (the first rung on the housing ladder), and families with children have all moved to Havelock in response to the size and relative price of its accommodation. Finally, there is the considerable size of its "residual" pensioner group. [Crook et al. 1976, p. 11]

The social reputation of the area at the time of this 1975 survey was very distinctive and can be summed up quite easily: it was, and had been for at least a decade, the main red-light district of Sheffield. While there was a small area of prostitution on the other side of the city, Havelock was the city's notorious prostitution location. The area was also widely known as a high-drug-use district, particularly for cannabis, and this was related both to the relatively large Afro-Caribbean group and to the number of students in the area. Less notoriously, but no less important, work done at this time for the Sheffield crime study showed that the area had the highest recorded notifiable offender and offense rate of any residential district in the city (Mawby 1979), a status that received confirmation in a 1975 victimization survey (Bottoms et al. 1986).

Some of Havelock's high offense rate at this time can be accounted for by the opportunities presented by the area. For example, multi-occupation of houses fostered burglary in obvious ways; cars parked on the streets, including the cars of those with business or professional interests in the surrounding districts, were a fairly easy target for thefts;[21] and once such an area became known as a red-light district, it attracted prostitutes to come and solicit there even if they lived elsewhere. However, as with the other area case examples, Havelock was

[21] Mawby (1979, p. 46–47) found that Havelock's high officially recorded offense rate included an exceptionally high proportion of offenses against nonresidents, most relating to cars.

also a high offender area as a result of the subsequent social interactions and socialization processes attributable to the kinds of people and social groups for whom it provided a home. Even with prostitution, while not all the prostitutes lived in the area, research in the 1970s showed that there was a social hierarchy among the women, that those with the highest status and the most influence did live in the area, and that this was a goal to which many of the others aspired.

Havelock, then, was a classic interstitial criminal area, and its criminality, especially as far as prostitution was concerned, was highly visible. For all that, there was at this time a certain degree of social accommodation about the area's deviant status. While some of the longer-stay residents protested about the activities of prostitutes, this produced no major or sustained response from social control agencies.[22] The local authority and other official agencies were reluctant to take any initiatives in the area because it was earmarked for redevelopment.[23] Participant observation research in the area suggested that, while the police patrolled the district nightly and did sometimes arrest for soliciting (see n. 22), their main object was to contain the activity within socially acceptable bounds. The general status of the area as a red-light district was accepted, and only the more extreme behavior was sanctioned. The overall result was that those residents who did protest were effectively marginalized, and thus protest went largely unheeded.

There is no reason to suppose that, other things being equal, this situation could not have continued. The most likely future for Havelock at this time would have been a continuation of its deviant identity while the area continued to decline because of planning blight. Eventually, this situation would have been brought to an end by the physical clearance and redevelopment of the area.

This is not what has happened. Indeed, by the winter of 1983–84, the deviant status of Havelock had become a controversial issue in the

[22] In the ten years up to and including the year when Havelock obtained "housing action area" (HAA) status (1978), there was an average prosecution rate for soliciting of only two cases per week in the whole of Sheffield (mainly Havelock). This rate fluctuated dramatically from time to time, partly in response to occasional pressure from Havelock residents, but it never exceeded an annual average of three per week.

[23] An exception was the probation service, which bought a house in the area as a focus for "detached probation work" (see Hugman 1977). However, this annoyed rather than placated the disaffected residents since they saw it as an illegitimate initiative aimed at helping prostitutes and other undeserving deviants. The probation unit in Havelock was closed in 1980.

city's politics. To understand why this happened we have to explicate changes in Havelock's position in the housing market.

The most significant element in changing this position was that government policy toward the nation's housing stock changed. The social disadvantages of both local authority green-field estates and high-rise apartment blocks led to a reexamination of whether clearance was the best policy for old and decaying property. The alternative was that government subsidies in the housing market would no longer be channeled only through tax relief to owner-occupiers and through grants for local authority building—but also would be given to owners of older houses in the form of improvement grants. The Housing Act, 1969, introduced "general improvement areas" (GIAs), but much of the money so made available was used by local authorities to improve their older property. The Housing Act, 1974, then introduced "housing action areas" (HAAs), a move intended by the then Conservative government to concentrate grants in more difficult, decaying, mainly private rental inner-city areas. Although public expenditure cuts necessitated by yet another Sterling crisis muted the effect of this measure, it was nevertheless fostered by the Labour government that came to power later in 1974. There was henceforth a mechanism by which government subsidies could be channeled into areas that had a high proportion of private rental tenures.

Havelock was to take advantage of this new possibility. It was able to do so because it was small, was surrounded by nondecaying areas, and was in a part of the city generally regarded as desirable and worth preserving. Most important of all, the area, partly because of its location, had become a focus for the attention of a number of middle-class professionals who wished to improve it.

A public meeting was held in the area in February 1975 and was attended by forty people, at which Havelock's owner-occupiers were overrepresented. This meeting set up an action committee to oppose clearance and redevelopment of the area and to press instead for the granting of HAA status. Such status would provide priority treatment for the area for up to five years and up to 90 percent grants for improvements. To achieve this, the action committee, with the assistance of the university's Town Planning Department, conducted a social and physical survey of the area as the basis for its case. (It is this survey we have referred to earlier in describing the social composition of the area at this time.) The survey formed the basis of a report to the city council requesting HAA status, which was granted. In spite of the notorious reputation of Havelock, the survey report hardly mentions prostitution. Indeed, while the physical decay of the area is stressed, the report seeks to emphasize elements of social normality (e.g., "Havelock is a more stable community in terms of residential mobility than it has been customary to believe in recent years" [Crook et al. 1976, p. 6]). This is hardly surprising since the political purpose of the report was to try to achieve HAA status.

The granting of HAA status in 1978 was to begin a process of change in Havelock. It removed planning blight and therefore redlining by the building societies. This was to prevent any future decline in owner occupation in the area, and indeed there has been a slight increase in that tenure (see table 7, part A). The other main tenure change has been a significant decline in privately rented dwellings in the area and their replacement by "housing association" properties.

The same legislation that allowed the creation of HAAs also made public money more available to housing associations, and two such bodies bought properties in Havelock after 1978. Housing associations are private, non-profit-making bodies but have access to government funds for building and improving property; they have played a small but increasing role in British housing policy and provision (see Donnison and Ungerson 1982, pp. 198 ff). Housing associations are able to rent their properties to specifically defined groups, and, although they have to take account of economic considerations, they may also use other criteria. Hence we have here another (if small-scale) example of a bureaucratic allocation mechanism for housing. The effect in Havelock has been that new tenants moving into housing-association property after 1978 have come from groups selected by the associations, and overall this has aided a gentrification process.

We can chart the process of population change in Havelock because the university's Department of Town Planning conducted a second survey five years after the granting of HAA status to examine its effect (Crook and Darke 1983). The survey showed that in the preceding five years no fewer than three-fifths of the residents of the area had changed. Young single adults dominated these newcomers, with the result that there had been a proportionate decline of childless couples and the elderly.

There is also evidence of gentrification from the survey. It is somewhat difficult to assess because of the high contemporary level of unemployment and because Havelock remains a poor area. However, as table 7, part B, illustrates, there has been a significant increase in the

TABLE 7

Tenure and Population Change in Havelock after the Granting of Housing Action Area Status in 1978

A. Tenure Change

| Tenure by Household | 1975 Survey | 1982 Survey |
|---|---|---|
| Owner occupied | 32 | 39 |
| Public housing | 68* | 7 |
| Privately rented | | 39 |
| Housing association | † | 15 |
| Total | 100 | 100 |

B. Population Change

| Socioeconomic Status of Heads of Households Resident in 1982 | Household Living in Havelock before 1978 | Household Moved to Havelock after 1978 |
|---|---|---|
| All households: | | |
| Never economically active | 12 | 42 |
| Nonmanual | 18 | 32 |
| Manual | 70 | 26 |
| Total | 100 | 100 |
| Owner-occupiers: | | |
| Never economically active | 15 | 16 |
| Nonmanual | 22 | 52 |
| Manual | 63 | 32 |
| Total | 100 | 100 |

SOURCE.—Crook and Darke (1983, pp. 9, 12).

NOTE.—Data are in percentages.

* Data not separately available from Town Planning Department survey. A criminological survey in the same year (1975) in Havelock, conducted with a slightly different area definition, produced the following figures. Owner occupied, 33%; public housing, 2.5%; privately rented, 64.5% (Bottoms et al. 1986).

† Negligible.

proportion of nonmanual heads of households in spite of a rising unemployment level in the city as a whole. This is especially apparent among owner-occupiers, and they were to be a critical group in future events in Havelock.

This process of gentrification threatened the continuation of the lifestyles that had previously contributed to the deviant identity of the area. Some of the newcomers added their voices to those who protested about the activities of prostitutes and their clients. More important, the changed status of the area meant that these protestors were no longer marginalized. The local authority was increasingly prepared to listen to their complaints in the context of the general policy to improve the area. As part of a traffic management scheme, the local authority prevented through traffic in Havelock; this made it more difficult for the prostitutes' clients to drive through the area and increased their vulnerability. More direct attempts were also made to discourage clients. Roads in the area were made into cul-de-sacs and one-way streets, and "sleeping policemen" were built at strategic points. This attempt at using physical crime-reduction techniques, however, failed to make any significant effect on the amount of "cruising" in the area. Havelock continued to be the major red-light area of Sheffield, a status that was confirmed in a blaze of publicity when the notorious murderer the Yorkshire Ripper—many of whose victims had been prostitutes—was finally caught in the area in January 1981. Prior to his arrest, the Yorkshire Ripper had terrified prostitutes throughout the north of England, and there were suggestions that prostitutes' activity declined in Havelock as the girls sought safer areas in the south. After his arrest, however, there were counterallegations that girls from all over now regarded Havelock as a particularly safe area because of the guardianship of the South Yorkshire constabulary! None of this did anything to calm the more respectable residents of Havelock, and their protests continued to grow.

A final twist to their mounting protests was provided as an unintended consequence of the Criminal Justice Act, 1982, which removed the sanction of imprisonment for soliciting. While the Sheffield magistrates had never used imprisonment for prostitutes to any significant extent, its removal was seen by sections of the Havelock community as a denial of the only effective deterrent. Prostitution had now become a major political problem in Havelock. The 1983 survey showed that "[p]rostitution, the reputation of the area, the specific problems associated with these, account for one-third of the negative comments about living in Havelock. Prostitution was spontaneously mentioned most frequently as the worst disliked feature of the Havelock area" (Crook and Darke 1983, p. 35). Complaints about prostitution were not, however, evenly distributed throughout the area. The reasons for this are complex, but the main factors seem to be that a combination of the processes of gentrification spreading down the area from the northern end (mainly because of the nature of the property and tenure distribution), together with the new road schemes already referred to, pushed the prostitutes toward the southern end of Havelock. Whatever the reasons, the effects were clear enough: "We found that households in the 'northerly' parts of Havelock tended to be more satisfied (and less dissatisfied) than those people we interviewed in the southern area . . . only a third of people living in the south of Havelock were indifferent to prostitution, and nearly all the rest felt it to be a negative feature of the locality. . . . In effect, the concern that people have about prostitution seems directly related to how close they are to the main area where 'business' is contracted" (Crook and Darke 1983, pp. 32–33). One consequence of this southern push of soliciting was to bring the center of the trade nearer to the socially desirable conservation area to the southwest, known as Broomhall Park. The Broomhall Park Association was a formidable middle-class pressure group, and it began actively to lobby against the prostitutes on its border. They were joined in this by the residents' group from Havelock, on which owner-occupiers were overrepresented.

Both local councillors and members of parliament received numerous complaints about prostitution and demands for action. In October 1983 the Broomhall Park Association produced a report on the problem of prostitution. Since this was part of a successful campaign, its main points are worth summarizing. The report claimed that there were 300 prostitutes operating in the quarter-square-mile of Havelock and compared this with a claimed 500 prostitutes in the notorious vice area of London. In fact the figures were based on police statistics of girls known to have been prostitutes at some time in the city and almost certainly grossly overestimated the number of girls who were active in the area. Nevertheless, it was claimed that Sheffield had proportionately the highest number of prostitutes of any city in England. It was alleged that pimps were importing girls into Havelock from all over the country, and the residents lived in fear of a general crime wave. The Yorkshire Ripper was alluded to to justify these fears. Most significant for present purposes, the report suggested that, in the absence of the sanction of imprisonment, the fines for prostitution in residential areas should be significantly increased. The report received wide publicity in the local press, but it was also part of a more specific campaign to bring pressure to bear on the magistrates and the police in the city.

As early as April 1983 the magistrates had been lobbied to reexamine their policy of fining prostitutes for soliciting. It was suggested that the fines being imposed varied between individual benches, were ridiculously low relative to the girls' earnings, were in any case not being paid by the girls, and, because they were lower than in neighboring towns, were encouraging a flood of prostitutes into the city. The magistrates set up a special committee to examine the problem, and this committee took evidence from the Broomhall Park Association and the relevant police divisional commander. The evidence of the police commander supported the residents' complaints; he told us that he was concerned that "respectable" residents of Havelock and Broomhall might turn to vigilante solutions and that "[t]he local authority has made many recent improvements in the area, with the result that the aspirations of the residents have been raised whilst their tolerance to undesirable happenings has correspondingly been reduced."

The political campaign was so intense that the magistrates took the unusual step of issuing a press statement announcing a new "get tough" policy on prostitution in the city. Fines for soliciting were significantly increased, and, although some convicted prostitutes appealed against the new sentencing policy, the appeal court upheld it. In addition, the police began to use new tactics against both the girls and their clients. The most unusual aspect of this was the use of an act of 1361 to take the male clients to court and bind them over not to commit a public nuisance.[24] Publicity and stigma were being used in an attempt to destroy the demand side of the prostitutes' business. The old, somewhat uneasy accommodation between the prostitutes and the agencies of social control had now totally broken down. What had once been the (informally) accepted red-light district for the city is now, at least potentially, threatened with extinction. Powerful attempts are being made radically to shift the deviant career of this particular small neighborhood.

Although allegations have been made of a large increase in prostitution in Havelock, we can find no real evidence that the deviant activity in the area has significantly changed in the last decade. What has changed is the social composition of the area. This change was brought about by housing policy decisions that transformed a decaying inner-city area into a more desirable residential district and that may well

[24] The Justices of the Peace Act 1361 allows justices to bind over persons "not of good fame" in "sufficient surety and mainprise of their good behaviour towards the King and his people." This binding over does not constitute a conviction. The use of the statute against prostitutes' clients was not common in Britain, but it had been so used in at least one other town before its application in Sheffield. Subsequently, the British Parliament has made "kerb-crawling" a statutory offense.

eventually change the dominant tenure status of the area. These changes occurred in spite of the deviant reputation of Havelock. Notwithstanding the changes in the social composition of Havelock, those who are actively campaigning to change its deviant identity are still in a minority, but they are no longer socially marginalized and have received powerful support from the neighboring Broomhall area.

How successful will this attempt to change the deviant career of Havelock be? It is too early to say with certainty, but the question of what can happen to prostitution in Sheffield is clearly the key. There has been some worry expressed to and by the local member of parliament that the girls will simply be displaced to other areas. This may happen to a small extent, but another possibility has begun to develop. We are seeing the development in Sheffield of the use of sauna parlors for prostitution. These saunas exist in a number of areas in the city, and it may be that the traditional red-light district will be replaced by a more scattered distribution of prostitutes. As we have already explained, it is difficult to see a red-light district existing in any tenure sector except that of private rental. Havelock is one of the last such areas left in Sheffield, and this area is being changed. A move of prostitution to saunas or to cheap hotels could get around this difficulty by separating the girls' place of residence from their place of work but still providing a clear geographical locus for clients to approach. If this happens, then changes in housing policy and tenure patterns will have changed both the deviant career of an area and the form of illicit activity. This is something quite different from the crime-reduction strategies in the public sector discussed in the last section. Interestingly, the police commander is not opposed to such a move since he believes that it presents the police with an easier control problem and that it is a way of responding to citizen pressure for protection that is a key element in the new philosophy of policing emerging in England.

However, prostitution is not the only constituent of Havelock's crime. The area still has one of the highest offender and offense rates in Sheffield. Burglary rates are high, and the area continues to be a center for minor drug trafficking. The changes in the social composition of the area and in the use of property may begin to affect both the offender and the offense rate generally. Interestingly, as part of the police-community dialogue, the residents were encouraged to set up a neighborhood-watch scheme. The effect of this further attempt to change the community crime career of Havelock is not yet known but will be worth watching in light of the changes we have outlined.

## IV. Conclusions and Speculations

In this final section we summarize our argument about community crime careers. We also speculate on the future of residential community careers in response to further changes in housing policy and tenure patterns.

### A. *Housing and Residential Community Crime Careers*

We have argued that changes in residential community crime careers are, at least in Britain, only intelligible in the context of a rigorous analysis of developments in housing and housing policy, and such analysis itself demands some attention to macroeconomic change and national political development.

It could be objected that our claims are trivial. Obviously, one might say, a changing residential community crime career can be understood only if we understand where that community fits into the other communities in the city; the study of comparative areas of cities and their criminality is scarcely new; and it is obviously the case that to study a particular area of the city we need to know how the residents moved there in the first place, that is, something about the housing market; but the most important housing market differentials are those based on social class, the staple diet of criminological interest for many years.

We do not wish in any way to minimize the importance of class in studying residential community crime careers, but we do want to insist that it is not enough. In the first place, it is unambiguously clear that two areas of similar class composition can nevertheless have very different criminal careers and that such differences can be understood only by reference to housing allocation processes (consider Gardenia and Stonewall). Second, it is also clear that a change in national housing policy can provide the occasion for decisive effects on area criminal careers at the local level (consider the effect of the HAA legislation in Havelock). More generally, if indeed it is obvious that to study the criminality of a particular area we need to know something about how the residents got there in the first place, we can only say that most criminologists have shown a remarkable lack of interest in the details of this process.

The lack of criminological interest in housing policy and the housing market probably has several sources. They include the dominance of price market mechanisms in North American housing (and the assumption that these mechanisms are simple and not worth detailed analysis); a lack of realization that the operations of the housing market are not reducible simply to social class; a tendency to be diverted to interesting side issues such as Oscar Newman's (1972) "defensible-space" hypothesis; and, in Britain, a lack of interest created by the manifest failure of the widespread postwar assumption that new and better housing would reduce crime.

We believe there is now sufficiently clear evidence about the relation between housing markets and residential community crime careers to justify more research. Indeed what has been done so far has merely scratched the surface of the topic. In particular, much more work needs to be done on the subject on a comparative basis.

### B. *Housing Market and Social Structure*

The operation of the housing market and of its effects on residential community crime careers cannot be fully understood except within the context of the overall political economy of the state. It was the two types of state subsidy that fostered the emergence of the two dominant tenure types in Britain, and it was the ideology of the welfare state that produced the unique British public rental sector as more than a residual, safety-net housing for the poor. We have also explained how a crisis in the political economy of Britain has begun to alter this position. Before returning to this, however, let us examine some major effects of the housing market on the social structure of modern Britain.

The effect of tax relief on mortgage repayments was that, during the inflation of the 1960s and 1970s, owner-occupiers possessed an asset whose capital value was increasing in real terms. This is a capital asset that under British tax law can be passed on by inheritance. It is therefore hardly surprising that children of owner-occupiers are themselves more likely to become owner-occupiers (United Kingdom 1985, p. 128, table 8.11). The inflationary benefit for local authority housing stock, however, was not necessarily passed on to tenants since this depended on the different rent levels set by local authorities. It certainly did not take the form of an appreciating capital asset that could be inherited: the most a child could hope to inherit in this sector was his or her parents' tenancy, and even that was difficult. This difference created a huge incentive to become an owner-occupier but also meant that the gap between those who did and those who could not was a social distance that increased generationally. This gulf, which cuts across normally defined class boundaries, will become increasingly important in the future.

A further effect was that house purchase became one of the best and

TABLE 8

Asset Composition of Gross Personal Wealth in the United Kingdom, 1960 and 1975

| Holdings | 1960 | 1975 |
|---|---|---|
| Land | 1.9 | 3.6 |
| Dwellings | 19.1 | 38.9 |
| Other physical assets | 7.1 | 6.5 |
| Company securities | 21.2 | 8.7 |
| Life policies | 11.0 | 13.8 |
| Building Society deposits | 5.0 | 6.8 |
| Other financial assets | 34.7 | 21.7 |
| Total gross wealth (£ thousand millions) | 55.3 | 210.3 |

SOURCE.—Royal Commission on the Distribution of Income and Wealth (1977), after Donnison and Ungerson (1982, p. 219).

NOTE.—Data are percentages of assets in holdings.

safest forms of investment in postwar Britain. As table 8 shows, the percentage of gross personal wealth in the United Kingdom accounted for by dwellings increased from just under 20 percent to just under 40 percent in the fifteen years from 1960 to 1975. Quite apart from the social cleavage this created, it also diverted investment attention away from industry and so helped to make the reversal of economic decline more difficult. It was the failure to halt this decline that created the crisis in public spending out of which the changes in housing policy of the last seven years were to emerge. We must now turn to these changes and speculate on their possible effect on residential community crime careers.

### C. *The Future of Residential Community Crime Careers*

What then can we say about the future of residential community crime careers in Britain in relation to housing allocation mechanisms? Contemporary attempts to alter tenure patterns in Britain mean that anything we say must be highly speculative. Nevertheless, some trends can be discerned and the possible consequences of these for crime examined.

If we take private rental tenure first, then the trend is fairly clear. While there are some pressures to reverse the trend (National Federation of Housing Associations 1985), nevertheless the tenure will almost certainly continue to decline with the minor exception of housing association rentals. While there will still be a demand for private rental and especially for furnished property, the supply will be small and will consist mainly of odd houses within basically owner-occupied areas. Much of this may be in the tenure for a short period, for example, after the death of a relative or while a family is away, and some will double as holiday lettings for part of the year. What will especially decline will be dominantly private rental areas. Some of these may remain in the center of large cities—especially London—but we have seen what has happened to such an area in Sheffield, which is the fifth-largest city in England. Where private rental areas do remain in the center of large cities, there is a danger that their poor quality will lead to their becoming ghettos for the most disadvantaged groups. Here, high offense and offender rates are likely, with the added possibility of social disorder.

Where private rental is declining, the criminal careers of such areas will either be brought to an abrupt end because the area is pulled down for redevelopment or will probably eventually decline as a result of the processes of gentrification we have described in Havelock. As in Havelock, the most interesting aspect of this will relate to inner-city areas that have provided convenient locations for the supply of illicit goods and services. Since the demand for such goods and services is not likely to decline, changes will occur in the social organization of the supply. In the case of prostitution, for example, either street work will continue (but in nonresidential areas using cars) or new commercial locations, such as saunas or hotels, will be used. This will change the social organization of prostitution and especially the autonomy of job control allowed to the women and the role of the pimp. Street work allows a fair degree of job control for the women, and the pimp is as much protector and boyfriend as procurer. Prostitutes have often objected to brothel situations because they reduce, or remove, this job autonomy (see Jaget 1980). Saunas are near to the brothel in form, although there is some evidence that (at any rate for the moment in Sheffield) the women have managed to maintain a degree of autonomy by only renting space from the sauna owner.

This may, however, be only a transitory phase created by a generation of prostitutes with a cultural tradition derived from the autonomy of street work. The use of hotels brings the pimp into a much more direct role as procurer. The change in the criminal careers of areas like Havelock will probably affect in this way the careers of other areas. Prostitution, instead of being concentrated in one red-light district, may be dispersed among a number of much less concentrated locations (nonresidential areas or small commercial enterprises within a mainly residential area). The effect of prostitution on the general criminality of residential areas is likely to be very limited, and, because it will be small-scale and nonstreet work, it is less likely to generate significant public complaints. For these reasons, although some of these locations for prostitution may in fact be relatively easy for the police to prosecute, they may instead operate a discretionary toleration. A new informal accord about prostitution will have been created to replace the one fractured by the structural changes in the old red-light area.

One thing that could upset these trends in private rental areas would be if the present government could succeed on a large scale in selling off whole local authority estates for private rental. This would halt the decline of the tenure. While they have done this to some small extent, it is very doubtful whether they can do so more generally. If they did succeed, the effects on tenure distribution and crime careers would be very complex and beyond the scope of this essay.

As far as the two main tenure types in Britain are concerned, the future is uncertain and complicated, and therefore speculation on residential community crime careers is difficult. As long as the present government remains in power, it will encourage the further proportional growth of the owner-occupied sector. It will do so both by fostering more new building in the sector by restricting public expenditure and by selling off local authority housing to tenants as owner-occupiers.[25] Even a new government will find it difficult to halt this trend since the crisis in the political economy of Britain over the funding of the public sector has not been solved. The latest household tenure statistics, which are quoted in table 2, show a halt in the previous growth of local authority tenures. Future figures will almost certainly show a decline in this tenure. The general trend is likely to be an increase in owner occupation and a decline in local authority rentals.

Within this general trend there will be considerable regional variation, perhaps further exacerbating the differences we have already noted. If such trends were to continue for some time, then, in the more affluent south, local authority tenures would probably decline to a small percentage of households. In the economically depressed areas

[25] There is, however, some evidence that sale of local authority houses to tenants is running into difficulties as unemployment and depressed wage levels make it difficult for these new occupiers to meet their mortgage repayments. Furthermore, the government has reduced the incentive even to politically sympathetic local authorities to sell off their housing stock by now not allowing them to keep the profits.

this would probably not occur. In such areas the funding for owner occupation is less available, the local political authorities are more likely to resist such movement, and the current proportion of local authority housing is at a much higher level.

While there will be considerable variation, such a projection presents us with two extreme models: on the one hand, a city where owner occupation is the overwhelming majority of tenures but with a small local authority sector and, on the other hand, a city where local authority tenures may still be occupied by almost half the households. The latter model is not dissimilar to the general position for much of the postwar period in Britain and is close to what we have discussed in Sheffield (except with an even smaller privately rented sector). In this model we would expect offender rates to be correlated with tenure but with considerable offender rate variation within the local authority sector. The effects and mechanisms will be similar to those we have already described. The first model, however, represents a new situation that needs to be examined in a little more detail.

If a city has very little private rental housing and its local authority rental sector shrinks to a small proportion, then the latter will become a residual tenure. Here will be concentrated all the households who cannot gain access to the price market of owner occupation. They will be the low paid, the unemployed, single parents, and the large and "problem" families. Such areas are also likely to be the locations of the operations of the "black economy," which high unemployment rates in Britain have fostered. In other words, this residual tenure will concentrate together those social groups with a high criminogenic potential. In extreme cases this will probably mean that local authority tenure areas will have uniformly high offender rates with a continuing community crime career. The crime career reversal techniques discussed earlier will be very difficult to apply to such cases since the key control of allocation mechanisms to prevent "tipping" will be impossible.

What then of community crime careers in the owner-occupied sectors of such a city? One hypothesis is that the move of households to this different tenure actually reduces their offending. If so, this would result either in a reduction in overall crime rates in such a city or, failing that, in an increased offender rate concentration in the public sector. Some very tentative evidence for such a hypothesis can be found in Herbert's (1982) work in Cardiff, following a suggestion from early work in Sheffield (Baldwin and Bottoms 1976). Herbert found that "at the 5 percent level of significance, the correlation between low delinquency rate and owner-occupancy remains valid even when social class effects are controlled" (Herbert 1982, p. 87). The evidence, however, is slender (as Herbert readily concedes), and we remain doubtful whether a change of tenure will necessarily reduce offending. If it does not, then offender rates in a city with enhanced owner occupation will correlate with tenure, but within the owner-occupied sector there will be considerable area variation in offending—the opposite of what we have described in Sheffield. In such a situation, tipping could occur in the criminal careers of an owner-occupied area, and a detailed study of the operation of the price market would be necessary to understand the mechanism of this. In this regard, comparative research from a country with dominantly owner-occupier tenures (such as Australia) would be very useful to future British research.

The picture we have painted in this model of a low-proportion local authority tenure city is, however, a simplification of what will actually occur in the near future. It should be obvious from current tenure distribution that a move to such a model would, at least in the short term, depend on the sale of local authority houses to tenants. The result would be mixed tenure areas. But the situation is even more complicated than that. Given the relation we have already discussed between community crime careers of public sector estates and the allocative desirability of the estates, it is not unreasonable to suppose that the local authority houses that are sold will be particularly located in areas with low offender rates. Indeed we would hazard a guess that one of the best predictors of the level of sales in an area would be the relative offender rate. This could mean that estates with low offender rates are more likely to change tenure type or that subareas with lower offender rates within estates will change their dominant tenure type. Such complex situations will have a considerable effect on attempts at reversing community crime careers. On the one hand, a growth of owner occupation on an estate would produce improvements in an area that local authority management would reinforce as part of a crime-reduction strategy, provided the position in the authority as a whole allowed them to control any allocative support for tipping. On the other hand, a growth of owner occupation in only one part of an estate may produce a separated owner-occupier culture that will not cooperate with such local authority policies. The effect of this may be to split the estate into two distinct areas with different offender rates and possibly different community crime careers. Whether this happens will crucially depend on whether socialization effects between the two areas can be avoided. Interestingly, schools in Britain, because they had geographical catchment areas, often made this difficult, but the provisions of the Education Act, 1980, which enjoins parental choice of school, may make this more possible.

Some of these final considerations are necessarily very speculative, but we have included them to demonstrate the possibilities of criminological thinking that seriously take into account the relations between housing tenure, the dynamics of the housing market, and residential community crime careers.

## APPENDIX

In the introduction to this essay, we drew the general and familiar distinction between area *offender rates* (i.e., the extent to which residents in an area commit crimes) and area *offense rates* (i.e., the extent to which offenses are committed in an area). In this note we amplify this general distinction, adding also the separate concept of the *victimization rate*; and we also spell out the data sources that can be used to measure each concept.

### I. Offender Rates

In examining offender rates for a given area, one takes the total number of offenders (however measured—see below) among the residents and divides by the population base. As a refinement, one can also distinguish, if desired, the *total offender rate* (i.e., residents committing offenses anywhere) and the *within-area offender rate* (i.e., residents committing offenses within the area only).

If relying only on police-recorded data, the numerator for the total offender rate in Britain will usually be obtained by adding together persons convicted of and persons cautioned for "notifiable offenses" (see n. 4) in a given time period (persons both convicted and cautioned are counted only once for this purpose). This is a person-based measurement, so that if an offender is convicted of a notifiable offense on three separate occasions within the measured period (say, a year), he still counts only once. In the United States the nearest equivalent is the *arrest rate*, but this is not a person-based measurement as described above and is also deficient as an indicator of offending since significant numbers of people may be arrested for crimes but then not proceeded against because of insufficient evidence.

Offender rates for areas may also, in principle, be measured by carrying out a self-report study in the relevant districts; but in practice, area-based self-report studies are very rare.

## II. Offense Rates

In examining the offense rate for a given area, the numerator is the total number of offenses (however measured—see below) committed in the area. The denominator is often a population base, but this can be unsatisfactory in nonresidential (or mixed residential and nonresidential) areas, and various suggestions for alternative denominators have been made (Boggs 1965; Harries 1981).

If relying only on police-recorded data, the numerator for the offense rate will be the number of recorded offenses in the relevant area over the relevant time span. So far as crimes with victims are concerned, this overall offense rate will be made up of (1) household and personal crimes against residents living in the area; (2) crimes against nonresidents visiting the area (e.g., theft from car or assault); or (3) crimes against commercial or industrial enterprises in the area. (The distinction between 1 and 3 may sometimes in practice be difficult to draw, e.g., in the case of a crime against the owner of a small corner shop that is not a limited company.)

In going beyond police-recorded data to measure offense rates, the usual index is, of course, the set of offenses revealed in a household victimization survey. However, it should be noted that this covers only the first of the three kinds of crime types listed above, and this needs to be borne carefully in mind when making comparisons between police and survey data. (A separate commercial victimization survey could be carried out if it is desired to include the third type of crime in the comparison.) Additionally, it should be noted that comparability with police data for offenses against residents will be achieved only, in the offense rate context, if the household victimization survey offense data are restricted to offenses occurring within the area being studied (see further below).

## III. Victimization Rates

The victimization rate for an area measures the extent to which individual residents of that area have been the victims of offenses within a relevant time span. It differs from the offense rate, in that (1) it excludes crimes against visitors to the area; (2) it excludes crimes against commercial or industrial enterprises in the area; and (3) it includes all crimes committed against residents of a given area, whether these crimes were committed in the area or outside it (e.g., theft of a purse while shopping in the city center). (Within-area household/personal victimization is, by definition, identical to the area offense rate against residents for such offenses—see above.)

The victimization rate, in the sense used here, is not routinely available from police-recorded data, but, by going back to the original data sources, it is usually possible to compute a police-recorded victimization rate for a given area (an example is given in table A1). Going beyond police-recorded data, victimization rates are of course obtainable from household victimization surveys and are the usual measurement derived from such surveys (i.e., the surveys record victimizations to residents of given areas but normally do not distinguish where the victimization took place).

The following example from data for the Gardenia and Stonewall estates in

TABLE A1

Criminal Indices for Gardenia and Stonewall Estates

| | Gardenia | Stonewall |
|---|---|---|
| Police-recorded offender rate for notifiable offenses (1971) | 9.7 | 3.2 |
| Self-report offender rate | . . . | . . . |
| Police-recorded offense rate for notifiable offenses committed in the area (1971): | | |
| Household/personal offenses against residents | 8.5 | 2.4 |
| Personal offenses against visitors | .9 | 1.1 |
| Offenses against industrial/commercial enterprises | 10.2 | 4.0 |
| Total offense rate (includes crimes without victims) | 20.4 | 7.6 |
| Victim-survey offense rate for offenses against residents within area only (1975) | 51.0 | 15.0 |
| Police-recorded victimization rate for notifiable offenses against residents inside or outside area (1971) | 11.3 | 3.2 |
| Victim-survey victimization rate for offenses against residents inside or outside area (1975) | 65.0 | 25.0 |

Sheffield (see table A1) may help to clarify the above distinctions. (In each case, data are given "per hundred households." Note in this connection that size of household was similar in the two areas—see table 3. All rates given are annual rates.)

## REFERENCES

Baldwin, J. 1974. "Problem Housing Estates: Perceptions of Tenants, City Officials and Criminologists." *Social and Economic Administration* 8:116–35.

———. 1975. "Urban Criminality and the Problem Estate." *Local Government Studies*, n.s., 1:12–20.

Baldwin, J., and A. E. Bottoms. 1976. *The Urban Criminal*. London: Tavistock.

Boggs, S. L. 1965. "Urban Crime Patterns." *American Sociological Review* 30:899–908.

Bottoms, A. E., R. Mawby, and M. A. Walker. 1986. "A Localised Crime Survey" (in press).

Bottoms, A. E., and P. Xanthos. 1981. "Housing Policy and Crime in the British Public Sector." In *Environmental Criminology*, edited by P. J. Brantingham and P. L. Brantingham. Beverly Hills, Calif.: Sage.

Brantingham P. J., and P. L. Brantingham, eds. 1981. *Environmental Criminology*. Beverly Hills, Calif.: Sage.

Bright, J., and G. Petterson. 1984. *The Safe Neighbourhoods Unit*. London: National Association for the Care and Resettlement of Offenders.

Burbidge, M. 1984. "British Public Housing and Crime: A Review." In *Coping with Burglary*, edited by R. Clarke and T. Hope. Boston: Kluwer-Nijhoff.

Crook, A., and R. Darke. 1983. "Havelock Housing Action Area: Achievements after Five Years: The Residents' Perspective." Mimeographed. Sheffield: University of Sheffield, Department of Town and Regional Planning.

Crook, A., B. O'Leary, D. Skinner, and J. Watson. 1976. "Havelock: The Case for Priority Treatment." Mimeographed. Sheffield: Broomhall Community Group.

Damer, S. 1974. "Wine Alley: The Sociology of a Dreadful Enclosure." *Sociological Review* 22:221–48.

Donnison, D., and C. Ungerson. 1982. *Housing Policy*. London: Penguin.

Farrington, D. P., and E. A. Dowds. 1985. "Disentangling Criminal Behavior and Police Reaction." In *Reactions to Crime*, edited by D. P. Farrington and J. Gunn. Chichester: Wiley.

Gaskell, S. M. 1976. "Sheffield City Council and the Development of Suburban Areas Prior to World War I." In *Essays in the Economic and Social History of South Yorkshire*, edited by S. Pollard and C. Holmes. Barnsley: South Yorkshire County Council.

Gill, O. 1977. *Luke Street*. London: Macmillan.

Harries, K. D. 1981. "Alternative Denominators in Conventional Crime Rates." In *Environmental Criminology*, edited by P. J. Brantingham and P. L. Brantingham. Beverly Hills, Calif.: Sage.

Hedges, A., A. Blaber, and B. Mostyn. 1980. *Community Planning Project: Cunningham Road Improvement Scheme*. London: Social and Community Planning Research.

Herbert, D. T. 1982. *The Geography of Urban Crime*. London: Longman.

Herbert, D. T., and S. W. Hyde. 1984. *Residential Crime and the Urban Environment*. Report to the Economic and Social Research Council. Swansea: University College of Wales, Department of Geography.

Hugman, B. 1977. *Act Natural*. London: Bedford Square.

Jaget, C. 1980. *Prostitutes: Our Life*. Bristol: Falling Wall.

Jeffrey, C. R. 1971. *Crime Prevention through Environmental Design*. Beverly Hills, Calif.: Sage.

Johnson, P. B. 1968. *Land Fit for Heroes: The Planning of British Reconstruction*. Chicago: University of Chicago Press.

Kemeny, J. 1981. *The Myth of Home Ownership*. London: Routledge & Kegan Paul.

Macrae, I. 1974. "The Twilight Area: Its Function in Sheffield." Master's thesis, University of Sheffield.

Malpass, P., and A. Murie. 1982. *Housing Policy and Practice*. London: Macmillan.

Mawby, R. 1979. *Policing the City*. Westmead: Saxon House.

Merrett, S. 1979. *State Housing in Britain*. London: Routledge & Kegan Paul.

Middlemas, K. 1980. *Politics in Industrial Society*. London: Deutsch.

Morris, T. P. 1957. *The Criminal Area.* London: Routledge & Kegan Paul.

National Federation of Housing Associations. 1985. *Enquiry into British Housing.* Report of the National Federation of Housing Associations, H.R.H. Prince Philip, chairman. London: NFHA.

Newman, O. 1972. *Defensible Space.* New York: Macmillan.

Niner, P. 1975. *Local Housing Policy and Practice.* Birmingham: University of Birmingham, Centre for Urban and Regional Studies.

Royal Commission on the Distribution of Income and Wealth. 1977. *Third Report on the Standing Reference, Cmnd 6999.* London: H.M. Stationery Office.

Shaw, C. R., and H. D. McKay. 1942. *Juvenile Delinquency and Urban Areas.* Chicago: University of Chicago Press.

United Kingdom. 1981. *Regional Trends.* London: H.M. Stationery Office.

———. 1982. *Social Trends,* no. 12. London: H.M. Stationery Office.

———. 1983. *Social Trends,* no. 13. London: H.M. Stationery Office.

———. 1984. *Social Trends,* no. 14. London: H.M. Stationery Office.

———. 1985. *Social Trends,* no. 15. London: H.M. Stationery Office.

Wilson, S. 1980. "Vandalism and Defensible Space in London Housing Estates." In *Designing Out Crime,* edited by R. Clarke and P. Mayhew. London: H.M. Stationery Office.

Xanthos, P. 1981. "Crime, the Housing Market and Reputation: A Study of Some Local Authority Estates in Sheffield." Ph.D. dissertation, University of Sheffield.

*Scott C. McDonald*

# Does Gentrification Affect Crime Rates?

ABSTRACT

The emergence of gentrification in American cities during the 1970s surprised most urban observers because it contradicted the general trend of urban decline. The middle class was suddenly and unexpectedly moving into neighborhoods where crime rates were notoriously high. A number of hypotheses have been offered concerning gentrification and crime. One is that high-income newcomers offer more lucrative targets, this being conducive to increased crime. Another is that middle-income people commit less crime than do low-income people, and the displacement of low-income residents by newcomers should reduce crime. In this study, time-series data from fourteen gentrified neighborhoods in Boston, New York, San Francisco, Seattle, and Washington, D.C., were analyzed to determine if gentrification had an effect on crime rates in central city neighborhoods. The neighborhoods resembled one another in architectural or locational amenities, attracted young middle-class professionals with nonfamily living arrangements, and experienced a rapid appreciation of property values. Additional factors lent a distinctive character to each neighborhood. Analysis of crime rates between 1970 and 1984 in the fourteen neighborhoods tentatively indicates that gentrification leads to some eventual reduction in personal crime rates but that it has no significant effect on rates of property crime. Relief from long-term trends of urban decline may be only temporary in gentrified neighborhoods. Crime may act as a feedback mechanism to deter neighborhood stability resulting from gentrification.

For many decades sociologists and demographers have had little optimism to offer for the future of America's central cities. Indeed, through-

Scott C. McDonald is Director of Research, Time, Inc.


0-226-80802-5/86/0008-0005$01.00

out most of the last thirty years, observers and writers on urban affairs compiled a formidable list of discouraging trends: the "flight" of the white middle class to the suburbs (Berry and Kasarda 1977), the increasing concentration of poor nonwhites in central cities (Pettigrew 1980), the polarization of city and suburb according to race and class (Schnore 1972), the deterioration of central city housing stock (Muth 1969), the migration of people and jobs out of central business districts (Berry and Cohen 1973), the resulting erosion of the city's tax base (Kasarda 1976; Peterson 1981), the declining quality of city services, the upward trend of crime rates, and other indicators of anomie. Indeed the increasingly inhospitable character of our central cities seemed to be confirmed by census data that charted appreciable net out-migration from the cores of most central cities during recent years (Berry 1976).

Since 1975, some scholarly and journalistic comment on the prospects for central cities has taken an optimistic turn. A growing body of popular and technical literature now argues that, after decades of unrelieved economic and demographic decline, at least some of America's cities are showing signs of revival. This revival is said to manifest itself in several ways. Central business districts have replaced their declining manufacturing and retail sectors with the burgeoning financial, insurance, real estate, and professional services sectors. This turnover not only has made America's downtown districts the bastions of well-paid white-collar occupations but has also spawned the construction of gleaming new office towers—highly visible monuments to the new urban prosperity. In their shadows, elegant and inventive restaurants, sophisticated boutiques, mirrored health clubs, and stylish bars have sprung up to minister to the needs and whims of this growing and affluent downtown clientele. Inspired by the success of San Francisco's Ghirardelli Square and Boston's Faneuil Hall Marketplace, numerous cities have undertaken major commercial restorations of historic downtown sites, and to varying degrees these efforts have all succeeded in luring shoppers and tourists back to downtown venues.

While these commercial developments have provided the most glittering examples of central city resurgence, it is the apparent revitalization of central city private housing markets—in the lay vernacular, "gentrification"—that has provoked the most scholarly attention and controversy. Controversy has raged over such issues as whether gentrification exists (Black 1979; Lipton 1980; Spain 1980), how it is best defined (Clay 1979), whether it is actually a "back to the city" movement or merely a "stay in the city" movement (Gale 1976), whether it is significant for the future of cities (Sternlieb and Hughes 1980), whether it creates expensive service demands for cities (Laska and Spain 1980), whether it inflicts misery and displacement on vulnerable populations (Cicin-Sain 1980; Schill and Nathan 1983; Gale 1984), and whether it stems more from speculator greed and manipulation (Hartman 1979), from demand-side demographic forces in the metropolitan housing market (McDonald 1983), from the constricted supply of new suburban housing (Muller, Sobel, and Dujack 1980; Segal 1980), from natural cycles of aggregate capital flows (Smith 1979), or from dynamics inherent to its own unique development (Pattison 1977). Numerous case studies have described the local circumstances of gentrification in cities across the country, the characteristics of in-movers, the escalation of property values, the effect on architectural tastes, and so forth. Curiously, though numerous studies have suggested that fear of crime remains high in gentrified neighborhoods (Gale 1976, 1979; Laska and Spain 1980; McDonald 1983; Schill and Nathan 1983), none have investigated gentrification's effect on crime rates. It is this neglected issue that this essay addresses.

From the perspectives of both urban history and urban development theory, gentrification is quite anomalous. As such, it flies in the face of many of our most venerable assumptions about urban processes. Indeed, gentrification probably attracts many researchers precisely *because* it is such a theoretical and historical anomaly. Such subjects tempt one to argue more from theory than from statistical facts, but this essay will struggle to resist that temptation if only because its data cannot resolve the most alluring of the theoretical issues. Though one can find theoretical considerations woven throughout, the essay's core is simple, descriptive, and empirical: an examination of neighborhood crime statistics between 1970 and 1984 in fourteen gentrified neighborhoods of five American cities.

In the pages that follow, the essay will first review the research on gentrification and neighborhood change that is relevant to the issue of crime. It will then describe the process of gentrification in the neighborhoods included in the study, at least to the extent that those processes can be reconstructed from the case-study literature and from census statistics. Having laid this foundation, the essay will review the fourteen-year crime trends amassed for this study, trends that suggest that rates of "personal" crime decline as neighborhoods gentrify. Finally, the essay will revisit the theoretical issues with which it began and evaluate the implications of the study's findings.

## I. Should Gentrification Affect Crime Rates?

Gentrification's relation to crime is highly problematic. Since Adam and Eve fell from grace and were expelled from Eden into the first city, Western culture has associated the city (i.e., the man-made environment) with crime, pollution, and corruption, especially when contrasted to the benign, simple, sturdy, and honest ways of the pastoral (God-given) rural life (McDonald 1983). This tendency to equate cities with crime is not merely a quaint residue from our cultural past since cities have, indeed, usually always suffered higher crime rates than have rural areas, small towns, and suburbs. Central city neighborhoods have typically been the most dangerous of all, especially those scarred by physical and economic deterioration. Indeed, research has shown that the fear of crime is one of the main reasons that middle-class people flee urban neighborhoods (Taub, Taylor, and Dunham 1984; Skogan, in this volume). Gentrification, then, appears to be both anomalous and counterintuitive, for why would middle-class people (who have other choices) begin moving into the very teeth of the crime problem? What kind of people are these? What effect should one expect them to have on the safety of the new neighborhoods they occupy?

One's expectations about gentrification's relation to crime rates should depend to some extent on one's definition of gentrification itself. Journalists use the term rather loosely to describe variously the redemption of architectural treasures, the in-migration of middle-class residents to once disreputable city neighborhoods, the rapid escalation of residential property values, and the proliferation of "fern bars," boutiques, and quiche-serving cafes along formerly shabby city boulevards. These assorted definitions reflect the diverse usages of "gentrification" in common parlance, but they do not satisfy the academic demand for precision. While physical improvements to property may accompany gentrification, they cannot per se define it; indeed, as Clay (1979) and Goetze (1979) note, neighborhoods may be physically ameliorated through the sole efforts of the indigenous residents, just as prices may soar merely as a result of a general inflation in housing markets (Grebler and Mittlebach 1979). Similarly, the taste for fern bars, croissants, quiche, and the like may also flourish in unflaggingly affluent suburban shopping malls; thus one cannot divine the presence of gentrification simply by their presence. As a result, most scholarly treatment of gentrification accepts Clay's (1979) distinction between "gentrification" (where newcomers in old neighborhoods make physical improvements in houses) and "incumbent upgrading" (where the housing stock is improved by the existing residents, and little or no population change takes place). Accordingly, scholars tend to make population change a necessary (but not sufficient) condition of gentrification: gentrification is said to take place whenever high-income people replace low-income people in central city neighborhoods and when that turnover is accompanied by capital reinvestment in the neighborhood's housing stock. Though the scholarly literature has paid virtually no attention to forms of commercial gentrification, a similar definitional standard would seem to be appropriate: a boutique opening in an affluent suburban shopping mall would not indicate commercial gentrification, but a boutique replacing a pawnshop or a shoe repair shop on a central city avenue would.

Thus gentrification necessarily implies a turnover process in which lower-class neighborhood incumbents are succeeded by (at least) middle-class ones and in which the housing stock improves through reinvestment. This process never happens all at once, and indeed it may be drawn out over many years. In the interim the neighborhoods are often a curious mixture of old and new ways. Elegant townhouses may coexist in the same set of blocks with subsidized housing projects and single-room-occupancy (SRO) hotels. Working-class ethnic residents with staunchly traditional and familistic values may witness with dismay the invasion of their neighborhood by younger, affluent, but nontraditional households—artists, bohemians, gays, singles, and childless couples—the social and demographic groups reported to be the "shock troops" of gentrification. During the transitional periods, humble corner stores and beauty parlors may sit next to discos and charcuteries.

As several writers have noted, this coexistence is not always peaceful. In some "urban villages" where strong ethnic bonds regulated neighborhood norms and social behavior, the invasion of affluent newcomers who did not share those norms triggered vocal resentment by incumbents at the newcomers' life-styles. In the Fairmount (Philadelphia) neighborhood studied by Levy and Cybriwsky (1980), conflict between the two groups even boiled into violence against the newcomers and their property. In this sense the social conflicts attending a neighborhood's gentrification contributed *directly* to the crime statistics for that neighborhood. But conflict of this magnitude is relatively rare. One expects that the relation between gentrification and crime rates is considerably more complex. Indeed, from the case study literature, one can find as many reasons why gentrification might depress crime rates as reasons why it might stimulate them.

In the simplest of scenarios, gentrification should reduce crime rates in several ways. (1) Affluent neighborhoods have, for the most part, long enjoyed lower crime rates than have poor neighborhoods; thus, as central city neighborhoods once again become more affluent, their crime rates should increasingly approach those of other affluent neighborhoods—simply as a function of the social class of their residents. (2) The renovation of buildings by newcomers has, in some cases, encouraged upgrading by long-time incumbents of the neighborhood, presumably because they become more optimistic about their potential return on investment. These enhancements should instill greater neighborhood pride and reduce such minor "environmental" crimes as vandalism and graffiti writing. (3) Case studies report that, in response to their fear of crime, newcomers to these gentrifying neighborhoods frequently organize "citizen patrols," "neighborhood watches," or similar groups. In theory, activity of this sort should deter crime (though research on the subject has failed to show that it does). (4) The affluent newcomers usually have more political clout than do their predecessors in the neighborhood. As they increasingly come to speak for their neighborhood, they are likely to demand and receive better services from city hall. In particular, studies have shown them to be vocal and effective petitioners for improved street lighting and greater police protection—both of which should serve to dampen local crime rates. (5) Displacement of the poor may remove not only the elderly and the vulnerable, who are the focus of much policy concern, but also the young and the criminal. If public housing projects and SRO hotels—filled with impoverished welfare families, drug dealers and users, and anomic teenagers—are the principal domiciles of a neighborhood's "criminal element," then their removal could have a salutary effect on local crime rates.

On the other hand, one can imagine other scenarios in which gentrification actually increases crime rates. (1) Displacement itself could be a two-edged sword. Crime-prone teenagers and young adults may only be displaced to adjacent neighborhoods or even to adjacent blocks, and they may regard the burgeoning bourgeoisie of their old neighborhood as very attractive targets. Furthermore, the process of being displaced may lead them to objectify the newcomers or to regard them as enemies worthy of retribution. (2) Gentrification could subject neighborhoods to long transitional periods in which economic inequality is very salient. As research by Blau and Blau (1982) has suggested, economic inequality (particularly, economic inequality between the races) increases rates of criminal violence. As such, crime may be the "cost" that society pays for inequality—and one might expect gentrification to increase this "cost" for the affected neighborhoods. (3) When gentrification occurs in cohesive ethnic neighborhoods (rather than in disorganized ghetto neighborhoods), it may destroy the bonds that maintained order in those neighborhoods. As rents increase and old-timers are forced or encouraged to leave, fewer people know their neighbors. Systems that disciplined "rule-breakers" dissolve and are not replaced by any comparable "organic" form of social organization. For example, the Philadelphia neighborhood of Fairmount had, according to local testimony, long managed to maintain order without police interference; however, the social dislocations resulting from gentrification caused a "breakdown" in the neighborhood's internal organization so severe that residents ultimately had to petition the police for protection from youth gangs (Levy and Cybriwsky 1980). (4) As noted already, gentrification can lead to community conflicts that spill over into criminal activity. While these types of crimes are usually infrequent and minor (vandalism, minor physical altercations classified perhaps as non-aggravated assault, and so forth), they can be more serious, as when a newly renovated house in Philadelphia's Spring Garden neighborhood was firebombed, causing $40,000 in damage (Levy and Cybriwsky 1980). (5) Finally, it is quite possible that gentrification has no significant effect in either direction on crime rates. Rather the crime rates of individual urban neighborhoods—even those with crime rates well above the citywide average—may merely move up and down with the tides of national and metropolitan crime rates. In such instances a neighborhood's crime rate may decline in step with its city's crime rate, and gentrification's claim to having influenced the decline would vanish. If this were the case, then an empirical investigation of the relation between gentrification and crime might prudently look not for absolute changes in crime rates but for changes relative to metropolitan rates.

## II. The Study Neighborhoods

This study examines a sample of fourteen neighborhoods in which gentrification has been reported. As is generally the case in such studies, the selection of neighborhoods was somewhat arbitrary; however, it was guided by a few principles. First, this study sought crime data for neighborhoods in which some case-study literature already existed or with which the author had direct familiarity. Second, the selection of neighborhoods was to some extent driven by the crime data available on those neighborhoods. Neighborhood-level crime statistics are available only from local police departments. Police departments that could not or would not provide such statistics effectively eliminated their neighborhoods from the study. In the researcher's ideal world, accurate and comparable crime statistics would be available on the neighborhood level for all years between 1970 and 1984. Alas, crime statistics are very far from that ideal. Crime reporting categories change; neighborhood reporting areas shift boundaries; and in some cases, information more than three years old is simply not retrievable—at least without commissioning major data-retrieval projects by police agencies that often are ill-suited even to minor ones. These difficulties conspired to eliminate some sought-after neighborhoods from this study and to reduce the number of years in the time series for other neighborhoods. The third principle guiding the selection of neighborhoods was the principle of geographic comparability. While the author recognized at the outset that the crime statistics might very well show that gentrification had not affected crime rates at all, he also anticipated possible variations among the sampled neighborhoods. Any attempt to explain these variations would be aided enormously by tract-level data from the 1970 and 1980 censuses. Thus, though a perfect fit between police reporting area boundaries and census tract boundaries was too much to hope for, a reasonable fit was essential. This requirement also led to the elimination of some neighborhoods. Fourth, and finally, an attempt was made to select a variety of neighborhoods—neighborhoods that had experienced only residential gentrification and ones that had also experienced commercial gentrification; and neighborhoods that had previously been organized ethnic enclaves, ghettos, warehouse districts as well as ones that had merely been declining lower-middle-class residential districts.

This set of criteria led to the selection of fourteen neighborhoods in five cities.[1] For each neighborhood and for each city, data were gathered from local police agencies on the reported incidence of "Part One Index Crimes," those major felonies that are tabulated for reporting to the Federal Bureau of Investigation for its Uniform Crime Reports. These include the "personal crimes" of homicide, rape, robbery, and assault and the "property crimes" of burglary, larceny (theft), and

[1] For information on the specific census tracts and police reporting areas used to define neighborhood boundaries, see App. table A1.

motor-vehicle theft. Though arson has been added in recent years to the property-crime reporting category, its reporting remains erratic among local police departments and is available only for recent years; thus arson data were not tabulated here.

## III. Gentrification in the Study Neighborhoods

Though neighborhoods can have much in common, each is somewhat unique—marked by a distinctive history, populated by a different assortment of members of the human tribe, neither geographically nor economically identical to any other neighborhood. Statistics, of the variety collected by the Census Bureau, can direct our attention to both the unique and the various aspects of neighborhoods, but they cannot tell enough of the history that is critical to understanding gentrification in these particular neighborhoods. Thus this section relies not only on census statistics but also on the case studies found in the literature on gentrification.

Table 1 summarizes most of the statistical information contained in the neighborhood vignettes that will follow in this section. Before proceeding to those vignettes, it is worth noting some of the statistical regularities common to most, if not all, of the study neighborhoods.

First, most neighborhoods lost population despite the onset of gentrification. However, many neighborhoods added to their housing stock during the 1970s, and even those that lost dwelling units did so at a rate lower than their rate of population loss. These dynamics allowed the remaining population of the neighborhoods to "spread out" into the existing housing stock. Thus densities declined in all but one neighborhood. These less intensely used housing units usually came to be occupied by smaller households, generally nonfamily households and often just single individuals. Thus table 1 displays succinctly two demographic hallmarks of the gentrified neighborhood: lower-than-average residential densities and higher-than-average concentrations of nonfamily households.

One can spot another demographic regularity here: nearly all neighborhoods saw a decline in their young male population. This of course mimicked the national oscillations in age structure that stemmed from the maturation of the postwar baby boom. Its significance here derives from the fact that young males are the most criminogenic segment of the population.

The other data in table 1 bear more on the variations among the neighborhoods than on the uniformities; accordingly, their interpreta-

## TABLE 1

### Selected Population and Housing Characteristics in Study Neighborhoods, 1970–80

| City/Community | Population (% Change) | Dwelling Units (% Change) | Persons per Dwelling Unit (1970) | Persons per Dwelling Unit (1980) | Households (% Change) | Nonfamily Households | | | Males Aged 15–24 | | |
|---|---|---|---|---|---|---|---|---|---|---|---|
| | | | | | | % 1970 | % 1980 | % Change | % 1970 | % 1980 | % Change |
| Boston: | | | | | | | | | | | |
| Citywide | −7.5 | 3.8 | 2.76 | 2.46 | .4 | 35.2 | 46.7 | 33.2 | 9.6 | 11.3 | 9.0 |
| North End | −14.3 | 11.1 | 2.45 | 1.89 | 6.7 | 32.9 | 58.2 | 88.6 | 8.1 | 12.9 | 37.6 |
| South End | 29.4 | 64.3 | 2.13 | 1.67 | 82.8 | 53.8 | 69.1 | 134.6 | 7.3 | 8.2 | 46.0 |
| New York City: | | | | | | | | | | | |
| Citywide | −10.4 | −4.4 | 2.71 | 2.54 | −1.7 | 28.0 | 37.0 | 30.0 | 7.5 | 7.9 | −5.0 |
| East Village | −30.5 | −18.3 | 2.11 | 1.80 | −21.0 | 48.7 | 65.1 | 5.6 | 9.8 | 8.9 | −37.5 |
| West Village | 5.0 | 13.3 | 1.73 | 1.60 | 12.5 | 62.9 | 73.3 | 31.2 | 6.8 | 7.1 | 9.9 |
| Upper West Side | −1.7 | 4.7 | 1.72 | 1.62 | 9.5 | 60.0 | 71.3 | 30.0 | 5.2 | 4.7 | −10.6 |
| Park Slope | −19.1 | −8.0 | 2.31 | 2.03 | −3.5 | 42.1 | 57.1 | 31.0 | 7.3 | 5.7 | 37.1 |
| San Francisco: | | | | | | | | | | | |
| Citywide | −5.1 | −3.7 | 2.31 | 2.27 | 1.2 | 44.3 | 53.1 | 21.2 | 8.4 | 8.0 | −9.2 |
| Haight-Ashbury | −15.7 | −10.6 | 2.29 | 2.16 | −2.9 | 50.5 | 70.0 | 34.7 | 9.2 | 11.0 | 1.2 |
| Eureka Valley | −15.3 | −1.0 | 2.17 | 1.85 | 2.3 | 52.3 | 74.3 | 45.6 | 8.4 | 7.0 | −29.7 |
| Seattle: | | | | | | | | | | | |
| Citywide | −7.0 | 3.6 | 2.39 | 2.15 | 6.5 | 35.3 | 48.0 | 44.7 | 9.2 | 9.7 | −1.3 |
| Capitol Hill | 47.1 | −2.5 | 1.09 | 1.64 | 7.2 | 63.3 | 73.9 | 25.2 | 15.6 | 9.3 | −12.8 |
| Madrona | −9.2 | −6.0 | 2.62 | 2.52 | 3.8 | 24.9 | 34.6 | 43.9 | 7.7 | 8.4 | −.9 |
| Downtown | 16.0 | −14.8 | 1.23 | 1.67 | −14.9 | 87.2 | 89.2 | −13.0 | 6.4 | 13.0 | 136.3 |
| Washington, D.C.: | | | | | | | | | | | |
| Citywide | −15.6 | −.6 | 2.72 | 2.31 | −3.6 | 38.0 | 47.2 | 19.6 | 8.7 | 9.4 | −8.8 |
| Mount Pleasant | −2.8 | 14.2 | 2.32 | 1.97 | 10.6 | 51.0 | 62.8 | 36.1 | 10.1 | 8.6 | −17.7 |
| Dupont Circle | −10.9 | −17.3 | 1.50 | 1.44 | −12.5 | 74.9 | 73.4 | −14.3 | 10.8 | 7.7 | −36.6 |
| Capitol Hill | −28.4 | 2.1 | 2.70 | 1.89 | −.4 | 40.3 | 59.7 | 47.3 | 8.1 | 6.6 | −42.0 |

| City/Community | Blacks % 1970 | Blacks % 1980 | Blacks % Change | Persons in Poverty % 1970 | Persons in Poverty % 1980 | Persons in Poverty % Change | Female-headed Families % of Families 1970 | Female-headed Families % of Families 1980 | Female-headed Families % Change | Percentage of Children under Age 18 Living in Female-headed Families 1970 | Percentage of Children under Age 18 Living in Female-headed Families 1980 |
|---|---|---|---|---|---|---|---|---|---|---|---|
| Boston: | | | | | | | | | | | |
| Citywide | 16.3 | 21.3 | 20.5 | 15.5 | 18.0 | 7.6 | 14.7 | 16.2 | 11.0 | 21.7 | 34.1 |
| North End | .1 | 1.3 | 1416.7 | 16.1 | 12.0 | −35.9 | 11.5 | 9.2 | −14.7 | 9.9 | 6.5 |
| South End | 53.3 | 42.8 | 3.8 | 31.2 | 15.8 | −34.5 | 12.2 | 9.8 | 46.7 | 27.8 | 37.6 |
| New York City: | | | | | | | | | | | |
| Citywide | 21.1 | 25.2 | 7.0 | 14.8 | 19.7 | 19.5 | 12.5 | 16.6 | 30.9 | 19.5 | 30.9 |
| East Village | 14.3 | 10.8 | −47.6 | 29.7 | 32.3 | −24.3 | 11.1 | 11.1 | −21.0 | 28.2 | 32.6 |
| West Village | 4.2 | 3.1 | −23.0 | 10.8 | 11.5 | 11.6 | 4.9 | 4.1 | −5.9 | 14.7 | 18.8 |
| Upper West Side | 7.2 | 5.8 | −20.6 | 10.4 | 12.0 | 13.7 | 6.1 | 4.9 | −11.1 | 18.8 | 17.7 |
| Park Slope | 38.9 | 16.1 | −95.2 | 15.4 | 10.7 | −43.8 | 10.4 | 10.3 | −4.2 | 19.0 | 27.5 |
| San Francisco: | | | | | | | | | | | |
| Citywide | 13.4 | 12.7 | −10.1 | 13.6 | 13.4 | −6.6 | 9.2 | 10.0 | 9.1 | 18.7 | 21.2 |
| Haight-Ashbury | 40.5 | 25.5 | −46.9 | 20.2 | 18.7 | −22.0 | 12.1 | 10.1 | −18.7 | 30.7 | 36.7 |
| Eureka Valley | 4.7 | 4.6 | −18.7 | 12.3 | 10.1 | −30.6 | 8.8 | 5.8 | −32.3 | 18.9 | 26.1 |
| Seattle: | | | | | | | | | | | |
| Citywide | 7.1 | 9.5 | 23.5 | 10.0 | 10.7 | −.4 | 8.3 | 9.1 | 17.3 | 14.5 | 22.1 |
| Capitol Hill | 28.9 | 16.9 | −13.8 | 27.8 | 18.3 | −3.2 | 8.3 | 7.7 | −.3 | 29.7 | 39.2 |
| Madrona | 72.2 | 62.2 | −21.3 | 14.3 | 14.1 | −10.4 | 16.0 | 20.3 | 31.8 | 24.7 | 26.4 |
| Downtown | 6.6 | 12.7 | 124.4 | 19.7 | 15.9 | −6.4 | 2.5 | 1.7 | −43.8 | 29.3 | 12.9 |
| Washington, D.C.: | | | | | | | | | | | |
| Citywide | 71.1 | 70.3 | −16.5 | 16.3 | 17.8 | −7.9 | 15.6 | 19.3 | 18.9 | 25.9 | 37.3 |
| Mount Pleasant | 93.5 | 49.3 | −25.8 | 19.3 | 17.8 | −10.2 | 12.4 | 11.1 | −.6 | 20.7 | 30.0 |
| Dupont Circle | 31.9 | 17.7 | −50.6 | 16.4 | 13.0 | −29.6 | 5.5 | 6.8 | 9.3 | 25.2 | 32.6 |
| Capitol Hill | 60.5 | 31.3 | −62.9 | 21.8 | 17.7 | −41.7 | 13.6 | 8.2 | −39.7 | 18.8 | 17.8 |

tions are best embedded in a substantive review of gentrification in the individual study neighborhoods.

*Boston: The North End.* Boston's North End is one of the oldest neighborhoods in the United States. A center of colonial shipping activity and home to Paul Revere and the Old North Church, it has, for at least the past fifty years, been a tightly knit enclave of ethnic Italians. Long reputed to be Boston's safest neighborhood, the North End has had a reputation for "taking care of itself" (i.e., using indigenous norms to control social behavior). Nevertheless, the North End's population has continued to drop—from over 15,000 in 1950 to 7,038 in 1980. The city government spent over $2 million to renovate public facilities in the North End in the late 1960s and early 1970s, but no public works project had as profound an effect on the North End as did the privately funded rehabilitation in the mid-1970s of the Faneuil Hall–Quincy Market complex just beyond the perimeter of the North End. This enormously successful redevelopment served its intended purpose of making the area a tourist attraction; however, it also began to attract young professionals to nearby condominium apartments carved out of abandoned warehouses. By 1978 the Quincy Market housing boom had begun to spill over into the North End, particularly along the rundown waterfront area at its eastern edge. A 1981 report by the Boston Redevelopment Authority noted that eighty-three housing units in the North End had already been converted to condominium apartments, and a recent visit to the neighborhood showed that, if anything, the pace of change has quickened. Condominiums have become more prevalent, pressing farther west into the core of the neighborhood. Though the commercial enterprises of the neighborhood still retain their old character, the old and cluttered salumerias now face new and elegantly appointed real estate offices with signs that proclaim "Condominium and Townhouse Specialists." In this study, the North End is our paradigmatic example of the organized, relatively safe ethnic neighborhood invaded by gentrification.

*Boston: The South End.* The South End was Boston's first example of gentrification, and to many minds it remains its finest example. Originally built in the 1840s as part of an ambitious public landfill project, its graceful squares of London-style bowfront townhouses became, by the turn of the century, a teeming and squalid district of rooming houses. By the 1950s the housing stock of the South End had deteriorated to such a degree that city officials worried that it might be irretrievably lost. Gentrification in the South End has mostly resulted from the private investments of individual and small-time developers, and, compared to other Boston neighborhoods, condominium conversion has not been very pronounced. The invasion of newcomers, which began in the mid-1960s and accelerated considerably in the mid-1970s, was attended by considerable controversy and public conflict (Auger 1979). Public concern about the negative effects of displacement led city officials to enact policies to keep the poor in the neighborhood—but in publicly funded housing projects. Thus the South End today is an odd amalgam of genteel, restored townhouses on charming English squares, adjacent to sterile public housing projects. The city's policy has guaranteed that the South End not only will retain its considerable heterogeneity but also will encapsulate within its borders a very high degree of socioeconomic inequality. For more than 100 years the South End has had the reputation of being a very dangerous part of Boston, a reputation that, on the testimony of crime statistics, it apparently deserved. Indeed Kevin Lynch's (1960) study of Bostonians' images of Boston found the South End to be completely missing from citizens' "mental maps" of Boston; if recalled at all, the South End was said to be a dangerous no-man's-land to be scrupulously avoided. Perhaps partly because of this unsavory reputation, the South End has never enjoyed much commercial activity. Even now its residents tend to go to the neighboring Back Bay to shop for groceries, clothing, and household items. Gentrification in the South End has been, first and last, a residential affair.

*New York: East Village and West Village.* Greenwich Village has long savored its reputation as a bohemian magnet for artists, intellectuals, and literati of various persuasions. Moreover, the pervasive influence of New York University at Washington Square has ensured high rates of turnover in the Village population. This built-in turnover makes it a bit difficult to spot any classic cycle of ecological invasion and succession in Greenwich Village. Nevertheless, changes have been evident. In the late 1960s and early 1970s the West Village came increasingly to be identified with New York's homosexual minority. With the emergence of this identity and of the tolerant ambience that it inspired, gays began to settle in the West Village in increasing numbers. Gays were also attracted to the West Village because it was already a fairly stable middle-class neighborhood with an architecturally attractive housing stock. Renovation of the Federal Period row houses prevalent in the neighborhood was much in evidence throughout the decade, and the appreciation in property values reflected the heightened stature of the West Village as a residential neighborhood. While the median value of homes in New York doubled from $30,420 to $60,500 in the decade between 1970 and 1980, median values in the West Village nearly quadrupled, rising from $50,000 to $175,000. New York's strict rent-control laws have limited displacement throughout the city, and there is little evidence of conflict inspired by displacement in the West Village.

The transformation of the East Village has been somewhat more rancorous. For most of the past thirty years, the East Village has been a somewhat run-down transitional zone between the more stable core Village neighborhood around Washington Square, and the seedy Lower East Side. As one proceeds east from Washington Square each block seems to get progressively poorer, culminating in the bleak tenements around Tompkins Square Park. Indeed, the 1980 census found that 32 percent of the East Village population lived below the official poverty line and that of that number a full 65 percent were more than 200 percent below the poverty line. In the late 1970s and early 1980s the East Village became notorious as a hub of the illicit drug trade in New York—a neighborhood where cocaine and heroin could be purchased openly on the streets or in drive-through arrangements reminiscent of fast-food franchises. Into this sordid milieu came, in the early 1980s, New York's burgeoning art community. Squeezed by the increasing cost of loft and gallery space in nearby Soho (a neighborhood transformed in the 1960s and 1970s from industrial to art-oriented commercial and residential uses), artists began to move into this comparatively inexpensive neighborhood. Avant-garde galleries have attracted middle-class people into this neighborhood that, only a few years ago, they would have scrupulously avoided, and the galleries have now been matched by an assortment of trendy restaurants and shops. Partly as a result of this new population of the East Village, in 1983 the New York Police Department initiated "Operation Pressure Point," a massive crackdown on the East Village drug trade that forced some of the traders out of the neighborhood and impelled others to peddle their wares more discreetly. However, the middle-class invasion of the East Village has also provoked fear of displacement among poor neighborhood residents. Conflicts between old and new residents are occasionally reported, and visitors to the East Village cannot fail to notice the antigentrification banners and graffiti that are very much in evidence. Since the process of gentrification is not yet very far advanced in the East Village, one would expect that any effect on crime rates would be quite recent.

*New York: Upper West Side.* Like Boston's South End, the Upper West Side was originally built to provide attractive housing for the city's growing middle class. The mansions lining Central Park West and Riverside Drive were connected by side streets lined with thousands of row houses. In the first thirty years of this century the Upper West Side was the site of construction of New York's first large apartment houses, many with spacious rooms and fine architectural features. The building boom fell victim to the Great Depression, but the neighborhood's population continued to swell. In the postwar years, New York's middle class fled in increasing numbers to the suburbs. Though Central Park West, Riverside Drive, and West End Avenue retained their middle-class residential character, the row houses and brownstones were commonly subdivided to make them more affordable for the low-income residents who now occupied them. In the area above 87th Street, just beyond the area under study here, urban renewal led to the construction of vast housing projects in the 1950s and 1960s. For quite a while the "West Side Story" looked fairly bleak. However, the construction of Lincoln Center in the early 1960s forced the demolition of vast numbers of tenements on the southern perimeter of the neighborhood. The transformation of Lincoln Square helped to make the Upper West Side more attractive again for middle-class residents. Throughout the 1970s and the early 1980s building renovation flourished on the Upper West Side, assisted in part by the city's J-51 tax-abatement program. Between 1970 and 1980 the occupied housing stock of the Upper West Side increased by 5.9 percent, and owner occupancy increased 92.9 percent, compared with a 16.5 percent increase for Manhattan as a whole (New York Department of City Planning 1984). Furthermore, the number of overcrowded units declined on the Upper West Side by 36 percent, compared with a 16.8 percent drop for Manhattan. The principal agents of this change were the young professionals moving to New York to work in its growing financial, media, and professional services occupations. Though the twenty-five- to forty-four-year-old age group grew in the 1970s by 12 percent in Manhattan, it grew by 31 percent on the Upper West Side. Indeed, this age group was the only one to grow in both absolute and relative terms during the decade. This age group also provided a ready market for the commercial gentrification much in evidence on the Upper West Side—mostly concentrated along Columbus Avenue and Broadway but now also extending to Amsterdam Avenue. Except for early opposition to the razing of tenements to make way for Lincoln Center (and the concomitant relocation of residents into public housing), relatively little conflict attended the gentrification of the Upper West Side. Thus, in this study, the Upper West Side represents the "twin" form of gentrification (i.e., both commercial and residential), accomplished with only modest levels of displacement and conflict.

*New York: Park Slope.* Like the Upper West Side, Park Slope in Brooklyn was a very fashionable neighborhood in the early years of this century. The grand mansions facing Prospect Park formed something of a "gold coast" for affluent Brooklyn families. Also, like the Upper West Side, Park Slope suffered severe losses of middle-class population and serious housing deterioration in the years between 1930 and 1960. Though it is difficult to date exactly, it appears that private market reinvestment in Park Slope began to be noticeable in the mid-1960s, and the pace accelerated throughout the 1970s. Partly to protect their investment, the initial brownstoners organized themselves into community improvement organizations to lobby for local improvements with the city officials, banks, and public utilities. They also worked to reduce the number of SRO hotels and rooming houses in the neighborhood, seemingly to good effect since the number of such dwellings declined by eighty-four buildings during the 1970s. Furthermore, in an attempt to dodge local rent-control laws that make it hard to evict tenants, owners held many apartments vacant for cooperative or condominium conversion; thus the neighborhood's rental vacancy rate increased by 52.8 percent during the decade. The number of overcrowded units declined by 43.9 percent, compared with the borough average of 28.1 percent; and owner occupancy increased in Park Slope by 8.6 percent, compared to Brooklyn's decrease of 7.8 percent (New York Department of City Planning 1984). These statistics suggest that displacement was fairly pronounced in Park Slope. Indeed, the Park Slope population declined by 19 percent between 1970 and 1980, though the number of housing units declined by only 8 percent. Nonwhites accounted for much of this exodus, their number dropping from 39 percent of the neighborhood's 1970 population to 16 percent in 1980. Similarly, the percentage of the Park Slope population living below the poverty line declined from 15 percent in 1970 to only 11 percent in 1980. Unlike the Upper West Side, residential redevelopment in Park Slope has not spawned significant commercial redevelopment; thus the neighborhood retains an essentially residential flavor. However, like the Upper West Side, Park Slope's gentrification has not altered its geographic proximity to the unreconstructed ghettos (and thus to very high crime neighborhoods).

*San Francisco: Haight-Ashbury.* Haight-Ashbury has had a curious history. Like many San Francisco neighborhoods devastated in the catastrophic 1906 earthquake, Haight-Ashbury had rebuilt in the prevailing Victorian style. In the postwar years it retained a modicum of working-class stability until the 1960s, when the first of a series of ecological invasions took place. First, of course, came the hippies and "flower children," celebrated in song and verse, from throughout the country. Attracted by the neighborhood's reputation for tolerance, drugs, and free love as well as by its proximity to Olmstead's vast Golden Gate Park, they made the Haight, for a short period at least, into something of a tourist attraction. However, the hippies' communal and low-income life-style entailed high-density uses of the housing stock, and during this period many of the old Victorians began to show signs of wear. As the hippie movement faded, Haight-Ashbury decayed into a very disorganized state. Drug addiction was rampant as the subculture of "street people" remained as a sad reminder of the more innocent days recently passed. During this period disinvestment accelerated, and the housing stock was allowed to fall into ever-greater disrepair.

By the mid-1970s, the Haight was becoming indistinguishable from the impoverished and anomic Fillmore District that it adjoins. However, since the late 1970s and early 1980s, the Haight's fortunes have turned once again. Spurred by the growth of gentrification in other San Francisco neighborhoods and by a citywide scarcity of housing, young middle-class investors have again begun buying houses in the Haight. Median home values have soared to $147,250, compared to the citywide average of $103,900. Rising rents and use conversions have caused considerable displacement of the black population, but economic inequality remains high within the neighborhood. As of 1980, a date that must be regarded as early in this neighborhood's gentrification process, 19 percent of the Haight's population still lived below the official poverty line, compared to the city's average of 13 percent. Nonfamily households have long been an important component of the San Francisco population profile, but the Haight's earlier hippies apparently coexisted with traditional families: the 1970 census found that about half of the Haight's households were family households. However, the latest waves of newcomers have altered that mix substantially; nonfamily households accounted for 70 percent of the Haight households in 1980.

*San Francisco: Eureka Valley.* In some ways the gentrification of Eureka Valley parallels the development of New York's West Village. Both neighborhoods contain an attractive and architecturally distinct housing stock. Both neighborhoods had been relatively stable lower-middle-class neighborhoods prior to gentrification, though Eureka Valley had a stronger ethnic (Italian) component than did the West Village. Both experienced a mixture of commercial and residential gentrification during the 1970s. Most important, both became centers of the gay subcultures of their respective cities, and gays played a prominent role in the transformation of both neighborhoods. However, conflicts between the ethnic incumbents and the newcomers were more manifest in Eureka Valley—owing more to life-style differences than to gentrification per se. In terms of economic class, Eureka Valley did not undergo changes as profound as did some neighborhoods: the neighborhood's median income went from slightly below the citywide median in 1970 to slightly above it in 1980, and the percentage of the population living below the poverty line only declined from 12 percent to 11 percent between the two censuses. Nevertheless, changes in the neighborhood were profound. A gay-oriented commercial district developed and flourished along the blocks near the intersection of Market Street and Castro Street. Between 1970 and 1980, nonfamily households rose from 52 percent of Eureka Valley households to 74 percent, and males increased their fraction of the neighborhood's population from 50 percent to 61 percent. In 1970 Eureka Valley's median home value lagged behind the city median, $26,940 to $28,100; however, by 1980 it had climbed to well above the citywide median, $140,100 to $103,900. Perhaps most dramatic of all, the gays who moved to Eureka Valley formed the nucleus of a gay political movement in San Francisco that not only won national media attention and the respect of local politicians but also led to the 1978 election of the first openly gay elected city official, Harvey Milk. Because this political movement was fundamentally liberal in its outlook, the gentrifiers of Eureka Valley were loathe to organize simply to protect their property investments, to demand police protection, to remove SRO hotels, or the like. Indeed, that political movement found much of its strength from the coalitions it formed with other "disenfranchised" groups—renters, minorities, the poor, union groups, and so forth. The intergroup conflicts that did develop during the gentrification of Eureka Valley stemmed from the expansion of the neighborhood's gay enclave into the neighboring Mission District, a primarily poor and Hispanic neighborhood that was wary both of gay social behavior and of the threat of displacement. However, compared to many other neighborhoods cited in the case-study literature, the transformation of Eureka Valley proceeded with relatively little conflict. The conflicts that did emerge focused more on the issue of public homosexuality than on gentrification per se, though in the case of Eureka Valley the two social phenomena were inextricably entwined.

*Seattle: Capitol Hill.* Capitol Hill in Seattle rises gently above the central business district of the city and affords splendid views of Puget Sound and the downtown skyline. It has a long tradition of bohemianism and of racial and life-style diversity (Hodge 1980), which, in the 1960s and 1970s, made it hospitable first to hippies and political activists, then later to gays and an assortment of nontraditional households. Its housing stock includes large Victorian houses in the blocks adjacent to Volunteer Park, smaller and plainer houses near its eastern perimeter, and apartment buildings along its principal commercial streets. During the 1960s Capitol Hill showed signs of increasing impoverishment, reflecting closely Seattle's economic decline during that decade. Beginning in the early 1970s, a commercial renaissance along Capitol Hill's main business street, Broadway, brought an urbane and stylish population to Capitol Hill for food and entertainment. As commercial rents rose, small neighborhood-oriented shops closed and were replaced by establishments catering to the more cosmopolitan tastes of the newcomers. The commercial renaissance triggered a resurgence of the Capitol Hill residential market. New apartment construction has been matched by the widespread renovation of older apartment buildings. The median house price has risen steeply from its $16,700 level in 1970 (compared to the citywide median of $19,600) to a 1980 level of $85,000 (compared to the 1980 citywide median of $65,100). The influx and transformation has provoked rather severe community conflicts that have played themselves out in community councils, on street corners, and on the graffiti-flayed walls of fancy Broadway commercial establishments (Hodge 1980). Yet by the mid-1980s the newcomers seemed to have established themselves as the new status quo of the neighborhood, and Broadway's transformation into a fashionable commercial district seems complete. Within the metropolitan context, however, Capitol Hill has maintained its identity as a neighborhood that specializes in life-style diversity and, indeed, that has been a cornerstone of its appeal to gentrifiers.

*Seattle: Madrona.* Like Capitol Hill, Madrona sits on a hill facing the water, though in this case the body of water is Lake Washington. Like Capitol Hill, it has a combination of exceptionally spacious and graceful housing and of housing that is more modest and plain. Like Capitol Hill, it underwent serious decline during the economically stressful 1960s, though its decline started somewhat earlier. In other respects, it is different from Capitol Hill. Its character has always been thoroughly residential, lacking the distraction of a major commercial thoroughfare. It has never cultivated Capitol Hill's reputation as a bohemian enclave, and thus its population has always been more familistic. It has, however, been a racially diverse neighborhood. In fact blacks represented a full 72 percent of Madrona's population by 1970. However, as Hodge (1980) noted, individual blocks within the neighborhood were quite differentiated racially. Racial violence in the aftermath of the assassination of Martin Luther King, Jr., in 1968 heightened tensions in the neighborhood considerably and served to sully the neighborhood's reputation. However, the appeal of the nicer houses on the eastern edge of the neighborhood (the edge that borders Lake Washington) and of the neighborhood's proximity to downtown proved irresistible to Seattle's growing population of young professionals. Beginning in the mid-1970s they moved into the neighborhood with ever-greater enthusiasm, provoking a rapid rise in property values (Leach 1978). Madrona greeted gentrification with some discomfort, though with considerably less conflict than had occurred in Capitol Hill. Data from the 1980 census show that, despite gentrification, Madrona remains racially diverse (62 percent black), familistic (65 percent of households are family households), and with an age distribution that mirrors Seattle's. Home values have recovered from their 1970 level that was slightly below the citywide median to a 1980 level that, at $75,000, is somewhat more than $10,000 higher than the Seattle median. Indeed, it appears that elements of Seattle's black middle class were accomplices in Madrona's gentrification and that the course of events encouraged many long-term residents to reinvest and upgrade their properties. Thus Madrona provides us with an example of gentrification of a slightly different flavor: more familistic, more black, involving significant incumbent upgrading as well as in-migration and investment by newcomers.

*Seattle: Downtown.* This neighborhood is a bit anomalous in this study, in that it is not really a residential district. However, the district has undergone pronounced commercial gentrification—modeled somewhat on the successful transformation of Boston's Faneuil Hall–Quincy Market and San Francisco's Ghirardelli Square mentioned earlier. The centerpiece of this transformation has been the old Pike's Place Market, a large open-air fish and produce market at the downtown waterfront. Though Pike's Place Market has always attracted shopping traffic to downtown, it has been somewhat redecorated and expanded. Vendors now hawk a variety of ethnic foods for strollers. Specialty shops purvey exotic wares. High-status restaurants lure a business clientele to lunch and an evening crowd to dinner. The streets adjacent to the market have seen a proliferation of "new-style" boutiques, shops, and restaurants that, through their facades (exposed brick, abstract shapes, and landscaping), their names, their amenities (valet service), or their goods (wine bar, mesquite grill, and so on) offer the cultural cues that differentiate them from the district's more gritty traditions. This neighborhood has a very low residential population and has undergone virtually no discernible residential gentrification. It is included just to provide a more pure example of commercial gentrification and its effects on crime rates.

*Washington, D.C.: Mount Pleasant, Dupont Circle, and Capitol Hill.* These three Washington, D.C., neighborhoods are grouped together because their processes of gentrification have been fundamentally similar. Two of the three neighborhoods began the 1970s as predominantly black neighborhoods in a city that was over 71 percent black: in 1970, Mount Pleasant was 94 percent black, and Capitol Hill was 61 percent black; only Dupont Circle (40 percent black) had more whites than blacks among its residents. During the course of their gentrification, whites became the majority in all three neighborhoods—51 percent in Mount Pleasant, 82 percent in Dupont Circle, and 69 percent in Capitol Hill. Noteworthy levels of displacement have been the natural corollaries of this demographic shift (though it may be noteworthy mostly because gentrification has been studied more closely in Washington than in any other city). The other (by now) familiar statistical hallmarks of gentrification are also present in these three neighborhoods. Young adults, aged twenty-five to thirty-four, represent more than 35 percent of the populations of these neighborhoods, compared with their 19 percent in the District of Columbia. The percentage of the population having at least a college education approaches and surpasses 50 percent in these neighborhoods, while in the city as a whole it amounts to only 27 percent. Though nonfamily households have increased remarkably in Washington as a whole (from 38 percent in 1970 to 47 percent in 1980), nonfamilies represent 60 percent of the households in Capitol Hill, 63 percent of the households in Mount Pleasant, and 73 percent of the households in Dupont Circle. In a city in which 33 percent of the labor force works in professional or managerial occupations, the percentage in these neighborhoods surpasses 50 percent. It is clear that a high degree of economic inequality exists in at least two of these three neighborhoods—Mount Pleasant and Dupont Circle. Despite the influx of well-heeled newcomers, the neighborhood median incomes lag the citywide average for all but Capitol Hill. Mean incomes are substantially higher than median incomes in all three cases—an indication of a highly skewed income distribution. Indeed, 18 percent of the Mount Pleasant population, 13 percent of the Dupont Circle population, and 18 percent of the Capitol Hill population live below the poverty line (compared to a citywide average of 18 percent). Neighborhoods change block to block in Washington, and the motor of central city economic growth that has fueled gentrification in other cities has been less significant in this most federal of cities. Thus the gentrified neighborhoods of Washington, D.C., do resemble "islands of renewal in a sea of decay" (to borrow Brian Berry's imagery). Straying a few blocks beyond any of these neighborhoods, the unwary stroller is likely to find himself in a vastly poorer, less attractive, and more dangerous neighborhood. In Dupont Circle these dangers are mitigated somewhat by a flourishing commercial district that keeps pedestrian traffic lively until late in the evening. However, none of these three Washington neighborhoods can claim to be "distant" from impoverished, high-crime sections of the city.

In summary, this study encompasses a wide range of neighborhoods for which gentrification has been noted. Though the neighborhoods bear resemblance in (1) their architectural or locational amenities, (2) their ability to attract affluent young professionals who often live in nonfamily living arrangements, and (3) the rapid appreciation of their property values, they also differ in several respects that may have importance for interpreting trends in their crime rates. Commercial developers, artists, gays, families, and black professionals have combined in various ways to stamp their distinctive characters on the gentrification process in each of these fourteen neighborhoods. In some of the study neighborhoods, gentrification unraveled the "organic" bonds of self-regulating ethnic communities, while in others it invaded disorganized and anomic ghettos. Some neighborhoods experienced only residential gentrification, one only commercial gentrification, and most some combination of the two. Some have undergone the transition quietly, others with deafening cacophony. The severity of displacement has varied, as has the level and style of community conflict occasioned by the gentrification. Some neighborhoods have become racially and economically homogeneous, while others have retained their polyglot character; neighborhoods of the latter variety have, of course, become small microcosms of the economic inequalities of the larger society. It is not too difficult to imagine that at least some of the poorer residents of those neighborhoods harbor malevolent feelings toward their more affluent neighbors. Even homogeneous neighborhoods often abut other, less fortunate tracts, districts that certainly must pose some threat to the security and the serenity of the gentrified enclave. The foregoing description of these study areas has attempted to highlight these variations, which in theory at least, ought to influence the incidence of crime in gentrified neighborhoods. Readers who are now reeling under the burden of recalling the idiosyncrasies of fourteen different neighborhoods will be grateful for the summary presented in table 2. And all readers may find it useful to refer back to tables 1 and 2 when puzzling over the review of neighborhood crime trends that now follows.

## IV. The Effect of Gentrification on Crime Rates

Table 3 presents the crimes reported per capita for all neighborhoods and their cities in 1970, 1975, 1980, and 1984.[2] Crime rates of this variety can be deceptive since the "per capita" denominator of the equation can cause the rates to change just as surely as can shifts in the incidence of crimes. In this instance, recall that in nearly every venue population declined between 1970 and 1980. (Exceptions were Seattle's Capitol Hill with its 47 percent population increase; the South End,

[2] Geographic inconsistencies in the data-retrieval capabilities of the different police departments involved in this study required that some of the cells in table 3 remain blank. However, the data are complete for the 1980s. In the interest of tabular simplicity, the column headings for table 3 (and for subsequent tables in the paper) report results for a uniform set of years when, in fact, cities were only able to provide data for slightly different sets of years. Boston data are for 1976, 1980, and 1984. New York City data are for 1970, 1975, 1980, and 1983. San Francisco data are only for 1980 and 1984. Seattle data are for 1970, 1975, 1980, and 1983. Washington, D.C., data are for 1976, 1980, and 1984. Crime rates for noncensus years were computed using an estimate of neighborhood population as the denominator. Population estimates for noncensus years were derived using the simple demographic logarithmic extrapolation/interpolation technique (Rives and Serow 1984).

## TABLE 2

### Summary Characteristics of Neighborhoods in Study

| Neighborhood | Pregentrification Character | Type of Gentrification | Initiators | Current Stage | Displacement | Community Conflict | Proximity to High-Crime Neighborhoods |
|---|---|---|---|---|---|---|---|
| North End, Boston | Working class; ethnic; Italian | Residential | Real estate and condos developed | Early | Little so far | Very little | Distant |
| South End, Boston | Very poor; rooming-house district | Residential | Gays; bohemians; young professionals; black; middle class | Advanced, though still polyglot, area | Extensive relocation to public housing in neighborhood | Extensive | Near |
| East Village, New York | Very poor; Hispanic and black | Residential and commercial | Artists | Early | Unknown | Extensive | Near |
| West Village, New York | Stable lower-middle class | Commercial and residential; gay influence | Gays | Advanced | Little | Little | Distant |
| Upper West Side, New York | Moderate and low income; mixed residential | Commercial and residential | Redevelopment of Lincoln Center | Advanced | Extensive | Moderate | Near |
| Park Slope, Brooklyn | Low income; mixed residential | Residential | Both family and nonfamily households | Advanced | Extensive | Little | Near |

| | | | | | | | |
|---|---|---|---|---|---|---|---|
| Haight-Ashbury, San Francisco | Declining residue of "hippie"era | Mostly residential | Young professionals | Early | Unknown | No | Near |
| Eureka Valley, San Francisco | Lower-middle class; ethnic; Italian | Commercial and residential | Gays | Advanced | Unknown | Some | Near |
| Capitol Hill, Seattle | Bohemian; mixed | Commercial and residential | Gays; bohemians; commercial developers | Advanced | Moderate | Extensive | Distant |
| Madrona, Seattle | Poor; racially mixed | Residential | Young professionals; black middle-class; neighborhood incumbents | Intermediate | Moderate | Little | Distant |
| Downtown, Seattle | Declining; waterfront; commercial | Commercial | Commercial developers | Intermediate | Nil | None | Near |
| Mount Pleasant, Washington, D.C. | Poor; predominantly black | Residential | Young professionals; black middle-class; neighborhood incumbents | Advanced | Extensive | Little | Near |
| Dupont Circle, Washington, D.C. | Mixed poor black; commercial and institutional | Commercial and residential | Gays; young professionals | Advanced | Extensive | Little | Near |
| Capitol Hill, Washington, D.C. | Poor; predominantly black | Residential | Young professionals | Advanced | Extensive | Little | Near |

## TABLE 3

### Crime Rates in Selected Cities and Neighborhoods, 1970–84

| | Personal Crime[a] | | | | Property Crime[b] | | | | Total Index Crime[c] | | | |
|---|---|---|---|---|---|---|---|---|---|---|---|---|
| City/Community | 1970 | 1975 | 1980 | 1984 | 1970 | 1975 | 1980 | 1984 | 1970 | 1975 | 1980 | 1984 |
| Boston: | | | | | | | | | | | | |
| Citywide | N.A. | 21.69 | 28.91 | 26.91 | N.A. | 113.78 | 116.85 | 102.50 | N.A. | 130.36 | 139.45 | 122.50 |
| North End | N.A. | 12.02 | 15.77 | 14.21 | N.A. | 228.13 | 256.32 | 169.14 | N.A. | 240.15 | 272.09 | 183.34 |
| South End | N.A. | 124.16 | 105.23 | 68.27 | N.A. | 315.72 | 317.82 | 237.24 | N.A. | 439.88 | 423.06 | 305.51 |
| New York City: | | | | | | | | | | | | |
| Citywide | 12.13 | 15.58 | 18.87 | 16.98 | 43.61 | 44.83 | 64.52 | 58.56 | 61.96 | 65.91 | 88.47 | 80.42 |
| East Village | 37.34 | 47.60 | 52.98 | 50.51 | 82.14 | 72.80 | 102.87 | 108.17 | 138.28 | 139.71 | 174.04 | 181.70 |
| West Village | 19.55 | 20.68 | 28.16 | 18.43 | 100.70 | 70.26 | 109.83 | 111.63 | 128.33 | 96.90 | 144.61 | 134.20 |
| Upper West Side | 18.67 | 19.98 | 19.35 | 12.59 | 64.36 | 58.46 | 88.71 | 83.79 | 94.52 | 84.49 | 110.95 | 97.80 |
| Park Slope | 56.03 | 65.57 | 89.35 | 75.93 | 125.40 | 144.65 | 204.38 | 166.64 | 213.35 | 235.49 | 314.06 | 259.96 |
| San Francisco: | | | | | | | | | | | | |
| Citywide | N.A. | N.A. | 17.99 | 17.11 | N.A. | N.A. | 79.37 | 78.07 | N.A. | N.A. | 98.03 | 94.60 |
| Haight-Ashbury | N.A. | N.A. | 31.12 | 24.96 | N.A. | N.A. | 105.67 | 121.65 | N.A. | N.A. | 136.79 | 146.61 |
| Eureka Valley | N.A. | N.A. | 27.50 | 19.71 | N.A. | N.A. | 98.85 | 107.39 | N.A. | N.A. | 126.36 | 127.10 |
| Seattle: | | | | | | | | | | | | |
| Citywide | 5.98 | 7.81 | 10.53 | 9.97 | 77.62 | 82.30 | 97.38 | 101.64 | 89.58 | 96.68 | 107.92 | 110.41 |
| Capitol Hill | 20.72 | 22.80 | 21.87 | 21.77 | 120.39 | 124.30 | 171.45 | 190.00 | 295.64 | 307.26 | 386.64 | 423.64 |
| Madrona | 15.78 | 16.04 | 17.78 | 15.47 | 90.47 | 74.43 | 84.19 | 108.70 | 122.25 | 101.79 | 101.97 | 125.14 |
| Downtown | 86.19 | 78.38 | 145.17 | 127.04 | 951.10 | 1243.58 | 1057.47 | 1031.35 | 1094.34 | 1400.35 | 1202.64 | 1163.07 |
| Washington, D.C.: | | | | | | | | | | | | |
| Citywide | N.A. | 15.22 | 20.35 | 19.68 | N.A. | 57.56 | 81.10 | 75.57 | N.A. | 73.15 | 102.03 | 95.86 |
| Mount Pleasant | N.A. | 17.18 | 21.06 | 21.73 | N.A. | 58.75 | 68.79 | 71.31 | N.A. | 75.93 | 102.32 | 108.89 |
| Dupont Circle | N.A. | 25.04 | 32.12 | 29.47 | N.A. | 145.40 | 241.10 | 203.67 | N.A. | 170.44 | 299.05 | 262.98 |
| Capitol Hill | N.A. | 26.11 | 40.58 | 30.85 | N.A. | 70.69 | 132.58 | 95.64 | N.A. | 96.79 | 201.48 | 142.88 |

NOTE.—Crime rates are expressed as crimes per 1,000 population.

[a] Includes homicide, rape, robbery, and aggravated assault.

[b] Includes burglary, theft, and auto theft.

[c] Includes both personal and property crimes.

where gentrification brought population growth of nearly 30 percent; Seattle's Downtown, which grew by 16 percent; and the West Village, which grew by about 5 percent during the decade.) Under conditions of population decline, a constant incidence of crimes would yield an increased crime rate. Thus in most of these study neighborhoods the demographic forces of population decline favored increases in per capita crime rates.

The first thing that is striking about table 3 is that all these gentrified neighborhoods have total Index crime rates above the averages for their respective cities. In some cases, such as the South End, the East Village, and Seattle's Capitol Hill and Downtown districts, the total crime rates are substantially higher than the citywide averages. Only in Madrona and Mount Pleasant do the neighborhood Index crime rates approach the citywide rates. On closer inspection one sees that the pattern of higher crime rates in gentrified neighborhoods generally holds true both for personal crimes and for property crimes. Exceptions to this pattern, at least for some reported years, can be found in the personal crime rates of the North End of Boston and the Upper West Side of New York and in the property crime rates of Seattle's Madrona neighborhood and Mount Pleasant in Washington, D.C. In general, however, at any given point in time gentrified neighborhoods appear to be less safe than the "average" neighborhoods in their cities.

On the evidence presented in table 3 it is safe to say that, whatever effect gentrification has on crime rates, it is not a linear effect. Nearly all the city- and neighborhood-level time series rise to a terrifying crescendo in 1980 before falling back somewhat in the latest reported year. Thus one's judgment about gentrification's effect on crime rates will be seriously affected by the time frame one employs. The longer one's time horizon, the more pessimistic are one's conclusions. Compared to their 1970 or 1975 rates, only four neighborhoods experienced a decline in personal crime rates (West Village, Upper West Side, South End, and Madrona), and most of these declines were slight. And before their late decline, the personal crime rates rose during intervening years in all neighborhoods except the South End. Applying a similar yardstick to property crimes and to total Index crimes, one finds long-term declines in crime rates only in the Boston neighborhoods of the North End and the South End. By contrast, if one considers only the 1980–84 period, much happier conclusions are in store. Every neighborhood experienced a decline in its personal crime rates between 1980 and 1984; half of the total sample of neighborhoods enjoyed similar declines in their property crime rates in the 1980s, and total Index crime rates declined during the period in eight of the fourteen neighborhoods.

Of course, in all cities except Seattle, the citywide crime rates followed the same general pattern of rising during the 1970s and retreating during the 1980s. Thus it is useful to evaluate each neighborhood's crime trends in its citywide context. Table 4 does this by recasting the data from table 3 so that each neighborhood's crime rates appear as ratios to their citywide rates for that year.

Table 4 brings the patterns into sharper relief. Even controlling for citywide trends, gentrification appears to have significantly reduced personal crimes from 1970 or 1975 levels in six of the study neighborhoods: South End, West Village, Upper West Side, and all three Seattle neighborhoods. More modest declines can be seen in all other neighborhoods except Mount Pleasant. Furthermore, personal crime rates declined appreciably in both San Francisco neighborhoods, for which only more recent data were available; this suggests that, were a longer time series available for those neighborhoods, it might well reveal similar patterns of long-term decline. Among the neighborhoods that were blessed with deeper longitudinal data, the decline in personal crime rates was palpable regardless of whether the gentrification was residential or commercial in nature. This amelioration affected equally the neighborhoods that endured conflict and displacement and the neighborhoods in which the transitions had been pacific; it also showed equanimity toward both neighborhoods that border ungentrified poor districts and those that do not. Happily, the biggest improvements came to the neighborhoods that had been the most dangerous, relative to their citywide averages. Among the neighborhoods in which gentrification began in the 1960s or early 1970s and developed to advanced stages by 1984, only Park Slope showed no substantial reduction in personal crime rates.

Gentrification's effect on property crime rates is less clear. Only one neighborhood registered a significant, stable, long-term decline in its property crime rate—Seattle's Downtown. Other neighborhoods registered modest improvements, particularly in the 1980–84 period; these improvements touched both the North End and the South End in Boston, Park Slope in Brooklyn, and the Washington, D.C., neighborhood of Mount Pleasant. However, gentrification seems to have visited higher property crime rates on the residential neighborhoods of Seattle and San Francisco as well as on the East Village and the Upper West

TABLE 4

Crime Rates of Selected Neighborhoods, Indexed to the Crime Rates of Their Cities, 1970–84

| | Personal Crime[a] | | | | Property Crime[b] | | | | Total Index Crime[c] | | | |
|---|---|---|---|---|---|---|---|---|---|---|---|---|
| City/Community | 1970 | 1975 | 1980 | 1984 | 1970 | 1975 | 1980 | 1984 | 1970 | 1975 | 1980 | 1984 |
| Boston: | | | | | | | | | | | | |
| North End | N.A. | .55 | .55 | .53 | N.A. | 2.01 | 2.19 | 1.65 | N.A. | 1.84 | 1.95 | 1.50 |
| South End | N.A. | 5.72 | 3.64 | 2.54 | N.A. | 2.77 | 2.72 | 2.31 | N.A. | 3.37 | 3.03 | 2.49 |
| New York City: | | | | | | | | | | | | |
| East Village | 3.08 | 3.06 | 2.81 | 2.97 | 1.88 | 1.62 | 1.59 | 1.85 | 2.23 | 2.12 | 1.97 | 2.26 |
| West Village | 1.61 | 1.33 | 1.49 | 1.09 | 2.31 | 1.57 | 1.70 | 1.91 | 2.07 | 1.47 | 1.63 | 1.67 |
| Upper West Side | 1.54 | 1.28 | 1.03 | .74 | 1.48 | 1.30 | 1.37 | 1.43 | 1.53 | 1.28 | 1.25 | 1.22 |
| Park Slope | 4.62 | 4.21 | 4.74 | 4.47 | 2.88 | 3.23 | 3.17 | 2.85 | 3.44 | 3.57 | 3.55 | 3.23 |
| San Francisco: | | | | | | | | | | | | |
| Haight-Ashbury | N.A. | N.A. | 1.73 | 1.46 | N.A. | N.A. | 1.33 | 1.56 | N.A. | N.A. | 1.40 | 1.55 |
| Eureka Valley | N.A. | N.A. | 1.53 | 1.15 | N.A. | N.A. | 1.25 | 1.38 | N.A. | N.A. | 1.29 | 1.39 |
| Seattle: | | | | | | | | | | | | |
| Capitol Hill | 3.47 | 2.92 | 2.08 | 2.18 | 1.55 | 1.51 | 1.76 | 1.87 | 3.30 | 3.18 | 3.58 | 3.84 |
| Madrona | 2.64 | 2.05 | 1.69 | 1.55 | 1.17 | .90 | .86 | 1.07 | 1.36 | 1.05 | .94 | 1.13 |
| Downtown | 14.42 | 10.04 | 13.78 | 12.74 | 12.25 | 15.11 | 10.86 | 10.15 | 12.22 | 14.48 | 11.14 | 10.53 |
| Washington, D.C.: | | | | | | | | | | | | |
| Mount Pleasant | N.A. | 1.13 | 1.03 | 1.14 | N.A. | 1.02 | .85 | .94 | N.A. | 1.04 | 1.00 | 1.14 |
| Dupont Circle | N.A. | 1.65 | 1.58 | 1.50 | N.A. | 2.53 | 2.97 | 2.70 | N.A. | 2.33 | 2.93 | 2.74 |
| Capitol Hill | N.A. | 1.72 | 1.99 | 1.57 | N.A. | 1.23 | 1.63 | 1.27 | N.A. | 1.32 | 1.97 | 1.49 |

NOTE.—Index is created by dividing specific neighborhood crime rates by the comparable citywide rate; thus coefficients greater than one indicate higher-than-average crime rates per 1,000 population, and coefficients less than one indicate the opposite.

[a] Includes homicide, rape, robbery, and aggravated assault.

[b] Includes burglary, theft, and auto theft.

[c] Includes both personal and property crimes.

Side of New York. At first blush the examples of Seattle's Downtown and of Dupont Circle might make it appear that high levels of commercial gentrification help to protect neighborhoods against rising rates of property crime. However, this theory does not withstand closer scrutiny since commercial gentrification did not serve to protect the Upper West Side or Seattle's Capitol Hill. Nor can commercial gentrification explain the modest improvements in the Boston and Brooklyn neighborhoods. Alas, the other variations in neighborhood characteristics summarized in table 2 cast no further light on this puzzle. Given criminological research that indicates that middle-class people are more likely than are poor people to report property crimes, one might naturally expect these official statistics (of reported crime) to increase as the middle class moves into these neighborhoods. However, the neighborhoods that absorbed their largest influxes of middle-class people during the 1970s (e.g., Upper West Side) should, by 1984, have begun registering improvements in their property crime rates—if, indeed, gentrification serves to reduce those rates. On the basis of the data collected here, there seems to be little evidence to support such a claim—and what evidence does exist remains painfully weak.

As noted earlier, the populations of these neighborhoods were changing throughout the period covered by this study. For the most part, populations were declining, though the South End, Seattle's Downtown Capitol Hill, and the West Village all saw some population growth during the period. This analysis of crime trends has thus far relied on per capita crime statistics, statistics that are potentially sensitive to shifts in population. Though it is unlikely that these population shifts would seriously distort the findings, it is clear that per capita rates can overstate and understate the "dangerousness" of particular neighborhoods. Perhaps the clearest example of this in the present study is Seattle's Downtown, a sparsely populated district that nevertheless has an enormous daytime (workday) population. Per capita crime statistics for this neighborhood, based as they are on the census's count of full-time residents, make it appear to be far more treacherous than in reality it is. A different type of distortion arises from the differing population densities of neighborhoods. For example, New York's West Village, composed of row houses rather than of large apartment buildings, has by Manhattan standards a comparatively low density. By contrast, the tenements and projects of the East Village are far more densely packed, and as a result the East Village's population is considerably larger than the West Village's. In absolute terms, crimes occur more frequently in the East Village than in the West Village, but in per capita terms the West Village looks nearly equally dangerous. Perhaps the ideal statistics for analyses of this type might be "crimes per square mile," or some other geographically based measure; however, such statistics would be very difficult to compute given existing reporting procedures. It is possible, however, to calculate, as table 5 does, whether the neighborhoods in this study have increased or decreased their shares of their respective cities' crimes. Statistics of this sort have their own biases, of course, since larger neighborhoods naturally take larger shares. However, this alternative perspective allows the analyst to remove possible population-based distortions from the analysis.

The "share indexes" of table 5 echo the per capita findings in most respects. Personal crime rates dropped in almost all gentrified neighborhoods. The major exception here is Seattle's Downtown district, a neighborhood that, from the per capita perspective, had experienced a substantial decline in personal crimes. Apparently, that optimistic finding was unduly influenced by the neighborhood's population growth since, indeed, Downtown increased its share of the city's personal crimes. Similarly, table 5 puts the South End's "successful" battle against property crimes in a less favorable light by showing that the neighborhood actually increased its share of such crimes within Boston; here, too, the per capita statistics could be misleadingly optimistic for this neighborhood that grew by more than 30 percent during the fourteen years covered by this study. In general, however, the picture that emerges from the two alternative approaches is much the same: gentrification appears to reduce a neighborhood's personal crime rates but to have little clear-cut effect on its property crime rates.

It is of course possible that this convergence of neighborhood and citywide crime rates represents nothing more than yet another example of the statistical law of "regression toward the mean." From this perspective, neighborhoods with higher-than-average crime rates would, over a period of time, naturally move toward their citywide averages regardless of whether gentrification was taking place. This argument would seem to gain support from our discovery that the neighborhoods whose crime rates deviated most widely from their citywide averages (e.g., the South End and Seattle's Capitol Hill and Downtown districts) tended to be the neighborhoods that made the greatest progress in reducing their crime rates; on the other hand, both Park Slope and the East Village also began with crime rates substantially higher than New York City's average, and neither were blessed with a similar "regres-

TABLE 5

Share Index: Percentage of Citywide Crimes Reported in Selected Neighborhoods, 1970–84

| | Personal Crime[a] | | | | Property Crime[b] | | | | Total Index Crime[c] | | | |
|---|---|---|---|---|---|---|---|---|---|---|---|---|
| City/Community | 1970 | 1975 | 1980 | 1984 | 1970 | 1975 | 1980 | 1984 | 1970 | 1975 | 1980 | 1984 |
| Boston: | | | | | | | | | | | | |
| North End | N.A. | .69 | .68 | .65 | N.A. | 2.50 | 2.74 | 2.04 | N.A. | 2.30 | 2.44 | 1.85 |
| South End | N.A. | 6.08 | 4.57 | 3.72 | N.A. | 2.95 | 3.42 | 3.39 | N.A. | 3.58 | 3.81 | 3.66 |
| New York City: | | | | | | | | | | | | |
| East Village | .55 | .58 | .43 | .41 | 6.20 | 3.77 | 3.87 | 4.19 | 2.04 | 1.91 | 2.43 | 2.45 |
| West Village | .24 | .26 | .29 | .22 | 6.25 | 3.73 | 5.28 | 6.32 | 1.55 | 1.36 | 2.58 | 2.64 |
| Upper West Side | .36 | .38 | .28 | .21 | 6.28 | 4.65 | 6.11 | 6.59 | 1.80 | 1.77 | 2.84 | 2.68 |
| Park Slope | .25 | .26 | .25 | .23 | 2.83 | 2.42 | 2.68 | 2.36 | .94 | 1.04 | 1.53 | 1.28 |
| San Francisco: | | | | | | | | | | | | |
| Haight-Ashbury | N.A. | N.A. | 2.44 | 2.01 | N.A. | N.A. | 1.88 | 2.15 | N.A. | N.A. | 1.97 | 2.14 |
| Eureka Valley | N.A. | N.A. | 3.73 | 2.75 | N.A. | N.A. | 3.04 | 3.28 | N.A. | N.A. | 3.15 | 3.21 |
| Seattle: | | | | | | | | | | | | |
| Capitol Hill | 5.45 | 4.75 | 3.50 | 3.76 | 2.44 | 2.46 | 2.97 | 3.22 | 5.19 | 5.17 | 6.04 | 6.60 |
| Madrona | 6.97 | 5.35 | 4.35 | 3.97 | 3.08 | 2.36 | 2.22 | 2.73 | 3.60 | 2.74 | 2.43 | 2.90 |
| Downtown | 11.00 | 9.08 | 13.11 | 12.95 | 9.35 | 13.67 | 10.33 | 10.31 | 9.32 | 13.10 | 10.60 | 10.71 |
| Washington, D.C.: | | | | | | | | | | | | |
| Mount Pleasant | N.A. | 1.67 | 1.61 | 1.70 | N.A. | 1.51 | 1.32 | 1.45 | N.A. | 1.54 | 1.56 | 1.75 |
| Dupont Circle | N.A. | 2.19 | 2.16 | 2.00 | N.A. | 3.37 | 4.07 | 3.60 | N.A. | 3.11 | 4.01 | 3.67 |
| Capitol Hill | N.A. | 1.64 | 1.76 | 1.34 | N.A. | 1.18 | 1.44 | 1.08 | N.A. | 1.27 | 1.74 | 1.27 |

[a] Includes homicide, rape, robbery, and aggravated assault.
[b] Includes burglary, theft, and auto theft.
[c] Includes both personal and property crimes.

sion." To resolve this causal issue one would need comparable time-series data on the crime rates of both gentrifying and nongentrifying neighborhoods—data that are beyond the scope of this rather limited, exploratory inquiry.

While it would be foolish to dismiss the explanatory power of the regression argument, it seems unlikely that it could account for all of the reductions in neighborhood crime rates observed here. It has long been known that crime is distributed unevenly across the urban landscape. Most of our explanations for this differentiation derive from the human ecology models developed by the "Chicago School" in the early decades of this century. These models, based on an essentially biological metaphor, posit that through continuing cycles of invasion and succession most areas close to the central business district continually "filter downward" as more noxious land uses drive out the less noxious ones. This classical model explains the mechanisms of urban decay, but it does not anticipate any ultimate "regression toward the mean" whereby declining neighborhoods eventually recover. Gentrification might be viewed as an example of the classical model stood on its head: cycles of invasion and succession (i.e., gentrification and displacement) lead to "reverse filtering" in which urban neighborhoods improve, investment is encouraged, land uses ameliorate, crime rates fall, and so forth. In this sense, gentrification could be the engine, the mechanism of a neighborhood's regression toward the mean. Yet there is nothing to suggest that neighborhoods are predestined to undergo gentrification. Indeed, the sad experience of the South Bronx (to name only one notorious example) would suggest that whole neighborhoods can decline to such extremes that recovery is virtually unimaginable. If all urban neighborhoods, gentrified and otherwise, eventually move toward crime rates typical of their citywide averages, then gentrification would appear to be nothing more than a style—a single exemplary, but not exclusive, path for neighborhood recovery. If, on the other hand, *only* those neighborhoods undergoing gentrification and reinvestment manage to "regress" toward their citywide crime averages, then the regression itself does not really explain very much. Indeed, by implying a determinism that may not be justified, the regression argument may mystify and obscure rather than illuminate the key causal processes. Hopefully, future research will gather the more comprehensive neighborhood data necessary to resolve this issue.

All this of course begs the question of how these trends affect the crime rates in *other* neighborhoods. Just as even the displaced poor must live somewhere, the displaced criminals must also move on to find new targets. Nowhere does this seem to be as transparently true as in New York City, where periodic campaigns to clean up one district (e.g., Times Square and Union Square) visit disaster on other districts. Again, examination of this issue would require more complete neighborhood-level data than were gathered for this study. A truly comprehensive study of the effects of gentrification upon crime rates and criminal behavior would need to examine the entire ecological balance of larger parts of the urban landscape. If it is indeed true that urban crime is something of a zero-sum game, then one neighborhood's boon may merely be another's bane. In such a light, gentrification would affect only the distribution of crime, not its absolute levels. Accordingly, from the policy perspective, gentrification and housing policy would ultimately come to appear irrelevant to urban crime problems.

The data presented here are more suggestive than conclusive. The indications that gentrification may reduce rates of personal crime should be assessed with larger samples of neighborhoods. Indeed, with substantially more than fourteen cases, one could buy enough degrees of freedom to test with some statistical rigor the hypotheses explored here. Future research could also profit from better information on the incidence of the "lesser" crimes—misdemeanors, vandalism, prostitution, and the like—activities that might signal to criminals the potential impunity offered by the neighborhood. Similarly, the ideal study of gentrification and crime would obtain better data on the processes by which the neighborhoods change—the level of conflict, the degree of displacement, and, most important, the rate at which the transformation takes place. Given the limitations of the case-study literature and the infrequency of national censuses, future research will probably find this a challenging goal; nevertheless, it is worth pursuing.

Caveats aside, it still seems clear that gentrification is altering the traditional patterns of "downward filtering" that have long characterized urban development and that this, in turn, offers new hope for safer, more civilized, and less predatory central city environments. Yet it would be a mistake to cast gentrification as the new savior of our central cities—for gentrification itself may prove to be only a transitory respite from the long-term trends of urban decline. Those neighborhoods that have been settled by particular subcultures (gays, artists, and so on) may enjoy some modicum of stability because the subcultures themselves may reinforce commitments to stay in the central city neighborhoods. However, neighborhoods that have been settled by more diffuse groups of young urban professionals and cohabiting or childless couples may again find themselves victims of the traditional patterns of life-cycle-driven housing demand; that is to say, many such couples may, on arriving at the thresholds of marriage and parenthood, opt for the safer, more bucolic, and more familistic suburbs. For the moment they can probably be quickly replaced by other, young urban professionals and childless couples. However, by the time the youngest members of the enormous generation born in the postwar baby boom reach their thirties (i.e., in the mid-1990s), demand for central city housing may again slacken. The single study that tried to assess the future effects of such life-cycle shifts on a gentrified neighborhood concluded that they posed little threat to the stability of the neighborhood's housing demand; the neighborhood, however, was one in which gays had played a significant role in the gentrification process (McDonald 1983). In other neighborhoods the story could be quite different.

Moreover, crime itself may dampen the prospects for gentrified neighborhoods regardless of improvements in fundamental crime rates. The data presented here suggest that most gentrified neighborhoods still have crime rates well above their citywide averages. Even the "risk-oblivious" individuals who move into these high-crime neighborhoods may grow to be more averse to risk as they age and as they make deeper investments into their properties. Those who cavalierly dismissed warnings about the dangers lurking in these city neighborhoods may treat the warnings far more soberly after being mugged or burglarized (or after hearing of similar misfortunes among neighbors). On the testimony of the case-study literature, crime remains foremost among the concerns of the gentry. Numerous studies have shown that the in-migrants to these neighborhoods value police protection over all other neighborhood services, a clear indication that the threat of crime is ever on their minds. My own detailed study of the South End (McDonald 1983) suggested that worry about crime was the single reason that could prompt an otherwise very committed group of homeowners to abandon their urban neighborhood in favor of safer, more suburban environments. One particularly perceptive South End home buyer characterized crime in the neighborhood as "low-level noise, quite like an air conditioner or traffic—noise that you get used to but that you never lose track of. I hear that noise whenever I have to decide whether I *really* want that carton of milk from the all-night market on the corner, whenever I barricade myself behind these door locks, whenever I hear the approach of footsteps from behind me." Noise of that sort slowly undermines people's affection for their neighborhood. Even if the noise hums at a constant decibel level, it may slowly wear on residents, fatiguing them and straining their attachments to the neighborhood. If the volume of the noise rises so that fear roars on every corner, even the heartiest of the "urban pioneers" will have second thoughts about staying.

Thus, though this study has suggested that gentrification tends at least to have some salutary effect on personal crime rates, crime *itself* serves as a feedback mechanism to deter the stability of the gentrification process. On the basis of the limited evidence presented here, there is at least some cause for optimism that the forces pushing the resurgence of central city housing markets are stronger than the forces deterring it; but the balance is often delicate, and the outcome is never predetermined.

## APPENDIX

### TABLE A1

Census Tract and Police Reporting Areas Used to Define the Boundaries of Each of the Neighborhoods in the Study

| Neighborhood | Census Tracts | Police Areas |
|---|---|---|
| Boston: | | |
| North End | 301, 304, 305 | 79–91 |
| South End | 706, 707, 708 | 147–160, 163, 164, 166, 168, 170 |
| New York City: | | |
| East Village | 20, 22.02, 26.01, 26.02, 28, 30.02, 32, 34, 36.02, 38, 40, 42 | 9 |
| West Village | 55.01, 55.02, 57, 59, 61, 63, 65, 67, 69, 71, 73, 75, 77, 79 | 6 |
| Upper West Side | 145, 147, 149, 153, 155, 157, 159, 161, 163, 165, 169, 171 | 20 |
| Park Slope | 155, 157, 159, 165 | 78 |
| San Francisco: | | |
| Haight-Ashbury | 165, 166 | 264, 266, 502, 506 |
| Eureka Valley | 169, 170, 203, 205, 206 | 528, 530, 532, 546, 548 |
| Seattle: | | |
| Capitol Hill | 75, 76 | 110, 111 |
| Madrona | 77, 78, 88 | 100, 101, 102 |
| Downtown | 81, 82 | 130, 131 |
| Washington, D.C.: | | |
| Mount Pleasant | 27.01, 27.02 | 271, 272 |
| Dupont Circle | 42.2, 53.1, 53.2 | 422, 531, 532 |
| Capitol Hill | 66, 67 | 660, 670 |

## REFERENCES

Auger, Deborah. 1979. "The Politics of Revitalization in Gentrifying Neighborhoods: A Case of Boston's South End." *Journal of the American Planning Association* 45(4):515–22.

Berry, Brian J. L. 1976. "The Counterurbanization Process: Urban America since 1970." In *Urbanization and Counterurbanization*, edited by Brian J. L. Berry. Urban Affairs Annual Review, vol. 11. Beverly Hills, Calif.: Sage.

Berry, Brian J. L., and Yehoshua Cohen. 1973. "Decentralization of Commerce and Industry: The Restructuring of Metropolitan America." In *The Urbanization of the Suburbs*, edited by Louis Mazotti and Jeffrey Hadden. Urban Affairs Annual Review, vol. 7. Beverly Hills, Calif.: Sage.

Berry, Brian J. L., and John Kasarda. 1977. *Contemporary Urban Ecology*. New York: Macmillan.

Black, J. Thomas. 1979. "Central City Investment Activity." Working Paper no. 1. Chicago: Urban Land Institute, May 1979.

Blau, Judith R., and Peter M. Blau. 1982. "The Cost of Inequality: Metropolitan Structure and Violent Crime." *American Sociological Review* 47:114–29.

Cicin-Sain, Biliana. 1980. "The Costs and Benefits of Neighborhood Revitalization." In *Urban Revitalization*, edited by Donald B. Rosenthal. Urban Affairs Annual Review, vol. 18. Beverly Hills, Calif.: Sage.

Clay, Phillip. 1979. *Neighborhood Renewal: Middle Class Resettlement and Incumbent Upgrading in American Neighborhoods*. Lexington, Mass.: Lexington.

Gale, Dennis. 1976. "The Back to the City Movement . . . or Is It? A Survey of Recent Homebuyers to the Mount Pleasant Neighborhood of Washington, D.C." Occasional Paper Series. Washington, D.C.: George Washington University, Department of Urban and Regional Planning, September.

———. 1979. "Middle Class Resettlement in Older Urban Areas." *Journal of the American Planning Association* 45(3):293–304.

———. 1984. *Neighborhood Revitalization and the Postindustrial City*. Lexington, Mass.: Lexington.

Goetze, Rolf. 1979. *Understanding Neighborhood Change: The Role of Expectations in Urban Revitalization*. Cambridge, Mass.: Ballinger.

Grebler, Leo, and Frank G. Mittlebach. 1979. *The Inflation of Housing Prices*. Lexington, Mass.: Lexington.

Hartman, Chester. 1979. "Comment on 'Neighborhood Revitalization and Displacement: A Review of the Evidence' by Sumka." *Journal of the American Planning Association* 45(4):488–90.

Hodge, David C. 1980. "Inner-City Revitalization as a Challenge to Diversity? Seattle." In *Back to the City: Issues in Neighborhood Renovation*, edited by Shirley Broadway Laska and Daphne Spain. New York: Pergamon.

Kasarda, John. 1976. "The Changing Occupational Structure of the American Metropolis: Apropos the Urban Problem." In *The Changing Face of the Suburbs*, edited by Barry Schwartz. Chicago: University of Chicago Press.

Laska, Shirley Broadway, and Daphne Spain. 1980. "Anticipating Renovators' Demands: New Orleans." In *Back to the City: Issues in Neighborhood Renovation*, edited by Shirley Broadway Laska and Daphne Spain. New York: Pergamon.

Leach, Valerie. 1978. "Upfiltering and Neighborhood Change in the Madrona Area of Seattle, Washington." Master's thesis, University of Washington.

Levy, Paul R., and Roman A. Cybriwsky. 1980. "The Hidden Dimensions of Culture and Class: Philadelphia." In *Back to the City: Issues in Neighborhood Renovation*, edited by Shirley Broadway Laska and Daphne Spain. New York: Pergamon.

Lipton, S. Gregory. 1980. "Evidence of Central City Revival." In *Back to the City: Issues in Neighborhood Renovation*, edited by Shirley Broadway Laska and Daphne Spain. New York: Pergamon.

Lynch, Kevin. 1960. *The Image of the City*. Cambridge, Mass.: MIT Press.

McDonald, Scott Cameron. 1983. "Human and Market Dynamics in the Gentrification of a Boston Neighborhood." Ph.D. dissertation, Harvard University.

Muller, Thomas, Carol Sobel, and Susan Dujack. 1980. *The Urban Household in the 1970s—a Demographic and Economic Perspective*. Washington, D.C.: Urban Institute, April.

Muth, Richard F. 1969. *Cities and Housing*. Chicago: University of Chicago Press.

New York Department of City Planning. 1984. *Private Reinvestment and Neighborhood Change*. New York: New York City Department of City Planning, March.

Pattison, Timothy. 1977. "The Process of Neighborhood Upgrading and Gentrification." Master's thesis, Massachusetts Institute of Technology.

Peterson, Paul. 1981. *City Limits*. Chicago: University of Chicago Press.

Pettigrew, Thomas. 1980. "Racial Change and Intrametropolitan Distribution of Black Americans." In *The Prospective City*, edited by Arthur P. Solomon. Cambridge, Mass.: MIT Press.

Rives, Norfleet W., and William J. Serow. 1984. *Introduction to Applied Demography: Data Sources and Estimation Techniques*. Sage Series on Quantitative Applications in the Social Sciences. Beverly Hills, Calif.: Sage.

Schill, Michael H., and Richard P. Nathan. 1983. *Revitalizing America's Cities: Neighborhood Reinvestment and Displacement*. Albany: State University of New York Press.

Schnore, Leo. 1972. *Class and Race in Cities and Suburbs*. Chicago: Markham.

Segal, David. 1980. "A Model to Forecast Neighborhood Change: The Example of New York City." Unpublished manuscript. Harvard University, Department of City and Regional Planning.

Skogan, Wesley G. In this volume. "Fear of Crime and Neighborhood Change."

Smith, Neil. 1979. "Toward a Theory of Gentrification: A Back-to-the-City Movement by Capital, Not People." *Journal of the American Planning Association* 45(4):538–48.

Spain, Daphne. 1980. "Indicators of Urban Revitalization: Racial and Socioeconomic Changes in Central-City Housing." In *Back to the City: Issues in Neighborhood Renovation*, edited by Shirley Broadway Laska and Daphne Spain. New York: Pergamon.

Sternlieb, George S., and J. W. Hughes. 1980. "Back to the Central City: Myths and Realities." In *America's Housing: Prospects and Problems*, edited by George Sternlieb and James Hughes. New Brunswick, N.J.: Rutgers University Press.

Taub, Richard B., D. Garth Taylor, and Jan D. Dunham. 1984. *Paths of Neighborhood Change: Race and Crime in Urban America*. Chicago: University of Chicago Press.

*Wesley Skogan*

# Fear of Crime and Neighborhood Change

ABSTRACT

Crime rates and the quality of life do not necessarily change in direct response to changes in the physical and social characteristics of neighborhoods. Developments that have an indirect effect on increasing crime rates and fear of crime include neighborhood disinvestment, demolition and construction activities, demagoguery, and deindustrialization. Other factors such as government programs, collective neighborhood action, and individual initiatives and interventions help to maintain neighborhood stability. Fear of crime in declining neighborhoods does not always accurately reflect actual crime levels. It is derived from primary and secondary knowledge of neighborhood crime rates, observable evidence of physical and social disorder, and prejudices arising from changes in neighborhood ethnic composition. Regardless of its source, fear of crime may stimulate and accelerate neighborhood decline. Increasing fear of crime may cause individuals to withdraw physically and psychologically from community life. This weakens informal processes of social control that inhibit crime and disorder, and it produces a decline in the organizational life and the mobilization capacity of a neighborhood. Fear may also contribute to the deterioration of business conditions. The importation and local production of delinquency and deviance may also be influenced by perceptions of neighborhood crime rates. Changes in the composition of the resident population may be stimulated by the cumulative effects of fear. Fear of crime does not inevitably encourage or result in urban decline as "gentrification" demonstrates.

Recent research on fear of crime and neighborhood change suggests that neighborhoods change only slowly unless "triggering" events shift them from a position of relative stability into one of demographic and

Wesley Skogan is Professor of Political Science and Urban Affairs at Northwestern University.


0-226-80802-5/86/0008-0006$01.00

economic flux. Those precipitating events include disinvestment, demolition, and demagoguery plus regional and national economic forces. Once areas begin to decline, "feedback" processes can take command of neighborhood conditions. Problems such as crime, physical deterioration, and social disorder emerge. Resulting increases in fear of crime in turn undermine the capacity of the community to deal with its problems. Fear stimulates withdrawal from the community, weakens informal social control mechanisms, contributes to the declining mobilization capacity of the neighborhood, speeds changes in local business conditions, and stimulates further delinquency and disorder. These problems feed on themselves, spiraling neighborhoods deeper into decline. There is evidence that some areas can break out of this downward spiral, and the examples illustrate the place of crime among the factors that determine a neighborhood's eventual fate. However, there is little evidence that those hard-won victories are common, and in the aggregate the effect of fear on the fabric of American society has been very consequential.

The dynamic aspects of this theory largely are hypothetical, for there has been virtually no research over time on fear of crime in which people are linked to their neighborhood environment. Research using census data and measures of reported crime (which are available across time) suggests that in small urban areas important changes can take place rapidly. Neighborhoods apparently can move from low- to high-crime status within a decade (Kobrin and Schuerman 1981). Fear of crime, residential commitment, and other factors that in theory provide the linkages between aspects of community change and levels of reported crime are better measured by sample surveys. However, most surveys concerning crime problems in cities or particular neighborhoods can provide only a one-time, cross-sectional view of residents' fears and intentions. Further, most of those studies have been conducted since 1965 in northern industrial cities marked by generally declining populations and shifting economic fortunes. Much less is known about crime, fear, and neighborhood change in lower-density southeastern and southwestern cities that have prospered and grown during the same period. Perhaps the small-area social *processes* that link fear and neighborhood change are similar across U.S. cities, with differences among them being confined to the *magnitude* of those problems or the number of neighborhoods affected. This is suggested by the fact that national surveys reveal about the same relations between fear and other factors as do neighborhood studies (cf. Baumer 1985). However, the generality of research on fear and neighborhood factors to cities of all types is not entirely clear.

Here is how this essay is organized. Section I discusses triggering factors that have a strong influence on neighborhood change. Declining neighborhoods offer an environment in which crime rates and levels of fear change. Neighborhood-level sources of fear of crime are the topic of Section II. In Section III, I examine the effect of fear on community life. Neighborhood decline in the urban setting is not inevitable; factors that are important to reversing the process are described in Section IV. The final section briefly examines some of the consequences of fear of crime for American society.

## I. Factors Triggering Neighborhood Decline

Although some studies of fear of crime convey suggestions for theory involving neighborhood factors and change over time (one of the most explicit being Goodstein and Shotland [1980]), few have much systematic data on these points. Moreover, most (like their "crime causes crime" model) seem to assume that a glacial, sociologically inexorable downward slide characterizes urban neighborhoods. It is more likely that the reverse is true, that residential areas are fairly stable social systems, which is why they are identifiable as "neighborhoods." At various times this stability may be upset, but old patterns persist, and generally the future resembles the past. Analytic models of stable systems feature "negative feedback loops," or sketches of mechanisms in the system that react to events, set things right, retard change, and keep most problems within bounds (Przeworski and Teune 1970). In the case of residential areas, these feedback mechanisms can include government programs, collective neighborhood action, and individual initiatives and interventions. However, when things happen that disrupt the processes by which neighborhoods continually renew themselves, real change is set off. If these changes spark feedback forces that are positive rather than negative, they stimulate further changes rather than dampen them. In such areas, one change leads to another. Systems characterized by positive feedback change rapidly. These changes do not necessarily make crime or the quality of life in those areas worse (see McDonald, in this volume), but, when they do, neighborhoods caught up in them can quickly decline.

"Stability" does not mean that things are "the same." Neighborhoods never remain the same. Even in places that on the surface appear tranquil, families move in and out, the building stock ages, and economic forces continually affect the price and demand for housing. However, if about the same number of people move into a neighborhood as move out, and if they resemble each other, the area can be counted as stable. Areas are stable if the housing stock is continually repaired and renewed and if people can sell and buy or rent homes there at prices appropriate for the structures and the social class of the residents. Stability means that the neighborhood as a social system reproduces itself.

Forces that affect the pace of this regeneration have profound consequences for the viability of communities. The inventory of events that could trigger neighborhood change is very large. Some of them are in the hands of local actors, but others are determined outside. The effect of these on crime and fear is indirect through their effect on an area's population and housing stock. Four key factors that affect neighborhood stability are described below.

*Disinvestment.* Decisions by landlords and homeowners to repair and rehabilitate their buildings are critical for maintaining the attractiveness of a neighborhood as a place to live. These decisions reflect the value and demand for housing, whether or not buildings have reached the end of their depreciable life, and if they can be sold profitably. An important factor in these calculations is institutional decisions about the viability of particular neighborhoods. When mortgaging institutions and insurance companies refuse to make reasonable purchase or construction loans or to issue policies in certain neighborhoods, this effectively "writes off" those areas (Bradford and Rubinowitz 1975; Urban-Suburban Investment Study Group 1975). "It is a sign for all that the neighborhood is 'going.' Powerful and influential interests have lost faith in it, and that stands as a warning to any home-seekers or commercial investors to look elsewhere if they have the means to do so" (Goodwin 1979, p. 60).

*Demolition and Construction.* The residential quality of neighborhoods can be severely affected by nearby land-use patterns. The freeway networks driven through the hearts of many American cities in the 1950s greatly reduced the desirability of surrounding neighborhoods. Typically, they were channeled through—and destroyed—low-income, minority neighborhoods, where land was cheaper. This forced area residents into other neighborhoods, a consequence not appreciated by those already living there (Altschuler 1965). The planning and construction activities of government often create what Bursik (in this volume) dubs "artificial neighborhoods" and upset the stability of city areas of a variety of social class levels. Concentrating high-rise public housing in a few areas has had disastrous consequences for those communities. Even locating a few community-based drug or mental health treatment centers in an area can arouse a storm of protest from residents.

*Demagoguery.* Key actors profit greatly from the fragility of urban neighborhoods. Cagey real estate agents (known as "panic peddlers") can reap enormous profits trading on fear. Stirring concern about crime and racial change, they frighten white residents into selling their homes at reduced prices; then the homes are resold at inflated prices to blacks and Hispanics desperate for better and safer housing, a practice often known as "block-busting" (Goodwin 1979). An ambitious politician seeking to build a neighborhood political base can make somewhat different use of the same raw materials.

*Deindustrialization.* Factory closings, the shift of jobs from the central city to the suburbs, a decline in the number of jobs at a particular wage and skill level, and extralocal economic trends can undermine the locational advantages of particular neighborhoods or the economic well-being of the kind of people who live there. These changes may be slow and evolutionary, but they also can be precipitous; the city of Chicago, for example, lost more than 21 percent of its manufacturing jobs between 1980 and 1983 (Exter 1985, table 2).

It should be clear that the triggering events discussed above all stem from conscious, often corporate decisions by persons in positions of power. They reflect the interests of banks, manufacturing firms, government agencies, and others with large economic and political stakes in what they do. None is individually "sociologically inexorable," although they obviously may be driven by still larger economic and demographic forces. The volitional nature of these decisions has not been lost on community organizations that have tackled redlining, blockbusting, zoning, and economic development issues, and they highlight the larger—but often invisible—political context in which studies of individual concerns about crime are set. To the extent that those concerns are driven by neighborhood conditions, they can be seen as manifestations of political decisions.

The critical role of these triggering events appears to be their effect on the number and mix of people moving into and out of a neighborhood. The engine of neighborhood change is selective out-migration from the neighborhood (Frey 1980). Few residents will want to live in an area characterized by mounting crime and fear. Measures of both are strongly related to residential dissatisfaction and the desire to move to a safer place (Droettboom et al. 1971; Kasl and Harburg 1972). However, studies of actual moving—as opposed to dissatisfaction or desire—document the harsh realities of economics and race (Duncan and Newman 1976). A comparison of "movers" and "stayers" in the Chicago metropolitan area indicates that households that left the central city were more affluent, had more education, and more often were intact nuclear families. This was despite the fact that blacks, unmarried adults, and the poor were far more likely to be fearful and unhappy with their city neighborhood. Those who moved out were "pulled" by the attractiveness of safe suburban locations as well as "pushed" by fear and other concerns (Skogan and Maxfield 1981).

Flight from neighborhoods may carry away somewhat less fearful residents, leaving those who are more fearful—but stuck there—to deal with the area's problems. A few elderly and long-time residents may remain behind after this transition because they are unwilling to move or cannot sell their homes for enough to buy another in a nicer neighborhood. They find themselves surrounded by unfamiliar people whom they did not choose to live with. Loneliness and lack of community attachment are significant sources of fear among the urban elderly (Jaycox 1978; Yin 1980), especially among women (Silverman and Kennedy 1984). Interestingly, it appears that perceived social diversity (measured by questions about whether neighbors are "the same" or "different" from the respondent) has a strong effect on fear only among the elderly (Kennedy and Silverman 1985).

Demographic changes are significant for the local housing market and even for its very physical composition. If fewer or poorer people want to move in, real estate values shift. A soft demand for housing due to the undesirability of the area can be stimulated by reducing its price and changing standards for tenant selection, but this further affects the mix of in-movers. Schuerman and Kobrin (1983) find that changes in the socioeconomic status of residents of destabilizing areas *follow* population turnover. Income-level decline probably is slowed by the inertia of initial housing prices and the nature of the housing stock. During these periods, the invasion-succession process produces a number of positive benefits for new residents. Since World War II, the flight of the better off to the suburbs, combined with generally decreasing rates of migration into northern industrial cities, allowed blacks and others who remained behind to take advantage of the softer housing market by moving into better-quality buildings in nicer neighborhoods. It was the value of the overcrowded, deteriorated tenements that *they* abandoned as rapidly as possible that was most affected by early population shifts (Frey 1984).

If residential buildings are fully depreciated for tax purposes, it can be unprofitable to maintain them adequately or even to pay the real estate and utility bills. If there is no demand for them, they may sit boarded up. The arson rate is sensitive to such calculations (Sternlieb and Burchell 1983). Urban residential fires in general are concentrated in cities sheltering the poor, unemployed, renters, minorities (Munson and Oates 1983), and where crime rates are higher (Pettiway 1983). Future investments in a neighborhood appear to be affected by a relatively low level of building abandonment, perhaps 3–6 percent (Department of Housing and Urban Development 1973). It appears that abandonment has increased as migration into many northern industrial cities has slowed to a trickle; the "way station" role historically played by the worst housing in inner-city, mixed land-use areas, which gave it continued economic value, has vanished with the disappearance of new migrants. Where there still is a demand for housing, demographic shifts can be exacerbated by changes in the use of the housing stock. One adaptation to declining real estate values is to intensify its use; large single-family homes can be cut up—often illegally—into multiple-unit dwellings. This further affects the area's demography.

If an area's crime rate mounts, it may further reduce real estate values (Frisbie et al. 1977). However, most regression-based studies of the crime-property value nexus find area-level crime rates so highly correlated with other physical and social determinants of property values that the independent effect of crime cannot be estimated. Taub, Taylor, and Dunham's (1984) survey data indicate that individuals' market evaluations and investment plans are affected by dissatisfaction with safety, perceived risk of victimization in the area, and actual victimization. Crime affects the upkeep of the neighborhood, and together the two affect perceptions that the neighborhood is going sour and the residents' desire to move away.

## II. The Effect on Fear of Neighborhood Decline

Schuerman and Kobrin's research (in this volume), using census figures and recorded crime, places demographic change near the beginning of the decay process. Land use, housing, and population changes at first lead shifts in crime rates. The consequences can stimulate even further change, including mounting levels of fear. Neighborhood-level sources of fear of crime are numerous. They include local victimization rates, rumors of nearby crimes and victims, physical deterioration, social disorder, and group conflict over the control of living space.

### A. *Victimization and Fear*

Several researchers have examined the relation between levels of crime and fear. In one Chicago study, people who reported feeling "unsafe outside after dark" were concentrated in community areas with higher rates of reported crime (Skogan and Maxfield 1981). McPherson (1978) found a general correspondence between fear and official crime rates for residents of Minneapolis. In England, people's ratings of how common various offenses are in their neighborhood rise directly with area-level victimization rates (Maxfield 1984*a*). When asked to rate the magnitude of various neighborhood problems, Chicagoans who ranked specific crimes as "big problems" in their neighborhood lived in areas with higher rates for those types of incidents. Both relations were stronger for robbery and aggravated assault than for burglary rates. However, burglary is both more frequent than personal crime and more widely dispersed, hitting high-income households as well as the poor (Bureau of Justice Statistics 1983, p. 7). As a result, it stimulates fear in more places and is responsible for "spreading it around" city and suburban areas (Skogan and Maxfield 1981).

The conclusion that people who live in crime-ridden areas are more fearful is not surprising. However, the relation is not as strong as might be expected. There are other sources of fear. Women and the elderly report higher levels of fear and fear-related behaviors, probably reflecting their self-perceived vulnerability to victimization and its more serious outcomes. People are not particularly geographically concentrated along these dimensions, so they provide a kind of background level of fear in virtually every community. (There is evidence that distinctively high levels of fear for the elderly are found only in big cities and not in smaller places; see Baumer [1985]). Some residents of higher-crime areas do not report excessive levels of concern (Lewis and Maxfield 1980; Taylor, Gottfredson, and Brower 1984). The reason may be, in part, one of pluralistic ignorance. People in a neighborhood may not have good individual knowledge of their collective experiences. Most crimes that strike individuals and households or commercial establishments leave no outward sign of their visitation. Area residents know of them only indirectly, through crime statistics, media stories of individual crimes or trends, or rumors. Their own direct victimization experiences typically are few or nonexistent (even in big cities most people are not victimized at all in any recent period) and may be discounted as atypical of their neighborhood (Hindelang, Gottfredson, and Garofalo 1978). Thus, although crime is very real, many residents of a neighborhood only know of it indirectly via channels that may inflate, deflate, or garble the picture. The official picture of levels of crime in various neighborhoods may be fear provoking because those figures are known to the public as well as to the police (Garofalo 1981).

### *B. Secondhand Information*

Research suggests that the most important secondary sources of information about crime are neighborhood based, produce fear levels that are somewhat at odds with the real distribution of crime, and provide a mechanism that may accelerate neighborhood decline. People make extensive use of information gathered secondhand through social networks. Surveys of dense neighborhoods in industrial cities indicate that neighbors talk frequently about crime and that, as a result, large proportions of them know people in their vicinity who have been victimized. In one study of three such cities, fully 48 percent of those interviewed knew a local robbery victim. In contrast, city victimization surveys indicated that only 5.5 percent of residents had been robbed in the past year (Skogan and Maxfield 1981). Little is known about the frequency with which residents of low-density, automobile-oriented, air-conditioned cities of the South and Southwest participate in such neighborhood-oriented rumor networks.

Talking with neighbors about crime and knowing local victims appears to affect levels of fear and individual estimates of the risk of victimization (Bishop and Klecka 1978; Tyler 1980; Lavrakas, Herz, and Salem 1981; Skogan and Maxfield 1981; Greenberg, Rohe, and Williams 1982). People also tend to talk about serious violent crimes rather than more typical property offenses. There is evidence that individuals who hear about people like themselves being victimized rather than about victims with a different demographic profile are even more fearful (Skogan and Maxfield 1981). Crime messages can spread fast in tight-knit communities; Lawton, Nahemow, and Yaffe (1976), in their study of elderly residents of a low-income housing project, report that one-half could describe a crime against a fellow tenant. Ironically, neighborhoods with well-developed social ties, extensive communication networks, and an active organizational life, which can spread such stories widely, also tend to enjoy lower levels of victimization.

It is adaptive and efficient for people to use indirectly acquired information to judge their risks and make decisions about what to do about crime, for it is an infrequent, yet potentially high-consequence, event. Rumor networks (unlike the mass media) are informative about local events and conditions. They can convey messages of personal significance, and there is evidence that their messages are integrated into people's views of their immediate environment (Tyler 1984). However, they may work most effectively in areas where the events about which stories are being spread actually are less frequent. As we shall see below, the consequences of this may be considerable.

### C. *Deterioration and Disorder*

Unlike most serious crimes, which are widely experienced only secondhand, there are neighborhood conditions that provide readily observable evidence of the extent of local decline. They are visual signs of physical deterioration and social disorganization: junk and trash in vacant lots, boarded-up buildings, stripped and abandoned cars, bands of teenagers congregating on street corners, street prostitution, panhandling, public drinking, verbal harassment of women, open gambling and drug use, and other incivilities (Hunter 1978; Gardner 1980; Lewis and Maxfield 1980; Taub, Taylor, and Dunham 1981). More than fifteen years ago, Biderman et al. (1967) argued that people's major impressions about area crime are derived from "the highly visible signs of what they regard as disorderly and disreputable behavior in their community."

Many surveys asking about the extent of these problems have found that the answers are closely related to fear of crime and to perceptions that serious crimes are neighborhood problems. Some research suggests that visible disorderly activity by people has a greater effect than does deterioration but that both independently are important determinants of fear and some fear-related behaviors (McPherson, Silloway, and Frey 1983). This parallels Hunter's conceptual distinction between "social" and "physical" signs of incivility. Deterioration and disorder can be discomforting and run counter to many adults' expectations about proper public conditions (although, of course, they will vary in their tolerance of such situations). They may take them as signs of the disintegration of the standards that guide local public life. The anxiety that deterioration and disorder generate among area residents can be a constant psychological irritant. Stinchcombe et al. (1980) and Hunter (1978) argue that such conditions are one of the most debilitating sources of fear. They are associated in the minds of many with the level of area crime, and their presence is taken as an early warning of impending danger. If they are common, the warning flag flies constantly.

The effect of deterioration and disorder may be conditioned by other factors. Taylor, Schumaker, and Gottfredson (1986) find that physical decay (measured observationally) has its greatest effects in blue-collar rather than in poor or more well-to-do areas of Baltimore. In wealthy areas, instances of these problems may be ignored as atypical and nonthreatening, and residents of poor areas have many things to worry about. However, in moderate-income areas of the city, where market conditions for housing are insecure, residents may be more sensitive to such barometers of decline. This may account as well for the high negative correlation between indicators of decay and neighborhood confidence found in those areas.

Wilson and Kelling (1982) also argue that disorder actually spawns more serious crime as well as erodes the commitment of stable, family-oriented residents to the neighborhood. They allude to a "developmental sequence" by which unchecked rule breaking fosters petty plundering and even more serious street crime and theft. The nature of the relation between crime and disorder is still unclear, and Maxfield (1984*b*) illustrates how perceptions of crime and disorder are differentially related to fear, depending on their absolute level. However, several studies report high correlations (+.45–+.60) between area-level measures of crime and perceived disorder. That there are few high-disorder, low-crime neighborhoods suggests that the effect of one condition on the other is either quite powerful or that the relation is due to their strong joint association with some other set of factors.

### D. *The Built Environment*

There is some evidence that the physical composition of the housing stock may wield independent influence on fear. Newman (1972), Newman and Franck (1980), Maxfield (1984*a*), and others, reviewed in Greenberg, Rohe, and Williams (1984), report that fear of crime is higher among residents of high-rise buildings and large flats than among those living in smaller buildings. Residents of low-rise and less congested areas have a stronger sense of territoriality as well (Taylor, Brower, and Drain 1979). High-rise living seems to be related to feelings of alienation and powerlessness, although it is not clear that people do not "self-select" themselves into such environments. Several randomized experiments do indicate that building size affects neighboring and the strength of neighborhood ties (cf. Greenberg et al. 1984). Such effects may differ by subgroup; my unpublished calculations suggest that elderly persons living in larger buildings are more fearful than others, controlling for a number of important determinants of fear and group conflict.

### *E. Group Conflict*

A final source of fear, and a traditional engine of neighborhood change, is group conflict over the control of neighborhood "turf." As various racial and ethnic groups grow or shrink in size, their demand for living space follows. This threatens change, which can be translated into concern about crime when contending groups differ in class, family organization, and life-style. To a large extent, neighborhood succession takes the form of spillover or invasion from one area to the next (Aldrich and Reiss 1976). When the encroaching community is a crime-exporting area, residents of nearby crime-importing areas are more fearful (Greenberg et al. 1984). Often the newcomers are younger and have more children than do the old-timers, so intergenerational conflicts about public deportment overlay other differences between them. Merry (1979) reports that neighborhood crime can sometimes be an extension of such conflict. In her anthropological study of a housing project, black, white, Hispanic, and Asian residents viewed each other with suspicion. No individual or group enjoyed any overarching moral authority, and there were no mechanisms for informally resolving disputes among residents who crossed ethnic lines. Instead, disputants sometimes resorted to violence to settle them.

Noncrime factors are, of course, at work as well. Talk about the threat of crime can serve as an outlet for other concerns in neighborhoods undergoing racial change. Taub et al. (1984) found a strong correlation between fear and white Chicagoans' beliefs about black neighborhood succession, crime rates, and property values. Working-class whites in particular believed that the movement of blacks into a neighborhood brought with it higher rates of crime. This belief was reflected in their evaluations of the market value of homes in their area. The same study found that two measures of fear (fear of walking alone at night and dissatisfaction with area safety) were negatively related to whites' estimates of the ability of their neighborhoods to resist racial change and positively related to levels of prejudice against incoming black families. And fear was a strong correlate of their desire to move out of the neighborhood.

Outsiders who are in the process of violating a community's space can threaten a broad range of values and conjure up many stereotypes about their behavior. Market forces battle discrimination, politics, and even collective violence in determining how rapidly the demand for housing by expanding groups is translated into shifting residential patterns. They usually win out in the conflict over living space in American cities, although sometimes local skirmishes can delay that victory, so change of this sort seems inevitable (Molotch 1972; Goodwin 1979).

## III. The Effect of Fear on Community Life

Fear has further consequences for communities. It can work in conjunction with other factors to stimulate more rapid neighborhood decline. Together, the spread of fear and other local problems provide a form of positive feedback that can further increase levels of crime. These feedback processes include (1) physical and psychological withdrawal from community life; (2) a weakening of the informal social control processes that inhibit crime and disorder; (3) a decline in the organizational life and mobilization capacity of the neighborhood; (4) deteriorating business conditions; (5) the importation and domestic production of delinquency and deviance; and (6) further dramatic changes in the composition of the population. At the end lies a stage characterized by demographic collapse.

### A. *Withdrawal*

One of the most significant consequences of fear is physical withdrawal from community life. Fearful people report that they stay at home more often, especially after dark. When they do go out, they carefully avoid coming into contact with strangers or potentially threatening situations, and they confine their path to the safest times and routes possible. They do not talk to people they do not know, and not getting involved seems a wise course. Among women, in particular, adoption of such defensive tactics is related to levels of neighborhood disorder as well as to perceived risk of victimization (Riger, Gordon, and Lebailly 1982). In its best light, this can result in a form of "ordered segmentation" of the community that enables diverse and potentially conflictful people to share the same turf without coming into contact (Suttles 1968). However, the effects of fear extend further.

There are other psychological and behavioral consequences of fear. People feel powerless, impotent, and vulnerable in the face of crime. They are passive in response to events around them, for fear generates a kind of "learned helplessness" (Kidd and Chayet 1984). High levels of perceived crime and disorder appear to undermine people's belief that problems can be solved locally. It increases their feeling of personal isolation and spreads the perception that no one will come to their rescue when they find themselves in trouble (Lewis and Salem 1985). Not surprisingly, fear does not stimulate constructive, preventive responses to crime (Lavrakas 1981; Tyler 1984). Surveys and experiments indicate that fear reduces people's willingness to take positive actions when they see crimes, including simply calling the police. The reduction in the number of legitimate users of the streets caused by fear, coupled with the unwillingness of bystanders to intervene because they are afraid, can create easy opportunities for predators.

### *B. Informal Control*

Fear also decreases the spatial radius that individuals feel responsible for defending. "Territoriality" is a set of attitudes and behaviors regarding the regulation of the boundary that surrounds people's personal and household space (Taylor et al. 1980; Brown and Altman 1981). When that boundary is expansive, individuals monitor more strangers, youths, and suspicious sounds and activities. Where territories encompass only people's homes and families, untended persons and property are fair game for plunder. Territoriality thus is an important component of the larger process of surveillance and may be an important mechanism for controlling crime. Surveillance entails both "watching" and "acting." Acting is facilitated by personal recognition, shared standards about appropriate public behavior, a sense of responsibility for events in the area, and identification with potential victims.

There is some evidence (summarized in Shotland and Goodstein [1984]) that crime is encouraged by low levels of surveillance of public places and reduced by people willing to act to challenge strangers, supervise youths, and step forward as witnesses. Research on "crime prevention through environmental design" (Newman 1972) focuses in part on how subtle features of the built environment facilitate surveillance. Its effect on levels of crime is as yet ill-understood (Murray 1983; Taylor et al. 1984), but people feel less safe in low-traffic, unsupervised, less visible locations where no one would intervene if there were trouble. Fear seems dampened by the availability of social support, including that offered by neighbors and the police (Sundeen and Mathieu 1976). "The perceived availability of helping resources in the neighborhood . . . has the effect of reducing fear, particularly among those living in a threatening environment. . . . The perception that assistance is available from neighbors when needed may act as a buffer between the individual and the environment" (Greenberg et al. 1984, p. 88). Such conditions may be less common in high-fear communities, and more fear can lead to even less foot traffic, smaller territories, and less watching and intervention.

Beginning with Maccoby, Johnson, and Church (1958), there has been a great deal of research on the effect of the strength of "local social ties" on interventions (or intentions to intervene) of a variety of kinds, especially to control juveniles. The effect of local social ties is strong but is particularly affected by fear. In stable neighborhoods, residents supervise the activities of youths, watch over one another's property, and challenge those who seem to be up to no good. Neighborhood change brings to the neighborhood newcomers, changes in patterns of street life, and unpredictable people. This further redounds to the disadvantage of such areas through the effect of dense social relationships on fear. Surveys often find that the strength of local social ties is a strong and independent correlate of feelings of safety. They have such further consequences as increasing the scope of individual territoriality, cementing identification to one's area, and encouraging participation in organized community activity (Hunter 1974; DuBow and Emmons 1981; Taylor et al. 1984).

### C. *Organizational Life*

Both fear and demographics work against organized community life in neighborhoods caught in the cycle of decline. Research indicates that fear does not stimulate participation in collective efforts to act against crime; rather, it often has the effect of undermining commitment to an area and interest in participation (Lavrakas et al. 1981). Where fear promotes suspicion in place of neighborliness, it can be difficult to forge formal linkages between residents to attack neighborhood problems.

When neighborhoods spiral into decline, demographic factors related to participation in community organizations can shift unfavorably. Inmovers tend to be harder to organize; they are renters, single-parent families, the poor and less educated, younger and unmarried persons, and nonfamily households. They report having little economic or emotional commitment to the community and usually expect to move again.

As a result of these demographic changes, the mobilization capacity of the area—affecting the ability of residents to effectively demand that landlords and governments act on their behalf—is diminished. Where that capacity is strong, organization can combat community deterioration and disorder. One important function of community organizations is to convey the image—to residents and outsiders alike—of a mobilized community that will resist unwelcome change (Unger and Wandersman 1983). Organizations can restore or reinforce a local value consensus and emphasize the shared interests of people living together (DuBow and Emmons 1981). Where informal organization is limited, there may be few other mechanisms for generating community cohesion around the issues of crime, disorder, and decline. For example, Cohen (1980) finds that street prostitution flourishes only where community consensus is weak and there is no organized resistance to deviant public behavior.

Another role of neighborhood groups is to extend face-to-face contacts between residents and generate optimism about the future of the area, both important factors facilitating crime-prevention efforts (DuBow and Emmons 1981). Perceptions registered in surveys that neighbors help each other are an important source of morale in urban communities and seem to stimulate a variety of positive actions against crime (Lavrakas 1981). Participation in neighborhood organizations seems to stimulate homeowner investments as well (Taub et al. 1984). However, in neighborhoods in decline, mutual distrust and hostility are rampant, and antipathy between newcomers and long-term residents prevails. Residents of poor, heterogeneous areas tend to be more suspicious and feel less commonality with one another (Taylor, Gottfredson, and Brower 1981; Greenberg et al. 1982; Taub et al. 1984). Greenberg (1983) concludes that crime prevention programs requiring social contact and neighborhood cooperation are less often found in heterogeneous areas and those with high levels of fear. This is perhaps why Titus's (1984) review of neighborhood burglary programs found that participating areas had lower levels of crime. The best hypothesis probably is that the relation between area levels of fear and collective neighborhood responses to crime is curvilinear, with participation lowest in the low-fear areas (few problems) and the high-fear areas (too many problems) and highest in the middle.

### *D. Delinquency and Disorder*

A further consequence of individual passivity, weak informal social control, and collective incapacity is that neighborhoods caught in decline lose the ability to control problems caused by youths living in the area. They may import problems, attracting crime and disorder from the outside.

Rising victimization rates can be especially unsettling when they are due to an increase in the local prevalence of *offenders* and not just offenses. A question about who people thought caused local crime was asked in the U.S. Census Bureau's surveys of twenty-six big cities. It reveals that people are more fearful than otherwise when they believe that it is people from within the neighborhood rather than outsiders who are responsible for local crime (my unpublished calculations). This concern is a corrosive one, for it undermines trust among neighbors. It certainly violates one of the assumptions behind Neighborhood Watch and other programs that attempt to promote mutual cooperation to prevent crime—it may not seem wise to inform the neighbors that you will be out of town when it is their children whom you fear (Greenberg 1983).

Wilson and Kelling (1982) argue that a reputation for being tolerant of social disorder also serves as a neighborhood invitation to outside troublemakers. Areas that tolerate (or cannot counter) rowdy taverns, dirty bookstores, public drinking, prostitution, and other incivilities will quickly attract street robbers to prey on the trade. Thieves will sense the limited surveillance capacity of the area and that it presents easy pickings for burglars.

### *E. Commercial Decline*

One barometer of trends in urban neighborhoods is commercial activity. Because they are located on major streets and intersections, small retail shops are one of the most visible features of a community, so their appearance and character may help determine those trends as well (McPherson et al. 1983). Research by Aldrich and Reiss (1976) and McPherson (1978) indicates that disorder and crime hurt small retail establishments by affecting their profitability and not by direct victimization, so business factors are critical. When an area enters the cycle of decline, there will be fewer prosperous shoppers, outsiders will not come into the area to shop, and fewer customers of any kind will be out after dark. Existing stores may close because the market they once served no longer exists. Others may change their hours, prices, and types of goods in order to stay open. Convenience stores stocking fewer goods at somewhat higher prices grow in number.

In neighborhoods with a reputation for disorder, economic forces will favor bars, seedy transient hotels, X-rated movie theaters and bookstores, and massage parlors (Cohen 1980). The trade these attract, along with groups of unsavory males drinking (and urinating) in nearby side streets and alleys, will further decrease the desirability of the area for families and others with a lower tolerance for deviance. In areas in decline, increasing numbers of shops will stand empty or be converted to nonretail uses (karate parlors, evangelistic churches, social clubs, and the like).

### *F. Collapse*

Finally, the effect of all these processes can rebound in the form of even more dramatic changes in the population composition of an area. Where levels of fear are extreme, neighborhoods collapse and are transformed into entirely different, nonresidential places.

After a while, their history of crime and disorder becomes the driving force in the population composition of areas deep in the cycle of decline. The affluent are long gone, but now women, children, and the elderly shun those areas. As in large parts of Woodlawn (Chicago) and the South Bronx (New York City), such a high tolerance for risk is required to live in these places that the population drops precipitously. Disorder can continue to occur, but there is virtually no "community" remaining to define it as a problem. Unattached males, the homeless, and the aimless live there in boarded-up buildings, seedy residential hotels, and flophouses. Skid row saloons are the only commercial establishments open after dark. Abandoned buildings become "shooting galleries" where drugs are distributed and consumed. Street prostitution will have moved elsewhere, however, for it depends on customers feeling that they can cruise an area safely (Cohen 1980). As collapse approaches, residential and commercial buildings in the area stand empty or are demolished, and arson becomes a common problem. In Newark, for example, vacant residential buildings burn at four times the city's overall rate; the rate for vacant commercial structures is even higher (Sternlieb and Burchell 1983). Vacant lots thus multiply, filled with the rubble of demolition. The crime count can even drop in such areas because there are dramatically fewer people to be victimized. When collapse spreads, cities develop hollow cores where the worst areas have burned. They have reached the bottom of the cycle of decline.

## IV. Reversing the Process of Decline

Despite the power of the social forces reviewed above, shifting into decline is not the inevitable fate of urban neighborhoods, even where fear is high. They can go "up" (in common parlance) as well as "down," both through gentrification and through "incumbent upgrading" (cf. McDonald, in this volume). Concern about crime is merely one feature of urban life, and it is not necessarily the most important determinant of decisions to move or to invest in an area. Taub et al.'s (1981, 1984) studies of fear of crime and real estate prices in Chicago neighborhoods suggest that fear has substantial negative effects on moving and investment decisions only if other neighborhood factors are pushing in the same direction. If they are, people who live there view crime as a leading indicator of community decline. Among white Chicagoans, for example, fear was related to the perception that investment in the neighborhood was risky among only those who thought their area was racially unstable. In generally deteriorating areas, crime takes on great significance as a sign of neighborhood decay, and people who live there report feeling helpless in the face of the large-scale social forces that seem to be working against them.

However, factors other than concern about crime are important in determining the demand for property or rental housing that pushes real estate values up or down. These include closeness to the downtown, the quality and style of the housing stock, access to amenities and transportation, and the availability of loans. When other factors are positive and (especially) when property values are appreciating, residents find ample reason to be satisfied with the area, and they tolerate surprisingly high levels of crime. The same seems to be true for small retail businesses in urban residential areas. McPherson et al. (1983) found that even in disorderly, problem-ridden, high-crime areas, owners were more likely to plan to remain in business and make future investments if they believed the future of their market area looked bright and if they were optimistic about local development efforts. Concern about crime does not in itself determine levels of investment, the confidence of residents in the future, or property values. Rather it is one strand in a bundle of features that make up a community's character. Where people are optimistic about the bundle as a whole, crime counts for less.

This does not mean that residents of higher-crime, but appreciating, areas are not personally fearful. McDonald (in this volume) summarizes several studies indicating that residents of inner-city gentrifying neighborhoods *are* fearful of crime; the difference is that they are willing to tolerate that condition despite their ability to move elsewhere. One reason they can do so is that residents of gentrifying areas often are childless and thus able to ignore a number of local problems, including school safety. A survey in poor neighborhoods in Philadelphia found that the safety of their children in and on the way to school was the number one crime-related concern among parents. Interviews with their children revealed that they also saw schools as dangerous places (Savitz, Lalli, and Rosen 1977). Economically advantaged areas also may succeed in steering more city resources into building the stock of local amenities that underlie appreciating property values. "Rehabbers" often prove to be effective petitioners for better services, including police protection, and they understand how to change neighborhood dynamics by stimulating negative rather than positive feedback processes. This means, first, dealing with population turnover. Taub et al. (1984) found that defensively "stabilizing the real estate market" was the first concern of community organizations in the Chicago neighborhoods they studied and that "[m]ost of the strong community organizations considered in this book arose in response to impending or actual racial change" (p. 184). At best, they found that this was accomplished by self-consciously promoting the virtues of racial integration and by appealing to class interests instead. They also found that neighborhood efforts to reverse tendencies toward decline primarily were successful when supported by large but immobile corporate actors (e.g., hospitals, banks, and universities) with a sunk investment to protect.

## V. The Systematic Consequences of Fear

This essay argued first that neighborhoods change only slowly and proposed that critical triggering events and conditions shift some of them from relative stability into a state of demographic and economic change. Those precipitating events include disinvestment, demolition, and demagoguery plus regional or national economic forces out of the hands of local decision makers. Once areas slip into the cycle of decline, feedback processes take control of neighborhood conditions and increase levels of fear. The problems that emerge include crime, physical deterioration, social disorder, and group conflict over the control of neighborhood turf. Fear in turn undermines the capacity of the community to deal with these problems. It stimulates physical and psychological withdrawal from the community, a weakening of informal social control mechanisms, a decline in the organizational life and mobilization capacity of the neighborhood, deterioration of local business conditions, and further disorder and crime. These problems feed on themselves, spiraling neighborhoods deeper into decline. As Schuerman and

Kobrin (in this volume) report, in the worst areas crime shifts from being just a "dependent" variable to being an "independent" variable as well in areas characterized by twenty years of decline. At the extreme end of the cycle, they may no longer be recognizable as neighborhoods but take on an entirely different social function.

There is a great deal of interest in identifying which neighborhoods are entering the cycle of decline. Schuerman and Kobrin (in this volume) have some hope for what they dub "emerging crime areas." These are middle-aged rather than old residential areas, with changing populations but substantial pockets of middle-class residents. Here they recommend "deceleration of demographic and socioeconomic change." Wilson and Kelling (1982) focus on "the ratio of respectable to disreputable people" in an area to foresee its fate. Neighborhoods not too far past their tipping point are those with substantial levels of legitimate street use and a critical mass of residents interested in keeping the area in good repair. Schuerman and Kobrin argue that areas deeply in the cycle of decline—characterized by at least three decades of high crime—are lost territory to the rest of society. Wilson and Kelling would seem to write off places somewhat more quickly. They all favor triage, consigning areas mired in crime, disorder, and fear to some urban scrap heap—although, like nuclear waste, neighborhood problems have a half-life that will scar those who wander too close to them for the foreseeable future.

Individually disastrous as the cycle of decline is for the areas involved, when aggregated at the metropolitan level they are collectively even more important. They help explain (but do not completely determine) some central features of contemporary urban life. The most important of these is "white flight" from central cities. The massive and racially selective suburbanization of the United States following World War II may be the most consequential effect of crime on American society. The suburban ring often dominates the political balance of power in many urban states. Socially, it has driven another cleavage between whites and blacks, browns, and Asians, who uneasily huddle together at the core; urban areas have divided into what Farley et al. (1978) dubbed "chocolate cities" and "vanilla suburbs." There has been a corresponding pattern of disinvestment in inner-city areas. This includes a mammoth outward shift in the location of jobs and concomitant changes in the ratio of services to taxes, which favors suburban over center-city locations. The growth of shopping centers at the expense of central business districts has eroded city tax bases. Further, there is evidence that suburban rings cast a shadow back over the cities they surround. For example, the extent of suburbanization is correlated with higher central-city tax burdens, partially because of the volume of services and the maze of roadways required by those living outside the taxing jurisdiction of the city (Kasarda 1972).

Thus, partially as a result of fear, American society is faced with the concentration in inner cities of structurally unemployable public service consumers who are excluded from economic and social developments in the mainstream. (Another source of this tendency toward concentration has been the increasing flow of younger, more affluent blacks into the suburbs; see Frey [1984].) Many cities are threatened with becoming dumping grounds for those locked out of other sectors. There is some evidence of a modest reversal of these processes, with a return to the cities affecting areas with location advantages and housing suited to affluent, childless households (Laska and Spain 1980). Gentrification can force up rents, increase the value of land, and upgrade the housing stock in small areas through economic pressures that act just in reverse of the more familiar trends described above (McDonald, in this volume). However, there is no evidence that the pace of such developments is outstripping the hollowing out of many city centers.

## REFERENCES

Aldrich, Howard, and Albert J. Reiss, Jr. 1976. "Continuities in the Study of Ecological Succession: Changes in the Race Composition of Neighborhoods and Their Businesses." *American Journal of Sociology* 81:846–66.

Altschuler, Alan A. 1965. *The City Planning Process.* Ithaca, N.Y.: Cornell University Press.

Baumer, Terry L. 1985. "Testing a General Model of Fear of Crime: Data from a National Sample." *Journal of Research in Crime and Delinquency* 22:239–55.

Biderman, Albert D., Louise A. Johnson, Jennie McIntyre, and Adrianne W. Weir. 1967. *Report on a Pilot Study in the District of Columbia on Victimization and Attitudes toward Law Enforcement.* Washington, D.C.: U.S. Government Printing Office.

Bishop, George, and William Klecka. 1978. "Victimization and Fear of Crime among the Elderly Living in High Crime Urban Neighborhoods." Paper presented at the annual meeting of the Academy of Criminal Justice Sciences.

Bradford, Calvin P., and Leonard S. Rubinowitz. 1975. "The Urban-Suburban Investment-Disinvestment Process: Consequences for Older Neighborhoods." *Annals of the American Academy of Political and Social Sciences* 422:77–86.

Brown, Barbara B., and Irwin Altman. 1981. "Territoriality and Residential Crime." In *Environmental Criminology*, edited by Paul Brantingham and Patricia Brantingham. Beverly Hills, Calif.: Sage.

Bureau of Justice Statistics. 1983. *Criminal Victimization in the United States 1981*. Washington, D.C.: Bureau of Justice Statistics.

Bursik, Robert J., Jr. In this volume. "Ecological Stability and the Dynamics of Delinquency."

Cohen, Bernard. 1980. *Deviant Street Networks: Prostitution in New York City*. Lexington, Mass.: Lexington.

Department of Housing and Urban Development. 1973. *Abandoned Housing Research: A Compendium*. Washington, D.C.: Department of Housing and Urban Development.

Droettboom, Theodore, Ronald J. McAllister, Edward J. Kaiser, and Edgar W. Butler. 1971. "Urban Violence and Residential Mobility." *Journal of the American Institute of Planners* 37:319–25.

DuBow, Fred, and David Emmons. 1981. "The Community Hypothesis." In *Reactions to Crime*, edited by Dan A. Lewis. Beverly Hills, Calif.: Sage.

Duncan, Gregg, and Sandra Newman. 1976. "Expected and Actual Residential Moves." *Journal of the American Institute of Planners* 42:174–86.

Exter, Thomas G. 1985. "Major Metropolitan Markets." *American Demographics* 7:46–48.

Farley, Reynolds, Howard Schuman, Suzanne Bianchi, Diane Colasanto, and Shirley Hatchett. 1978. "Chocolate City, Vanilla Suburbs." *Social Science Research* 7:319–44.

Frey, William H. 1980. "Black In-Migration, White Flight, and the Changing Economic Base of the Central City." *American Journal of Sociology* 85:1396–1417.

———. 1984. "Lifecourse Migration of Metropolitan Whites and Blacks and the Structure of Demographic Change in Large Central Cities." *American Sociological Review* 49:803–27.

Frisbie, Douglas, Glenn Fishbein, Richard Hinz, Mitchell Joelson, and Julia B. Nutter. 1977. *Crime in Minneapolis*. St. Paul, Minn.: Governor's Commission on Crime Prevention and Control, Community Crime Prevention Project.

Gardner, Carol B. 1980. "Passing By: Street Remarks, Address Rights, and the Urban Female." *Sociological Inquiry* 50:328–56.

Garofalo, James. 1981. "The Fear of Crime: Causes and Consequences." *Journal of Criminal Law and Criminology* 72:839–57.

Goodstein, Lynn I., and Lance Shotland. 1980. "The Crime Causes Crime Model: A Critical Review of the Relationships between Fear of Crime, Bystander Surveillance, and Changes in the Crime Rate." *Victimology* 5:133–51.

Goodwin, Carol. 1979. *The Oak Park Strategy: Community Control of Racial Change*. Chicago: University of Chicago Press.

Greenberg, Stephanie W. 1983. "External Solutions to Neighborhood-based Problems: The Case of Community Crime Prevention." Paper presented at the annual meeting of the Law and Society Association, June.

Greenberg, Stephanie W., William M. Rohe, and Jay R. Williams. 1982. *Safe and Secure Neighborhoods: Physical Characteristics and Informal Territorial Control in High and Low Crime Neighborhoods*. Washington, D.C.: National Institute of Justice.

———. 1984. "Informal Citizen Action and Crime Prevention at the Neighborhood Level: Synthesis and Assessment of the Research." Grant report from the Research Triangle Institute, Chapel Hill, N.C., to the U.S. Department of Justice, National Institute of Justice, Washington, D.C.

Hindelang, Michael, Michael Gottfredson, and James Garofalo. 1978. *Victims of Personal Crime*. Cambridge, Mass.: Ballinger.

Hunter, Albert. 1974. *Symbolic Communities*. Chicago: University of Chicago Press.

———. 1978. "Symbols of Incivility: Social Disorder and Fear of Crime in Urban Neighborhoods." Paper presented at the annual meeting of the American Society of Criminology.

Jaycox, Victoria H. 1978. "The Elderly's Fear of Crime: Rational or Irrational." *Victimology* 3:329–33.

Kasarda, John D. 1972. "The Impact of Suburban Population Growth on Central-City Service Functions." *American Journal of Sociology* 77:1111–24.

Kasl, Stanislav V., and Ernest Harburg. 1972. "Perceptions of the Neighborhood and the Desire to Move Out." *Journal of the American Institute of Planners* 38:318–24.

Kennedy, Leslie W., and Robert A. Silverman. 1985. "Perception of Social Diversity and Fear of Crime." *Environment and Behavior* 17:275–95.

Kidd, Robert F., and Allan F. Chayet. 1984. "Why Do Victims Fail to Report: The Psychology of Criminal Victimization." *Journal of Social Issues* 40:39–50.

Kobrin, Solomon, and Leo A. Schuerman. 1981. *Interaction Between Neighborhood Change and Criminal Activity*. Los Angeles: University of Southern California, Social Science Research Institute.

Laska, Shirley, and Daphne Spain, eds. 1980. *Back to the City: Issues in Neighborhood Renovation*. New York: Pergamon.

Lavrakas, Paul J. 1981. "On Households." In *Reactions to Crime*, edited by Dan A. Lewis. Beverly Hills, Calif.: Sage.

Lavrakas, Paul J., Lisa Herz, and Greta Salem. 1981. "Community Organization, Citizen Participation, and Neighborhood Crime Prevention." Paper presented at the annual meeting of the American Psychological Association.

Lawton, M. Powell, Lucie Nahemow, Silvia Yaffe, and Steven Feldman. 1976. "Psychological Aspects of Crime and Fear of Crime." In *Crime and the Elderly*, edited by Jack Goldsmith and Sharon Goldsmith. Lexington, Mass.: Lexington.

Lewis, Dan A., and Michael G. Maxfield. 1980. "Fear in the Neighborhoods." *Journal of Research in Crime and Delinquency* 17:160–89.

Lewis, Dan A., and Greta W. Salem. 1985. *Fear of Crime: Incivility and the Production of a Social Problem*. New Brunswick, N.J.: Transaction.

Maccoby, Eleanor, Joseph P. Johnson, and Russell Church. 1958. "Community Integration and the Social Control of Juvenile Delinquency." *Journal of Social Issues* 14:38–51.

Maxfield, Michael G. 1984*a*. *Fear of Crime in England and Wales*. Home Office Research Study no. 78. London: Home Office Research and Planning Unit.

———. 1984*b*. "The Limits of Vulnerability in Explaining Fear of Crime: A Comparative Neighborhood Analysis." *Journal of Research in Crime and Delinquency* 21:233–50.

McDonald, Scott. In this volume. "Does Gentrification Affect Crime Rates?"

McPherson, Marlys. 1978. "Realities and Perceptions of Crime at the Neighborhood Level." *Victimology* 3:319–28.

McPherson, Marlys, Glenn Silloway, and David Frey. 1983. "Crime, Fear, and Control in Neighborhood Commercial Centers." Grant report from the Minnesota Crime Prevention Center, Inc., to the U.S. Department of Justice, National Institute of Justice, Washington, D.C.

Merry, Sally E. 1979. "Going to Court: Strategies of Dispute Management in an American Urban Neighborhood." *Law and Society Review* 13:891–925.

Molotch, Harvey L. 1972. *Managed Integration*. Berkeley: University of California Press.

Munson, M., and W. E. Oates. 1983. "Community Characteristics and the Incidence of Fires: An Empirical Analysis." In *The Social and Economic Consequences of Residential Fires*, edited by C. Rapkin. Lexington, Mass.: Lexington.

Murray, Charles A. 1983. "The Physical Environment and Community Control of Crime." In *Crime and Public Policy*, edited by James Q. Wilson. San Francisco: Institute for Contemporary Studies Press.

Newman, Oscar. 1972. *Defensible Space: Crime Prevention through Urban Design*. New York: Macmillan.

Newman, Oscar, and Karen Franck. 1980. "Factors Influencing Crime and Instability in Urban Housing Developments." Report from the Institute for Community Design Analysis to the U.S. Department of Justice, National Institute of Justice, Washington, D.C.

Pettiway, L. 1983. "Arson and American City Types." *Journal of Environmental Systems Inquiry* 13:157–76.

Przeworski, Adam, and Henry Teune. 1970. *The Logic of Comparative Social Inquiry*. New York: Wiley.

Riger, Stephanie, Margaret T. Gordon, and Robert Lebailly. 1982. "Coping with Urban Crime." *American Journal of Community Psychology* 10:369–86.

Savitz, Leonard D., Michael Lalli, and Lawrence Rosen. 1977. *City Life and Delinquency: Victimization, Fear of Crime, and Gang Membership*. Washington, D.C.: U.S. Department of Justice, National Institute for Juvenile Justice and Delinquency Prevention.

Schuerman, Leo A., and Solomon Kobrin. 1983. "Crime and Urban Ecological Processes: Implications for Public Policy." Paper presented at the American Sociological Conference, November.

———. In this volume. "Community Careers in Crime."

Shotland, R. Lance, and Lynne I. Goodstein. 1984. "The Role of Bystanders in Crime Control." *Journal of Social Issues* 40:9–26.

Silverman, Robert A., and Leslie W. Kennedy. 1984. "Loneliness, Satisfaction and Fear of Crime." *Canadian Journal of Criminology* 27:1–13.

Skogan, Wesley G., and Michael G. Maxfield. 1981. *Coping with Crime: Individual and Neighborhood Reactions.* Beverly Hills, Calif.: Sage.

Sternlieb, George, and R. W. Burchell. 1983. "Fires in Abandoned Buildings." In *The Social and Economic Consequences of Residential Fires*, edited by C. Rapkin. Lexington, Mass.: Lexington.

Stinchcombe, Arthur, R. Adams, Carol Heimer, Kim Scheppele, Tom Smith, and D. Garth Taylor. 1980. *Crime and Punishment in Public Opinion.* San Francisco: Jossey-Bass.

Sundeen, Richard A., and James T. Mathieu. 1976. "The Fear of Crime and Its Consequences among the Elderly in Three Urban Areas." *Gerontologist* 16:211–19.

Suttles, Gerald D. 1968. *The Social Order of the Slum.* Chicago: University of Chicago Press.

Taub, Richard P., D. Garth Taylor, and Jan D. Dunham. 1981. "Neighborhoods and Safety." In *Reactions to Crime*, edited by Dan A. Lewis. Beverly Hills, Calif.: Sage.

———. 1984. *Patterns of Neighborhood Change: Race and Crime in Urban America.* Chicago: University of Chicago Press.

Taylor, Ralph B., Sidney Brower, and W. Drain. 1979. "Towards a Resident-based Model of Community Crime Prevention: Urban Territoriality, Social Networks, and Design." Unpublished paper, Johns Hopkins University, Center for Metropolitan Planning and Research.

Taylor, Ralph B., Stephen D. Gottfredson, and Sidney Brower. 1980. "The Defensibility of Defensible Space." In *Understanding Crime*, edited by T. Hirschi and M. Gottfredson. Beverly Hills, Calif.: Sage.

———. 1981. "Informal Control in the Urban Residential Environment." Report from the Center for Metropolitan Planning and Research, Johns Hopkins University, to the U.S. Department of Justice, National Institute of Justice, Washington, D.C.

———. 1984. "Block Crime and Fear: Defensible Space, Local Social Ties, and Territorial Functioning." *Journal of Research in Crime and Delinquency* 21:303–31.

Taylor, Ralph B., Sally Schumaker, and Stephen D. Gottfredson. 1986. "Neighborhood-Level Linkages between Physical Features and Local Sentiments: Deterioration, Fear of Crime, and Confidence." *Journal of Architectural Planning and Research* (in press).

Titus, Richard. 1984. "Residential Burglary and the Community Response." In *Coping with Burglary*, edited by Ronald Clarke and Tim Hope. Boston: Kluwer-Nijhoff.

Tyler, Tom R. 1980. "Impact of Directly and Indirectly Experienced Events: The Origin of Crime-related Judgments and Behaviors." *Journal of Personality and Social Psychology* 39:13–28.

———. 1984. "Assessing the Risk of Crime Victimization: The Integration of Personal Victimization Experience and Socially Transmitted Information." *Journal of Social Issues* 40:27–38.

Unger, Donald, and Abraham Wandersman. 1983. "Neighboring and Its Role in Block Organizations." *American Journal of Community Psychology* 11:291–300.

Urban-Suburban Investment Study Group. 1975. *The Role of Mortgage Lending Practices in Older Urban Neighborhoods*. Evanston, Ill.: Northwestern University, Center for Urban Affairs and Policy Research.

Wilson, James Q., and George Kelling. 1982. "Broken Windows." *Atlantic* (March), pp. 29–38.

Yin, Peter. 1980. "Fear of Crime among the Elderly." *Social Problems* 27:492–504.

*Richard M. McGahey*

# Economic Conditions, Neighborhood Organization, and Urban Crime

ABSTRACT

Analyses of neighborhoods and their role in urban decline and revival, and mainstream sociological theories of crime, have focused attention on neighborhood crime and crime control patterns. Although much has been learned from such work, the effects of economic change on neighborhood social organization have not been taken into account. For example, poor local economic conditions and inadequate participation in the labor market can both cause and result from social disruption. The Vera Institute of Justice recently conducted a study of the effects of metropolitan labor markets and housing patterns on high-crime neighborhoods. Survey and ethnographic research among three Brooklyn, New York, neighborhoods indicated that persistent unemployment among adult residents limited the development of stable households and youth employment opportunities. The resulting lack of informal social controls contributed to the persistence of crime in some poor urban neighborhoods. Property crime, drug sales, and other illegal activities provided income to youths in neighborhoods where legitimate employment options were scarce or provided low wages and sporadic hours. Public policy on crime control in poor neighborhoods has concentrated on providing delinquents with vocational training. The results have not been encouraging, however.

Richard McGahey is Director of Policy and Program Development, New York State Department of Commerce. Special thanks to Jim Jacobs and Al Reiss for their criticisms of earlier drafts. Thanks also to David Greenberg, Bob Korstad, Lloyd Ohlin, Mercer Sullivan, and Michael Tonry for their comments and to Lisa Ewell, Susan Sebbard, and Linda Wheeler Reiss for manuscript preparation. Preparation of this essay was supported in part by grants from the Charles H. Revson Foundation, the National Institute of Justice, and the National Science Foundation. The statements made and views expressed are solely the responsibility of the author.


0-226-80802-5/86/0008-0007$01.00

Community action programs, inspired by the Mobilization for Youth program, attempted more profound social reforms and met with varying degrees of success.

In recent years the role played by neighborhoods and community organizations in the process of urban decay and revival has captured the attention of social scientists and public officials. In spite of large-scale federal efforts in housing, education, employment, and crime control, urban poverty and related social distress, including crime, has persisted and intensified in many cities. Often these problems are concentrated in a relatively small group of neighborhoods. The perceived failure of large-scale programs—along with a recognition that other national policies in local finance, housing, and transportation favored the development of suburbs—has led many analysts to focus on urban neighborhood organization as a possible source for stabilization and positive change (Schoenberg and Rosenbaum 1980; Downs 1981). Several observers have concentrated on the role of "mediating institutions," social organizations such as the family, school, churches, clubs, and other nongovernmental organizations (Berger and Neuhaus 1977; Novak 1982).

New analyses of crime and crime control policy have contributed to this revived interest in neighborhoods and community organization (Podolefsky and DuBow 1981; Woodson 1981). These analyses concentrate on the informal social controls provided by stable neighborhoods rather than on the effects of economic forces or criminal justice policy. These analyses have helped to illuminate how stable neighborhoods control or manage street crime but have not said much about how neighborhoods decay and lose control, in part because the effects of economic change on neighborhood economies, organization, and crime have not been fully addressed.

To help bridge this gap, this essay examines urban and neighborhood economies and their effects on social organization and crime. The relative abilities of different neighborhood economies and social organizations to cope with urban, regional, and national economic transformations may help explain why some neighborhoods turn into persistently high-crime communities and others do not. By viewing urban crime in relation to particular neighborhood economies and the broader urban labor market, we may be better able to understand crime's generation and persistence and to devise more effective policies for its control and reduction.

This essay begins with a brief consideration of the tension between economic change and social stability since the benefits and costs of socioeconomic change, including crime, are unevenly distributed among urban neighborhoods. Section II discusses legitimate economies in impoverished urban neighborhoods. Drawing on recent research, especially work conducted by the Employment and Crime Project at the Vera Institute of Justice, neighborhood employment and economic patterns are detailed. Some of this work echoes themes found in older sociological analyses of delinquency, but special attention is given here to the broad structure of the urban labor market, to its effects on youth unemployment, and to diverse economies in urban neighborhoods. Section III focuses on neighborhood crime patterns in relation to employment and social organization and details relations between employment and crime in poor neighborhoods. The role of illicit drugs, the perceptions of risk and reward for crime and legitimate employment, and community supports for certain types of crime all interact to form specific neighborhood crime patterns. Sections IV and V take up the role of previous public policy in stabilizing neighborhoods and influencing crime, giving special attention to the experience of the Mobilization for Youth program of the early 1960s. The final section outlines questions for future research and policy experiments.

## I. Unstable Economies, Destabilized Neighborhoods, and the Persistence of Crime

Joseph Schumpeter once described economic development in capitalist free-market economies as a process of "creative destruction" (1947, chap. 7), in which older techniques of production, resource use, employment, and associated social patterns were continuously transformed into new economic and social arrangements. Among other issues, Schumpeter was particularly concerned with the tension between a dynamic market economy, premised on the constant mobility of people and resources, and the social benefits provided by stable social organization.

Urban development in the United States has been profoundly affected by this tension, and the problems generated by this "creative destruction" have been unevenly distributed. Most Americans enjoyed a rising standard of living in the post–World War II period, but the population in central cities remained disproportionately poor, disproportionately nonwhite, and disproportionately victimized by crime. General prosperity rose throughout much of this period, but research does not show an automatic link between economic growth and improvement in black economic circumstances (Harris 1982).

This uneven distribution of socioeconomic costs and benefits is tied to the development of neighborhood organization. Although economic changes can disrupt social organization, the effects are not uniform. Affluent suburbs or wealthy central city residential districts often do not have extensive informal social networks, voluntary organizations, or ethnic solidarity, but they do not generate high levels of street crime. Crime remains concentrated in a relatively small number of persistently high-crime central city neighborhoods that also have high levels of chronic poverty and unemployment, substandard housing, illegitimate births to teenagers, and narcotic drug use. Of course, urban crime affects all residents through its effect on economic development, the fiscal burdens imposed by increased criminal justice spending, and its effects on property values. But its effects are greatest on the residents of decayed high-crime neighborhoods.

Labor market changes, demographic shifts, housing patterns, and public policy all influenced the rise in crime during the 1960s and the 1970s. Most of the rise in crime was concentrated in cities and further concentrated in the poorest neighborhoods, which also contained disproportionate numbers of nonwhites. Affected by broad economic changes that were a primary influence on migration and urban employment patterns (Wilson 1980; Johnson and Campbell 1981), social organization suffered in these impoverished neighborhoods, helping to create crime-prone environments.

The specific nature of high-crime communities needs to be emphasized. Crime did not rise uniformly in all cities during the 1960s and the 1970s nor in all neighborhoods in any particular city. This uneven change may help explain why macroeconomic analyses have not been able to confirm systematic links between overall indicators of economic distress and crime (Long and Witte 1981; Thompson et al. 1981; Freeman 1983*a*). Schuerman and Kobrin (in this volume) identify a process by which neighborhoods move from emerging to enduring high-crime areas. This process operates at the neighborhood level and generates enduring high-crime areas that contribute disproportionately to the city's crime rate (Reiss 1983).

Socioeconomic forces affect the growth of urban crime but do not fully determine the particular neighborhood structures that allow crime to persist. The following sections discuss the way in which broad economic forces along with local legitimate and illegitimate economies influence social organization and formal and informal social control. These patterns differ between neighborhoods; the resulting environments shape the relative returns from legitimate and illegitimate enterprise. Although economic changes are a central driving force of these problems, there are reciprocal social and neighborhood effects that account for crime's persistence, effects that are somewhat independent of economic forces.

The erosion of social institutions is one main source of persistent crime. Economic pressures and inadequate family structures fail to socialize and control children, who both encounter and create trouble in their inadequate schools and who fail to get decent educations. Because of this limited education, a lack of adult labor market connections, and an overall lack of jobs, they cannot find adequate jobs in their local labor market and engage in income-oriented crime, including predatory theft and drug sales. This increased crime helps drive out law-abiding citizens and legitimate economic activity from poor neighborhoods. Thus poor local economic conditions and inadequate participation in the labor market come to be the results of social disruption in addition to being causes of it.

## II. Neighborhood Connections between the Economy and Crime

Recent research on the interaction of economic patterns and crime patterns in poor urban neighborhoods can help disentangle the interplay of these factors. The Vera Institute of Justice, with the support of the National Institute of Justice, concentrated on some of these issues in a study of employment and crime patterns among "high-risk" youths living in Brooklyn, New York. The project had two central research strategies: statistical analysis of a randomly selected cohort of arrestees ($N$ = 903), using self-reported labor market information and official criminal histories, and an ethnographic analysis and comparison of white, Hispanic, and black neighborhoods.[1]

The Vera project set out to study the complex links among poverty, unemployment, and crime, especially for youth. The sample of arrestees was used for quantitative analyses of employment and crime rela-

[1] I was deputy project director of this project for several years with primary responsibility for the survey work and analysis of economic and labor market issues. I left the project prior to the completion of the final reports, although I remained in close contact with the project's progress. The interpretations of that project's findings presented in this essay are my own.

tions. Interviewed during the summer of 1979 with twenty-four-hour sampling every day of the week, arrestees were approached within a few hours of their arrest prior to arraignment and asked if they would participate in the survey. A 40 percent sample of arrestees was originally selected. Almost 40 percent of this original group was not interviewed due to refusals to participate or to removal from the holding area prior to completion of the interview. Analysis by the Vera staff indicated that the remaining sample was broadly similar to the overall group of arrestees in Brooklyn for the same time period (Sviridoff and McElroy 1984, pp. 26–31).

The ethnographic analysis focused on qualitative issues that cannot be examined through survey research. This phase of the project examined the variations in employment and crime among low-income urban neighborhoods through intensive fieldwork and life-history interviews with small groups of young men living in different neighborhoods. The project staff selected Brooklyn neighborhoods with substantial concentrations of poverty, looking for variations in crime opportunities, ethnicity, neighborhood organization, and special government programs. Project researchers maintained contact with some of the youths for up to four years (Sviridoff and McElroy 1984, pp. 31–35).

Analyses of these data tested different versions of the "economic model of crime"—the idea that most human behavior can be understood as a rational choice and that criminals choose crime on the basis of the relative costs and benefits of crime versus other activities. Little support was found for this simple economic model of crime (McGahey 1982; Thompson, Cataldo, and Lowenstein 1984). Although the experiences of some arrestees (and some of the subjects in the ethnographic work) showed that such choices occur between employment and crime, in most cases the relations were more complex (McGahey 1982). These findings suggested that the research should examine group patterns of criminal behavior and the neighborhood setting for crime. The quantity and quality of jobs available to various groups living together in local neighborhoods influence the ways that people form households, regulate public behavior, and use public services such as schools, welfare, police, and social programs. The resulting neighborhood atmosphere in turn helps to shape the incentives for residents to engage in legitimate employment and in income-oriented crime.

There seemed to be similar age-graded patterns of criminal involvement in all three neighborhoods that were reflected in the survey analysis. But as youth aged, these patterns diverged sharply, and the economic and social organization of the respective neighborhoods was a principal factor in these differences. For example, among fourteen- to sixteen-year-olds, crime often is not an alternative to work. Crime, especially petty theft, usually precedes legal employment, often by several years. In the later teenage years early employment experience is combined with some continued crime, which moderates among most youths as they age. Crime often ceases altogether for youths by their early twenties, with a few individuals involved in full-time crime.

So far this pattern merely confirms the general statistical profile of young criminals and the well-known process of "aging out." But the Vera research found significant variations when comparing youth crime patterns among different demographic groups and across different neighborhoods and found that more sustained income crimes were committed by nonwhites. In the arrestee survey, 61 percent of blacks and Hispanics had an income-oriented charge as their top charge compared with 52 percent of whites. Specific types of income offenses also varied: 22 percent of all black arrestees were charged with robbery, while Hispanics and whites were more likely to be charged with burglary (25 and 22 percent, respectively). Current income and drug charges were associated with higher frequencies of recent subsequent arrests (Sviridoff and McElroy 1984, pp. 132–75).

The neighborhood study mirrored the findings from the survey. In all three study neighborhoods "involvement in street crime was a relatively common phenomenon" for youths (Sviridoff and McElroy 1984, p. 204). Black and Hispanic youths were more likely to be systematically involved in theft and income-oriented crimes than were whites of the same age, but age remained the dominant factor related to criminal involvement in all three neighborhoods.

These findings are reminiscent of Shaw and McKay's (1969) studies of delinquency in Chicago neighborhoods. Shaw and McKay's initial research and policy prescriptions concentrated on youth-oriented activities such as recreational programs and schools and on work with criminal justice agencies, especially local police and parole. There was a relative lack of attention to direct employment and economic issues, partly because such problems were seen as outside the control or influence of the local community. Although Shaw in particular started with high hopes for grafting anticrime programs onto existing community structures, recent research has cast serious doubt on whether those Community Action Projects had any measurable effect on delinquency (Schlossman et al. 1984).

Neighborhood crime patterns and forms of community organization continued as a theme in later research. Cloward and Ohlin, direct heirs to this tradition, felt that Shaw and McKay had overlooked the degree and form of social organization in high crime areas: "Although they [Shaw and McKay] consistently referred to illegitimate activities as 'organized,' they nevertheless tended to label high-rate delinquency areas 'disorganized' because the values transmitted were criminal rather than conventional" (1960, p. 154). Seeing poor youths as caught between aspirations for legitimate success and the inability to meet those goals, Cloward and Ohlin looked for specific forms of delinquency and crime that would allow youths to mediate these needs. Their theories were associated directly with work on a major antidelinquency program, the Mobilization for Youth project on New York's Lower East Side. (This project and its effect on urban policy are discussed in more detail in Sec. IV.)

The idea that poor neighborhoods have their own forms of organization became a major theme of sociological research. Whyte's (1955) study of the "Cornerville" community found that crime and legitimate work were linked through a hierarchical community structure that provided the key to understanding both the legitimate and the illegitimate behavior in this community: "[I]n every group there was a hierarchical structure of social relations binding the individuals to one another and that the groups were also related hierarchically to one another" (p. viii). Spergel (1964), in his comparative study of delinquency in three lower-class urban neighborhoods, discovered distinctive patterns of crime and delinquency that were only partially related to local illegitimate enterprises. Blocked or socially unacceptable routes to legitimate or illegitimate success gave rise to new forms of delinquency.

### A. *The Role of Employment in Poor Communities*

Most of these studies assessed youth crime in relation to adult criminal opportunities and neighborhood social organization. These studies' major flaw is a lack of attention to the overall urban labor market and local economy. The quantity and quality of employment for local residents, adults as well as youths, is a central factor in explaining neighborhood and social disorganization and high crime.

Harrison (1972) describes a stylized "dual economy" in American cities, where the legitimate labor market is divided into a "primary" and a "secondary" sector. The primary market features steady jobs with reasonable wages and prospects for advancement; workers in this sector tend to be older, better educated, and more motivated. These favorable personal characteristics are reciprocally strengthened by the high quality and stability of the jobs. In contrast, workers in the secondary labor market sector are in low-wage, sporadic, dead-end jobs. They tend to be less skilled, educated, and reliable, again both mirroring and influencing the character of their jobs.[2] When they work, many adults in crime-prone communities work in secondary-sector jobs.

Harrison's typology points to the variety of income sources that supports poor communities. Stable, low-crime communities tend to draw their incomes and livelihood almost exclusively from primary-sector employment, while impoverished, high-crime communities do not subsist solely on the low returns to legitimate secondary jobs. Government transfers, participation in employment and training programs, and crime and illegal "hustles" constitute important additional sources of income, social organization, and identity for the urban poor.

Crime-plagued urban neighborhoods have substantial concentrations of unemployment and poverty. Crime is highest among young males in these economically deprived neighborhoods, where youth and adult employment problems have persisted throughout the post–World War II period, especially among nonwhites. Nonwhite teenagers traditionally suffer higher rates of unemployment than do whites, but the gap between these groups actually has grown since the early 1970s. The ratio of black to white unemployment rates for eighteen- and nineteen-year-olds grew from 1.72 in 1964 to 2.43 in 1983, indicating that the oft-discussed problem of youth unemployment "has not taken the form so much of joblessness among white youths as of high joblessness among black youths" (Freeman and Holzer 1985, pp. 18–19). Of course youths generally have higher levels of unemployment than have adults as the exploratory nature of youth labor market behavior is mutually reinforced by employers' reluctance to offer them stable job opportunities (Osterman 1980). But the growing black-white teenage unemployment gap cannot be explained by such factors, which are common to all teenagers (McGahey and Jeffries 1985, pp. 11–18).

Adult unemployment rates, while lower than those of teenagers, are disproportionately concentrated among residents of poor urban neigh-

[2] The dual economy model has come in for a great deal of criticism and refinement; see, among others, Freedman 1976; Kalleberg and Sorenson 1978; Beck, Horan, and Tolbert 1978. Nevertheless, its central insights remain valid: that urban labor markets are sharply divided by the type of jobs available; that workers are distributed unevenly in these jobs by race, sex, and education; and that poor communities must use a variety of income sources to get by.

borhoods. Even when employed, many blacks continue to be concentrated in lower-paying occupations and in the lower tiers of specific occupational groups, which are in those economic sectors most vulnerable to cyclical economic downturns (Westcott 1982). Although some nonwhites, especially those with college educations, have moved into better occupations with higher and more stable earnings, many remain stuck at the bottom of the occupational and earnings structure (Wilson 1980; McGahey and Jeffries 1985).

In the Vera research such differences in employment were tied to crime among the arrestees sample and in the study neighborhoods. The cohort of felony arrestees reported higher levels of legitimate labor market behavior than might be expected. Eighty-five percent of them were either working or looking for work at the time of their arrest. (Although there may have been some overreporting of job seeking in an effort to impress the interviewers, the employment/population ratios for the arrestees were very similar to their respective 1980 census cohorts.)[3] The black arrestees had a 51 percent employment/population ratio, compared with 57 percent among all Brooklyn black males sixteen and older; among Hispanics, arrestees were employed at a 54 percent rate relative to a total cohort employment population rate of 60 percent; and among whites, the respective figures were 67 percent for arrestees and 62 percent for the overall cohort (Sviridoff and McElroy 1984, p. 77, table 3.1). Fifty-four percent of the arrestees reported legitimate employment at the time of their arrest, and 86 percent of them reported working at some time within the previous two years. The occupation and industry of their current or previous jobs were disproportionately in the secondary-labor market, especially when compared with overall employment patterns for Brooklyn males.

Even within this group of felony arrestees, there were striking employment differences by race and ethnicity. White arrestees reported better employment than did blacks or Hispanics; indeed the white felony arrestees reported higher employment rates than did all Brooklyn blacks or Hispanics in the 1980 census. All the arrestee groups were more likely to work in blue-collar jobs, and whites were more often in higher-skilled and higher-paying craft jobs. White arrestees reported higher average wages than did blacks or Hispanics, and the gaps in-

[3] The employment/population ratio is the ratio of all employed people to the total working-age population; many analysts consider this a better measure of ghetto employment problems than the unemployment rate, which does not count those not actively seeking work.

creased with age. All three groups of sixteen- to nineteen-year-olds reported average hourly wages within thirty cents of the minimum wage, with whites the highest paid; for arrestees twenty-five and older, whites' average hourly wages were more than $1.80 above those of blacks and Hispanics (McGahey 1982, chap. 2; Sviridoff and McElroy 1984, pp. 80–90).

Differential employment patterns were also observed in the neighborhood study; in fact, they were one of the principal characteristics that distinguished the three neighborhoods: "The single most striking difference among the neighborhoods was the greater amount of employment and lesser amount of systematic economic crime during the middle teen years among the . . . [white teenagers] . . . in comparison to the two, poorer minority groups" (Sullivan 1984, p. 319).

The lack of teenage employment is linked to the employment problems of parents and other adults: underemployed adults cannot easily place youths in temporary or permanent jobs as the adults have little or no access to stable job openings. Neighborhood differences in adult poverty and employment "also contributed to differences in patterns of delinquency and youth crime" as parents were unable to provide spending money, fueling youths' early income-oriented crime (Sullivan 1984, pp. 320–21). Each group of youths—white, Hispanic, and black—had strong desires to settle into a stable labor market niche, but their respective ideas of what that would be varied sharply. For white youths, blue-collar, unionized jobs in construction or building maintenance looked like the best route to employment stability. For the Hispanic youths, blue-collar jobs with some sort of craft skills seemed the most desirable. Blacks focused mostly on civil service and government employment.

These aspirations mirror the employment experiences of adults in the three communities. Whites had the best chance to get the jobs they desired because of prior connections among families, friends, and locally based networks. Blue-collar, skilled manufacturing work is attractive to young Hispanic males because of language, training, and network barriers in growing white-collar jobs. But these jobs are less frequently available than they were in the past. These jobs have been shrinking in New York and in other cities (as they have in the U.S. economy) throughout the last several decades with especially dramatic losses during the mid-1970s (Yago et al. 1984). Blacks in turn focused on government employment, which was by far the largest source of stable jobs for blacks (including professionals) during the 1960s and the

1970s (Rumberger 1983). Government employment began to shrink in New York City during the late 1970s as a result of the city's fiscal crisis, and the legal and civil service apparatus that increased formal access to government employment also lessened nonwhite parents' ability to get entry-level jobs for their children.

Inadequate adult employment in turn causes a lack of youth jobs in two ways. First, unemployed adults cannot provide networks for their own children or for the children of extended family members and friends (Granovetter 1974; Freedman 1976). Second, diminished income among unemployed adults means less affluent residential neighborhoods with fewer youth jobs. The ideal job for a school-age youth is a local part-time job that is coupled with school attendance; retail and service jobs are the major source of such employment (Bailey and Waldinger 1984).

Impoverished, unstable neighborhoods with many unemployed adult residents do not have thriving retail sectors that offer such jobs. Sullivan's (1984) description of conditions in the black study neighborhood underscores this problem: "The only business activity in the area during the research period was concentrated in a rapidly dwindling commercial section. Most of the stores there were owned by people from outside the neighborhood. . . . During the research period, these businesses disappeared rapidly, succumbing to fires on an almost weekly basis" (p. 101). The lack of part-time locally based retail and service employment combined with inadequate family income drives teenagers to choose between school and income; there is no part-time work to reinforce continued schooling. This search for income then becomes one of the major forces driving acquisitive property crime.

### B. *Housing Investment and Neighborhood Economies*

In addition to employment patterns among adult residents and locally based employment for teenagers, the other major economic factor that distinguishes stable neighborhoods is the pattern of housing ownership and investment. Downs (1981, chap. 1) points out that "stability" in urban neighborhoods is actually a process of constant fluctuation. Residents are always moving in and out, and a neighborhood remains stable to the extent that new residents are similar to the old and that housing is maintained or improved. If low-income families suddenly move in and housing begins to deteriorate, current residents either move out or try to defend the neighborhood against such changes. Many families have a substantial capital investment in their homes, and without an expectation that the neighborhood will prosper, they may not continue to invest in housing upkeep. With the perception that neighborhood and property values will deteriorate, many residents will move. This reinforces the fears of others, and without strong neighborhood organization or other incentives to remain, housing may turn over very rapidly, with changes in the social makeup of households to poorer and less stable families.

Economists have only recently begun to study such neighborhood housing changes; a recent collection of economic analyses states that the authors "believe that a neighborhood can be analyzed like a good" (Segal 1979, p. 10), considering social factors primarily for their effect on housing prices.[4] Neighborhood characteristics are viewed as a public cost or benefit (an "externality") that individuals consume not through the result of direct private market transactions but by the indirect effects of location, principally through their purchase of, and investment in, housing. Segal (1979) presents the results of several economists' analyses of this version of neighborhood as an externality affecting housing prices; most of these analyses do not take crime explicitly into account. These analyses concentrate on the effect of local characteristics on housing prices and the decisions of individuals and households to stay or to move and give little attention to the interplay of the social factors that distinguish different neighborhoods.

A recent study that examines individual housing investment and neighborhoods combines this issue with older sociological interests in local organization and residential composition, especially racial invasion and succession and the fear of crime. Echoing other studies that find residents more likely to remain in neighborhoods when they are involved in a wide range of community activity, Taub, Taylor, and Dunham (1984) report that the effect of crime on residential decisions is complex: "[I]t is one's net judgement of the seriousness of the crime problem, not victimization experiences per se or even perceptions of the level of threat, that influence mobility intentions, expectations of neighborhood tipping, and willingness to invest in property maintenance" (p. 170). In the Chicago neighborhoods that they studied, the fear of crime and neighborhood tipping is bound up with racial factors but not solely as a matter of prejudice. Rather, the factors of perceived "crime, deterioration, and dissatisfaction" are associated with higher probabili-

[4] Downs (1981) is an exception. He goes beyond the issue of individual housing investments, linking demographic, economic, and policy changes to patterns of housing ownership and development.

ties that current residents will move out. The housing that then opens up is often taken by nonwhites who are looking to improve their own housing and to leave a bad neighborhood, sometimes leading to racial tensions between new black and Hispanic residents and those whites who cannot or do not want to leave.[5] Stable or rising housing investment and ownership in a neighborhood is tied to the employment and income of adult residents. Taub et al. (1984) found significantly higher levels of professional employment and income in some Chicago neighborhoods that were changing rapidly but not declining. Higher household incomes with a more traditional employment mix were found in neighborhoods that were stable and that were resisting racial turnover (pp. 30–31, tables 2.8–2.11). As McDonald (in this volume) points out, not all high-income neighborhoods are low in crime; wealthier "gentrifying" neighborhoods do not automatically have low crime rates. Rather, new urban residents and investors in gentrifying areas seem willing to tolerate higher levels of crime in return for other amenities such as proximity to employment and cultural institutions. Property crime in these neighborhoods seems to spill over from adjacent poor neighborhoods with the new affluent residents providing targets for property crime.

Low-crime neighborhoods often are characterized by stable, relatively affluent households, many of whom own their residence and have substantial capital investments in them. In contrast, much of the housing in poor neighborhoods is not owner occupied, because of a lack of income and stable employment among residents. During the 1950s and the 1960s the rapid expansion of suburban housing created an oversupply of older housing in cities that often was filled in marginal neighborhoods by renting to poor nonwhites. This rental pattern entailed the conversion of older properties into cheaper and less well maintained housing; in turn, older slum housing was not maintained at all, and some was abandoned entirely (Matusow 1984, pp. 232–37). Renters are more likely to be mobile and less committed to their communities than are owners. Downs identifies a high percentage of renters as one of the factors that is linked to declining neighborhoods along with high proportions of low-income households, old and poorly designed buildings, a loss of overall urban population, a lack of strong

[5] Rieder (1985) provides a graphic account of such tensions in the Brooklyn neighborhood of Canarsie, whose residents in the 1970s felt that a combination of white liberal politicians and lower-class blacks were destroying their neighborhood and schools.

community organizations, high turnover and transiency among residents, and high crime (1981, p. 66, table 5-1). Of course many American cities during the 1960s and the 1970s had some or most of these characteristics, especially in high-crime neighborhoods. In contrast to the interaction of the legitimate employment market and housing ownership and investment that helps create stable low-crime environments, the absence of these factors contributes to sustained street crime in impoverished neighborhoods.

## III. Neighborhood Organization and the Persistence of Crime

One sobering finding from the Vera research is the widespread prevalence and persistence of property crime among nonwhites in poor communities. Most crimes are property crimes, and the research reflects this: both blacks and Hispanics in the arrestees sample had income-oriented charges as their top charge 61 percent of the time, while income charges for white arrestees were the top charge in 52 percent of the cases. The nature of the income charges varied by race and ethnicity; robbery arrests were concentrated among young blacks with robberies falling off among all older arrestees. Among sixteen- and seventeen-year-olds, blacks were arrested for robbery in 39 percent of the cases, while there was a 15 percent rate of arrests among sixteen- and seventeen-year-old Hispanics for robbery and 11 percent among whites. In the two years preceding the current arrest, eighteen- and nineteen-year-olds were most likely to have greater numbers of prior arrests (22 percent of the eighteen- and nineteen-year-old arrestees had four or more prior arrests in the two-year period) (Sviridoff and McElroy 1984, pp. 140, 144).

This pattern varied by neighborhood with property crime much more widespread in the nonwhite communities and more persistent among black and Hispanic youths. White youths were involved in a wide variety of delinquent crime but were not as systematically involved in property crime. The Vera researchers summarized the relations between crime and employment in "Hamilton Park," the white working-class neighborhood they studied: "Although in Hamilton Park, employment for the very young (14–16) did not entail the cessation of exploratory property crime, it seemed that employment, working in concert with other social, institutional, and ecological influences, strongly affected the frequency and severity of early adolescent criminal activity, the duration of the period of exploratory property crime, and the prevalence of income-oriented street crime during mid-adolescence" (Sviridoff and McElroy 1984, pp. 264–65).

The other neighborhood contribution to persistent crime problems is the existence of quasi-organized criminal enterprises. Sullivan (1983) classified youth crime in the Vera study neighborhoods as "peer recruited" and "adult recruited." In the white neighborhood, adults recruited youths for racketeering and loan sharking; in the Hispanic neighborhood, adults recruited youths into auto theft and chop shops. In the black neighborhood, there was less organized crime and more peer-recruited theft and drug sales (although some drug selling took place in all three communities).

These findings recall previous sociological analyses of crime patterns in poor neighborhoods. Cloward and Ohlin (1960) theorized that differences in local opportunity structures would strongly influence distinctive youth-gang organization. Spergel (1964) examined three New York City communities in the early 1960s and found very specific patterns of delinquency and crime, although these patterns were not always closely linked to the particular character of local legitimate opportunities. In "Racketville," youth crime was closely tied to preparation for participation in adult criminal networks, while there was a weaker link between youth and adult crime in the other two neighborhoods.

Such analyses discovered that youthful criminal behavior often varies in different neighborhoods in relation to adult criminal enterprises and networks. The latter must coexist with the legitimate local economy. Analysts such as Kobrin (1951), Whyte (1955), Cloward and Ohlin (1960), and Spergel (1964) have noted the curious coexistence of legitimate and illegitimate enterprise in stable neighborhoods.

The distinct patterns postulated in this earlier research were more mixed in the Vera research; some of the crimes that are theoretically associated with different neighborhoods were found in all of the study neighborhoods. In addition, some neighborhoods lack either stable legitimate or stable illegitimate structures. This is especially true in very poor neighborhoods. Cloward and Ohlin (1960) refer to these areas as "disorganized," or "unintegrated," neighborhoods, where neither legitimate resources nor illegitimate structures are available: "This is not to say that crime is nonexistent in such areas, but what crime there is tends to be individualistic, unorganized, petty, poorly paid, and unprotected" (p. 173).

Where there is little steady legitimate opportunity, stable patterns of crime may not arise. The Vera study found few stable criminal networks in the two nonwhite study neighborhoods. Crimes among nonwhites were more likely to be individualized. Although many of these crimes, especially robberies, are done by groups, they are not highly organized.

A high level of predatory property crime is tied to the lack of stable adult employment in the larger urban economy and to the prevalence of poverty in nonwhite neighborhoods. Impoverished neighborhoods are disproportionately populated with unstable households that cannot exercise authority or control over young people and that also cannot provide them with spending money. The lack of adult income feeds the decline of local retail and service employment, which means fewer jobs for local youths. These youths drop out of school without a viable alternative in contrast to white youths who drop out for legitimate jobs.

### A. *The Role of Illicit Drugs*

Illicit drugs also provide a source of income and employment in some poor neighborhoods as well as providing a steady supply of users. Sales and use are often intertwined; a study of active black and Chicano addicts found that drug sales accounted for 35.7 percent of self-reported crime, "vice crimes" such as pimping and prostitution accounted for another 32.9 percent, and property crimes accounted for 26.3 percent (Chambers, Dean, and Pletcher 1981, p. 148). The property crime and fear for children's health that is associated with drug dealing lend it much less community legitimacy than do other types of crime. Nevertheless, it persists as a major source of illegitimate opportunity in some poor neighborhoods.

The rising use of illicit drugs, especially heroin, has played a significant role in the deterioration of urban neighborhoods. Although there is no perfect indicator of changing heroin use, a variety of indicators shows the rising severity of the drug problems, mainly in northern cities. After stabilizing and actually declining between 1930 and 1945, total prosecutions for narcotics in the United States rose sharply from slightly over 4,000 in 1945, to around 18,000 in 1955, and to over 34,000 in 1962 (Helmer 1975, p. 86, fig. 5-3). Wilson (1983, p. 177) cites a report that estimated a tenfold increase in Boston heroin users during the 1960s. Preble and Casey (1969) found that the New York heroin epidemic that began in the early 1950s was concentrated primarily among the young, who began injecting the drug rather than inhaling it as older addicts did.

The epidemiology of heroin use indicates that the spread of addiction is neighborhood based and occurs in areas where some significant amount of drug use already exists and where friends and peers are the main source of supply (Kaplan 1983, pp. 27–32). Such epidemics can take place in a relatively short period of time; Claude Brown, in his memoir of growing up in Harlem during the 1950s, says that "if anyone had asked me around the later part of 1957 what I thought had made the greatest impression on my generation in Harlem, I would have said 'Drugs.' . . . Just eight years earlier, in 1949, this wouldn't have been true" (1965, p. 263).

Like many other social problems, the upsurge in heroin use was concentrated in urban areas, especially in poor nonwhite neighborhoods. Large numbers of younger addicts became involved, and heroin prices were reported to rise sharply in the late 1950s and early 1960s (Preble and Casey 1969). This rise in drug use was contemporaneous with a rise in urban crime, and the relation between drug use and crime has been illuminated by recent research. The image of the unemployed addict, driven by an uncontrollable need for ever-greater quantities of heroin with no income option other than crime, has been replaced by a more sophisticated picture of the drug-crime relation. Involvement with heroin seems more a part of certain criminal patterns and lifestyles than an independent cause of crime; heroin use often begins some time after involvement in other crimes. But there are still strong ties between the volume and type of crime and drug use. The amount of crime committed by users seems to be directly related to the size of the habit. Although many heroin users have jobs and other legitimate sources of income (Goldstein 1981), their property offenses rise sharply during times of peak drug use (Inciardi 1979; Gandossy et al. 1980, pp. 44–52; Ball et al. 1981; Chambers et al. 1981).

### *B. Relations between Employment and Crime in Poor Neighborhoods*

The relations between employment and crime in poor neighborhoods, especially persistent crime among nonwhite teenagers, must be understood against the backdrop of persistent poverty, unstable households, and related social problems such as illicit drug use. Although one may not want to go as far as Charles Silberman and claim that "theft is in the very air that lower-class youngsters breathe" (1980, p. 124), chances for criminal participation are widespread and well-known within poor communities, while legitimate employment options are sparse.

The migration of nonwhite populations into central cities from rural areas influenced these crime and employment patterns. Nonwhite urban populations grew in three successive ways: immigration of prime-age workers; immigration of wives, extended families, and older relatives; and birth of children to the new immigrants (Johnson and Campbell 1981). This pattern is typical for most immigrant groups and is important for understanding crime patterns. First-generation migrants do not assimilate fully into urban life but retain values and behavioral standards from their birthplaces often with the goal of returning to their birthplace. It is the children of immigrants who adopt new urban values, including the desire for immediate material success (Piore 1979). These second-generation urban dwellers are not in the labor force in their early teens, and thus their choices are often not between employment and crime but between school and income. If their parents cannot provide them with income, then their other options include crime and employment. For young teens this often means crime because of the age-graded job structure and other labor market barriers, including discrimination and a lack of neighborhood employment. Criminal networks also grow among the new immigrants, providing alternative routes to material success.

There are a number of barriers that affect both legitimate employment and crime among residents of poor neighborhoods. In addition to the lack of jobs there seems to be an information paradox operating in these neighborhoods. Poor youths often have very limited information about the types of jobs available in the legal labor market, although they know that legitimate jobs pay quite poorly (Bullock 1973). Conversely, they know about criminal options but may overestimate the potential returns from property crime, drug sales, and the like.

Crime competes with school and work for the time and labor resources of poor youths, but several myths about the monetary returns from urban youth crime cloud most analyses. Crime is not a lucrative income option despite claims that high black youth unemployment rates can be explained by rich opportunities in the "underground economy" and in crime. In fact returns from crime tend to be sporadic and low for most young criminals, rather like the low wages and sporadic hours offered by legitimate secondary labor market jobs.

This conclusion is based in part on work done for the Vera project. For instance, the analysis of the survey data on felony arrestees found no evidence of crime and employment trade-offs, in part because the monetary returns from street crime are estimated to be low (McGahey 1982). Most teenage crime is spontaneous and unplanned and is performed for short-run income needs that are not met by parents or other adults and that cannot be met through legal work.

This contrasts with studies conducted as part of the National Bureau of Economic Research (NBER) project on inner-city minority youth employment, which suggested that crime presents an attractive alternative source of income (Viscusi 1983). In an article summarizing the NBER findings, Freeman and Holzer (1985) conclude that "crime and employment are alternatives" and that a lack of good legitimate job options "can lead to participation in crime" (p. 29). But the Vera project's econometric studies of felony arrestees found little evidence of systematic trade-offs between crime and employment among youths (McGahey 1982, chap. 4). It may be that youths' perception of high illegal earnings is tied to their criminal participation; the NBER survey relied on youths' perceptions of illegal earnings and risks of punishment, while the Vera study computed total monetary returns for crimes by extrapolating crime frequencies from arrest data. But if youths are trading off crime against legal employment opportunities, they are doing it in a prospective manner as criminality (in terms of the widest criminal participation among their cohort) peaks before substantial cohort involvement in the legal labor market.

The Vera research explored the issue of perceptions of risk and return to crime with a subset ($N = 160$) of the original arrestees sample. Respondents were asked to rank six types of crime for risks of arrest and personal injury and then to estimate the potential weekly earnings from these crimes. They estimated weekly earnings in a relatively wide range: $348 for shoplifting, $461 for robbery, $466 for "grab and run" theft, $623 for marijuana sales, $787 for burglary, and $861 for con games such as three-card monte. Estimated risks of injury and arrest were highest for burglary, robbery, and "grab and run," and lowest for marijuana sales (Sviridoff and McElroy 1984, pp. 170–72). All these figures are substantially above the weekly earnings for a full-time minimum-wage job (approximately $135 for a forty-hour week).

Estimates for net dollar returns to single crimes for Brooklyn in 1979 give some idea of the likely frequency of crime needed to produce the earnings estimated by the subsample. The average net value of a single larceny was roughly estimated at $80.15, robbery at $134.09, burglary at $451.81, and weekly marijuana sales at $200. (Details of the estimation procedure are given in McGahey [1982, pp. 197–206]; these estimates include discounts on stolen property purchased by fences, the cost of purchasing marijuana for resale, and so on. They are not adjusted for neighborhood differences in wealth.) The figures vary in some cases from the estimates provided by the arrestees (for instance, in the case of marijuana sales), while other figures could be in close proximity, depending on the frequency of particular crimes. The subsample's estimated weekly earnings could be achieved with fewer than four average robberies and with fewer than two average burglaries. This frequency of robbery and burglary would quickly use up the available crime targets in a neighborhood, especially in a poor neighborhood where the average take is likely to be lower. This level of frequency would also increase the chances of arrest and punishment or of retaliation.

A favorite story among participants in crime involves the "big score"—a lucky robbery or burglary in which some (often apocryphal) criminal happened on a victim with lots of money. This parallels the role of lotteries in poor communities and fits with a belief among the urban poor that success often is a matter of luck. Although desires for success tend to be shared by different classes in the United States, there is little belief among the poor that adherence to "middle-class values" provides any assurance of achieving success (Howell 1973; Stack 1974; Coleman and Rainwater 1978). As Silberman (1980) noted, "To the 'children of poverty,' those who want something badly enough usually do not get it, no matter how hard they work or how long they wait" (p. 119).

The effect of aspirations, attitudes, and values also relates to legitimate employment patterns but is complicated by race and ethnicity. The young whites observed in the Vera ethnographic study dropped out of high school about as frequently as did the blacks and Hispanics but were significantly more able to find jobs through their superior family networks and superior local markets. With the contraction of New York's blue-collar job market, these connections were not as rewarding as they were in the past, but they remained much more effective than did labor market networks among nonwhites. Whites in the arrestees survey had markedly superior labor market experiences that were not explained statistically by their educations, skills, or work experiences (McGahey 1982, chap. 3).

Variations in employment are also not easily explained by differences in expressed values or commitments to education. The Hispanic youths were the strongest believers that blue-collar craft skills would provide steady employment. The black youths expressed stronger commitments to formal schooling as a route to success than either the

Hispanics or the whites. The whites valued schooling for the formal credential of a high school diploma, which would allow them to "benefit fully from family and neighborhood-based connections to jobs" (Sullivan 1984, p. 54).

So young urban males have reasonably good information about the returns to minimum-wage legal work and about the jobs that their parents and adult relatives hold, although they have little reliable information on the actual requirements for, or the daily content of, those jobs. Conversely, they know a fair amount about how to engage in crime in their neighborhoods. They may overestimate the long-run potential monetary returns from crime, or they may simply not be thinking about long-run effects as do many youths in the legitimate labor market. Youths of all races and ethnic groups leave school to earn income, but white youths move more easily from school into legal work. Nonwhites more frequently use crime as a sustained source of income. For high-risk young men in cities, the immediate trade-off is not between work and crime but between school and income. Often school is not highly valued as a route to labor market success. Even when it is, the possibility of higher future returns from education must be weighed against immediate needs for income—and the two available sources of income in impoverished neighborhoods are employment and crime. Although many youths mix these sources, the continuing lack of employment among nonwhite neighborhoods relative to whites helps to explain their higher levels of crime.

### *C. Crime and Social Organization in Poor Neighborhoods*

Neighborhoods with little stable adult and youth employment are vulnerable to predatory crime, partly because of the effect of persistent unemployment on household stability. Unstable households account for a disproportionate amount of total unemployment and poverty in the United States (Freeman 1981, p. 115). These unstable households and impoverished neighborhoods often put a premium on male aggressiveness as a means of dealing with limited opportunity and of providing a social identity (Glasgow 1980; Poussaint 1983). A lack of legitimate neighborhood economic activity also reduces the number of older people on the street; the result is domination of street life by idle youths. Such patterns contribute to the fear of crime and may create opportunities for predatory crime that is not easily controlled by police (Podolefsky and DuBow 1981; Wilson and Kelling 1982). It is difficult for such neighborhoods to mobilize formal or informal defenses against crime.

Although impoverished neighborhoods suffer from this disorganization, community and social organization should be viewed as a continuum and not as a dichotomy between "organization" and "disorganization." A variety of studies have documented the surprising strength and creative nature of familial and quasi-kin networks among the urban poor, white and nonwhite alike (Howell 1973; Stack 1974; Bochert 1980). But the ability of families and neighborhoods to cope under socioeconomic pressure should not be romanticized; high levels of crime and social disruption in many poor neighborhoods attest to the relative weakness of their social organizations.

Many forces that affect a neighborhood's strength emanate from outside its boundaries. The national and metropolitan economy, which is the primary source of jobs, money, and social status, provides the economic basis to establish intact households and to maintain housing. Problems such as the continuing supply of illegal drugs cannot be controlled by neighborhoods alone; neither can residential segregation, cutbacks in social welfare spending, or inadequate schools. Impoverished communities are not without resources for social control, but their resources seem to vary directly with the amount and type of legitimate employment available to adults who reside in the community. The resulting patterns of social organization lead to different degrees of acceptance or resignation regarding different types of crime.

Different crimes are accorded different levels of acceptance, toleration, and, sometimes, active support. Silberman cites studies that found the numbers business to be the single largest employer in Bedford-Stuyvesant, a black Brooklyn neighborhood; most of the money spent on the numbers remained in the community, lending it a strong degree of legitimacy and community support (1980, pp. 134–40).

In the Hispanic neighborhood studied by the Vera researchers, youths burglarized local factories, often selling the stolen goods to neighborhood residents at a discount. Most of the factories were owned and managed by people who did not reside in the neighborhood, and local residents held ambivalent views regarding the immorality of these burglaries. Residents did disapprove of heroin sales and residential theft, although the Hispanic youths claimed not to conduct many such crimes in their own neighborhoods. When they did, they faced retaliation from neighborhood residents, especially for violent robberies.

Robberies also led to swifter and more severe punishment from criminal justice agencies. The only organized criminal activity in which the Hispanic youths engaged was auto theft, and some were recruited into relatively stable theft rings.

In the black study neighborhood there were almost no opportunities for commercial burglaries because of a lack of businesses. Crime was of two kinds: predatory theft (including a wave of gold-chain snatching) and drug sales (both marijuana and harder drugs). As in the Hispanic neighborhood, predatory theft by individual youths ended fairly quickly, although new thieves often took their place. Targets and local crime opportunities dry up as young criminals become known, and residents defend themselves and retaliate, sometimes violently. Drug sales provided a more steady income although still in a rather individualistic and disorganized way. A fair amount of the drug sales were to local residents sometimes through the establishment of "reefer stores," that is, shops that set up for a few weeks in a storefront operation and deal drugs along with candy, gum, and cigarettes.

In the white study neighborhood, the patterns of youth crime strongly resembled the patterns described in earlier sociological work on delinquency, although diverse types of violent crime, theft, and drug use coexisted. Although this neighborhood had substantial levels of poverty, criminally involved youths were somewhat the exception unlike the other two study neighborhoods. The white youths were more likely to run into trouble with the community at an early age and to reduce or halt their criminality fairly quickly. The white neighborhood had more stable intact households with primary labor market jobs and networks, more quasi-organized criminal networks, and a higher degree of overall social control. Crime among the white youths was still strongly motivated by economic goals, but it usually ended when young men obtained legitimate jobs through locally based family and neighborhood networks. (These neighborhood crime patterns are detailed extensively in Sullivan [1984].)

## IV. The Effect of Public Policy

With a few notable exceptions, the public policy debate on crime in the 1960s and early 1970s did not focus on the economies of neighborhoods and cities. Calls for increased employment and social welfare relied on the premise that rational criminals would abandon street crime in favor of employment, while advocates of deterrence felt that crime would be reduced in response to increased threats of punishment.

Many analysts have debated the effect of public policy on poverty and crime in poor urban communities. Piven and Cloward (1971) argued that the structure of public welfare and social service agencies during the 1960s and the 1970s undercut autonomous behavior by poor people, fostering dependency on institutions that were out of the poor's control. A parallel analysis has come to play a major role in recent debates on social policy, although the policy suggestions are associated with the political Right. It is expressed most fully in the work of Walter Williams (1982), Charles Murray (1984), Thomas Sowell (1984), and others who implicate American welfare state policies in the continued deterioration of life among the urban poor. Murray (1984) sees the urban poor's behavior as deteriorating, noting that they fell further behind while social programs increased:

> The most compelling explanation for the marked shift in the fortunes of the poor is that they continued to respond, as they always had, to the world as they found it, but that we—meaning the not-poor and un-disadvantaged—had changed the rules of their world. . . . The first effect of the new rules was to make it profitable for the poor to behave in the short term in ways that were destructive in the long term. Their second effect was to mask these long term losses—to subsidize irretrievable mistakes. We tried to provide more for the poor and produced more poor instead. [P. 9]

Murray and other analysts claim not to rely on a subcultural argument that the poor hold different values than do other Americans. Rather they assert that crime is a rational response to changing incentives.[6] Murray suggests doing away with virtually the entire structure of social programs and government support for housing, employment, and income support; in their place government can offer mainly penalties (1984, p. 177).

Murray's work exemplifies a marked correspondence that links diverse analyses of urban crime. For those who see a strong direct tie

[6] Murray's analysis is in reality a curious admixture of economically rational and value-oriented subcultural arguments. The most consistent construction of his views might be that changed incentives caused changed behavior among the urban poor. These behavioral changes isolated the poor, furthering their segregation from mainstream society, including middle-class blacks. Such segregation in turn fosters further isolating behavior, deepening the socioeconomic gaps. For some seeming inconsistencies in Murray's analysis, see the exchange between Murray and Robert Greenstein (1985).

between unemployment and crime, crime is viewed as a rational response to a lack of legitimate opportunity and to inadequate public aid (Gordon 1973); for analysts such as Murray, the growth and persistence of crime and unemployment together is a rational response to declines in the threat of punishment and to the relatively higher returns from public programs. Both sides view much of criminal behavior as individually rational, and both implicate public policy as a principal cause of changing individual behavior. But both sides of this debate and much of public policy may have been limited by not viewing neighborhoods as the meeting ground of individual behavior and broad socioeconomic forces.

This can be illustrated by examining the results of employment and training programs aimed at improving labor market experiences and at reducing crime. These programs were expected to improve individuals' legal labor market position, which would then reduce the comparative attractiveness of crime. But analyses of individual employment and criminal behavior show little or no effects on labor market status or recidivism.

Most vocational programs aimed at delinquents were "so under-evaluated as to make it difficult to judge program effectiveness" (Dixon and Wright 1974, p. 68). But even studies that used rigorous evaluation methods reported discouraging findings. Several employment-program efforts had an explicit anticrime focus and also benefited from experimental design evaluations, including the Job Corps, supported work projects under the Youth Employment Demonstration Projects Act, and the Transitional Aid to Released Prisoners program. Except for the Job Corps, none of these programs had a statistically significant effect on crime (Manpower Demonstration Research Corporation 1980; Rossi, Berk, and Lenihan 1980; Taggart 1982; Sadd, Kotkin, and Friedman 1983).

There are several possible explanations for the failure to find reduced crime as a result of these programs. First, the programs did not really improve individuals' job readiness. Labor market outcomes did not improve, and crime did not abate. Second, changes in individual human resources and capabilities or in labor market position are not immediately related to changes in crime. Crime and unemployment may be correlated in the aggregate, but the relation is highly complex for individuals. The programs did not generally improve the labor market position of participants, so this interpretation remains untested. Third, programs and public policy did not adequately understand the dynamics between employment and crime, especially for young people, and may have incorrectly perceived the reasons for lack of program results. Rather than providing a chance to advance, programs are only another temporary stop in the dead-end urban labor market and become another erratic source of low income along with regular ill-paying jobs, transfer payments, and crime (cf. Harrison 1972).[7]

Finally, the analyses and program designs may have failed to pay sufficient attention to the neighborhoods where youthful crime takes place and where released prisoners return. Urban anthropologists have documented extensive sharing of resources among the urban poor, and young people are no exception. Income is often seen as a temporary windfall to be shared with friends and neighbors, not a permanent stream to be reserved for one's own use. The income from an employment program is spent rapidly on consumption for friends, peers, and families, vanishing into the larger pool of community poverty.

This may help explain why the Job Corps reduced crime. Job Corps participants were physically and socially removed from their high-crime neighborhoods and crime-prone peer groups. Presumably, there were fewer opportunities for crime on Job Corps sites and diminished needs to share money with peers. But for participants in different programs living in high-crime communities, the level of overall need remained quite high. In addition to low individual wages, most programs serve only a fraction of those in need (Taggart 1981). Among the sample of felony arrestees in the Vera study, 10 percent of their current or most recent employment was in a government program; 14 percent of all black arrestees' jobs were government supported compared with 6 percent of Hispanics and 1 percent of the white arrestees (Sviridoff and McElroy 1984, p. 86, table 3.5).

## V. Community Policy and Its Limits—Mobilization for Youth and the Community Action Program

Most policies aimed at reducing crime have been focused either on individuals or on large socioeconomic aggregates. Labor market programs have tried to increase individual skills or job qualifications. Criminal justice policy has concentrated on apprehending and deterring individual criminals. Macroeconomic policies have aimed to create more job opportunities for the poor (along with everyone else) through

[7] In addition, both experimentals and controls often entered the research and programs at periods of high criminality. These rates would diminish over time among both groups, blurring any statistical effect from the programs.

general economic growth, leading to reductions in crime and in other social problems (McGahey and Jeffries 1985).

Both policy approaches have failed to incorporate neighborhood-level factors and have not considered the local neighborhood and economy as that environment where individual behavior, social institutions such as the family, physical infrastructures such as housing, and criminal justice policies come together to shape crime. Programs aimed exclusively at individuals, such as most training programs, did not account for the structural changes in the urban labor market, the local and sporadic nature of most youth employment, and peer influences on young men. Macropolicies do not specify the mechanisms through which broad economic changes are to be translated into specific material improvements among the urban poor nor how those individual improvements might strengthen poor communities.

Much of the public policy in the 1960s and the supporting social science analysis seemed to assume that communities are nothing more than aggregations of individual behaviors and interests. There was one notable exception—the Community Action Program (CAP) of the 1960s, launched as part of the War on Poverty. One of CAP's expressed goals was to involve the urban poor directly, advocating "maximum feasible participation" in programs affecting their lives. The CAP model was drawn from a historic effort to combat urban crime and delinquency—the Mobilization for Youth (MFY) program on New York's Lower East Side in the late 1950s, which was adopted by the Kennedy administration under its Juvenile Delinquency and Youth Offense Control Act in 1961. Mobilization for Youth advocated a wide variety of coordinated community-based programs that would involve community residents in different activities, including employment programs, recreational efforts, and community organizing; the original Mobilization for Youth proposal ran more than 600 pages, with dozens of specific recommendations for action and pages of supporting research (Mobilization for Youth 1961).

Mobilization For Youth's original complex design was based on the analysis offered by Richard Cloward and Lloyd Ohlin in their book *Delinquency and Opportunity: A Theory of Delinquent Gangs* (1960). Rather than concentrate on the rational individual offender model of economic theory or on deviance models that were not rooted in broader community and social structures, Cloward and Ohlin saw youthful criminals as sharing the goals of American society, especially the desire for material success. But poor young men were blocked in achieving these goals by a lack of legitimate opportunity and turned to crime both as a source of income and as a source of identity. For Cloward and Ohlin these structural issues were the key to understanding and preventing delinquency. As they stated, "delinquency is not . . . a property of individuals or even of subcultures; it is a property of the social systems in which these individuals and groups are enmeshed," and this analysis led them to a distinctive policy conclusion: "The major effort of those who wish to eliminate delinquency should be directed to the reorganization of slum communities" (Cloward and Ohlin 1960, p. 211).

But most of the efforts launched under the broad CAP program drifted far away from MFY's original goals. The program was expanded vastly beyond the original pilot experiment, with over 1,000 federally funded community action agencies (CAAs) created between October 1964 and June 1966. Many of the CAAs were captured by existing political organizations who were threatened by the development of new political power bases. This subverted the original goal of creating alternative social and political networks among the poor. Mobilization for Youth itself ended up with a more limited mission that stressed the delivery of legal services and vocational education. In his analysis of the Great Society, Matusow (1984) views the CAP model as the one program that attempted profound social reform through its attempt to "redistribute power, if only on the local level and in limited ways" (p. 126). But the "community empowerment" approach encountered a variety of problems, including the animosity of existing political institutions, the changes and dilutions introduced into the program as it was expanded, the depth of social disorganization among the poor, and the complexity and need for coordination to carry out the program's original design.[8]

## VI. Future Research and Policy

Although a variety of socioeconomic problems continue to foster crime in impoverished urban neighborhoods, the lack of stable legitimate employment among adult residents remains a principal cause of persistent crime. The paucity of financial and other resources in these communities means that informal social controls are very weak and have little prospect of strengthening on their own.

[8] Matusow's account of how the CAAs were first attacked and then taken over by existing urban political agencies is a sobering account of the difficulties and limits of "top-down" reform policy (see, esp., Matusow 1984, chaps. 4, 9).

But this diagnosis does not automatically reveal a simple policy agenda. Although unemployment is a central problem for high-crime areas, traditional employment programs do not offer much of a solution. Previous training efforts did not provide measurable long-term labor market improvement to poor youth, and employment and social policy in the past two decades has not been associated with significant reductions in the levels of crime, violence, and disruption in poor urban neighborhoods. Criminal justice policies that have concentrated on apprehending and punishing criminals also have not made much of a dent in these neighborhoods.

Future research and policy needs to concentrate in four areas: employment, housing, family and child care, and criminal justice policy.

1. *Employment.* Efforts must be made to increase stable employment among adult residents of poor neighborhoods. Traditional training programs, with their emphasis on short-run participation and immediate transitions to private-sector jobs, are not appropriate in many circumstances (McGahey and Jeffries 1985). Experiments such as the supported work models pioneered by the Manpower Demonstration Research Corporation are one promising avenue. (Supported work programs offer graduated exposure to the world of work along with social supports. They have been successful in reducing crime among some target groups, especially ex-addicts.) The educational and training needs of the poor need to be reexamined and delivered more effectively. Basic competency in mathematics and language is critical, but the best place to accomplish this is in the public schools, not in training programs. For adults and teenage dropouts, competency programs should be tied to work experience in a cooperative fashion. For youths still in school, cooperative part-time jobs should be linked with continued school attendance. (Models and resources for competency programs are reviewed in Center for Human Resources [1984–85].)

The role of informal networks should also be studied further to see how such networks might be developed and strengthened among the poor. But trying to expand such networks without actually expanding employment holds little promise. As Granovetter (1974) notes, "Blacks are at a disadvantage in using informal channels not because they have failed to 'develop an informal structure' . . . but because they are presently under-represented in the structure of employment itself" (p. 133).

Job-creation efforts should also be pursued, especially in poor neighborhoods. Some localities are experimenting with first-source agreements, in which private sector firms that receive tax breaks, financing, and infrastructure development pledge to use public training referrals as a "first source" of new hires. These placement programs are sometimes coupled with employer-specific skill training, where existing employees are upgraded and where the entry-level slots that open up are filled with clients of public agencies. There are also new models for generating economic development in poor neighborhoods through a combination of business relocations, start-ups of new enterprises (sometimes using welfare or unemployment funds as a source of capitalization), and alternative investments of pension funds and other capital sources. (These types of programs are presented in Corporation for Enterprise Development, various editions.)

2. *Housing.* Housing remains a critical problem in strengthening and revitalizing urban neighborhoods. With cutbacks in federal funds, cities and states will have to carry out many of these policies with their own resources; for both fiscal and political reasons this will limit the amount that can be done. Private reinvestment in impoverished neighborhoods is a helpful step, although this raises the problem of gentrification and displacement of the resident poor. But if cities will not provide massive subsidies to improve substandard housing, a refusal to allow private market reinvestment by restricting conversions and displacement effectively amounts to preserving slums (Downs 1981, p. 149). Cities would be better advised to develop policies for relocation and rehousing of the displaced as some cities are already doing by imposing taxes on commercial development or by requiring direct contributions from private real estate developers (Pickman and Roberts 1985). Relocation could also assist in "deconcentrating" the poor from their disorganized and troubled neighborhoods.

Investment in housing for distressed communities can come also from the involvement of major nongovernmental institutions such as churches, universities, and foundations. These institutions can help leverage further investment by private lenders and governmental agencies. Such investments ought to concentrate on rehabilitation rather than on new construction. City governments can facilitate this process by directly turning over ownership of existing housing to these agencies or to the poor, who will then have a larger stake in upkeep and investment. Conversion and rehabilitation can also be a source of local employment for adults and teenagers. A Vera Institute of Justice nonprofit corporation employs ex-convicts to rehabilitate housing to provide shelter for the homeless (Jacobs, McGahey, and Minion 1984). Cities should also consider relaxing building and zoning codes in poor neighborhoods, where such relaxation is consistent with safety; highly specific building and safety codes add a great deal to the cost of rehabilitating and constructing housing.

3. *Family and Child Care.* Future research should concentrate on how some individuals succeed in the difficult circumstances found in high-crime communities. Although many young men in poor neighborhoods become involved in the web of problems discussed in this essay, some do not, and these low-crime individuals deserve more attention. Recent studies suggest that work attitudes derived in the home and religious training are tied to later economic success (Datcher-Loury and Loury 1983; Freeman 1983*b*). In previous years many experimental labor market programs gathered substantial longitudinal data on program participants and controls; these data could be profitably reexamined by pooling all the subjects and seeing which factors (not only program participation) are associated with later legitimate success and diminished crime.

Efforts to aid younger children are also needed. Although early research on childhood interventions such as Head Start found no significant effects, new studies suggest that such programs can lead to improved employment and lower crime among participants at least relative to controls (Berrueta-Clement et al. 1984). Programs that work with troubled families to teach better parenting skills also deserve further attention (Hirschi 1983).

4. *Criminal Justice Policy and Community Stabilization.* There need to be stronger criminal justice links with the economic and social institutions that promote community safety and stability. Criminal justice policy alone cannot bear the full weight of a crime-control and -reduction strategy, especially in impoverished communities. Police departments should continue their promising experiments with community-oriented patrol and other tactics to encourage more effective informal social control in poor neighborhoods. Traditional apprehension strategies do not seem to have significantly lowered the crime rate in poor neighborhoods (Greenberg and Kessler 1982; Moore and Kelling 1983), and police departments are now experimenting with a variety of "order maintenance" approaches to help maintain and build informal control.

Police efforts to stabilize neighborhoods and business districts are also important for urban economic development; the fear of crime is a major barrier to business expansion and relocation in central cities (McGahey 1983). Reiss (1985) describes an innovative program in Oakland to reduce the fear of crime and to help foster investment in the decaying core business district. This program combines careful police management, a variety of targeted patrol strategies, and an innovative financing mechanism that uses contributions from private firms to increase police resources without drawing them from other parts of the city. Although the nature of the program and the limits to statistical inference make it hard to assess the program in terms of its discrete effect on crime rates, Reiss found that the program does seem to be associated with significant reductions in crime, especially theft.

Policies also have to be developed to deal with the reintegration of released prisoners. The current size of American prison populations means that released prisoners will be returning to poor communities in ever-greater numbers in coming years. This will require programs to prepare better those prisoners for reintegration along with employment efforts that meet their needs on release (Jacobs et al. 1984). Community corrections also need more development, but these programs must be sensitive to the limited ability of nonincarcerative sanctions to provide incapacitation of dangerous offenders (Glaser 1983; McDonald 1986) and to the problem of locating halfway houses in poor communities.

Policies to reduce drug use should be explored as traditional enforcement strategies alone are not likely to make much of a difference. A recent Rand Corporation study noted that the federal government spent over 70 percent of its more than $1 billion drug-related expenditures on law enforcement and that there is relatively little hope that even doubling that expenditure would have any significant effect on drug prices or use (Polich et al. 1984, p. x). Therefore, enforcement resources might be targeted on the illegal drug industry with more experimentation in education and prevention programs to cut consumption.

### A. *Future Research Questions on Neighborhood Economies and Crime*

There are many unanswered questions about the dynamics of urban neighborhoods, their economies, and crime. The results of the Vera studies and other interdisciplinary efforts (Taub et al. 1984) suggest that interdisciplinary work can provide a variety of insights that cannot be gleaned from studies that use a single disciplinary perspective. Future research should encourage studies that incorporate insights from economics, sociology, and urban anthropology and history.

The role of urban neighborhoods in the future also needs to be examined. The traditional neighborhoods that have been the basis of so much study and attention—that is, those that are ethnically solid and that have intact households and stable intergenerational labor market patterns—may be vanishing from our cities as the urban and national economies change. Taub et al. (1984) describe the pressures on Chicago's East Side, a neighborhood that "closely resembles the ideal, typical community that has been the subject of much sociological thinking" as the steel mills, which were the economic and social bases of the community, shut down (chap. 4). Although Downs notes that "stability" in urban neighborhoods actually means a process of constant change and renewal (1981, chap. 3), current economic and social trends do not promise much hope that older urban neighborhoods will be renewed through their historic reliance on stable, primary blue-collar employment.

Can new employment, investment, and residential patterns support stable neighborhoods either in the ways that older neighborhoods did or in new ways? Will newer affluent communities of professionals develop roots in the city, or will they move out as they have children? Does the continuing development of more dispersed urban areas and the changing employment structure of the economy mean that older neighborhoods, which provided critical buffers against larger social and economic forces (Jacobs 1961; Janowitz 1967), are gone? If these neighborhoods provided critical elements of crime control, what combination of new formal and informal organizations might provide effective substitutes? Studies of economic, crime, and neighborhood patterns among new urban immigrants might shed light on these issues, especially if those immigrants are coping with a different economic structure than did previous groups (Piore 1979).

### *B. Community Leadership and Economic Adjustment*

Even with such new research and policy experimentation, the problem of high-crime communities in urban areas will be with us for some time. Conditions in these neighborhoods developed over a long period of time, and the interlocking nature of current problems does not promise any quick fix. Public policies will have an important role to play, but they will be ineffective without strong nongovernmental leadership. As many high-crime urban neighborhoods are black and Hispanic, substantial leadership in addressing these problems will have to come from those communities. Anticrime efforts that build on traditional community values and strengths need to be fostered without falling into a false dichotomy that poses continued governmental support against community-based leadership (Woodson 1981; Loury 1985).

This agenda must be tempered by the memory of the Mobilization for Youth program, which concentrated on "empowerment" for the poor. It may be that Mobilization for Youth and programs like it were too optimistic about the organizational resources and abilities among the poor, especially when they confronted established political authority. But it is difficult, if not impossible, to imagine substantial reductions in crime and social dislocation among the urban poor without leadership and assistance from the minority community itself.

Continuing rapid shifts in the world and national economy are also likely to create more disruption and change in urban labor markets. Although it is clear that short-term employment programs did not have much effect on crime, developing stable employment for adults who reside in impoverished crime-prone communities is essential for any long-term crime-reduction strategy. The economy and the labor market continue to be essential factors for strengthening and stabilizing noneconomic institutions in high-crime communities. Traditional employment policies alone will not solve the problem of high-crime communities but neither will policies that do not help reduce continuing economic deprivation among the urban poor.

## REFERENCES

Bailey, Thomas, and Roger Waldinger. 1984. "A Skills Mismatch in New York's Labor Market?" *New York Affairs* 8:3–19.

Ball, John C., Lawrence Rosen, John A. Flueck, and David N. Nurco. 1981. "The Criminality of Heroin Addicts: When Addicted and When Off Opiates." In *The Drugs-Crime Connection*, edited by James A. Inciardi. Beverly Hills, Calif.: Sage.

Beck, E. M., Patrick M. Horan, and Charles M. Tolbert II. 1978. "Stratification in a Dual Economy: A Sectoral Model of Earnings Determination." *American Sociological Review* 43:704–20.

Berger, Peter L., and Richard John Neuhaus. 1977. *To Empower People*. Washington, D.C.: American Enterprise Institute.

Berrueta-Clement, John R., Lawrence J. Schweinhart, W. Steven Barnett, Ann S. Epstein, and David P. Weikart. 1984. *Changed Lives: The Effects of the Perry Preschool Program on Youths through Age 19*. Ypsilanti, Mich.: High/Scope.

Bochert, James. 1980. *Alley Life in Washington: Family, Community, Religion, and Folklife in the City, 1850–1970*. Urbana: University of Illinois Press.

Brown, Claude. 1965. *Manchild in the Promised Land*. New York: Macmillan.

Bullock, Paul B. 1973. *Aspiration vs. Opportunity: "Careers" in the Inner City*. Ann Arbor: University of Michigan, Institute of Labor and Industrial Relations.

Center for Human Resources. 1984–85. "Planning Youth Employment Competency Systems." *Youth Programs* (Spring).

Chambers, Carl D., Sara W. Dean, and Michael F. Pletcher. 1981. "Criminal Involvements of Minority Group Addicts." In *The Drugs-Crime Connection*, edited by James A. Inciardi. Beverly Hills, Calif.: Sage.

Cloward, Richard A., and Lloyd Ohlin. 1960. *Delinquency and Opportunity: A Theory of Delinquent Gangs*. New York: Free Press.

Coleman, Richard P., and Lee Rainwater. 1978. *Social Standing in America*. New York: Basic.

Corporation for Enterprise Development. Various editions. *The Entrepreneurial Economy*. Washington, D.C.: Corporation for Enterprise Development.

Datcher-Loury, Linda, and Glenn C. Loury. 1983. "The Effects of Attitudes and Aspirations on the Labor Supply of Young Black Men." Paper presented at the National Bureau of Economic Research Conference on Inner City Black Youth Unemployment, Cambridge, Mass., August.

Dixon, Michael C., and W. E. Wright. 1974. *Juvenile Delinquency Prevention Programs: An Evaluation of Policy Related Research on the Effectiveness of Programs. Report on the Findings of an Evaluation of the Literature*. Nashville, Tenn.: George Peabody College for Teachers.

Downs, Anthony. 1981. *Neighborhoods and Urban Development*. Washington, D.C.: Brookings Institution.

Freedman, Marcia K. 1976. *Labor Markets: Segments and Shelters*. Totowa, N.J.: Allanheld, Osmun.

Freeman, Richard B. 1981. "Troubled Workers in the Labor Market." Working Paper no. 816. Cambridge, Mass.: National Bureau of Economic Research.

———. 1983*a*. "Crime and Unemployment." In *Crime and Public Policy*, edited by James Q. Wilson. San Francisco: Institute for Contemporary Studies.

———. 1983*b*. "Who Escapes? The Relation of Church-Going and Other Background Factors to the Socio-economic Performance of Black Male Youths from Inner-City Poverty Tracts." Paper presented at the National Bureau of Economic Research Conference on Inner City Black Youth Unemployment, Cambridge, Mass., August.

Freeman, Richard B., and Harry J. Holzer. 1985. "Young Blacks and Jobs—What We Now Know." *Public Interest* 78:18–31.

Gandossy, Robert P., Jay R. Williams, Jo Cohen, and Henrick J. Harwood. 1980. *Drugs and Crime: A Survey and Analysis of the Literature*. Washington, D.C.: National Institute of Justice.

Glaser, Daniel. 1983. "Supervising Offenders Outside of Prison." In *Crime and Public Policy*, edited by James Q. Wilson. San Francisco: Institute for Contemporary Studies.

Glasgow, Douglas G. 1980. *The Black Underclass: Poverty, Unemployment, and the Entrapment of Ghetto Youth*. New York: Vintage.

Goldstein, Paul J. 1981. "Getting Over: Economic Alternatives to Predatory Crime among Street Drug Users." In *The Drugs-Crime Connection*, edited by James A. Inciardi. Beverly Hills, Calif.: Sage.

Gordon, David M. 1973. "Capitalism, Class, and Crime in America." *Crime and Delinquency* 19:163–86.

Granovetter, Mark A. 1974. *Getting a Job: A Study of Contacts and Careers*. Cambridge, Mass.: Harvard University Press.

Greenberg, David F., and Ronald C. Kessler. 1982. "The Effect of Arrests on Crime: A Multivariate Panel Analysis." *Social Forces* 60:771–90.

Harris, Donald J. 1982. "Economic Growth, Structural Change, and the Relative Income Status of Blacks in the U.S. Economy, 1947–78." *Review of Black Political Economy* 12:75–92.

Harrison, Bennett. 1972. *Education, Training, and the Urban Ghetto*. Baltimore: Johns Hopkins University Press.

Helmer, John. 1975. *Drugs and Minority Oppression*. New York: Seabury.

Hirschi, Travis. 1983. "Crime and the Family." In *Crime and Public Policy*, edited by James Q. Wilson. San Francisco: Institute for Contemporary Studies.

Howell, Joseph T. 1973. *Hard Living on Clay Street: Portraits of Blue Collar Families*. Garden City, N.J.: Anchor/Doubleday.

Inciardi, James A. 1979. "Heroin Use and Street Crime." *Crime and Delinquency* 25:335–46.

Jacobs, James B., Richard McGahey, and Robert Minion. 1984. "Ex-Offender Employment, Recidivism, and Manpower Policy: CETA, TJTC, and Future Initiatives." *Crime and Delinquency* 30:486–506.

Jacobs, Jane. 1961. *The Death and Life of Great American Cities*. New York: Vintage.

Janowitz, Morris. 1967. *The Community Press in an Urban Setting: The Social Elements of Urbanism*. 2d ed. Chicago: University of Chicago Press.

Johnson, Daniel M., and Rex R. Campbell. 1981. *Black Migration in America: A Social Demographic History*. Durham, N.C.: Duke University Press.

Kalleberg, Arne L., and Aage B. Sorenson. 1978. "The Sociology of Labor Markets." Discussion Paper no. 509–78. Madison, Wisc.: Institute for Research on Poverty.

Kaplan, John. 1983. *The Hardest Drug: Heroin and Public Policy*. Chicago: University of Chicago Press.

Kobrin, Solomon. 1951. "The Conflict of Values in Delinquency Areas." *American Sociological Review* 16:653–61.

Long, Sharon K., and Ann D. Witte. 1981. "Current Economic Trends: Implications for Crime and Criminal Justice." In *Crime and Criminal Justice in a Declining Economy*, edited by Kevin N. Wright. Cambridge, Mass.: Oelgeschlager, Gunn, & Hain.

Loury, Glenn C. 1985. "The Moral Quandary of the Black Community." *Public Interest* 79:9–22.

McDonald, Douglas C. 1986. *Punishment without Walls: Community Service Sentencing in New York City*. New Brunswick, N.J.: Rutgers University Press (in press).

McDonald, Scott. In this volume. "Does Gentrification Affect Crime Rates?"

McGahey, Richard. 1982. "Labor Market Segmentation, Human Capital, and the Economics of Crime." Ph.D. dissertation, New School for Social Research.

———. 1983. "Economic Development and the Perception of Crime." *New York Affairs* 83:17–30.

McGahey, Richard, and John Jeffries. 1985. *Minorities and the Labor Market: Twenty Years of Misguided Policy*. Washington, D.C.: Joint Center for Political Studies.

Manpower Demonstration Research Corporation. 1980. *Summary and Findings of the National Supported Work Demonstration*. Cambridge, Mass.: Ballinger.

Matusow, Allen J. 1984. *The Unraveling of America: A History of Liberalism in the 1960s*. New York: Harper & Row.

Mobilization for Youth. 1961. *A Proposal for the Prevention and Control of Delinquency by Expanding Opportunity*. New York: Mobilization for Youth.

Moore, Mark H., and George L. Kelling. 1983. " 'To Serve and Protect': Learning from Police History." *Public Interest* 70:49–65.

Murray, Charles. 1984. *Losing Ground: American Social Policy, 1950–1980*. New York: Basic.

Murray, Charles, and Robert Greenstein. 1985. "The Great Society: An Exchange." *New Republic*, no. 3664 (April 8), pp. 21–24.

Novak, Michael. 1982. "Mediating Institutions: The Communitarian Individual in America." *Public Interest* 68:3–21.

Osterman, Paul. 1980. *Getting Started: The Youth Labor Market*. Cambridge, Mass.: MIT Press.

Pickman, James, and Benson F. Roberts. 1985. "Tapping Real Estate Markets to Address Housing Needs." *New York Affairs* 9(1):3–17.

Piore, Michael J. 1979. *Birds of Passage: Migrant Labor and Industrial Societies*. Cambridge: Cambridge University Press.

Piven, Frances Fox, and Richard A. Cloward. 1971. *Regulating the Poor: The Functions of Public Welfare*. New York: Pantheon.

Podolefsky, Aaron, and Frederic DuBow. 1981. *Strategies for Community Crime Prevention: Collective Responses to Crime in America*. Springfield, Ill.: Thomas.

Polich, J. Michael, Phyllis L. Ellickson, Peter Reuter, and James P. Kahan. 1984. *Strategies for Controlling Adolescent Drug Use*. Santa Monica, Calif.: Rand.

Poussaint, Alvin F. 1983. "The Mental Health Status of Blacks—1983." In *The State of Black America 1983*, vol. 7, edited by James D. Williams. New York: National Urban League.

Preble, Edward, and John J. Casey, Jr. 1969. "Taking Care of Business: The Heroin User's Life on the Street." *International Journal of the Addictions* 4:1–24.

Reiss, Albert J., Jr. 1983. "Crime Control and the Quality of Life." *American Behavioral Scientist* 27:43–58.

———. 1985. *Policing a City's Central District: The Oakland Story*. Washington, D.C.: National Institute of Justice.

Rieder, Jonathan. 1985. *Canarsie: The Jews and Italians of Brooklyn against Liberalism*. Cambridge, Mass.: Harvard University Press.

Rossi, Peter H., Richard A. Berk, and Kenneth J. Lenihan. 1980. *Money, Work, and Crime: Experimental Evidence*. New York: Academic Press.

Rumberger, Russell W. 1983. "The Employment Impact of Government Spending." Palo Alto, Calif.: Stanford University, School of Education, Institute for Research on Educational Finance and Governance.

Sadd, Susan, Mark Kotkin, and Samuel R. Friedman. 1983. *Alternative Youth Employment Strategies Project: Final Report*. New York: Vera Institute of Justice.

Schlossman, Steven, Gail Zellman, Richard Shavelson, Michael Selak, and Jane Cobb. 1984. *Delinquency Prevention in South Chicago: A Fifty-Year Assessment of the Chicago Area Project*. Santa Monica, Calif.: Rand.

Schoenberg, Sandra Perlman, and Patricia L. Rosenbaum. 1980. *Neighborhoods That Work: Sources for Viability in the Inner City*. New Brunswick, N.J.: Rutgers University Press.

Schuerman, Leo, and Solomon Kobrin. In this volume. "Community Careers in Crime."

Schumpeter, Joseph A. 1947. *Capitalism, Socialism, and Democracy*. 2d ed. New York: Harper.

Segal, David. 1979. "Introduction." In *The Economics of Neighborhood*, edited by David Segal. New York: Academic Press.

Shaw, Clifford R., and Henry D. McKay. 1969. *Juvenile Delinquency and Urban Areas*. Rev. ed. Chicago: University of Chicago Press.

Silberman, Charles E. 1980. *Criminal Violence, Criminal Justice*. New York: Vintage.

Sowell, Thomas. 1984. *Civil Rights: Rhetoric or Reality?* New York: Morrow.

Spergel, Irving. 1964. *Racketville, Slumtown, Haulberg: An Exploratory Study of Delinquent Subcultures*. Chicago: University of Chicago Press.

Stack, Carol B. 1974. *All Our Kin: Strategies for Survival in a Black Community*. New York: Harper & Row.

Sullivan, Mercer L. 1983. "Youth Crime: New York's Two Varieties." *New York Affairs* 8(3):31–48.

———. 1984. "Youth Crime and Employment Patterns in Three Brooklyn Neighborhoods." Mimeographed. New York: Vera Institute of Justice.

Sviridoff, Michelle, with Jerome E. McElroy. 1984. "Employment and Crime: A Summary Report." Mimeographed. New York: Vera Institute of Justice.

Taggart, Robert. 1981. *A Fisherman's Guide: An Assessment of Training and Remediation Strategies*. Kalamazoo, Mich.: W.E. Upjohn Institute for Employment Research.

———. 1982. "Prepared Statement." In *Hearings on Unemployment and Crime*, U.S. House of Representatives, Committee on the Judiciary and Committee on Education and Labor. Washington, D.C.: U.S. Government Printing Office.

Taub, Richard P., D. Garth Taylor, and Jan D. Dunham. 1984. *Paths of*

*Neighborhood Change: Race and Crime in Urban America*. Chicago: University of Chicago Press.

Thompson, James W., James Cataldo, and George Lowenstein. 1984. *Employment and Crime: A Survey of Brooklyn Arrested Persons*. New York: Vera Institute of Justice.

Thompson, James W., Michelle Sviridoff, and Jerry E. McElroy, with Richard McGahey and Orlando Rodriguez. 1981. *Employment and Crime: A Review of Theories and Research*. Washington, D.C.: National Institute of Justice.

Viscusi, W. Kip. 1983. "Market Incentives for Criminal Behavior." Paper presented at the National Bureau of Economic Research Conference on Inner City Black Youth Unemployment, Cambridge, Mass., August.

Westcott, Diane N. 1982. "Blacks in the 1970s: Did They Scale the Job Ladder?" *Monthly Labor Review* 105(6):29–38.

Whyte, William F., Jr. 1955. *Street Corner Society*. 2d ed. Chicago: University of Chicago Press.

Williams, Walter E. 1982. *The State against Blacks*. New York: McGraw-Hill.

Wilson, James Q. 1983. *Thinking about Crime*. Rev. ed. New York: Basic.

Wilson, James Q., and George L. Kelling. 1982. "Broken Windows." *Atlantic* 249:29–38.

Wilson, William J. 1980. *The Declining Significance of Race: Blacks and Changing American Institutions*. 2d ed. Chicago: University of Chicago Press.

Woodson, Robert L. 1981. *A Summons to Life: Mediating Structures and the Prevention of Youth Crime*. Cambridge, Mass.: Ballinger.

Yago, Glenn, Hyman Korman, Sen-Yuan Wu, and Michael Schwartz. 1984. "Investment and Disinvestment in New York, 1960–80." *Annals of the American Academy of Political and Social Sciences* 475:28–38.

*Robert J. Sampson*

# Crime in Cities: The Effects of Formal and Informal Social Control

ABSTRACT

This study examines the structural determinants of robbery and homicide offending in 171 American cities with a population greater than 100,000 in 1980. A macro-level social control model is presented that focuses on the consequences for formal and informal social control of police aggressiveness, jail incarceration risk, state incarceration, and family structure. Controlling for known determinants of crime rates such as poverty, inequality, and racial composition, the general question posed is, Do variations in criminal justice sanctions and the structural arrangement of families influence criminal behavior? To disentangle possible confounding effects of city composition in terms of demographic attributes, crime rates were disaggregated by age, race, and sex of offender. At least three major conclusions emerged. First, local official sanctions appear to have significant deterrent effects on robbery offending: cities with a high risk of jail incarceration produce disproportionately low robbery rates regardless of both demographic attributes of offenders and other known determinants of criminality. Cities where the police make frequent arrests for public order offenses (e.g., disorderly conduct and driving under the influence) tend to have significantly lower rates of black adult robbery. In addition, cities located in states with a high risk of imprisonment tend to have lower rates of juvenile robbery offending.

Robert J. Sampson is Assistant Professor in the Department of Sociology at the University of Illinois at Urbana-Champaign. This essay was supported in part by a grant funded by the National Institute of Justice (84-IJ-CX-0067) entitled "The Effects of Sanctions on Prevalence and Incidence of Crime." Points of view expressed herein are those of the author and do not necessarily represent the official position of the Justice Department. The author would like to thank Alfred Blumstein and Jacqueline Cohen for their valuable contributions to the analysis and Albert J. Reiss, Jr., and Michael Tonry for helpful comments on an earlier draft.


0-226-80802-5/86/0008-0008$01.00

Second, the empirical results demonstrate the importance of family and marital disruption as determinants of both robbery and homicide. In general, cities with a high percentage of black and white households comprised of a married-couple family have low rates of black and white juvenile offending, respectively, while the divorce rate exhibits a strong positive effect on adult offending. Finally, the results confirm traditional sociological concerns with economic stratification, as cities characterized by racial income inequality, poverty, and low occupational status were shown to have significantly higher rates of robbery and homicide.

The roots of criminology can be traced to the work of early social ecologists (see, e.g., Levin and Lindesmith 1937; Morris 1958; Baldwin 1979; Bursik 1984). Whether one considers the contributions of Quetelet and Guerry in France in the 1800s (Morris 1958) or the seminal works of Shaw and McKay (1942) in Chicago, there is little doubt that early criminologists focused considerable attention on the conditions of ecological areas associated with criminality. However, as several reviews have noted (e.g., Harries 1980, p. 62; Bursik 1984; Byrne and Sampson 1986), the research of both early and recent social ecologists has been largely confined to subareas (such as census tracts) within individual cities. While intracity studies of crime and delinquency thus captured widespread attention (Shaw and McKay 1942; Lander 1954; Bordua 1958; Chilton 1964), *intercity* variations in crime rates have received little empirical analysis (e.g., Ogburn 1935; Schuessler 1962) and almost no theoretical development.

A growing body of research has begun to redress this imbalance by focusing on the structural determinants of variations in urban crime (see, e.g., Flango and Sherbenou 1976; Harries 1976; Blau and Blau 1982; Crutchfield, Geerken, and Gove 1982; Messner 1982, 1983*a*, 1983*b*; Carroll and Jackson 1983; Bailey 1984; Jackson 1984; Williams 1984; Sampson 1985*a*, 1985*c*; Byrne 1986; Rosenfeld 1986). In general, social structure refers to population distributions and arrangements among social positions (Blau 1977, pp. 1–11). Structural dimensions are defined in terms of such characteristics as race, income, occupation, marital status, and power. The general thesis of the social ecological model is that characteristics of cities defined by the distributions of structural dimensions such as income inequality, the division of labor, or percentage divorced have independent effects on crime that are not attributable to the characteristics of individuals (see Byrne and Sampson 1986). The goal of macro-level research is therefore not to explain individual involvement in criminal behavior but to isolate characteristics of communities, cities, or societies that lead to high rates of criminality (cf. Blau and Blau 1982, p. 114).

This essay describes a theoretical model that links structural characteristics of cities to serious criminal offending and reports the results of an empirical analysis designed to test hypotheses derived from the theoretical framework. Section I begins with a brief overview of limitations of recent macro-level research. The major argument is that the effects of official sanctions and community social control factors have been neglected in ecological theory and research. I also argue that an almost exclusive reliance in prior research on offense rates confounds effects of demographic composition with the effects of ecological factors. Section II presents a social control model that focuses on the deterrent effects of two aspects of official sanctions—the degree of police aggressiveness and the local incarceration risk. This section also explores the macro-level consequences for criminal offending of variations in family structure. Section III describes a research strategy and data base designed to test the predictions from this model. The units of analysis are cities in the United States with a population greater than 100,000 in 1980. Section IV presents the empirical results, and Section V discusses their theoretical implications.

## I. Theoretical Issues

There are numerous limitations to the existing literature on cities and crime.[1] One fundamental limitation is a failure to view cities as units of social control. Instead researchers have tended to focus on ecological stratification in terms of racial and class composition. For example, the primary issue addressed in many recent articles has been the independent effects of relative deprivation (e.g., inequality and poverty) and racial composition on urban crime rates (see esp. Blau and Blau 1982; Messner 1983*a*, 1983*b*; Bailey 1984; Williams 1984; Sampson 1985*c*). This focus in not surprising since social ecologists have long considered economic deprivation to be a primary determinant of crime and delinquency (see, e.g., reviews in Kornhauser [1978]; Byrne and Sampson [1986]).

But, while concerns with social stratification may be important, its dominance in guiding ecological inquiry has diverted attention from other sources of variation in urban crime such as family structure and

[1] Space limitations preclude a comprehensive review of the literature on cities and crime. Excellent reviews are available elsewhere (see, e.g., Georges-Abeyie and Harries 1980; Harries 1980; Byrne 1983, 1986).

criminal justice sanctions. This is regrettable because the structural arrangement of families may have important macro-level consequences for both informal and formal social control in urban areas. Moreover, the family structure of a community is related to racial and socioeconomic factors (Bane 1986; Wilson and Aponte 1985), suggesting that many recent studies have failed to disentangle the effects of various race, class, and family structure variables. There is a strong possibility that causal inferences attributed to race and poverty result from underlying patterns of family disruption.

Prior ecological research has also failed adequately to investigate criminal justice sanctions as a source of community social control. A few studies examine the effect of the size of the police force on city crime rates (e.g., Harries 1980), but it is doubtful that police-force size is a relevant indicator of sanctions. There appears to be little connection between *how many* police there are and *what* they do on the street (Wilson and Boland 1978, p. 370). Although a sizable body of research has used aggregate data to test propositions derived from deterrence theory (Blumstein, Cohen, and Nagin 1978), these studies typically examine only the effects of certainty and severity of enforcement actions or punishment on the crime rates of large areas such as states. Official sanctions relating to community control such as police aggressiveness and local incarceration risk have not been fully explored.

The dominant perspective of deterrence theorists is a utilitarian rational choice model (Becker 1968; Ehrlich 1975), which assumes that a person commits an offense if the expected benefit, or "utility," to him from the offense exceeds the utility he could achieve by using his time and other resources at other activities (Becker 1968, p. 176). Strict adherence to a rational choice model results in a general failure to test its explanatory power vis-à-vis competing sociological theories of crime.[2] Indeed Becker dismisses all noneconomic theory: "A useful theory of criminal behavior can dispense with special theories of anomie, psychological inadequacies, or inheritance of special traits and simply extend the economists' usual analysis of choice" (Becker 1968, p. 170).

Deterrence research has thus contributed little to either the development or the testing of sociological explanations of crime. By the same

[2] Several studies, e.g., have excluded socioeconomic status factors from the crime function. As noted by Fisher and Nagin (1978), these sorts of ad hoc identification restrictions seriously undermine confidence in the results of many econometric studies of deterrence.

token, investigations of communities and crime usually fail to test a social control model and concentrate instead on social stratification. The study reported here attempts to overcome these limitations by combining in one analysis previously unexplored official community sanctions, general aspects of informal social control, and stratification models concerned with inequality and economic deprivation.

Most ecological research investigates the independent effects of ecological variables on the crime rate. The dependent variable is usually the number of reported offenses for a particular crime per unit of population. The aggregate offense rates employed in most studies can be highly influenced by compositional differences. Cities, for example, vary significantly in their age and race composition, two of the strongest individual-level predictors of involvement in serious crime (Hindelang 1978, 1981). While statistical controls for these individual-level predictors can be included in multivariate analyses, this approach fails to account adequately for compositional effects. For example, the differences in offending rates by age are so sharp (see, e.g., Hirschi and Gottfredson 1983) that aggregate controls, such as the percentage aged fifteen to nineteen or twenty to thirty-four, may mask considerable variation among cities in the age mix within the fifteen-to-thirty-four category.

More important, however, aggregate offense rates do not allow for a partitioning of compositional and contextual effects. For example, the aggregate offense rate may be positively related to the percentage of the population that is black because blacks have a higher rate of offending than do whites (an effect of composition) or because blacks in cities with a large black population have higher offending rates than do blacks in areas where they are a minority (an effect of context). Certain variants of subcultural theory predict exactly such a contextual effect (Curtis 1975; Sampson 1985*a*).

It is also possible that economic factors such as inequality and poverty have different effects on different population subgroups. For example, Blau and Blau (1982) argue that the criminogenic consequences of income inequality have a greater influence on blacks than on whites because blacks suffer greater economic discrimination based on race. Aggregate offense rates do not distinguish offenders by race and hence cannot address these theoretical issues.

One way to partition compositional and contextual effects is to analyze separately the effects of community characteristics on the criminal behavior of demographic subgroups such as blacks and whites or males and females; that is, one way to attack the compositional problem is to calculate crime rates for more homogeneous demographic subgroups.

Demographic disaggregation also helps to disentangle the effects of economic and family structure. Prior research indicates not only that race is an important correlate of homicide and other FBI Index crimes (Hindelang 1978, 1981) but also that the economic and family structures of blacks and whites differ dramatically (Bane 1986; Wilson and Aponte 1985). The proportion of female-headed families and the percentage of families below the poverty line, for instance, are much higher among blacks than among whites. Moreover, we know that American cities are highly segregated along racial lines (Van Valey, Roof, and Wilson 1976), resulting in separate white and black communities within major cities (Guest 1984). If disaggregated crime rates are of interest, it is thus misleading to use aggregate poverty and family measures that confound differential racial conditions.

The pertinent theoretical questions require race-specific analyses. For example, Is poverty in the black community related to black criminality? Similarly, Is white poverty related to white crime in a comparable way? Does overall inequality have the same effect on black offending as it does on white offending? With regard to family structure, an important theoretical and policy question is, To what extent does black family disruption increase black criminality (cf. Sampson 1985*b*; Wilson and Neckerman 1986)? These questions cannot be answered by more studies that correlate poverty and reported offense rates. Improved understanding requires disaggregation both of the crime rate and of economic and family factors.

This study addresses the issues identified above. The contextual/compositional question is addressed by demographically disaggregating crime-specific offending rates by age, race, and sex for the 171 cities in the United States that in 1980 had a population greater than 100,000. Census data were collected and combined with data on official sanctions to produce a data set containing estimated demographic-specific offending rates, sanction measures, family structure, and sociodemographic characteristics for each of these cities.

## II. Macro-Level Sources of Social Control

In its most general sense, "social control" refers to the regulation of human behavior. Janowitz (1975, p. 83) notes that sociologists often define social control as the social psychology of conformity and repression. Hence the sources of social control are often located within the individual (see Kornhauser 1978, p. 74; Reiss 1951). However, macro-sociological conceptions of social control derived from thinkers such as Durkheim (1897) refer to the ability of societies and communities to realize common values. As Janowitz (1975, p. 82) notes, in the most fundamental sense social control refers to the capacity of a society to regulate itself according to desired principles and values. Similarly, Reiss (1951, p. 196) observes that "social control may be defined as the ability of social groups or institutions to make norms or rules effective." Given this conception, the study of macro-social control focuses on the ecological, technological, economic, and institutional dimensions of social organization (Janowitz 1975, p. 88).

Criminological investigations of macro-level social control usually concern legal controls, including official actions and sanctions such as arrest and imprisonment. Modern-day deterrence theory is limited almost exclusively to the general deterrence of legal sanctions (see, e.g., Gibbs 1981, p. 87). However, a generic concept of social control encompasses other ecological and structural features of the community. Kornhauser (1978, pp. 69–82) has noted how the organization and arrangement of families, schools, and neighborhood associations may influence the attempts of communities to achieve desired goals. Macro-level social control thus stems from many different forms of social organization, both legal and nonlegal. The present study concentrates on the consequences of formal and informal social controls that stem from variations in criminal justice sanctions and family structure.

### A. *Family Structure*

Family organization is theoretically important for several reasons. First, marital and family disruption may interfere with the realization of community goals by indirectly decreasing formal social controls. Communities with high levels of family disruption tend to be characterized by low rates of participation in formal voluntary organizations and local affairs (Tomeh 1964; Bloom 1966; Kasarda and Janowitz 1974; Kornhauser 1978). For example, Bloom (1966) found that areas with high levels of family disruption had low rates of participation in community politics, recreation (e.g., YMCA), and educational activities (e.g., library membership). At the individual level, married persons are likelier to participate in formal organizations than are divorced and unmarried people (e.g., Tomeh 1973). Community participation is important since formal organizations attempt to integrate individuals into the larger community (Tomeh 1973, p. 89). Kornhauser argues (1978,

p. 81) that the family has the potential to perform many functions that link youth to institutions, thus providing institutional routes to valued goals. As she notes, "By parents' efforts, both individual and collective, nonfamily institutions are made more responsive to the child's needs" (Kornhauser 1978, p. 81). It is thus reasonable to expect that high levels of family disruption in a community may interfere with the individual and collective efforts of families to link youth to the wider society through institutional means such as schools, religion, and sports.

A second consequence of family dissolution is the attenuation of *informal* controls. Examples of informal social control include neighbors taking note of or questioning strangers, watching over each other's property, assuming responsibility for supervision of general youth activities, and intervening in local disturbances (see Greenberg, Rohe, and Williams 1985). Although its theoretical importance has been noted (e.g., Shaw and McKay 1942; Kobrin 1971, pp. 110–12; Hirschi 1983, pp. 61–64), the informal nature of collective family social control has not often been studied. The effects of the family have largely been studied from the viewpoint of "children under the roof"; that is, the effect of the behavior and supervision of parents has traditionally been studied only in reference to the delinquency of their own children. But children are often supervised, watched, and even reprimanded by people other than their own parents. Skogan (in this volume, p. 217) notes that "in stable neighborhoods, residents supervise the activities of youths, watch over one another's property, and challenge those who seem to be up to no good." In a related vein, research on informal group participation has shown that married-couple families have a higher rate of contact with neighbors than do divorced and single people (Tomeh 1964, p. 33). Thus, in areas with a cohesive family structure, parents often take on responsibility for their own children and for other youth also.

Intervening in group processes may well be one of the more effective means of controlling delinquency (see Short and Strodtbeck 1965). By supervising and keeping track of youth other than just their own, parents maintain some degree of control over group activity that accounts for well over one-half of all juvenile delinquency (Zimring 1981). Two-parent households provide increased supervision not only for their own children and property (cf. Cohen and Felson 1979) but also for public activities in the neighborhood. For example, acts such as truancy and vandalism are more likely to be noticed, particularly if one parent is home during the daytime hours.

Cohesive family structures are probably effective not because they intervene in actual criminal acts but because they are aware of and control peer-group activities that often set the context for more serious crime. Riley (1985), for example, found that parental supervision of leisure-time activities was one of the most important predictors of juvenile delinquency. In particular, juveniles who spent their leisure time in unsupervised peer groups away from home were exposed to more opportunities for crime and hence were more likely to engage in deviance.

The awareness and supervision of peer groups is dependent on a network of control. Felson clearly makes the point: "The single parent household gives the community only one parent to know and hence reduces the potential linkages which can be evoked for informal social control" (1986, p. 10). There is some empirical support for these notions. Sampson (1983, p. 172) showed that of all neighborhood characteristics studied family structure was the strongest predictor of juvenile group offending. Juveniles tended to offend in groups more often in neighborhoods characterized by high family disruption (i.e., a high proportion of female-headed families) than by low family disruption. In addition, Cartwright and Howard (1966) found that family stability was significantly lower in Chicago neighborhoods with delinquent gangs than in nongang neighborhoods.

Note that the theory proposed here does not necessarily require that the children of divorced or separated parents engage disproportionately in crime. Rather the perspective focuses on how the structure of family arrangements may affect crime in the community. Youth in areas characterized by stable families—regardless of their own family situation—probably have more informal controls placed on their activities, particularly leisure-time activities with peer groups. This conception may help to resolve the apparent paradox concerning the tenuous relation sometimes found between delinquency and broken homes at the individual level (cf. Wilkinson 1980; McCord 1982). The paradox exists only if one conceives of family disruption as a strictly micro phenomenon. The available evidence, however, suggests that families and communities are mutually connected, and, thus, to the extent that the former is disrupted, so too will be certain aspects of community life (Kornhauser 1978, p. 67).

Some have argued that marital disruption is a proxy indicator for overall disorganization and alienation in personal relationships. As Blau and Blau (1982, p. 124) argue, "Disproportionate numbers of divorced and separated in a population may be indicative of much instability, disorientation, and conflict in personal relations. Marital breakups entail disruptions of profound and intimate social relations, and they generally occur after serious estrangement, if not prolonged conflict." The Blaus thus suggest that divorce is an indicator of conflict and disorganization in adult relationships. Therefore, while the hypothesized consequences of single-parent families with children may not be directly related to adult behavior, divorce and separation may have potentially important effects on adult criminality.

Felson and Cohen (1980; Cohen and Felson 1979) also note the important influence of family structure on the control of criminal targets and opportunities. They argue that traditional theories of crime emphasize the criminal motivation of offenders without considering adequately the circumstances in which criminal acts occur. In particular, predatory crime requires the convergence in time and space of offenders, suitable targets, and the absence of effective guardianship. The spatial and temporal structure of routine family activities may play an important role in determining the rate at which motivated offenders encounter criminal opportunities. Felson and Cohen (1980) argue that the proportion of divorced persons and primary individual households (e.g., singles and nonrelatives) are proxy indicators of guardianship. For example, those who live alone are more likely to be out alone than are married persons and are thus more vulnerable to personal crimes. Also, leaving the home unguarded increases vulnerability to household crimes. Therefore, a community with a high proportion of divorced persons and primary individual households presents a more attractive environment for crime than do areas with a strong family orientation.

The present study focuses on the effects of community family structure on the criminal offending of both blacks and whites. This issue has not been explored adequately in previous research. Some of the early ecological studies did examine what were termed "family status" measures such as female labor force participation, family size, and stage in the life cycle (see, e.g., Schuessler 1962; Quinney 1966; Harries 1980; Byrne 1983), but few research efforts have examined the independent effects of such factors as divorce, separation, and the proportion of children who live in single-parent families on city crime,[3] and none have focused on race-specific effects.

[3] Some investigators like Harries (1976) used family disruption measures (e.g., percentage of female-headed families) but included them in canonical correlation and factor analyses. Hence the independent effects of family structure were not assessed. And, while some studies (e.g., Bloom 1966; Willie 1967) have examined the relation between juvenile delinquency and single-parent families, they have been conducted at the census-tract level and have not examined serious crimes.

### B. *Official Sanctions*

Wilson and Boland (1978) hypothesize that police in "legalistic" police departments adopt an aggressive patrolling strategy, by which they mean a strategy that maximizes the number of observations and interventions in the community (see also Wilson 1968). Aggressive police patrols tend to stop motor vehicles, to issue citations, and to question or arrest suspicious and disorderly persons at a high rate (Wilson and Boland 1978, p. 370). An aggressive patrol strategy may affect the crime control process: "By stopping, questioning, and otherwise closely observing citizens, especially suspicious ones, the police are more likely to find fugitives, detect contraband (such as stolen property or concealed weapons), and apprehend persons fleeing from the scene of a crime" (p. 373).

Wilson and Boland thus argue that police aggressiveness affects the crime rate mainly by increasing the ratio of arrests to offenses. Police aggressiveness is assumed to influence the crime rate indirectly and is thus appropriately excluded from the crime equation. However, Wilson and Boland (p. 374) acknowledge that police aggressiveness may directly affect the crime rate by influencing perceptions in the community regarding the probabilities of apprehension for illegal behavior.

The second hypothesis is more plausible since police aggressiveness is the most visible indicator of police activity. The general public has only a vague notion about the actual probabilities of arrest, and arrests for the seven Index crimes are relatively rare. Consequently, most potential offenders rarely witness an Index crime arrest. In contrast, the vigorous intervention by police on driving violations, drunkenness, and public disorder is highly visible. Aggressiveness in police patrol practices in all likelihood sends a signal to potential offenders that one's chances of getting caught are higher than they actually are.

I hypothesize that police aggressiveness in patrol practices has a direct negative effect on the crime rate.[4] Even if an aggressive patrol style does not actually clear more crimes, the existence of aggressive policing may be one of the important channels by which information on

[4] Since the decision to implement an aggressive patrol style stems from city political culture and the professional ethos of the police department, Wilson and Boland (1978) argue that there is no simultaneity problem between the crime rate and police aggressiveness. This is even more true in this analysis since disaggregated offending rates are analyzed. Also the police spend very little of their time in actual law-enforcement situations (Wilson 1968). It is thus unlikely that the frequency of homicides and robberies (which are usually handled by special units) will influence the average rate at which officers make stops and intervene in social control-type offenses.

the certainty of punishment is communicated to potential criminals. As Cook (1980, p. 223) has argued, "If the police are seen frequently in an area, potential criminals may be persuaded that there is a high likelihood of arrest in that area due to presumed low police response time and the chance that they will happen on the scene while the crime is in progress." Therefore, my analysis focuses not on whether increasing police presence and an aggressive style of policing actually increase clearance rates but rather on their direct effect on offending rates.

### *C. Local Incarceration Risk*

A primary goal of this study is to assess how variations in the risk of incarceration affect crime rates. Increasing the risk of detention and incarceration may have a greater deterrent effect on crime than does a simple increase in arrest and incapacitation, especially for the offender population. Deterrence researchers usually concentrate on arrest probabilities and sanction patterns such as the death penalty and imprisonment risk. But execution and imprisonment are rare, and imposition of both is usually delayed. Moreover, evidence for both derives from state-level variations that mask considerable heterogeneity in sanction risks. All these factors serve to reduce the deterrent effect of sanctions.

An alternative approach is to examine the deterrent effect on crime rates of the use of local jails. Incarceration in local jails, particularly with regard to pretrial detention, poses an immediate risk that is contemporaneous with the offense. Indeed detention in jail may be a more salient factor in deterring crime than is the more distant likelihood of imprisonment. As Feeley (1979) has persuasively argued, the process of criminal justice processing is punishment in itself, and a narrow focus on the deterrent effect of final dispositions is quite incomplete. Furthermore, there is considerable variation among localities within a state; data on jailing by local jurisdictions are a more sensitive indicator of local incarceration and crime control practices than are statewide data. Using an indicator of the likelihood of local incarceration per crime committed, I hypothesize that, all other things being equal, the risk of jail detention or incarceration will have a significant inverse effect on the crime rate.

## III. Research Strategy and Variable Construction

This study concerns intercity relations among demographic and family variables, sanctioning policies, and crime rates. This section describes the variables used, the data sources drawn on, and the methods employed.

I controlled for factors that are either known or suspected determinants of urban crime, including population size, region (Western location),[5] racial composition (percentage black), racial income inequality, poverty, and occupational status. The inequality measure used was the ratio of white to black median family income (mean across cities = 1.53; standard deviation = .27). The proportion of a community's civilian work force in professional and managerial occupational positions is a predictor used to reflect variations in occupational stratification.

To account for variations in the lower ends of the income distribution, race-specific measures of absolute deprivation were also chosen. Census data on the percentage of black families and white families with family income below $7,499 in 1980 were collected to provide disaggregated poverty measures. Because of residential segregation by race in U.S. cities, these measures in essence reflect the economic level of the black and white communities across major cities. As Guest (1984, p. 303) has observed, "The most accurate descriptive summary of residential distributions in American metropolitan areas would be in terms of a basic racial dichotomy, with blacks and whites largely occupying separate communities which rarely overlap." Disaggregating the crime rate by race permits examination of the similarities and differences in the causes of crime in the white and black communities. This, in conjunction with the disaggregated measurement of the economic and family structure of black and white communities, is one of the major features of the research design.

"Family structure" is a central concept in the present research. Measures of two different aspects of family structure were derived from the theoretical model. The first is the extent of divorce and separation among ever-married adults. Specifically, the divorce rate is defined as the ratio of divorced and separated to the population of ever married, excluding those currently widowed. The mean divorce rate across the 171 cities is 18 percent, ranging from a minimum of 6 percent to a maximum of 32 percent.

The second dimension of family structure is the percentage of house-

[5] Many early studies included regional dummies for southern location (e.g., Loftin and Hill 1974) when analyzing state-level crime rates. In contrast, this study employs a regional dummy for western location because (1) recent studies show that crime rates may be higher in western cities (e.g., Sampson 1985*c*; Byrne 1983), (2) migration patterns of the last decade largely reflect population shifts from the North and Midwest to the West and Southwest, and (3) our measure of police aggressiveness is positively correlated with western location. Further analysis utilizing a southern dummy variable yielded essentially the same results, however.

holds composed of a married-couple family. Fortunately, the 1980 census permits the calculation of race-specific measures of this variable, thus allowing a refined partitioning of the effect of racial composition from the effect of family disruption. For example, the percentage of total households with a female head is correlated approximately .8 with percentage black. This reflects the well-documented fact that black families are characterized by much higher rates of divorce and separation than are white families (Wilson 1984). In contrast, the percentage of *black* households composed of a married-couple family is very weakly related with percentage black ($r = -.16$).

The family structure of the black community is also relatively independent of the divorce rate—they share only about 25 percent common variance. This reflects two things. First, a large portion of the divorces and separations occur among those with no children. That is, there are many divorced and separated adults living alone or in nonfamily arrangements; in contrast, the race-specific measures refer to *family* households, usually with children. Second, since blacks constitute only 20 percent of the urban population on average, divorce in the general population measures mostly white divorce. Consequently, the divorce rate and percentage of white households with two-parent families share considerably more common variance (60 percent) than is the case for blacks.

### A. *Measurement of Official Sanctions*

Wilson and Boland (1978) were unable to locate a direct measure of police aggressiveness across a number of cities, so they selected a proxy, namely, the number of citations for moving traffic violations issued per sworn officer. In the present study a similar proxy measure is used, namely, the number of arrests *per police officer* for disorderly conduct and driving under the influence. These offenses fall under the category of "social control" offenses that legalistic-style departments tend to enforce vigorously (see Wilson 1968). The mean of police aggressiveness across the 171 cities is 5.48, indicating on average that each officer makes about five social control arrests per year. However, there is considerable variation in aggressiveness, ranging from a low of .47 to a high of 20.38.

The construct validity of our police aggressiveness measure appears to be quite good. Wilson and Boland (1978) argue that police aggressiveness arises most often in legalistic-style police departments, which in turn stem from a political culture of professional city management. A professional city management philosophy is often indicated by the presence of a council-manager form of city government (Wilson and Boland 1978, p. 79). Legalistic- and professional-style departments are also usually found in the West, while the older "watchman"-style departments that do not stress aggressive policing are usually found in the older cities of the East and Midwest (Wilson and Boland 1978, p. 77). To test these notions, data from the International City Managers Association were collected for each of the cities in our sample. A dummy variable of 1 was assigned to cities with a council-manager form of city government and to cities with a Western location. Consistent with theoretical expectations, the correlation of police aggressiveness was significantly positively ($p < .01$) related both to Western location (.36) and to council-manager government (.23). Finally, our measure also correlates .33 ($p < .01$) with the Index crime arrest/offense ratio. By all accounts, then, the police aggressiveness measure satisfies tests of construct validity.

The measure of local incarceration risk used is the estimated jail population per 100,000 reported offenses. The basic data on jails were available in the 1978 Census of Jails (Bureau of Justice Statistics 1978). However, several approximations were required in measuring jail risk. First, jails in the United States are usually organized at the county level. Although some cities operate their own jail systems, most are located within larger county boundaries. Each city located in an area with a countywide jail was assigned the jail risk measure for that particular county. If there were several jails within the county, then the jail populations were aggregated to the county level. The assumption is that the jail risk of the county adequately reflects the jail risk faced by offenders in the central city within that county. Many of the cities account for the majority of the county or standard metropolitan statistical area population. But, more important, the central cities almost certainly account for the vast majority of both crimes and offenders. Thus each city was assigned both the jail population and the number of offenses of the county in which it is located. In only a few cases (e.g., Los Angeles County) were several cities assigned the same risk measure because they were situated within the same county. The denominator of the jail risk measure is the number of reported offenses in a county for the personal crimes of murder, rape, robbery, and aggravated assault.[6]

[6] Reported offenses by county were available only broken down by violent (murder, rape, robbery, and aggravated assault) and property (burglary, larceny, and motor vehicle theft) crimes. Since I am estimating the deterrent effect of jail risk on homicide and robbery, violent offenses are used as the denominator of the risk measure.

The jail census, conducted in 1978, represents a one-day census of the number of detainees and offenders serving sentences of one year or less in 1978. The city offending estimates, by contrast, are developed for 1980. To use the 1978 jail data directly requires that variations in incarceration risk in 1978 adequately reflect variations in incarceration risk in 1980, two years later. In view of rapidly rising jail populations over these years, this may not be a reasonable assumption. Fortunately, data are also available from a 1982 survey of the 100 largest jails in the United States (Bureau of Justice Statistics 1982). Remarkable stability between 1978 and 1982 was observed for a subset of fifty-one jails found in our city sample. Although county jail populations increased on average over 33 percent, the correlation of the raw number of inmates across years was .99, and the correlation for the risk of jail incarceration per violent offense was .95. Thus, while varying in magnitude across years, the variation in jail risk found in 1978 appears accurately to reflect the variation in this variable in 1980.

The risk of jail, as measured by daily jail population per offense, is used here to reflect variation across cities in the use of official incarceration. Cities vary substantially in this local incarceration risk. Boston, for example, with a population of over 500,000, has only 616 persons in the county jail, yielding a risk of jail detention of only 3,762 per 100,000 violent offenses. This compares to an overall mean jail risk of 16,326 (standard deviation = 8,415). At the other extreme, cities such as Huntsville, Alabama, and Columbus, Georgia, detain over 25,000 offenders per 100,000 reported violent crimes. In addition, cities with a low risk of jail detention per reported offense show a slight tendency to have a nonaggressive patrol strategy as well (e.g., Boston and San Francisco), while other cities score highly on both measures of official control (e.g., Stockton, California, and Huntsville). However, the police aggressiveness and jail sanction measures are only moderately related ($r$ = .23) and hence reflect independent dimensions of official social control.

Simultaneous causation between official sanctions and crime rates has been a problem in past analyses of deterrent effects (see Fisher and Nagin 1978; Nagin 1978). If the risk of incarceration in jail not only deters crime but also is simultaneously influenced by the crime rate, then estimates of the deterrent effect of sanctions will be biased. For example, counties with high crime rates may be overburdened with crowded jails, thus reducing the probability that an arrested offender will be incarcerated. If the allocation of jail space is in part determined by the crime rate, then the error terms of both the crime rate and sanction equations will be correlated, resulting in biased parameter estimates.

Simultaneity is not likely to be a problem in the present analysis because of the focus on the deterrent effects of sanctions on disaggregated offending rates for specific crimes such as homicide and robbery. It is doubtful whether homicide arrests, for example, would have much influence on jail population levels. Also, the jail risk measures pertain to county estimates, whereas the offending rates are city based. Finally, the jail data are temporally prior to the offending estimates. Nevertheless, simultaneity is a possibility that cannot be ignored, especially considering the strong correlation of jail risk measures over time.

A theoretical model developed by Nagin (1978) can be used to address the potential biases arising from simultaneity: constraints on prison capacity are key determinants of imprisonment levels, which in turn are simultaneously related to crime rates. Nagin used states as his unit of analysis and introduced the average state imprisonment rate in the previous decade as a measure of effective prison capacity. Since prison capacity was hypothesized directly to influence imprisonment risk but not the crime rate, Nagin used the capacity measure as an identification restriction to estimate the deterrent effect of imprisonment; that is, sanction effects were estimated by excluding effective prison capacity from the crime function (Nagin 1978, p. 354).

The same basic approach is adopted here; however, an alternative measure of population constraint is introduced—the *actual rated design capacity* of each jail. Data on the maximum number of offenders each jail was designed to hold from the 1978 census were used to construct a jail constraint measure (rated design capacity per offenses). The analysis supported the underlying theoretical model—jail capacity explained over 50 percent of the variance in sanction risk. Therefore, in the analysis below, rated design was used as an instrumental variable. Parameter estimates for the deterrent effect of incarceration risk on offending are thus unbiased in the face of a simultaneous relation between sanction levels and crime.[7] It should also be noted that there are

[7] A complete discussion of the simultaneity problem is beyond the scope of the present essay. For excellent reviews of this issue with regard to deterrence studies, see Fisher and Nagin (1978) and Nagin (1978). In general, the method of instrumental variables involves the selection of a new variable that is both highly correlated with the independent variable and, at the same time, uncorrelated with the error term in the crime equation.

no common terms in the sanction and crime rate measures, thus eliminating problems arising from statistical dependency in ratio correlations (see Fisher and Nagin 1978).

Finally, to avoid misspecification of sanction risks an estimate is used of a more severe sanction—imprisonment, or what might be termed "state punitiveness." Prison data from each state were collected from the Bureau of Justice Statistics survey of new inmates in state prisons in 1980 (Bureau of Justice Statistics 1980). We collected data on all *new admissions* to prison in 1980. The measure of statewide prison risk is defined as the number of new prison admissions in 1980 per 1,000 state Index offenses in 1979. A one-year lag was chosen to account for delays occurring between the time of arrest and incarceration in the state system. The punitiveness measure has a mean of 11.59 (per 1,000), with a range from 2.9 to a high of 27.2. The prison measure refers only to states, and thus all cities within the same state were assigned the same score. While intrastate variation is by definition eliminated, the measure should reflect important regional variations in punitiveness that may have implications for offending patterns. At the very least, its introduction into the model separates the effects of state sanctioning policies from city-level variations in incarceration risk.

In brief, the analysis below focuses on the following three specific dimensions of official sanctions, the first two of which are defined as measures of official community social control: *police aggressiveness, local incarceration risk, and state prison risk (punitiveness).* By examining the independent effects of these variables after accounting for alternative theoretical explanations that reflect factors such as poverty, inequality, racial composition, region, size, and family structure, I present a more demanding test of the direct effects of sanctions on crime than does prior research.

### *B. Validity of Official Data and the Estimation of Offending Rates*

The present study uses arrest data to estimate dimensions of serious criminal offending. Given the criticisms that have been leveled against official data in general (e.g., Chambliss and Seidman 1971) and arrest data in particular (e.g., Liska and Chamlin 1984; Messner and South 1986), some discussion of concerns regarding validity appears warranted. The framework employed here assumes that arrest rates are reasonable proxies for involvement in criminal offending for the most serious of the Uniform Crime Report (UCR) Index crimes (e.g., murder, rape, and robbery).

Several empirical facts justify this assumption. First, Hindelang (1978, 1981) has systematically compared UCR Index arrest rates with offending rates estimated from National Crime Survey victim surveys and found almost exact agreement. For example, Hindelang (1978) found that 62 percent of the robbery offenders reported by victims were black, compared with an identical 62 percent of black robbery arrestees in UCR arrest data for the same year. This similarity increases confidence in official arrest data.

Second, a large body of research on police decisions to arrest has found that the seriousness of the crime is the strongest predictor of arrest (see, e.g., Black and Reiss 1970; Reiss 1971; Lundman, Sykes, and Clark 1978; Gottfredson and Gottfredson 1980; Smith 1984). In contrast, little evidence has been mustered for the proposition that the police differentially arrest by race. For example, in one of the most thorough investigations of police-citizen encounters to date, Smith (1984) found that, regardless of type of police department, the suspect's race did not have a direct effect on the arrest decision. There is some evidence that race and other extralegal factors such as neighborhood socioeconomic status and delinquent peers affect police contacts for juvenile offenses (e.g., Morash 1984), but most police-juvenile encounters involve minor crimes such as vandalism, larceny, and shoplifting. The present research thus limits testing to the most serious and also the most reliably recorded of the seven Index crimes—homicide and robbery—thus reducing the likelihood of bias.

However, one must acknowledge that official arrest data are contaminated by sources of bias when compared *across* jurisdictions. But rather than deny the validity of official data, the procedure followed here is explicitly to model and account for variations across areas in the crime control process. Specifically, the most important variation across areas with respect to arrest data is the probability of arrest. Some cities simply arrest more offenders per reported offense than do others. For example, in the present data the mean ratio of reported offenses per arrests for robbery is 4.18, meaning that for approximately every four robberies committed, on average only one arrest is made. This ratio, however, varies considerably among cities, ranging from a low of 1.33 to a high of 15.14. Moreover, recent research has demonstrated that the arrest/offense ratio varies with structural characteristics of cities such as inequality and racial composition (Liska, Chamlin, and Reed 1985).

In short, a comparison of simple arrest rates across jurisdictions may be biased by differential arrest probabilities in conjunction with covariations with city characteristics. To eliminate this bias each raw arrest rate is multiplied by the offense/arrest ratio of each city to achieve an estimate of *offending*. In other words, each demographic-specific arrest rate is scaled up to offending by the ratio of crime-specific offenses to arrests.

The procedure employed assumes that offense data are measured on a comparable basis across cities and that there are no differences between subgroups in arrest probabilities. The first assumption appears reasonable, as offense data are generally considered by criminologists to be reliably and validly recorded across jurisdictions, especially with regard to robbery and homicide (cf. Hindelang 1978). Furthermore, there are no major differences between population subgroups (e.g., race) in reporting practices (i.e., crimes reported to police) for serious crimes such as robbery (Flanagan and McLeod 1983, p. 299).

The second assumption appears met by the findings on police-citizen encounters, which conclude that there are few if any racial differences in arrest probability for serious crimes such as robbery and homicide. There may be some differences between juveniles and adults, although such differences are probably slight with regard to the crimes considered here. In sum, the dependent variables have been transformed from arrest rates into offending rates using the ratio of offenses to arrest. This method differs from Messner and South (1986) and Sampson (1985*c*), where raw arrest rates were analyzed. Thus I not only address criticisms of official arrest data but also use the very information thought to be problematic to develop estimates of offending.

### C. *Methods*

Using the above procedures in conjunction with population estimates from the 1980 census, race-age and sex-age crime-specific offending rates were constructed for each of the 171 largest cities in the United States for the years 1980–82.[8] The analysis is limited by FBI reporting

[8] Studying only cities with populations of more than 100,000 necessarily truncates the variation in some city-level variables (see esp. Byrne 1986). However, robbery and homicide are sufficiently rare in smaller cities that disaggregated offending rates are inherently unreliable, requiring that analysis be limited to large cities. Using cities as units of analysis also raises the issue pointed out by Gibbs and Erickson (1976) concerning the effects of city ecological position on crime rates. They argue that the denominator (city population) used in conventional crime rates may be inappropriate since people from outside the city may be victims. This is not a problem in the present analysis since *offending* rates rather than offense rates are used. The evidence clearly indicates that offenders tend to commit crimes in or near their own neighborhoods and almost always in their city of residence (see Pyle 1974; Sampson 1983). Not surprisingly, then, introduction of a control for ecological position (city/standard metropolitan statistical area population) in preliminary analyses did not alter the substantive results.

rules, which do not permit calculation of age-race-sex rates and allow a race breakdown only by juvenile (under eighteen) and adult (eighteen and over) status.[9] Because of potential year-to-year variations in reporting and recording practices, a three-year average rate was computed to stabilize random fluctuations and reduce missing data, a practice followed in previous research (see, e.g., Loftin and Hill 1974; Messner 1983*a*; Sampson 1985*a*).

Preliminary analysis revealed that all correlations among independent predictors included in the same equation were less than .80 and that all except two were under .50. This level of intercorrelation is fairly low for aggregate data and does not present serious multicollinearity problems (see, e.g., Kennedy 1979, p. 131). Nevertheless, as a precaution the variance-covariance matrices of parameter estimates were examined for unreasonable values. In addition, models where inefficiency appeared to be a problem were reestimated by varying the model specification.

With a sample size less than 200, the potential problem of a single or small number of observations influencing the results becomes an issue. Recently emerging literature (Cook and Weisberg 1980; Weisberg 1980) recommends case analysis to detect the importance of influential observations in estimating regression parameters. In the present study, for example, it is possible that one particular city with deviant patterns may disproportionately influence the overall results. To protect against this possibility all regressions were subjected to a case analysis. Specifically, the variables—Cook's $D$ and Studentized residuals—were inspected for each city (see Weisberg 1980). These variables reveal the extent to which individual cases disproportionately influence the outcome of the analysis. Specifically, a case is defined as influential if its deletion from the model results in a substantial change in the estimate of the parameter vector. Generally, no city exerted a disproportionate

[9] The numerators of the race-specific arrest rates refer to offenses by adults (eighteen and over). However, we know from previous research on age distributions and crime (e.g., Hirschi and Gottfredson 1983) that there are very few if any elderly robbery and homicide offenders. This presents a problem since the denominator would then include a population at low risk for offending (i.e., the elderly). If the proportion of black and white elderly varies with structural characteristics across cities, then estimates of the effect of these characteristics on offending may be biased. In fact, the proportion of elderly does vary with racial composition among other variables. Therefore, each adult offending rate was constructed after eliminating those sixty-five and older from the denominator. A lower cutting point would have been used, but more refined census estimates by city on race-specific age groups were not available. Similarly, black and white juveniles less than age five were removed from the denominator of the race-specific juvenile rates.

influence in all regressions, although a few cities showed influential patterns for some demographic-specific models. For example, Hialea (Florida), Eugene (Oregon), and Irving (Texas) were excluded from the black juvenile equations. There are few blacks in these cities, and the resulting juvenile rates were very unreliable. As a general rule, all cities with fewer than 1,000 blacks were excluded in the black-offending analysis. After eliminating influential observations and missing data from the FBI arrest reports, the sample size was 158 and 150 for the white and the black equations, respectively.

Preliminary analysis revealed that many offending rates were skewed, and in addition there was some evidence of heterogeneity of variance in the disturbance terms. Regression analysis assumes that the disturbance (i.e., error) terms all have the same variance (Kennedy 1979, p. 36). To induce homogeneity of variances and to counteract skewness in the rates, natural logarithms were taken of each demographic-specific offending rate. Multivariate regression was the method of analysis used to estimate the models.

## IV. Results

The procedure followed is first to examine the theoretical model employing aggregate offense rates and then systematically to disaggregate by age and sex and then by race of offender. In disaggregating by race of offender, we also disaggregate the components of family and economic structure.

Table 1 presents the results for aggregate homicide and robbery rates. The models fit the data well—over 70 percent of the variance in both crimes is explained. The effects of sanctions vary dramatically by type of crime. Police aggressiveness and local incarceration risk have no effect on homicide, while state punitiveness has an unexpected *positive* effect, ironically suggesting that an increase in prison sanctions actually serves to increase levels of homicide.[10] The results for robbery are quite the opposite. First, cities that have high levels of police aggressiveness and jail risk also tend to have significantly lower robbery rates. Second,

[10] Although prison risk is highly correlated with a southern location (.77), when a dummy variable for South is entered, the prison effect is reduced but still positive. This finding is difficult to interpret and is theoretically implausible. It may be that unmeasured factors correlated with prison risk are responsible for the positive effect. On the other hand, the results below show that prison risk is *inversely* related to robbery rates. Further research is thus needed to determine whether the positive effect on homicide is artifactual.

TABLE 1

Regression Results for 1980 Homicide and Robbery Offense Rates in U.S. Cities

| Structural Characteristics | Homicide[a] | | | Robbery[b] | | |
|---|---|---|---|---|---|---|
| | *b* | Beta | *t*-Ratio | *b* | Beta | *t*-Ratio |
| Police aggressiveness | −.006 | −.02 | −.46 | −.029 | −.13 | −2.94** |
| Local incarceration risk[c] | −.023 | −.02 | −.42 | −.162 | −.16 | −3.82** |
| State prison risk | .025 | .16 | 2.65** | −.017 | −.13 | −2.31** |
| Divorce rate | 6.115 | .28 | 3.99** | 10.221 | .54 | 8.54** |
| Occupational status | −6.975 | −.42 | −7.87** | −4.577 | −.32 | −6.60** |
| Racial income inequality | 1.013 | .31 | 5.28** | .790 | .28 | 5.27** |
| Population size | .278 | .24 | 5.02** | .139 | .14 | 3.22** |
| West | .451 | .23 | 3.71** | .260 | .15 | 2.74** |
| Percentage black | 1.131 | .22 | 2.68** | .306 | .07 | .93 |

[a] $R^2 = .73; p < .01$.
[b] $R^2 = .78; p < .01$.
[c] To reduce the number of places to the right of the decimal, the jail risk coefficient is multiplied by 1,000.
* $p < .10$.
** $p < .05$.

state punitiveness significantly decreases city robbery rates. The data thus suggest that, all else equal, increases in official sanctions have a deterrent effect on the incidence of robbery. That homicide is less influenced by sanctions than is robbery is consistent with the often explosive and unplanned nature of the offense. In other words, it is plausible on a priori grounds to expect that sanction risks will have a weaker deterrent effect on expressive violent crimes such as murder than on more instrumental crimes such as robbery. Indeed, further analysis disclosed that jail incarceration risk had significant inverse effects on burglary as well.

The pattern of parameter estimates for the other independent variables conforms to theoretical expectations for the most part. Specifically, all nonsanction variables have a significant effect on homicide in the predicted direction, showing that cities with a high divorce rate, low occupational status, high inequality, large population, Western location, and high percentage of blacks have disproportionately high levels of homicide. The same general pattern holds for robbery, with the exception that racial composition has no independent

TABLE 2

Regression Results for 1980 Age-specific Rates of Male Robbery Offending in U.S. Cities

| Structural Characteristics | Males 15–17[a] | | | Males 18–19[b] | | |
|---|---|---|---|---|---|---|
| | *b* | Beta | *t*-Ratio | *b* | Beta | *t*-Ratio |
| Police aggressiveness | −.027 | −.10 | −1.80* | −.049 | −.19 | −3.21** |
| Local incarceration risk[c] | −.202 | −.17 | −3.25** | −.215 | −.19 | −3.46** |
| State prison risk | −.057 | −.35 | −5.24** | −.021 | −.15 | −2.03** |
| Divorce rate | 13.079 | .57 | 7.48** | 6.559 | .31 | 3.77** |
| Occupational status | −3.390 | −.19 | −3.35** | −5.618 | −.35 | −5.57** |
| Racial income inequality | 1.006 | .29 | 4.58** | .787 | .24 | 3.43** |
| Population size | .174 | .14 | 2.74** | .172 | .15 | 2.72** |
| West | −.123 | −.06 | −.89 | .431 | .22 | 3.12** |
| Percentage black | −.486 | −.09 | −1.01 | .900 | .17 | 1.88* |

[a] $R^2 = .68; p < .01$.
[b] $R^2 = .64; p < .01$.
[c] To reduce the number of places to the right of the decimal, the jail risk coefficient is multiplied by 1,000.
* $p < .10$.
** $p < .05$.

effect. The divorce rate has by far the strongest effect on robbery rates.[11]

Tables 2 and 3 present robbery offending rates disaggregated by age and sex of offender. There were so few homicides when broken down into fine age categories that disaggregated rates are not presented; however, the results were very similar to the patterns in table 1 for the homicide offense rate. Table 2 shows that all three official sanctions are related to male robbery rates. For eighteen- and nineteen-year-old males in particular, increases in police aggressiveness and both local and state incarceration risk are associated with significantly lower robbery offending. Police aggressiveness does not have as strong of an effect on male juveniles (fifteen to seventeen), but the other two sanction risks have highly significant effects. In fact, prison risk has an

[11] Although percentage black and divorce are significantly related (.62), multicollinearity does not present a serious problem. For example, note that *both* variables have independent effects on homicide. When percentage black is dropped from the robbery equation, the explained variable remains unchanged (.78) as does the effect of divorce (*b* = 10.9). However, when divorce rather than percentage black is dropped, the explained variance is reduced by over 11 percent. There is clearly sufficient independent variation in racial composition and divorce rates in our sample of cities, with the latter having the stronger effects on both homicide and robbery rates.

especially strong influence on fifteen- to seventeen-year-old male robbery, an effect that remains significant even if a southern regional dummy is substituted for West. This is somewhat unexpected since this age group does not generally face prison sanctions. However, to the extent that prison risk is essentially an indicator of general social control, the results are consistent with deterrence hypotheses. The other factors exhibit patterns similar to robbery offense rates; that is, cities with high rates of divorce and inequality and with low occupational status have a disproportionately high incidence of robbery.

The results in table 3 specify the factors that distinguish juvenile from adult offending. In particular, prison risk has no independent effect on twenty- to twenty-four- or on twenty-five- to twenty-nine-year-old male robbery. Hence the significant effect on the aggregate rate (table 1) stemmed from male juvenile (fifteen- to seventeen-year-old) and youthful (eighteen- and nineteen-year-old) offenders and not from adults. Police aggressiveness and local incarceration risk, on the other hand, continue to depress city robbery offending independent of stratification factors. High levels of divorce and racial inequality both increase robbery, with the former having the strongest effect on older

TABLE 3

Regression Results for 1980 Age-specific Rates of Male Robbery Offending in U.S. Cities

| Structural Characteristics | Males 20–24[a] | | | Males 25–29[b] | | |
|---|---|---|---|---|---|---|
| | *b* | Beta | *t*-Ratio | *b* | Beta | *t*-Ratio |
| Police aggressiveness | −.040 | −.16 | −2.93** | −.036 | −.14 | −2.73** |
| Local incarceration risk[c] | −.180 | −.17 | −3.21** | −.142 | −.13 | −2.61** |
| State prison risk | −.003 | −.02 | −.36 | −.005 | −.03 | −.52 |
| Divorce rate | 7.556 | .37 | 4.80** | 9.334 | .44 | 6.12** |
| Occupational status | −6.341 | −.41 | −6.95** | −6.000 | −.37 | −6.78** |
| Racial income inequality | .763 | .24 | 3.68** | .921 | .28 | 4.58** |
| Population size | .167 | .15 | 2.93** | .147 | .13 | 2.65** |
| West | .429 | .23 | 3.35** | .423 | .22 | 3.49** |
| Percentage black | .704 | .14 | 1.63 | .710 | .14 | 1.70* |

[a] $R^2 = .68; p < .01$.

[b] $R^2 = .72; p < .01$.

[c] To reduce the number of places to the right of the decimal, the jail risk coefficient is multiplied by 1,000.

* $p < .10$.

** $p < .05$.

male robbery rates. Overall, then, the sex- and age-specific patterns underscore the importance of variations in official sanctions, family disruption, and inequality for explaining intercity variations in robbery offending.

One of the major goals of the present study was to disaggregate both the crime rate and the key independent factors correlated with racial composition. Table 4 presents the results of this analysis with respect to race-specific adult homicide offending. Juvenile homicide is quite rare and is not considered. The disaggregated homicide rates exhibit similar patterns for the sanction measures, with the exception that local incarceration risk significantly decreases the black homicide rate. As in table 1, increasing risks of being sent to prison have a positive effect on homicide, tending to refute further the notion that use of state prison sanctions has a deterrent effect on criminal homicide. If anything, the

TABLE 4

Regression Results for 1980 Race-specific Rates of Adult Homicide Offending in U.S. Cities

| Structural Characteristics | White Adults[a] | | | Black Adults[b] | | |
|---|---|---|---|---|---|---|
| | *b* | Beta | *t*-Ratio | *b* | Beta | *t*-Ratio |
| Police aggressiveness | .000 | .00 | .04 | .018 | .10 | 1.22 |
| Local incarceration risk[c] | −.060 | −.07 | −1.15 | −.132 | −.17 | −2.03** |
| State prison risk | .036 | .30 | 3.61** | .023 | .22 | 1.94** |
| Divorce rate | 6.879 | .38 | 2.60** | 2.965 | .18 | 1.39 |
| White two-parent households | .020 | .23 | 1.82* | ... | N.I. | ... |
| Black two-parent households | ... | N.I. | ... | −.018 | −.20 | −1.90* |
| White poverty | 6.801 | .33 | 4.49** | ... | N.I. | ... |
| Black poverty | ... | N.I. | ... | .480 | .05 | .46 |
| Occupational status | −4.755 | −.36 | −4.16** | −6.100 | −.51 | −4.88** |
| Racial income inequality | .715 | .26 | 3.68** | .673 | .27 | 2.34** |
| Population size | .288 | .32 | 5.46** | .087 | .11 | 1.38 |
| West | .688 | .44 | 5.31** | .533 | .37 | 3.50** |
| Percentage black | −.609 | −.14 | −1.36 | −1.411 | −.38 | −2.72** |

NOTE.—N.I. = not included in model specification.

[a] $R^2 = .63; p < .01$.

[b] $R^2 = .34; p < .01$.

[c] To reduce the number of places to the right of the decimal, the jail risk coefficient is multiplied by 1,000.

* $p < .10$.

** $p < .05$.

opposite is true, a rather disconcerting finding considering the huge increases in imprisonment in recent years (see, e.g., Bureau of Justice Statistics 1985). Whether this finding is artifactual is deserving of further research.

The pattern of effects for family dissolution varies somewhat by race of offender. In particular, cities with a high divorce rate have a significantly higher white homicide rate, while cities with a relatively large proportion of black two-parent families have significantly lower black homicide rates. The marginally significant effect of black two-parent families is apparently somewhat attenuated because of its overlap with divorce (.5); when the latter is dropped from the equation, the beta coefficient for black intact families increases to $-.28$ ($p < .05$). Hence both black and white adult homicide are significantly influenced by variations in family structure.[12]

For blacks the data suggest that relative inequalities in income and status are more criminogenic than is sheer economic deprivation. For example, racial inequality increases, and occupational status decreases, homicide for black adults as well as for white adults. But, while black poverty is unrelated to variations in black homicide, cities where whites are disproportionately poor tend to have significantly higher rates of white murder. This pattern for race-specific poverty was also apparent in 1970 for a smaller sample of cities (see Sampson 1985*c*).

In table 5 we turn to race-specific rates of juvenile *robbery* offending. While police aggressiveness is not significant, local incarceration risk has a significant deterrent effect on robbery by both black and white juveniles. Prison risk also significantly decreases robbery, but the magnitude of the effect is much stronger for black offenders than for white offenders. In fact, imprisonment risk has the largest beta coefficient in the black juvenile equation. This effect maintains despite introduction of a control for southern location (data not shown). Apparently, then, the effect of prison risk noted in table 2 for juveniles is due largely to the offending behavior of black juveniles. In any event it is clear that juvenile robbery is strongly influenced by patterns of community and state sanctions associated with deprivation of liberty.

The effect of family dissolution is also readily apparent. For black

[12] The effect of divorce on white homicide is significant and positive as expected. However, the marginally significant positive effect of white two-parent families is not expected. However, this apparently stems from problems with collinearity between divorce and percentage white two-parent families ($-.77$). Specifically, when divorce is dropped from the equation, the positive effect of white two-parent families is eliminated.

TABLE 5

Regression Results for 1980 Race-specific Rates of Juvenile Robbery Offending in U.S. Cities

| Structural Characteristics | White Juveniles[a] | | | Black Juveniles[b] | | |
|---|---|---|---|---|---|---|
| | *b* | Beta | *t*-Ratio | *b* | Beta | *t*-Ratio |
| Police aggressiveness | −.006 | −.02 | −.42 | −.023 | −.08 | −1.35 |
| Local incarceration risk[c] | −.206 | −.18 | −3.34** | −.274 | −.21 | −3.76** |
| State prison risk | −.023 | −.15 | −1.97** | −.060 | −.34 | −4.47** |
| Divorce rate | 3.206 | .15 | 1.07 | 6.737 | .25 | 2.87** |
| White two-parent households | −.029 | −.29 | −2.38** | ... | N.I. | ... |
| Black two-parent households | ... | N.I. | ... | −.047 | −.32 | −4.40** |
| White poverty | 5.655 | .23 | 3.36** | ... | N.I. | ... |
| Black poverty | ... | N.I. | ... | .240 | .02 | .19 |
| Occupational status | −5.130 | −.32 | −4.08** | −1.800 | −.09 | −1.22 |
| Racial income inequality | .537 | .17 | 2.56** | .685 | .17 | 2.08** |
| Population size | .145 | .13 | 2.38** | .085 | .06 | 1.20 |
| West | .592 | .31 | 4.05** | .339 | .15 | 2.00** |
| Percentage black | −.988 | −.19 | −1.97** | −2.062 | −.33 | −3.51** |

NOTE.—N.I. = not included in model specification.

[a] $R^2 = .67; p < .01$.

[b] $R^2 = .68; p < .01$.

[c] To reduce the number of places to the right of the decimal, the jail risk coefficient is multiplied by 1,000.

* $p < .10$.

** $p < .05$.

juveniles *both* elements of family disruption have independent effects on robbery. Specifically, the adult divorce rate increases, and the prevalence of two-parent black families reduces, the incidence of black juvenile robbery. The effect of two-parent black families is especially strong. For white juveniles the prevalence of two-parent white families also has rather large inverse effects on robbery, but the effect of divorce is insignificant. If divorce is dropped from the equations, the standardized effect of two-parent families on robbery increases to −.38 for white juveniles and to −.42 for black juveniles. Of all city characteristics, then, family structure clearly has the strongest effects on juvenile robbery offending for both races.

Economic structural factors continue to exhibit explanatory power, especially for white offenders. For example, both white poverty and low city occupational status contribute to increases in white juvenile robbery, whereas neither black poverty nor occupational status influence black juvenile robbery. The main influence on the latter stems from racial income inequality, which also increases white robbery. Finally, the results indicate that, all else equal, cities with a large population, a relatively low proportion of blacks, and a western location have disproportionately high race-specific rates of robbery offending.

Table 6 focuses on race-specific *adult* robbery offending. Like the juvenile equations, a considerable amount of variance (over 60 percent) is explained by the theoretical model. The effects of official sanctions are also similar to the juvenile results: cities with a high risk of jail incarceration have significantly lower rates of both black and white adult robbery offending. The main difference between the juvenile and adult results is the performance of state prison sanctions and police

TABLE 6

Regression Results for 1980 Race-specific Rates of Adult Robbery Offending in U.S. Cities

| Structural Characteristics | White Adults[a] | | | Black Adults[b] | | |
|---|---|---|---|---|---|---|
| | *b* | Beta | *t*-Ratio | *b* | Beta | *t*-Ratio |
| Police aggressiveness | −.018 | −.08 | −1.47 | −.042 | −.22 | −3.40** |
| Local incarceration risk[c] | −.169 | −.18 | −3.38** | −.219 | −.26 | −4.17** |
| State prison risk | .014 | .11 | 1.46 | −.006 | −.06 | −.66 |
| Divorce rate | 10.240 | .54 | 4.06** | 6.519 | .38 | 3.81** |
| White two-parent households | .012 | .13 | 1.15 | ... | N.I. | ... |
| Black two-parent households | ... | N.I. | ... | −.018 | −.18 | −2.26** |
| White poverty | 4.714 | .22 | 3.26** | ... | N.I. | ... |
| Black poverty | ... | N.I. | ... | −.568 | −.06 | −.68 |
| Occupational status | −6.355 | −.47 | −5.81** | −4.990 | −.39 | −4.96** |
| Racial income inequality | .865 | .31 | 4.66** | .748 | .29 | 3.24** |
| Population size | .176 | .19 | 3.49** | .051 | .06 | 1.00 |
| West | .723 | .45 | 5.84** | .425 | .28 | 3.47** |
| Percentage black | −1.688 | −.39 | −3.95** | −2.356 | −.58 | −5.65** |

NOTE.—N.I. = not included in model specification.

[a] $R^2 = .68; p < .01$.

[b] $R^2 = .62; p < .01$.

[c] To reduce the number of places to the right of the decimal, the jail risk coefficient is multiplied by 1,000.

* $p < .10$.

** $p < .05$.

aggressiveness. The former has no effect on adult robbery, while cities where the police make frequent arrests for public order offenses tend to have lower rates of black adult robbery. The parameter estimate for whites is also negative, but it fails to attain significance. These results thus establish the importance of demographically disaggregating offending rates by race. It is apparent that the deterrent effect of police aggressiveness on robbery (tables 1 and 4) is due almost solely to its effect on black adult offenders. Police aggressiveness simply does not have a strong effect on juvenile offenders of either race or on white adult offenders.[13]

The effect of the divorce rate on black and white adult offending is stronger than the effect of two-parent families. In fact the adult divorce rate has the single largest effect (beta = .54) on white adult robbery. Recall that just the opposite was the case for juveniles. The prevalence of two-parent households in a community thus appears to be closely connected to the social control of juveniles. Note, however, that both dimensions of family disruption have independent effects on black adult robbery. Moreover, if divorce is dropped from the equations, the standardized effect of intact families increases and is significant for both white adults (−.23) and black adults (−.33). The results thus underscore once again the importance of marital and family disruption in explaining the criminal behavior of whites and blacks.

The results for economic factors lend further credence to the notion that black offending patterns are determined more by structural inequality than by absolute deprivation in the black community. For example, racial income inequality and occupational status both have significant effects on black and white adult robbery. On the other hand, black poverty is unrelated to black adult robbery, whereas white poverty has a significant positive effect on white adult robbery. Finally, the patterns for city size, region, and racial composition are all similar to earlier results. Again the effect for percentage black is apparently counterintuitive—but only when compared to past research utilizing aggregated offense data. Once the compositional effect of race of offender is controlled, the results suggest that, all else equal, black of-

[13] These results are different from those found in Sampson (1985*c*) where police aggressiveness was either insignificant or had positive effects on white adult arrests. However, in that study a different measure of police aggressiveness was used, the sample was much smaller (55), and, most important, raw arrest rates were analyzed rather than offending rates estimated by the offense/arrest ratio.

fenders have higher offending rates in cities where there is a relatively small black population.[14]

## V. Discussion

The major concerns of criminologists in the past fifteen years or so have focused on the individual level of analysis. For example, the dominant perspectives on crime and delinquency have focused on the characteristics and motivations of offenders that distinguish them from nonoffenders (e.g., Hirschi 1969; Elliott, Huizinga, and Ageton 1985; Wilson and Herrnstein 1985). Similarly, policy efforts have moved increasingly toward a micro-level framework. Unlike early efforts at mobilizing entire communities, such as the Chicago Area Project (see Schlossman et al. 1984), current policy efforts such as selective incapacitation are aimed at individual crime control (see, e.g., Wilson 1983).

Ecological research, in contrast, is concerned with the attributes and processes that characterize aggregates such as neighborhoods and cities. Consequently, the ecological framework offers a distinctive alternative to the individual-level focus of mainstream criminology. As Berry and Kasarda observe, a fundamental assumption of the ecological approach is that social systems exhibit structural properties that can be examined apart from the personal characteristics of their members (Berry and Kasarda 1977, p. 13).

The present study adopted a macro-level framework by examining the structural determinants of homicide and robbery offending in large U.S. cities. The theoretical perspective focused on the macro-level consequences of official sanctions and family disruption for social control. The study of social control involves delineating the factors that increase or decrease the capacity of a community or society to achieve desired goals. Accordingly, the specific question posed was, Controlling for known determinants of crime rates (e.g., poverty, inequality,

[14] Liska and Chamlin (1984) argue that percentage black reduces black arrest rates because of victim discounting in high black areas. Since percentage black increases black intraracial crime (see, e.g., Sampson 1984), Liska and Chamlin hypothesize that the police either ignore or underarrest black offenders when victims are also black—a situation that would induce a negative correlation between percentage black and black arrest rates. This is unlikely to explain the current finding since arrest probability is controlled and since there is no evidence showing police bias by race in arrest practices for homicide and robbery. Furthermore, the arrest/offense ratio is not significantly related to racial composition and inequality in our sample (but see Liska et al. 1985). We thus believe that the finding is not merely an artifact of using arrests to estimate offending. However, a plausible substantive explanation is beyond the scope of the present essay.

region, racial composition, and size), do variations in criminal justice sanctions and the structural arrangement of families influence criminal behavior? To disentangle possible confounding effects of city composition in terms of demographic attributes, crime rates were disaggregated by age, race, and sex of offender.

At least two major conclusions emerged from the empirical analysis. First, official sanctions appear to have significant deterrent effects on criminal offending, with the effects conditioned by type of crime, age, and race of offender. More specifically, sanctions had either no effect on homicide or counterintuitive effects (e.g., prison risk was positively associated with homicide rates). By contrast, the effect of official sanctions on robbery offending conforms to theoretical predictions. Cities with a high risk of jail incarceration produce disproportionately low robbery rates regardless of both demographic attributes of offenders and other known determinants of criminality such as poverty and inequality.

Prison risk also has negative effects on robbery, but only for juvenile and youthful offenders. Indeed prison risk has a strong negative effect on both black and white juvenile robbery but no effect whatsoever on black and white adult robbery. The reason for this pattern is not immediately clear. It may be that juveniles are more impressionable regarding notions of punitiveness than are adults. Adult robbery offenders are also presumably more experienced and aware of the rarity of actual prison incarceration.

The effect of police aggressiveness also varies by type of crime and demographic attributes; that is, the significant inverse effect of police aggressiveness on the aggregate robbery rate (table 1) stems almost wholly from its deterrent effect on black offenders. The reason behind this particular interaction of sanctions with race is also not clear. A large part of the effect, however, may stem from differential patrolling policies in black neighborhoods. Even though racial composition was controlled for, it is still likely that police surveillance is lower in the white community than in the black community. The age-specific pattern is more easily interpreted—juveniles simply are not the primary targets of arrests for driving under the influence and disorderly conduct. Juveniles probably bear little of the brunt of aggressive police action (as defined in this study) and thus may not perceive it as a threat.

In any event, the results suggest that official sanctions—especially police aggressiveness and local incarceration—have important deterrent effects on robbery offending. This contrasts somewhat with recent conclusions regarding the effect of the criminal justice system on crime (e.g., Blumstein et al. 1978; Cook 1980). But it is important to keep in mind that the present analysis focuses on previously unexplored aspects of official social control. To our knowledge, the independent effects of jail risk have not been examined, and the *direct* effect of police aggressiveness has been explored only tangentially (e.g., Wilson and Boland 1978).

There are distinct theoretical advantages to the conceptual model used here. With regard to police aggressiveness, the theory did not focus on actual probabilities of getting caught but on threat communication; that is, the mechanism hypothesized to account for the results is the effect of highly visible police activities on changing the perceptions of potential offenders. Since the criminal justice system may be able to do very little in terms of changing actual probabilities of arrests for crimes such as robbery, it seems fruitful to continue exploring deterrent functions that operate at the perceptual level.

Second, the conceptualization of jail risk has the advantage of focusing on variations in official control at the local community level. Most previous studies examine only state-level variations in imprisonment. Since states are very large, they mask considerable variation in risk. It is doubtful that offenders in, say, New York either face or perceive similar risk factors as do offenders in Buffalo or Albany. One can argue that cities are also large units, but cities are still much smaller and more homogeneous than are states, and offenders in different cities face vastly different probabilities of official incarceration. Apparently, these differences have important implications for patterns and rates of offending. One reason for the effect of local variations in risk of being sanctioned may be the contemporaneous nature of jail risks. Incarceration in jail is more immediate than is imprisonment and more likely. The threat of immediate deprivation of liberty may thus serve as a more effective deterrent than does the more distant risk of imprisonment.

The empirical results also establish the importance of family structure as a determinant of variations in crime rates. Regardless of such related characteristics as racial composition, poverty, and inequality, family disruption has strong effects on robbery and homicide offending. The effect of family disruption derives from two sources—the overall divorce rate among adults and the proportion of black and white intact families. In general, both dimensions of family disruption proved important, although the prevalence of black and white two-parent families tends to have stronger effects on juvenile offending, while the divorce rate exhibits stronger effects on adult offending.

The direction and strength of the effects of family structure support the general community-level social control framework. However, as with most prior ecological research, direct measures of the hypothesized mediating constructs (e.g., supervision of peer groups and informal control) were not available. Future research efforts are needed to measure these factors directly and to partition the effects of social control of offenders from the control of targets and opportunities. For example, areas with high divorce rates may place fewer informal controls on potential offenders but may also provide more vulnerable targets of victimization. As noted by Felson and Cohen (1980, p. 401), "[I]solated [single, divorced] persons may be less subject to social control and thus more likely to engage in criminal activity. On the other hand, these persons may also be more suitable victims of crimes." Much future research is thus necessary to tackle some of the difficult measurement problems inherent in a definitive test of macro-social control models.

Given the limitations inherent in nonexperimental research in general and considering the specific limitations of the present study, policy implications are necessarily less than conclusive. The aim, however, was to assess a theory of informal and formal macro-level social control, not to determine how many crimes can be diverted given a certain policy. I do not suggest therefore that the police should start being more aggressive or that we should begin incarcerating more people in jail. Obviously, any crime control policy entails trade-offs, and the costs of enacting policies based on the current research might well be considered too high relative to expected gains. For instance, the restrictions on freedom entailed by aggressive policing may be an important concern. Similarly, both the moral and the financial costs of incarcerating more offenders in jail might be prohibitive. These concerns are beyond the scope of the present study, but they should not be ignored in future empirical and theoretical deliberations.

The implications of the family structure results also deserve some clarification. Some observers have noted that researchers typically view family disruption (e.g., divorce) as a sign of failure (Spitze 1985, p. 557). An alternative view suggests that divorce may have beneficial consequences (e.g., ending marital conflict and reducing spouse abuse), and viewing it as dysfunctional reflects a conservative bias in favor of the traditional American family (see, e.g., Furstenberg and Spanier 1984; Spitze 1985). Indeed the vociferous attacks on the Moynihan report in the 1960s are still well remembered in many circles (see Wilson 1984; Wilson and Aponte 1985).

Two comments seem to be in order. First, there is no necessary inconsistency in divorce having simultaneous positive and negative effects. Divorce may well have beneficial and adaptive consequences for particular individuals while at the same time generating negative consequences for community-level social controls. A similar point has been made by Cohen and Felson (1979)—many positive features of American society (e.g., economic growth and female labor force participation) may have unintended negative consequences for crime rates.

Second, while family disruption may have some positive adaptive features for some individuals, this is more likely to occur for whites than for blacks. There is an accumulating body of evidence suggesting that the disruption of black families has had profound negative implications for black women, particularly for those with children (Rainwater 1970; Wilson 1984; Wilson and Neckerman 1986). In particular, the pool of marriageable (i.e., economically stable) men is proportionately much smaller for black women than for white women, thus prolonging periods of financial stress and disruption for black families (Wilson and Neckerman 1986). In contrast, divorce and separation do not appear to have long-lasting negative consequences for either financial or family stability in the white population (Bane 1986). Whites are less likely to be separated than are blacks and more often remarry after divorce (Wilson and Neckerman 1986). Black teenagers also have much higher birth rates and out-of-wedlock births than do white teenagers (Wilson 1984). It is thus imperative that racial differences be taken into account in the study of family structure. Indeed there are a host of questions that remain to be examined regarding the causal linkages among black poverty, economic discrimination, family disruption, and black criminality.

The results suggest that it is misleading to make artificial distinctions between sociological and deterrence models of crime. Indeed one of the goals of this essay was to integrate a theory of official social control focusing on sanction risks with emerging perspectives on the macrolevel consequences of family dissolution. Traditional sociological concerns with inequality and poverty were also included in the theoretical model. This effort appears justified, as the dimensions of official sanctions, family structure, and economic stratification all had independent effects on homicide and robbery. Since all these dimensions are to some extent interrelated, it behooves investigators to continue to attempt to disentangle the structural components of communities and cities that foster criminal offending.

## REFERENCES


Bailey, William. 1984. "Poverty, Inequality, and City Homicide Rates: Some Not So Unexpected Findings." *Criminology* 22:531–50.

Baldwin, John. 1979. "Ecological and Areal Studies in Great Britain and the United States." In *Crime and Justice: An Annual Review of Research*, vol. 1, edited by Norval Morris and Michael Tonry. Chicago: University of Chicago Press.

Bane, Mary Jo. 1986. "Household Composition and Poverty: Which Comes First?" In *Antipoverty Policies: What Works and What Doesn't*, edited by S. Danziger and D. Weinberg. Cambridge, Mass.: Harvard University Press (in press).

Becker, Gary. 1968. "Crime and Punishment: An Economic Approach." *Journal of Political Economy* 78:169–217.

Berry, Brian, and John Kasarda. 1977. *Contemporary Urban Ecology*. New York: Macmillan.

Black, Donald, and Albert J. Reiss, Jr. 1970. "Police Control of Juveniles." *American Sociological Review* 35:63–77.

Blau, Peter. 1977. *Inequality and Heterogeneity*. New York: Free Press.

Blau, Judith, and Peter Blau. 1982. "The Cost of Inequality: Metropolitan Structure and Violent Crime." *American Sociological Review* 47:114–29.

Bloom, B. 1966. "A Census Tract Analysis of Socially Deviant Behaviors." *Multivariate Behavioral Research* 1:307–20.

Blumstein, Alfred, Jacqueline Cohen, and Daniel Nagin. 1978. *Deterrence and Incapacitation: Estimating the Effects of Sanctions on Crime Rates*. Washington, D.C.: National Academy Press.

Bordua, David. 1958. "Juvenile Delinquency and 'Anomie': An Attempt at Replication." *Social Problems* 6:230–38.

Bureau of Justice Statistics. 1978. *Census of Jails*. Washington, D.C.: U.S. Government Printing Office.

———. 1980. *Prisoners in State and Federal Institutions on December 31, 1980*. Washington, D.C.: U.S. Government Printing Office.

———. 1982. "Jail Inmates 1982." Bulletin. Washington, D.C.: U.S. Government Printing Office.

———. 1985. *Prisoners in State and Federal Institutions on December 31, 1984*. Washington, D.C.: U.S. Government Printing Office.

Bursik, Robert J., Jr. 1984. "Ecological Theories of Delinquency since Shaw and McKay." Paper presented at the annual meeting of the American Society of Criminology, Cincinnati, November.

Byrne, James. 1983. "Ecological Correlates of Property Crime in the United States: A Macroenvironmental Analysis." Ph.D. dissertation, Rutgers University.

———. 1986. "Cities and Crime: The Ecological/Nonecological Debate Reconsidered." In *The Social Ecology of Crime*, edited by James Byrne and Robert Sampson. New York: Springer-Verlag.

Byrne, James, and Robert Sampson. 1986. "Key Issues in the Social Ecology of Crime." In *The Social Ecology of Crime*, edited by James Byrne and Robert Sampson. New York: Springer-Verlag.

Carroll, Leo, and Pamela Jackson. 1983. "Inequality, Opportunity, and Crime Rates in Central Cities." *Criminology* 21:178–94.

Cartwright, D., and K. Howard. 1966. "Multivariate Analysis of Gang Delinquency." *Multivariate Behavioral Research* 1:321–71.

Chambliss, William, and Robert Seidman. 1971. *Law, Order and Power*. Reading, Mass.: Addison-Wesley.

Chilton, Roland. 1964. "Continuity in Delinquency Area Research: A Comparison of Studies for Baltimore, Detroit, and Indianapolis." *American Sociological Review* 29:71–83.

Cohen, Lawrence, and Marcus Felson. 1979. "Social Change and Crime Rate Trends: A Routine Activities Approach." *American Sociological Review* 44:588–607.

Cook, Philip J. 1980. "Research in Criminal Deterrence: Laying the Groundwork for the Second Decade." In *Crime and Justice: An Annual Review of Research*, vol. 2, edited by Norval Morris and Michael Tonry. Chicago: University of Chicago Press.

Cook, Dennis, and Sanford Weisberg. 1980. "Criticism and Influence Analysis in Regression." In *Sociological Methodology*, edited by S. Leinhardt. San Francisco: Jossey-Bass.

Crutchfield, Robert, Michael Geerken, and Walter Gove. 1982. "Crime Rates and Social Integration: The Impact of Metropolitan Mobility." *Criminology* 20:467–78.

Curtis, Lynn. 1975. *Violence, Race, and Culture*. Lexington, Mass.: Heath.

Durkheim, Émile. 1897. *Suicide: A Study in Sociology*, translated by J. Spaulding and G. Simpson. New York: Macmillan.

Ehrlich, I. 1975. "The Deterrent Effect of Capital Punishment: A Question of Life and Death." *American Economic Review* 65:397–417.

Elliott, Delbert, David Huizinga, and Susan Ageton. 1985. *Explaining Delinquency and Drug Use*. Beverly Hills, Calif.: Sage.

Feeley, Malcolm. 1979. *The Process Is the Punishment: Handling Cases in a Lower Criminal Court*. New York: Russell Sage.

Felson, Marcus. 1986. "Linking Criminal Choices, Routine Activities, Informal Social Control, and Criminal Outcomes." In *The Reasoning Criminal*, edited by Ronald Clarke and Derek Cornish. New York: Springer-Verlag.

Felson, Marcus, and Lawrence Cohen. 1980. "Human Ecology and Crime: A Routine Activity Approach." *Human Ecology* 8:389–406.

Fisher, Franklin, and Daniel Nagin. 1978. "On the Feasibility of Identifying the Crime Function in a Simultaneous Model of Crime Rates and Sanction Levels." In *Deterrence and Incapacitation: Estimating the Effects of Sanctions on Crime Rates*, edited by Alfred Blumstein, Jacqueline Cohen, and Daniel Nagin. Washington, D.C.: National Academy Press.

Flanagan, Timothy, and Maureen McLeod, eds. 1983. *Sourcebook of Criminal Justice Statistics, 1982*. Washington, D.C.: U.S. Government Printing Office.

Flango, V., and E. Sherbenou. 1976. "Poverty, Urbanization and Crime." *Criminology* 14:331–46.

Furstenberg, F., and G. Spanier. 1984. *Recycling the Family: Remarriage after Divorce*. Beverly Hills, Calif.: Sage.

Georges-Abeyie, Daniel, and Keith Harries, eds. 1980. *Crime: A Spatial Perspective*. New York: Columbia University Press.

Gibbs, Jack. 1981. *Norms, Deviance, and Social Control: Conceptual Matters*. New York: Elsevier.

Gibbs, Jack, and Maynard Erickson. 1976. "Crime Rates of American Cities in an Ecological Context." *American Journal of Sociology* 82:605–20.

Gottfredson, Michael, and Don M. Gottfredson. 1980. *Decision Making in Criminal Justice*. Cambridge, Mass.: Ballinger.

Greenberg, S., W. Rohe, and J. Williams. 1985. *Informal Citizen Action and Crime Prevention at the Neighborhood Level: Synthesis and Assessment of the Research*. National Institute of Justice Report. Washington, D.C.: U.S. Government Printing Office.

Guest, Avery. 1984. "The City." In *Sociological Human Ecology: Contemporary Issues and Applications*, edited by M. Micklin and H. Choldin. Boulder, Colo.: Westview.

Harries, Keith. 1976. "Cities and Crime: A Geographic Model." *Criminology* 14:369–86.

———. 1980. *Crime and the Environment*. Springfield, Ill.: Thomas.

Hindelang, Michael. 1978. "Race and Involvement in Common-Law Personal Crimes." *American Sociological Review* 43:93–109.

———. 1981. "Variations in Sex-Race-Age-specific Incidence Rates of Offending." *American Sociological Review* 46:461–74.

Hirschi, Travis. 1969. *Causes of Delinquency*. Berkeley: University of California Press.

———. 1983. "Crime and the Family." In *Crime and Public Policy*, edited by J. Wilson. San Francisco: Institute for Contemporary Studies Press.

Hirschi, Travis, and Michael Gottfredson. 1983. "Age and the Explanation of Crime." *American Journal of Sociology* 89:552–84.

Jackson, Pamela. 1984. "Opportunity and Crime: A Function of City Size." *Sociology and Social Research* 68:173–93.

Janowitz, Morris. 1975. "Sociological Theory and Social Control." *American Journal of Sociology* 81:82–108.

Kasarda, John, and Morris Janowitz. 1974. "Community Attachment in Mass Society." *American Sociological Review* 47:427–33.

Kennedy, Peter. 1979. *A Guide to Econometrics*. Cambridge, Mass.: MIT Press.

Kobrin, Solomon. 1971. "The Formal Logical Properties of the Shaw-McKay

Delinquency Theory." In *Ecology, Crime, and Delinquency*, edited by H. Voss and D. Petersen. New York: Appleton-Century-Crofts.

Kornhauser, Ruth. 1978. *Social Sources of Delinquency*. Chicago: University of Chicago Press.

Lander, Bernard. 1954. *Toward an Understanding of Juvenile Delinquency*. New York: Columbia University Press.

Levin, Yale, and Alfred Lindesmith. 1937. "English Ecology and Criminology of the Past Century." *Journal of Criminal Law and Criminology* 27:801–16.

Liska, Allen, and Mitch Chamlin. 1984. "Social Structure and Crime Control among Macrosocial Units." *American Journal of Sociology* 90:383–95.

Liska, Allen, Mitch Chamlin, and Mark Reed. 1985. "Testing the Economic Production and Conflict Models of Crime Control." *Social Forces* 64:119–38.

Loftin, Colin, and Robert Hill. 1974. "Regional Subculture and Homicide: An Examination of the Gastil-Hackney Thesis." *American Sociological Review* 39:714–24.

Lundman, R., R. Sykes, and J. Clark. 1978. "Police Control of Juveniles: A Replication." *Journal of Research in Crime and Delinquency* 15:74–91.

McCord, Joan. 1982. "A Longitudinal View of the Relationship between Parental Absence and Crime." In *Abnormal Offenders, Delinquency, and the Criminal Justice System*, edited by J. Gunn and David Farrington. New York: Wiley.

Messner, Steven. 1982. "Inequality and the Urban Homicide Rate." *Criminology* 20:103–14.

———. 1983*a*. "Regional and Racial Effects on the Urban Homicide Rate: The Subculture of Violence Revisited." *American Journal of Sociology* 88:997–1007.

———. 1983*b*. "Regional Differences in the Economic Correlates of the Urban Homicide Rate: Some Evidence on the Importance of Cultural Context." *Criminology* 21:477–88.

Messner, Steven, and Scott South. 1986. "Estimating Race-specific Offending Rates: An Intercity Comparison of Arrest Data and Victim Reports." Working paper. Albany: State University of New York at Albany, Department of Sociology.

Morash, Merry. 1984. "Establishment of a Juvenile Record: The Influence of Individual and Peer Group Characteristics." *Criminology* 22:97–112.

Morris, Terence. 1958. *The Criminal Area*. London: Routledge & Kegan Paul.

Nagin, Daniel. 1978. "Crime Rates, Sanction Levels, and Constraints on Prison Population." *Law and Society Review* 12:341–66.

Ogburn, W. 1935. "Factors in the Variation of Crime among Cities." *Journal of the American Statistical Association* 30:12–34.

Pyle, Gerald. 1974. *The Spatial Dynamics of Crime*. Monograph no. 159. Chicago: University of Chicago, Department of Geography Research.

Quinney, Richard. 1966. "Structural Characteristics, Population Areas, and Crime Rates in the United States." *Journal of Criminal Law and Criminology* 57:45–52.

Rainwater, Lee. 1970. *Behind Ghetto Walls: Black Families in a Federal Slum*. Chicago: Aldine.

Reiss, Albert J., Jr. 1951. "Delinquency as the Failure of Personal and Social Controls." *American Sociological Review* 16:196–207.

———. 1971. *The Police and the Public.* New Haven, Conn.: Yale University Press.

Riley, David. 1985. "Time and Crime." Paper presented at the annual meeting of the American Society of Criminology, San Diego, November.

Rosenfeld, Richard. 1986. "Urban Crime Rates: The Effects of Inequality, Welfare Dependency, Region, and Race." In *The Social Ecology of Crime*, edited by James Byrne and Robert Sampson. New York: Springer-Verlag.

Sampson, Robert. 1983. "The Neighborhood Context of Criminal Victimization." Ph.D. dissertation, State University of New York at Albany.

———. 1984. "Group Size, Heterogeneity, and Intergroup Conflict: A Test of Blau's *Inequality and Heterogeneity*." *Social Forces* 62:618–39.

———. 1985*a*. "Race and Criminal Violence: A Demographically Disaggregated Analysis of Urban Homicide." *Crime and Delinquency* 31:47–82.

———. 1985*b*. "Neighborhood and Crime: The Structural Determinants of Personal Victimization." *Journal of Research in Crime and Delinquency* 22:7–40.

———. 1985*c*. "Structural Sources of Variation in Race-Age-specific Rates of Offending across Major U.S. Cities." *Criminology* 23:647–74.

Schlossman, S., G. Zellman, R. Shavelson, M. Selak, and J. Cobb. 1984. *Delinquency Prevention in South Chicago: A Fifty Year Assessment of the Chicago Area Project.* Santa Monica, Calif.: Rand.

Schuessler, Karl. 1962. "Components of Variation in City Crime Rates." *Social Problems* 9:314–23.

Shaw, Clifford, and Henry McKay. 1942. *Juvenile Delinquency and Urban Areas.* Chicago: University of Chicago Press.

Short, James, and Fred Strodtbeck. 1965. *Group Process and Gang Delinquency.* Chicago: University of Chicago Press.

Skogan, Wesley. In this volume. "Fear of Crime and Neighborhood Change."

Smith, Doug. 1984. "The Organizational Context of Legal Control." *Criminology* 22:19–38.

Spitze, Glenna. 1985. "The Incomplete Institution." *Contemporary Sociology* 14:557–59.

Tomeh, Aida. 1964. "Informal Group Participation and Residential Patterns." *American Journal of Sociology* 70:28–35.

———. 1973. "Formal Voluntary Organizations: Participation, Correlates, and Interrelationships." *Sociological Inquiry* 43:89–121.

Van Valey, T., W. C. Roof, and J. Wilson. 1976. "Trends in Residential Segregation: 1960–1970." *American Journal of Sociology* 82:826–44.

Weisberg, Sanford. 1980. *Applied Linear Regression.* New York: Wiley.

Wilkinson, Karen. 1980. "The Broken Home and Delinquency." In *Understanding Crime*, edited by Travis Hirschi and Michael Gottfredson. Beverly Hills, Calif.: Sage.

Williams, Kirk. 1984. "Economic Sources of Homicide: Re-estimating the Effect of Poverty and Inequality." *American Sociological Review* 49:283–89.

Willie, Charles. 1967. "The Relative Contribution of Family Status and Economic Status to Juvenile Delinquency." *Social Problems* 14:326–34.

Wilson, James Q. 1968. *Varieties of Police Behavior.* Cambridge, Mass.: Harvard University Press.

———, ed. 1983. *Crime and Public Policy.* San Francisco, Calif.: Institute for Contemporary Studies Press.

Wilson, James Q., and Barbara Boland. 1978. "The Effect of the Police on Crime." *Law and Society Review* 12:367–90.

Wilson, James Q., and Richard Herrnstein. 1985. *Crime and Human Nature.* New York: Simon & Schuster.

Wilson, William Julius. 1984. "The Urban Underclass." In *Minority Report,* edited by L. Dunbar. New York: Pantheon.

Wilson, William Julius, and R. Aponte. 1985. "Urban Poverty." *Annual Review of Sociology* 11:231–58.

Wilson, William Julius, and K. Neckerman. 1986. "Poverty and Family Structure: The Widening Gap between Evidence and Public Policy Issues." In *Antipoverty Policies: What Works and What Doesn't,* edited by S. Danziger and D. Weinberg. Cambridge, Mass.: Harvard University Press (in press).

Zimring, Franklin E. 1981. "Kids, Groups, and Crime: Some Implications of a Well Known Secret." *Journal of Criminal Law and Criminology* 72:867–85.

*Douglas A. Smith*

# The Neighborhood Context of Police Behavior

ABSTRACT

A number of researchers have hypothesized that neighborhood context may influence police behavior. Data from sixty neighborhoods located in three large U.S. cities were analyzed using bivariate and multivariate analyses of five measures of police behavior and eleven neighborhood characteristics to test the neighborhood context hypothesis. Police offer more assistance to residents and initiate more contacts with suspicious persons and suspected violators in racially heterogeneous neighborhoods. They are also less likely to stop suspicious persons in high-crime areas. Suspects encountered by police in lower-status neighborhoods run three times the risk of arrest compared with offenders encountered in higher-status neighborhoods, regardless of type of crime, race of offender, offender demeanor, and victim preferences for criminal arrest. Variation in police use of coercive authority among neighborhoods is linked to the racial composition of neighborhoods but is not attributable to the race of individuals confronted by police. Police response to crime victims is also influenced by neighborhood characteristics. Officers appear less likely to file incident reports in higher-crime neighborhoods when other variables are taken into consideration. A threshold effect may operate in which offenses must reach a higher level of seriousness in higher-crime neighborhoods before police report incidents. Neighborhood characteristics and police departmental structure and policies may interact to produce systematic, and therefore predictable, patterns of police behavior.

Douglas A. Smith is Assistant Professor in the Department of Criminology and Criminal Justice at the University of Maryland at College Park. The author would like to acknowledge the helpful insights and comments of Professors Albert J. Reiss, Jr., Christy Visher, and Carl Klockars. The Police Services Study cited in Sec. II was funded by the National Science Foundation (grant GI43949) and the National Institute of Justice (grant 78NIAX0020).


0-226-80802-5/86/0008-0009$01.00

Over the last three decades, a considerable body of literature has evolved on the role and functioning of police in modern society. One of the more significant contributions is the "discovery" of police discretion (Rumbaut and Bittner 1979). Scholars in increasing number regard the law as only one factor influencing police behavior. Indeed, law justifies as well as determines police behavior (Bittner 1967, 1970; Manning 1977). In the search to discover factors besides law that influence the exercise of police discretion, researchers have primarily focused on situational characteristics of police-citizen encounters such as the race, sex, age, and demeanor of participants; the location of encounters; and the dispositional preferences of complainants (e.g., Black and Reiss 1970; Black 1971, 1976; Lundman 1974; Lundman, Sykes, and Clark 1978; Smith and Visher 1981). Some researchers have examined the organizational constraints and demands on police officers and their influence on officer behavior (e.g., Reiss and Bordua 1967; Wilson 1967, 1968; Friedrich 1977; Brown 1981; Smith 1984). This organizational perspective on police discretion stresses that any comprehensive attempt to understand police behavior must address the contexts in which such behavior occurs.

Another context of police behavior, the neighborhood, is examined in this essay.[1] The primary objective is to assess the degree to which discretionary police behaviors, such as making arrests, filing reports of victimizations, and exercising coercive authority toward citizens are influenced by the type of neighborhood in which encounters between police and citizens occur. Two specific issues are addressed. First, to what extent do characteristics of neighborhoods directly influence police behavior after controlling for the influence of encounter-specific or situational factors on police behavior? Second, to what degree do police respond differently to cues in encounters in different types of neighborhoods? Answers to these questions permit a preliminary assessment of the degree to which police actions are influenced by the neighborhood context in which encounters with citizens occur.

[1] The concept "neighborhood" has a variety of meanings in the literature. I use the term to refer to small residential areas within cities that are defined on the basis of police beats, census block groups, or enumeration districts. In the data used here, most neighborhoods have well-established geographic boundaries such as rivers, industrial parks, and major highways. Moreover, neighborhoods were selected for study, in part, because they represented meaningful geographic units to the police departments operating in these areas. For a complete discussion of the sampling design and definitional issues regarding the concept of neighborhood in these data see Caldwell (1977) and Dean and Parks (1977).

## I. Neighborhoods as Contexts

Speculation that police respond differently to similar situations has existed in the literature for over half a century. In 1936, Sophia Robison investigated whether delinquency can be accurately measured by using official police data on juvenile arrests. She speculated that one reason for the disproportionate representation of poor youth in the official delinquent population was that police tend to respond more formally to youth from "the wrong side of the tracks." Robison suggested that an arrest involved two elements: some rule-violating behavior and an assessment by police of the offender's moral character. Assessment of the latter element, she argued, was essentially an attribution process that worked to the detriment of those in poor areas. In short, police would be more likely to arrest youth from disadvantaged neighborhoods than from more advantaged neighborhoods. Unfortunately, no data were presented to assess this hypothesis.

William Whyte, in *Street Corner Society*, noted the sharply conflicting social pressures to which police must adapt in different neighborhoods. Whyte observed that an almost universal adaptation by police was the development of different standards of correct or acceptable conduct in different neighborhoods (1943, p. 136). Thus, what might be tolerated by police in one neighborhood would quickly be acted against in another.

Almost twenty years later, Michael Banton observed in his study of British and American police departments that "in different neighborhoods police provide different services" (1964, p. 181). He speculated that one explanation could be found in the degree to which police participate in the life of the society they patrol. The less social distance between police and the public, the more police would adopt a helping orientation in their encounters with citizens. As the social distance increased, two adaptations were possible: police might respond more formally to citizens or, alternatively, be reluctant to become involved at all.

Research in the late 1960s continued to develop the theme that to understand police behavior one must consider the environments in which police operate. Werthman and Piliavin (1967), for example, argued that police actions are motivated, in part, by a set of expectations regarding appropriate conduct in a given neighborhood. They suggest that "residence in a *neighborhood* is the most general indicator used by police to select a sample of potential law violators" (p. 76; emphasis in original). Thus, in constructing delinquent images police rely on pragmatic induction, in which past experiences guide immediate decisions. In many ways this is one example of Merton's (1968) self-fulfilling prophecy. Based on a set of internalized expectations derived from past experience, Werthman and Piliavin argued, police divide the population and the physical territory they must patrol into readily understandable categories. The result is a process of ecological contamination in which all persons encountered in bad neighborhoods are viewed by police as possessing the moral liability of the area itself. As a consequence, argued Werthman and Piliavin, the type of neighborhood in which police-juvenile encounters occur influences the actions taken by police.

Similar themes are found in works of Reiss and Bordua (1967) and Bayley and Mendelsohn (1969). Bayley and Mendelsohn argued that increased social distance between police and the poor results in a more aggressive or punitive police posture in lower-class areas. They also suggest that police will act more aggressively toward offenders encounted in high-crime areas. Specifically, in these neighborhoods, police will use greater coercion and make arrests more frequently. Reiss and Bordua (1967) also argue that police practices vary considerably from one context to the next. Indeed, they note that particularistic police responses are a necessary adaptive component of the police role. However, Reiss and Bordua differ from others by noting that police may act more aggressively in some disadvantaged areas yet be more reluctant to intervene in others. They note that police may refuse to take action against the use of violence between citizens in certain settings. Rubenstein (1973) observed a similar reluctance of police to make arrests in assaults involving blacks.

More recently, Donald Black (1976) proposed a theory to account for the "behavior of law." One indicator of law, according to Black, is the police decision to invoke the legal process either by making an arrest or by filing reports of victimizations. When Black refers to more or less "law," or the "quality of law," he is referring to the comparative extent to which social disorder provokes formal, legalistic responses, such as calling the police or, if police are called, their making an arrest or taking other official action, rather than informal responses. Black postulated that law varies with other aspects of social life, such as stratification. For example, police will exercise more law in high-status areas. In lower-status areas, police will invoke the legal process less often. In addition, the social, racial, and economic heterogeneity of an area may influence the quantity of law; that is, in more stratified communities police will invoke the legal process more often than in homogeneous communities. A similar idea was advanced earlier by Quinney (1970), who argued that law is the primary means of establishing order in heterogeneous communities to compensate for the declining significance of informal control mechanisms.

One common theme in these studies is the suggestion that police behavior may vary considerably from one neighborhood to the next. Despite this and the growing body of literature devoted to explain police discretion, little systematic evidence has directly addressed the questions raised by these studies. We simply do not know if police behavior varies systematically across neighborhoods or what specific characteristics of neighborhoods might explain such variation. A preliminary empirical assessment of these questions is presented in this essay. Two types of police behavior are examined. First, I construct two activity-based measures of police assistance and police investigation. Second, I use three conditional choice measures: (1) the probability of arrest given a contact with a suspected violator, (2) the probability that police will exercise coercive authority toward suspected offenders, and (3) the probability that police will file a report given a contact with an alleged victim.

## II. Data and Variables

Data were collected as part of a larger evaluation of police services conducted in 1977.[2] These data are comparable with previous observational data on police-citizen encounters (e.g., Black and Reiss 1970; Sykes and Clark 1975); 5,688 police-citizen contacts were observed and recorded by researchers riding on 900 patrol shifts. The observational data were collected in sixty study neighborhoods served by twenty-four police departments operating in three metropolitan areas: Rochester, New York; St. Louis, Missouri; and Tampa–St. Petersburg, Florida. Neighborhoods were defined on the basis of police beat boundaries, census block groups, and enumeration districts. Data on neighborhood characteristics were obtained from interviews with random samples of approximately 200 residents in each study neighborhood.[3]

[2] The Police Services Study was conducted under the direction of the Workshop in Political Theory and Policy Analysis at Indiana University and the Center for Urban and Regional Studies at the University of North Carolina at Chapel Hill.

[3] Samples were selected to obtain approximately 200 interviews per study neighborhood. Refusal rates ranged from 11 percent to 22 percent. For a more complete discussion of issues pertaining to the citizen interview, see Dean and Parks (1977).

These data allow us to aggregate individual or household responses to the neighborhood level to obtain measures of neighborhood characteristics. Most important, these data provide the opportunity to link police behavior with characteristics of the neighborhoods in which the behavior occurs.

*A. Police Behavior Variables*

Measures of police behavior come from direct observation of police-citizen encounters or police activity. Five measures of police behavior are examined. These items appear in table 1. The first two, *proactive investigation* and *proactive assistance*, are based on officers' use of discretionary or unassigned time. Discretionary time is defined as the total time each officer was observed less time spent on assignments from dispatchers or supervisors, time spent on administrative duties, and time spent on calls outside the study neighborhood.

*Investigative* acts are defined as police-initiated contacts involving suspects or suspicious persons. The measure used is the number of such encounters per 100 hours of assigned time. This variable ranges from 2.7 to 46.4 contacts per 100 hours in the sixty study neighborhoods with a mean of 20.5.

*Assistance* acts are police-initiated contacts with persons in need of assistance and contacts to check on someone about whom police are concerned. This variable ranges from 0 to 21.8 acts of assistance per 100 hours of unassigned time in the study neighborhoods with a mean of 6.01. These two measures reflect police styles since they are based on the types of activities police choose to undertake during their discretionary time.

Three additional measures of police behavior were constructed from the observational data on police-citizen encounters. The first of these, *arrest*, is the proportion of encounters involving suspected violators in a given neighborhood where the offender is taken into police custody. This measure ranges from 0 to .41 in the study neighborhoods with a mean of .13.

Following Blau (1964), who viewed physical coercion or its threat as the polar case of power, Bittner (1970) and others have argued that the capacity to use force is a central element of the police role. Thus, our next measure of police behavior, *coercive authority*, is the proportion of encounters where the suspect is unarmed in which police use or threaten to use force or enforcement activities. For example, if police threaten a suspect with arrest, surveillance, or physical harm, the encounter is classified as an instance of coercive authority. The proportion of encounters in which coercive authority is exercised ranges from 0 to .75 in the study neighborhoods, with a mean of .3.

The final measure of police behavior, *report*, is the proportion of encounters with victims in which police file an official report. This variable measures the degree to which law is extended to citizens by police. This variable ranges from .08 to .86 in the study neighborhoods with a mean of .45.

### *B. Neighborhood Variables*

Eleven characteristics of neighborhoods in eight categories are identified by aggregating responses from the citizen survey within neighborhoods (table 1).

*Crime Scale.* A crime scale was constructed from two victimization-based crime rates (violent and serious property victimizations) and two questions that asked residents to estimate the likelihood that they would be a victim of a robbery or a burglary in their neighborhood in the next year. These four measures have a mean interitem correlation of .75 in the study neighborhoods. Since these items are similar conceptually and empirically, a crime scale was created by converting each item into a standardized normal variable and then summing the four variables.

*Socioeconomic Scale.* A measure of neighborhood socioeconomic status was created by summing three normalized variables: median family income, the percentage of owner-occupied dwellings, and the percentage of households with annual family incomes above $5,000. The mean interitem correlation among these three variables across neighborhoods is .67.

*Residential Stability.* Several other dimensions of neighborhoods that may affect police behavior are included in the present analysis. One of these is a measure of transience or residential mobility within each neighborhood—the percentage of households that have resided in the neighborhood for less than five years. In the sixty study neighborhoods this measure ranges from 16.8 to 90.3 percent with a mean of 34.39 percent.

*Interaction.* A measure of interaction among neighborhood residents is created by asking respondents how often they get together with their neighbors. Responses to this question ranged along a six-point ordinal scale from very infrequently to almost daily and were aggregated within neighborhoods. The mean score on this variable within

TABLE 1

Description of Measures of Police Behavior and Neighborhood Characteristics for Sixty Study Neighborhoods

| | Description | Range |
|---|---|---|
| Police behavior: | | |
| Proactive investigation | No. of police-initiated contacts involving suspects or suspicious persons per 100 hours of unassigned officer time (mean = 20.5). | 2.7–46.4 |
| Proactive assistance | No. of police-initiated contacts with citizens in which police offer some assistance or check on someone they are concerned about per 100 hours of unassigned officer time (mean = 6.01). | 0–21.8 |
| Arrest | Proportion of encounters involving suspects in which offender is taken into custody by police (mean = .130). | 0–.41 |
| Coercive authority | Proportion of nondangerous encounters involving suspects in which police exercise some degree of coercion during the encounter such as physical force or verbal threats of arrest, force, or surveillance (mean = .30). | 0–.75 |
| Report | Proportion of encounters with victims in which police file an official report of the incident (mean = .45). | .08–.86 |
| Neighborhood characteristics: | | |
| Crime scale | A summated scale consisting of four standardized variables: victimization-based violent and serious property crime rates, mean neighborhood levels of perceived likelihood of being victimized by robbery and burglary (mean interitem correlation = .751). | −5.25–10.52 |

| | | |
|---|---|---|
| SES scale | A summated scale consisting of three standardized variables: median family income, percentage of owner-occupied dwellings, and percentage of households with annual incomes above $5,000 (mean interitem correlation = .667). | −5.71–4.75 |
| Residential mobility | Percentage of households who have lived in the neighborhood less than five years (mean = 34.39). | 16.83–90.32 |
| Interaction | Mean scores within each neighborhood to a question asking how frequently one gets together with other persons in neighborhood (mean = 3.49). | 2.77–3.95 |
| Single parents with children | Percentage of households with single parents containing children ages 12–20 (mean = 13.27). | 4.79–25.97 |
| Percent nonwhite | Percentage of population that is nonwhite (mean = 30.47). | 0–99.5 |
| Racial heterogeneity | Probability that two persons randomly drawn from the neighborhood will be in different racial groups, $K = 2$ (mean = .19). | 0–.5 |
| Income heterogeneity | Probability that two persons randomly drawn from the neighborhood will be in different income categories, $K = 7$ (mean = .76). | .58–.84 |
| Neighborhood instability | Percentage of households in neighborhood less than five years with household incomes below $5,000 annually (mean = 4.96). | 0–13.07 |
| Percent living alone | Percentage of single-person households (mean = 16.19). | 3.06–34.88 |
| Percent over sixty-five | Percentage of population over sixty-five years old (mean = 11.7). | 1.69–32.74 |

each neighborhood is used as that neighborhood's score on the interaction variable, and it ranged from 2.77 to 3.9.

*Household Composition.* Several variables reflecting household composition were also aggregated to the neighborhood level. For example, the resident survey obtained information on all persons living in each sampled household. Four measures of neighborhood composition are constructed from these data: percent living alone, the percentage of single-person households; percent over sixty-five, the percentage of the population over sixty-five years of age; single parents with children, the percentage of single-parent households with children between the ages of twelve and twenty; and percent nonwhite, the percentage of nonwhite population. The ranges and means of these variables in the sixty study neighborhoods are reported in table 1.

*Racial Heterogeneity.* Since some scholars have suggested that police may act differently in heterogeneous communities, we developed two measures of racial and income heterogeneity. Racial heterogeneity is defined as the probability that two persons randomly drawn from a neighborhood would be in different racial groups. Thus, a neighborhood that was 90 percent white and 10 percent black would have the same score on this measure as a neighborhood that was 90 percent black and 10 percent white. This variable approaches its maximum value (.5) as the white/nonwhite split in a neighborhood approaches fifty-fifty.

*Income Heterogeneity.* A measure of income heterogeneity was calculated, which represents the probability that two randomly selected households in a neighborhood would fall into different income categories. This variable is based on seven income categories and ranges from .58 to .84.

*Neighborhood Instability.* The last neighborhood measure combines information on residential mobility and household income. In examining these data, it was noted that residential mobility has both an upward and a downward dimension. That is, the most mobile neighborhoods tended to be at both ends of the socioeconomic spectrum. A neighborhood instability variable was constructed to measure the percentage of households with annual family incomes under $5,000 that have resided in a neighborhood for less than five years. It may reflect what might be conceptualized as neighborhoods of last resort for the economically disadvantaged. Neighborhoods containing powerless people and characterized by high transiency are perhaps the areas least able to exercise effective social controls over their residents.

A correlation matrix among these eleven neighborhood characteristics and the five indicators of police behavior is presented in table 2.

TABLE 2

Weighted Correlation Matrix among Neighborhood Variables and Indicators of Police Behavior ($N = 60$)

| | Proactive Investigation | Proactive Assistance | Arrest | Report | Coercive Authority | Crime Scale | SES Scale | Residential Mobility | Interaction | Percent Single Parents with Children | Percent Nonwhite | Income Heterogeneity | Racial Heterogeneity | Neighborhood Instability | Percent Living Alone | Percent over Sixty-five |
|---|---|---|---|---|---|---|---|---|---|---|---|---|---|---|---|---|
| Proactive investigation | 1.0 | | | | | | | | | | | | | | | |
| Proactive assistance | −.05 | 1.0 | | | | | | | | | | | | | | |
| Arrest | .24 | .05 | 1.0 | | | | | | | | | | | | | |
| Report | .37 | .22 | .24 | 1.0 | | | | | | | | | | | | |
| Coercive authority | .45 | −.19 | .42 | .03 | 1.0 | | | | | | | | | | | |
| Crime scale | .02 | −.02 | .42 | .08 | .37 | 1.0 | | | | | | | | | | |
| SES scale | −.05 | −.08 | −.60 | −.21 | −.30 | −.66 | 1.0 | | | | | | | | | |
| Residential mobility | −.14 | −.06 | .02 | −.14 | −.21 | .05 | .07 | 1.0 | | | | | | | | |
| Interaction | −.01 | .02 | .20 | .16 | −.15 | .19 | −.43 | .36 | 1.0 | | | | | | | |
| Percent single parents with kids | .09 | −.19 | .33 | .04 | .41 | .73 | −.60 | .09 | .19 | 1.0 | | | | | | |
| Percent nonwhite | .23 | −.07 | .44 | .11 | .54 | .63 | −.65 | −.13 | .02 | .81 | 1.0 | | | | | |
| Income heterogeneity | −.11 | −.07 | −.32 | −.22 | −.32 | −.38 | .73 | .34 | −.01 | −.44 | −.60 | 1.0 | | | | |
| Racial heterogeneity | .29 | .09 | .27 | .05 | .49 | .57 | −.34 | .10 | .01 | .48 | .57 | −.27 | 1.0 | | | |
| Neighborhood instability | −.05 | .04 | .51 | .27 | .18 | .67 | −.84 | .20 | .49 | .60 | .56 | −.50 | .33 | 1.0 | | |
| Percent living alone | −.07 | .15 | .45 | .21 | .01 | .31 | −.74 | .01 | .47 | .16 | .20 | −.41 | .19 | .63 | 1.0 | |
| Percent over sixty-five | .09 | .20 | .18 | .26 | −.16 | −.16 | −.26 | −.27 | .21 | −.40 | −.19 | −.18 | −.26 | .18 | .48 | 1.0 |
| Unweighted mean | 20.05 | 6.0 | .13 | .45 | .30 | .0 | .0 | 34.4 | 3.5 | 13.27 | 30.5 | .76 | .19 | 4.9 | 16.2 | 11.7 |
| Unweighted standard deviation | 10.6 | 5.3 | .10 | .18 | .19 | 3.6 | 2.6 | 11.9 | .26 | 5.5 | 34.4 | .07 | .16 | 3.8 | 7.6 | 6.3 |

Each of the neighborhood items is weighted by the number of households included in the sample for a given neighborhood. Since these measures of neighborhood characteristics are based on interview data collected from random samples of residents within each neighborhood, more weight was given to more reliable neighborhood estimates. For example, a measure based on the mean score for residents in a given neighborhood, such as neighborhood interaction, will be reliable in direct proportion to the number of persons interviewed in each neighborhood.

### C. *Bivariate Associations*

Some of the bivariate relations among variables in these data are of interest and help to convey how various neighborhood attributes are related. For example, neighborhoods with high-crime environments tend to be lower-status areas, have a high proportion of single-parent households with children between the ages of twelve and twenty, have racially heterogeneous or predominantly nonwhite populations, and are characterized by neighborhood instability. Neighborhoods with a high proportion of single-parent households with children between the ages of twelve and twenty tend to be nonwhite, lower-status, or unstable areas with high-crime environments. Indeed, the strongest correlate of the crime scale, which includes both victimizations and perceived risk, is the proportion of households headed by a single parent with children between the ages of twelve and twenty ($r = .73$). Unstable neighborhoods, in addition to being high-crime and lower-status areas, are characterized by an increasing percentage of single-person households and are more likely to have larger nonwhite populations. Finally, neighborhood socioeconomic status varies directly with income heterogeneity and inversely with the percentage of single-person households.

Bivariate relations between police behavior and neighborhood characteristics show that both police investigation and assistance are only modestly correlated with neighborhood characteristics. The strongest observed relation is between police-initiated investigation and the racial composition of neighborhoods, principally racial inequality ($r = .29$). The strongest correlate of police-initiated assistance contacts is the percentage of a neighborhood's population over sixty-five years of age ($r = .20$). These data suggest that police are more apt to initiate investigative actions, such as suspicious person stops, in racially heterogeneous neighborhoods and that police are more likely to offer assistance to residents in neighborhoods with a larger share of elderly residents.

While the types of encounters officers initiate with citizens during their discretionary time appear relatively unrelated to neighborhood characteristics, their actions, given a contact with a suspect or victim, do vary with properties of neighborhoods. For example, at the neighborhood level, the proportion of encounters with suspects that end in arrest varies directly with the neighborhood crime environment, the percentage of nonwhite residents, the extent of neighborhood instability, and the percentage of single-person households. Moreover, the lower the socioeconomic status of a neighborhood, the greater the probability that offenders encountered by police will be arrested. The probability that police will exercise coercive authority toward suspects also varies with racial heterogeneity and with increases in the percentage of nonwhite population. Police use more coercive authority in high-crime environments and in lower-status neighborhoods. Finally, the probability that police will file an official report given a contact with a victim does not correlate strongly at the neighborhood level with any of the measured neighborhood characteristics.

## III. Findings

A multivariate analysis to determine which neighborhood characteristics influence police actions at the neighborhood level is presented here. It begins with the analysis of police use of discretionary time.

### A. *Police Use of Unassigned Time*

Table 3 reports a series of regression models that regress the measures of proactive police activity on neighborhood characteristics. Two equations are presented for each measure of police behavior. One includes all neighborhood characteristics simultaneously, while the other reports results for the best subset of independent variables.[4]

1. *Investigation.* Results in table 3 indicate that five neighborhood characteristics accounted for 17 percent of the variation in proactive police investigations. The neighborhood characteristic exhibiting the strongest influence is the level of racial inequality characterizing a neighborhood ($t = 2.65$). As the percentage of neighborhood residents over sixty-five years of age increases, so does the propensity for investigative police activity. It appears that police may increasingly use their discretionary time to make suspicious person stops or conduct field interrogations in potentially volatile neighborhoods (i.e., racially

[4] Best subsets were obtained by using both backward elimination and forward entry. Both methods of inclusion resulted in identical solutions.

TABLE 3

Regression of Proactive Police Assisting and Investigating Acts on Neighborhood Characteristics ($N = 60$)

| | Assisting | | | | Investigating | | | |
|---|---|---|---|---|---|---|---|---|
| Independent Variable | $B^*$ | $t^\dagger$ | $B$ | $t$ | $B^*$ | $t^\dagger$ | $B$ | $t$ |
| Crime scale | −.02 | (.07) | ... | ... | −.28 | (1.15) | −.25 | (1.48) |
| SES scale | −.47 | (.88) | −.29 | (1.91) | −.37 | (.76) | ... | ... |
| Residential mobility | −.02 | (.10) | ... | ... | −.04 | (.23) | ... | ... |
| Interaction | −.03 | (.15) | ... | ... | .14 | (.78) | ... | ... |
| Percent single parents with children | −.49 | (1.40) | −.48 | (2.86) | .15 | (.48) | ... | ... |
| Percent nonwhite | −.08 | (.27) | ... | ... | .20 | (.07) | .28 | (1.76) |
| Income heterogeneity | .03 | (.13) | ... | ... | .11 | (.48) | ... | ... |
| Racial heterogeneity | .25 | (1.28) | .22 | (1.57) | .47 | (2.57) | .42 | (2.65) |
| Neighborhood instability | .02 | (.08) | ... | ... | −.36 | (1.27) | ... | ... |
| Percent living alone | −.14 | (.50) | ... | ... | −.40 | (1.59) | −.30 | (1.98) |
| Percent over sixty-five | −.01 | (.04) | ... | ... | .41 | (2.04) | .36 | (2.39) |
| $R^{2\ddagger}$ | −.05 | ... | .09 | ... | .12 | ... | .17 | ... |

* Standardized regression coefficient.

† Absolute value of $t$-statistic.

‡ Adjusted for degrees of freedom.

mixed) and in neighborhoods with a larger share of potentially vulnerable individuals (i.e., over sixty-five years of age). Finally, results from this model indicate that police are less likely to initiate suspicious person stops or proactively confront potential offenders in high-crime neighborhoods and in areas with a high percentage of single-person households once the effects of other measured variables have been taken into account.

2. *Assistance.* Results of the analysis for police initiated assistance to citizens confirm the low relation between assistance and neighborhood characteristics noted in the correlation matrix. The most parsimonious model accounts for only 9 percent of the between-neighborhood variation in officer assistance. Specific results indicate that officers engage in less assisting activity in higher-status neighborhoods, perhaps reflecting a lower need for assistance in these neighborhoods. Police also initiate somewhat more assistance in racially mixed areas and in neighborhoods with a larger proportion of single-parent households. This finding, coupled with the earlier result that police also initiate more aggressive actions in racially heterogeneous neighborhoods, may indicate that police are simply more active in these types of neighborhoods in both law enforcement and service activities.

### *B. Decision Making in Encounters: Aggregate Effects*

Independent effects of neighborhood characteristics on aggregate measures of police decision making are discussed in this section. Three measures of police activity are examined: (1) the proportion of encounters with suspects in which police take the offender into custody, (2) the rate at which police act coercively toward suspects in nondangerous encounters, and (3) the proportion of encounters with victims in which police file an official report of the incident. Conceptually, the proportion of suspects arrested is an indicator of the degree to which law is imposed by police, while the proportion of victimizations that result in an official report is a measure of the extent to which law is extended to citizens by police. Since the dependent variables are neighborhood averages of these events, the analysis focuses on the variation between neighborhoods in these measures.

Results of this analysis are presented in table 4. Two equations are presented for each aggregate measure of police behavior: one in which each measure of police behavior is regressed on all neighborhood characteristics simultaneously and another that uses only the most significant subset of neighborhood characteristics.

TABLE 4

Regression of Arrest, Coercive Authority, and Report on Neighborhood Factors ($N = 60$)

| | Arrest | | | | Coercive Authority | | | | Report | | | |
|---|---|---|---|---|---|---|---|---|---|---|---|---|
| Independent Variable | $B$* | $t$† | $B$ | $t$ | $B$* | $t$† | $B$ | $t$ | $B$* | $t$† | $B$ | $t$ |
| Crime scale | −.03 | (.14) | ... | ... | −.10 | (.49) | ... | ... | −.04 | (.17) | ... | ... |
| SES scale | −1.13 | (2.65) | −.97 | (5.04) | −.61 | (1.38) | ... | ... | .64 | (1.23) | .30 | (1.40) |
| Residential mobility | .13 | (.87) | ... | ... | −.15 | (1.01) | −.20 | (1.82) | −.24 | (1.35) | −.22 | (1.59) |
| Interaction | −.19 | (1.19) | −.22 | (1.66) | −.15 | (.90) | ... | ... | .20 | (1.02) | ... | ... |
| Percent single parents with children | −.27 | (.97) | ... | ... | .03 | (.09) | ... | ... | −.09 | (.27) | ... | ... |
| Percent nonwhite | .29 | (1.14) | ... | ... | .19 | (.63) | .32 | (2.50) | −.09 | (.28) | ... | ... |
| Income heterogeneity | .43 | (2.06) | .39 | (2.26) | .17 | (.81) | ... | ... | −.25 | (.98) | ... | ... |
| Racial heterogeneity | .04 | (.24) | ... | ... | .39 | (2.38) | .33 | (2.52) | .06 | (.34) | ... | ... |
| Neighborhood instability | −.11 | (.43) | ... | ... | −.14 | (.56) | ... | ... | .59 | (1.95) | .53 | (2.00) |
| Percent living alone | −.11 | (.49) | ... | ... | −.28 | (1.24) | ... | ... | .06 | (.22) | ... | ... |
| Percent over sixty-five | .06 | (.34) | ... | ... | −.01 | (.03) | ... | ... | .12 | (.57) | .17 | (1.37) |
| $R^2$‡ | .33 | ... | .38 | ... | .28 | ... | .34 | ... | .01 | ... | .09 | ... |

* Standardized regression coefficient.

† Absolute value of $t$-statistic.

‡ Adjusted for degrees of freedom.

1. *Arrest.* Three neighborhood characteristics account for 38 percent of the between-neighborhood variation in the probability of arrest. The most prominent factor affecting the probability of arrest across neighborhoods is the socioeconomic status of the community. Independent of other neighborhood properties, the probability that an encounter between police and a suspect will end in an arrest declines substantially with increasing community status. It is difficult to interpret this effect. Police may act more legalistically toward suspects in lower-status neighborhoods, or police in these neighborhoods may encounter a larger proportion of the types of offenses that are likely to result in arrest.

2. *Coercion.* While socioeconomic status of neighborhoods is the primary determinant of aggregate arrest probabilities, the racial composition of neighborhoods influences the likelihood that police will exercise coercive authority. Police are significantly more likely to use or threaten force against suspects encountered in primarily black or racially mixed neighborhoods. Police also use less coercive authority in more transient communities once other neighborhood characteristics are controlled for. Collectively, these three variables account for 34 percent of the between-neighborhood variation in police coerciveness.

3. *Reporting.* Finally, the percentage of victimizations in which police file an official report is not strongly influenced by the neighborhood characteristics available in these data. Results of this model indicate that police are somewhat more likely to file reports in higher-status neighborhoods and somewhat less likely in more transient communities. Reports are also more likely to be filed in less stable neighborhoods and in communities with a larger share of elderly residents.

In summary, the likelihood of arrest and coercive action by police toward suspects appears to vary with certain dimensions of neighborhoods. Increasing socioeconomic status decreases the probability of a legalistic police response at the neighborhood level. Moreover, police act more coercively toward suspects in nonwhite and racially mixed neighborhoods. The next section addresses possible interpretations of these observations.

### C. *Decision Making in Encounters: Contextual Effects*

Many scholars who argue that police behavior is affected by the context in which it occurs suggest that police will respond differently to similar situations in different types of neighborhoods. For example, police may be more tolerant of interpersonal violence between citizens

TABLE 5

Direct Effects Model of Neighborhood Characteristics on Arrest Decisions ($N = 762$)

| | Encounter-specific Covariates | | Neighborhood Characteristics | |
|---|---|---|---|---|
| Variable | *b** | *t*-Value | *b** | *t*-Value |
| Public location | .106 | .84 | .095 | .74 |
| Black suspect | .222 | 1.72 | .134 | .99 |
| Female suspect | −.223 | −1.23 | −.239 | −1.30 |
| Suspect antagonism | .473 | 5.79 | .452 | 5.47 |
| Violent offense | .574 | 3.32 | .512 | 2.91 |
| Property offense | .762 | 4.68 | .788 | 4.81 |
| Complainant requests arrest | .917 | 5.40 | .900 | 5.27 |
| Neighborhood SES scale | ... | ... | −.067 | −2.66 |
| Constant | −1.734 | ... | −1.713 | ... |
| Likelihood ratio test | 123.00 | ... | 130.12 | ... |
| Pseudo $R^{2\dagger}$ | .185 | ... | .200 | ... |

* Maximum-likelihood probit coefficient.
† See Judge et al. (1980, p. 601).

in nonwhite communities and hence make arrests less often in violent disputes in nonwhite neighborhoods. To address this and related questions, it is necessary to determine whether police are more likely to make arrests in certain types of neighborhoods after controlling for the characteristics of encounters between police and citizens.

1. *Arrest.* Results reported in table 5 address the question whether police arrest decisions are influenced by dimensions of neighborhoods after controlling for the characteristics of the individual police-suspect encounter. Drawing on the literature on determinants of police arrest decisions, the analysis includes measures of the sex, race, and demeanor of the suspect; the location of the encounter (public vs. private place); the type of problem (violent, property, or public order violation, which is used as a reference category for estimation); and whether the complainant requests arrest. The first two columns in table 5 report estimates of a probit model predicting individual arrest decisions with encounter-specific covariates. These results indicate that arrests are more likely in violent and property offenses, in encounters in which the complainant requests an arrest, and in encounters in which the suspect acts antagonistically toward police. Arrests are somewhat less likely when the suspect is female or white.

The next step involved reestimating this equation adding neighborhood characteristics to the encounter-level covariates in order to determine whether each neighborhood characteristic affects the decision to arrest. The first two columns in table 5 were reestimated eleven times, each time adding one of the eleven neighborhood characteristics. The neighborhood characteristic with the most significant effect on individual arrest decisions, after controlling for the encounter-level covariates, is neighborhood socioeconomic status. The probability of arrest decreases with increasing status of the neighborhood in which the encounter occurs. This effect is independent of the type of offense, suspect characteristics, and dispositional preferences of complainants. The next step was to reestimate the arrest equation including all encounter-level covariates and neighborhood socioeconomic status ten more times, each time adding one of the remaining ten neighborhood characteristics. These results indicate that, once neighborhood socioeconomic status and encounter-level variables are held constant, no other neighborhood characteristic has a significant effect on police decisions to arrest. Thus, my final contextual model of arrest decisions in individual encounters between police and suspect includes only the socioeconomic status dimension of neighborhoods and is presented in the third and fourth columns in table 5.

The results of this model indicate that the socioeconomic status of neighborhoods in which police encounter suspects has a direct negative effect on the probability that police will arrest the offender. Independent of the race, sex, demeanor of offenders, the type of problem, and the preferences of complainants, arrests are less likely to occur in higher-status neighborhoods.

2. *Coercion.* To determine whether neighborhood characteristics directly affect the propensity of police to exercise coercive authority toward suspects, the procedure discussed above was replicated. The results are presented in table 6. At the encounter level, police exhibit more coercive authority toward black and antagonistic offenders, but they act less coercively in encounters involving female offenders and in encounters that occur in public places. Two neighborhood characteristics appear independently to influence the probability of coercive police authority. Police are more likely to exercise coercive authority toward suspects encountered in nonwhite and racially mixed neighborhoods. Moreover, these effects are independent of the race, sex, and demeanor of the suspect; the type of problem involved; and whether the encounter occurs in a public or private setting. Thus, the propensity of

TABLE 6

Direct Effects Model of Neighborhood Characteristics on Coercive Authority ($N$ = 762)

| Variable | Encounter-specific Covariates *b** | Encounter-specific Covariates *t*-Value | Neighborhood Characteristics *b** | Neighborhood Characteristics *t*-Value |
|---|---|---|---|---|
| Public location | −.285 | −2.79 | −.281 | −2.71 |
| Black suspect | .344 | 3.35 | .105 | .83 |
| Female suspect | −.390 | −2.76 | −.389 | −2.72 |
| Suspect antagonism | .443 | 5.30 | .426 | 5.07 |
| Violent offense | .172 | .98 | .119 | .67 |
| Property offense | .120 | .82 | .164 | 1.12 |
| Complainant requests arrest | −.023 | −.13 | −.032 | −.17 |
| Percent nonwhite | ... | ... | .0036 | 1.95 |
| Racial inequality | ... | ... | .778 | 2.38 |
| Constant | −.559 | ... | −.745 | ... |
| Likelihood ratio test | 68.69 | ... | 81.81 | ... |
| Pseudo $R^{2\dagger}$ | .100 | ... | .117 | ... |

* Maximum-likelihood probit coefficient.
† See Judge et al. (1980, p. 601).

police to exercise coercive authority is not influenced by the race of the individual suspect per se but rather by the racial composition of the area in which the encounter occurs.

3. *Reporting.* A third issue is whether police decisions to file reports of incidents are influenced by the types of neighborhoods in which encounters between police and victims occur. The following encounter-level covariates were used: the race, sex, and demeanor of complainants; the type of problem involved; and whether the victim requests that police file a report. Results reported in table 7 indicate that police are more likely to file a report for violent and property offenses and if the victim requests that a report be made. Conversely, police are significantly less likely to file reports in instances involving female complainants. Two neighborhood characteristics independently influence the probability of police filing a report, namely, police are less likely to file victimization reports in high-crime neighborhoods and are more likely to file victimization reports in unstable neighborhoods.

Collectively, the results reported in tables 5, 6, and 7 indicate that police appear to respond differently to suspects and victims depending on the type of neighborhood in which these encounters occur. Suspects

TABLE 7

Direct Effects Model of Neighborhood Characteristics on Police Filing Official Reports ($N$ = 1,142)

| | Encounter-specific Covariates | | Neighborhood Characteristics | |
|---|---|---|---|---|
| Variable | $b$* | $t$-Value | $b$* | $t$-Value |
| Black victim | −.065 | −.76 | −.017 | −.19 |
| Female victim | −.185 | −2.23 | −.183 | −2.19 |
| Victim antagonism | −.249 | −.95 | −.244 | −.92 |
| Violent offense | .701 | 5.43 | .730 | 5.59 |
| Property offense | .780 | 8.02 | .798 | 8.12 |
| Interpersonal conflict | .136 | 1.02 | .159 | 1.17 |
| Victim requests report | 1.002 | 8.79 | 1.016 | 8.90 |
| Neighborhood crime scale | ... | ... | −.065 | −4.34 |
| Neighborhood instability | ... | ... | .055 | 4.15 |
| Constant | −.629 | ... | −.929 | ... |
| Likelihood ratio test | 223.12 | ... | 246.56 | ... |
| Pseudo $R^{2\dagger}$ | .185 | ... | .202 | ... |

* Maximum-likelihood probit coefficient.

† See Judge et al. (1980, p. 601).

confronted in lower-status neighborhoods have a higher risk of being arrested, while those encountered in nonwhite or racially mixed communities are more apt to be handled coercively by police. Victims in high-crime areas are less likely to have the incident reported by police. Hence there is some evidence in these data that certain characteristics of neighborhoods influence police decision making independently of the attributes of individual encounters between police and citizens.

### D. *Decision Making in Encounters: Conditional Effects*

The preceding analysis focused on the direct effects of neighborhood characteristics on police decision making in individual encounters. The behavioral model underlying these equations is a process of ecological attribution bias by police. That is, do police respond systematically to suspects and victims in all types of neighborhoods, or do they respond differently depending on the type of neighborhood in which the encounter occurs?

The following analysis examines a *conditional effects model*. This model addresses whether encounter-level variables interact with neighborhood characteristics to influence police decision making. Consequently, I relax the assumption of homogeneous or constant-within-neighborhood effects of encounter-level covariates. For example, table 5 indicates that police are more likely to arrest suspects if the complainant requests that an arrest be made. However, it is possible that police respond differently to complainants' requests for arrest in different types of neighborhoods. In high-status neighborhoods, for example, police arrest decisions may be more or less influenced by such requests than in low-status neighborhoods.

1. *Arrest.* Table 8 reports results of a conditional effects model for arrest decisions in individual encounters. I estimated a probit equation with arrest/no arrest as the dependent variable and included all encounter-level variables and neighborhood socioeconomic status as independent variables. Next I added to this equation a product interaction term between each encounter-level variable and each neighborhood characteristic. This equation was estimated once for each interaction term. The results are presented in table 8, which indicates that complainants' requests for arrest affect the probability of arrest differently depending on the racial heterogeneity of the neighborhood. Requests that the suspect be arrested have a much stronger effect on the likelihood of arrest in racially homogeneous communities. To see this more explicitly, the predicted probability of arrest for two hypothetical en-

TABLE 8

Conditional Effects Model of Police Arrest Decisions ($N$ = 762)

| Variable | $b$* | $t$-Value |
|---|---|---|
| Public location | .115 | .89 |
| Black suspect | .162 | 1.15 |
| Female suspect | −.234 | −1.27 |
| Suspect antagonism | .462 | 5.58 |
| Violent offense | .575 | 3.23 |
| Property offense | .765 | 4.60 |
| Complainant wants arrest | 1.453 | 5.08 |
| Neighborhood SES scale | −.064 | −2.50 |
| Racial heterogeneity | .177 | .43 |
| Complainant wants arrest × racial heterogeneity | −2.341 | −2.44 |
| Constant | −1.788 | ... |
| Likelihood ratio test | 136.50 | ... |
| Pseudo $R^{2\dagger}$ | .216 | ... |

* Maximum-likelihood probit coefficient.

† See Judge et al. (1980, p. 601).

TABLE 9

Conditional Effects Model of Police Use of Coercive Authority ($N$ = 704)

| Variable | $b$* | $t$-Value |
|---|---|---|
| Public location | −.285 | −2.76 |
| Black suspect | −.171 | −.89 |
| Female suspect | −.397 | −2.77 |
| Suspect antagonism | .424 | 5.03 |
| Violent offense | .128 | .71 |
| Property offense | .185 | 1.27 |
| Complainant wants arrest | −.035 | −.19 |
| Percent nonwhite | −.0023 | −.66 |
| Racial heterogeneity | 1.082 | 2.98 |
| Percent nonwhite × black suspect | .0083 | 1.96 |
| Likelihood ratio test | 85.72 | ... |
| Pseudo $R^{2\dagger}$ | .125 | ... |

* Maximum-likelihood probit coefficient.
† See Judge et al. (1980, p. 601).

counters was calculated. One calculation assumed that a complainant requested that an arrest be made in a racially homogeneous neighborhood (racial heterogeneity = .05). The second calculation assumed that a complainant requested that an arrest be made in a racially mixed neighborhood (racial heterogeneity = .40). The predicted probabilities of arrest in these two encounters, when all other variables in the model are evaluated at their means, are .59 and .30, respectively. Thus, police appear less willing to defer to citizens about arrests in racially mixed neighborhoods.

2. *Coercion.* Table 9 presents a conditional effects model for police use of coercive authority. Some scholars have suggested that police assess persons against the background in which interactions between police and citizens occur. One variation of this theme is the "out-of-context" thesis that police will act more aggressively toward persons encountered in areas where they appear out of place. Rubenstein (1973), for example, notes that police tend to act more aggressively toward blacks encountered in primarily white neighborhoods. My analysis also indicates a significant interaction between the suspect's race and the racial composition of the neighborhood in which the confrontation occurs. However, my analysis shows that police are more likely to exercise coercive authority toward black offenders in primarily *black* neighborhoods.

TABLE 10

Conditional Effects Model of Police Filing Official Reports ($N$ = 1,142)

| Variable | $b$* | $t$-Value |
|---|---|---|
| Black victim | −.506 | −2.67 |
| Female victim | −.190 | −2.26 |
| Victim antagonism | −.275 | −1.03 |
| Violent offense | .708 | 5.38 |
| Property offense | .790 | 8.02 |
| Victim requests report | 1.027 | 8.95 |
| Neighborhood crime scale | −.069 | −4.14 |
| Neighborhood instability | .054 | 3.92 |
| Percent nonwhite | .003 | 1.81 |
| Racial heterogeneity | −.669 | −1.64 |
| Black victim × racial heterogeneity | 1.609 | 2.83 |
| Constant | −.870 | . . . |
| Likelihood ratio test | 255.87 | . . . |
| Pseudo $R^{2}$† | .209 | . . . |

* Maximum-likelihood probit coefficient.
† See Judge et al. (1980, p. 601).

These results help explain an earlier finding (table 6) that the racial composition of neighborhoods has a significant effect on the propensity of police to exercise coercive authority toward suspects. To clarify this, the estimated probability of coercive police action for two hypothetical cases was calculated. The first calculation assumed that police confronted a black suspect in a predominantly white neighborhood (10 percent nonwhite). The second calculation assumed that police encountered a black offender in a predominantly black neighborhood (90 percent nonwhite). With other variables in the model evaluated at their means, the predicted probabilities of coercive police authority in these two cases are .26 and .44, respectively. Thus, in white neighborhoods, black suspects are handled less coercively by police than in black neighborhoods. Moreover, the probability of coercive authority directed toward white offenders remains fairly stable across different types of neighborhoods, fluctuating between .26 and .32.

3. *Reports.* The final conditional effects model concerns the probability that police will file a victimization report and is reported in table 10. This model identified one significant interaction involving the victim's race and the racial composition of the neighborhood in which the victimization occurred. This interaction was clarified by calculating the

estimated probability that police would file a victimization report in encounters involving black victims in three types of neighborhoods (90 percent white, 90 percent black, and 50 percent black). These were repeated in calculations for victimizations involving white victims. When other variables in the model are evaluated at their means, the predicted probabilities that police will file a report of a victimization involving a white victim in white, black, and mixed neighborhoods are .41, .50, and .52, respectively. However, for instances involving black victims, the corresponding estimated probabilities of police filing a report are .23, .32, and .48, respectively. Thus, in both white and black neighborhoods, police are much less likely to file reports of incidents involving black victims than of incidents involving white victims (.23 vs. .41 in white neighborhoods, and .32 vs. .50 in black neighborhoods). Only in neighborhoods where blacks and whites are equally represented in the population do police extend the law equally to blacks and whites.

## IV. Summary

Police patrol both people and places. This essay offers a preliminary examination of the territorial dimension of policing. The analysis suggests that police do act differently in different neighborhood contexts. Several dimensions of neighborhoods appear important. Police appear generally to be more active in racially mixed neighborhoods. In racially heterogeneous neighborhoods, police have a greater propensity to offer assistance to residents and to initiate more contacts with suspicious persons and suspected violators. An initial hypothesis was that police initiated more investigative contacts in racially mixed and minority areas because they were more actively looking for suspected offenders in these areas. However, this analysis also indicates that in high-crime areas police are less likely to stop suspicious persons, suggesting that the findings evidence a higher level of general police activity in racially mixed neighborhoods.

This analysis has examined police actions after a contact with a suspect or a victim. The data indicate that suspects confronted by police have a higher average probability of being arrested in lower-status neighborhoods than in higher-status areas. The data in table 5 indicate that, with other variables evaluated at their means, the predicted probability of arrest for a suspect encountered in the highest-status neighborhoods is .07. The corresponding probability in the lowest-status neighborhoods is .23. Put differently, suspects encountered in lower-status neighborhoods run three times the risk of being arrested as offenders encountered in the highest-status neighborhoods. It is difficult to interpret this finding without ambiguity. Specifically, no information is available on the status of citizens encountered by police in these data. Thus, I simply do not know whether the differences in arrest probability are independent of the influence of the individual offender's status on police arrest decisions. A number of plausible interpretations of this finding are possible. For example, police may regard arrest as less severe in lower-status areas since arrest may have far less reaching implications for those arrested. Thus, police may operate with different "arrest thresholds" in neighborhoods of differing socioeconomic status. Additionally, police may be able to obtain compliance in higher-status neighborhoods without resorting to arrest. Correlatively, suspects encountered in higher-status neighborhoods may regard arrest as more severe and be less likely to aggravate police to the point at which they make arrests. Despite these ambiguities, what remains clear is that offenders encountered in lower-status neighborhoods have a higher categorical risk of being arrested independent of factors such as type of crime, race of offender, offender demeanor, and victim preferences for arrest.

Police also vary in their exercise of coercive authority across neighborhoods, and these data indicate that this variation is linked to the racial composition of neighborhoods. Police are more apt to exert coercive authority in minority and racially mixed communities. Moreover, this variation in coercive authority is not attributable to the race of the individual offenders whom police confront. Several scholars have written about the social distance between police and minorities and the resulting tensions that such distance facilitates. While this may account for the more coercive posture of police toward individual minority offenders, it cannot account for the contextual effects identified in the current analysis. The neighborhoods in these data probably represent meaningful geographic units to the police agencies studied. Moreover, police assessments of individual offenders may reflect the officer's perceptions of the "kind of people" who live in a particular neighborhood. Thus individuals encountered in minority or racially mixed areas may be viewed by police as possessing moral liabilities connotative of the area itself. One consequence of this ecological contamination may be that the probability that police will exercise coercive authority reflects both who is involved and where the encounter occurs.

Neighborhood characteristics affect police responses to victims of crime. When encounter-level variables such as the type of problem and the race and sex of victims are controlled for, police are less likely to file reports of incidents in higher-crime neighborhoods. A threshold effect may operate here, in which offenses must reach a higher level of seriousness in high-crime neighborhoods before police will report the incident.

Findings such as these are disturbing on a number of grounds. First, they undermine our ability to develop general theories of police discretion or decision making. If police act differently in different neighborhoods, theories of police discretion must explicitly recognize the contextual variability of police decision making. On the positive side of this issue, however, is the set of null findings regarding conditional neighborhood effects. Specifically, police are more likely to arrest offenders for property and violent offenses and offenders who act antagonistically, and these effects are constant across different types of neighborhoods. Moreover, decisions to arrest appear independent of the race and sex of offenders and independent of the type of neighborhood in which police-suspect encounters occur. However, the degree to which police comply with complainants' requests for arrest does vary with the racial composition of the community.

Second, the finding that police are more likely to make arrests in lower-status neighborhoods raises a question of comparability of arrest-based measures of crime at the aggregate level. This would affect comparisons between cities or comparisons within cities. The same problem affects comparisons of crime rates based on police reports of offenses. Police appear less likely to file reports of victimizations involving blacks in both white and black neighborhoods. Thus, race-specific victimization rates based on police reports of victimizations may be differentially reliable in all but racially mixed communities.

Finally, the results reported here address the issue of equitable treatment of citizens by police. Several findings clearly show that police behave differently in different neighborhoods. Black offenders, for example, are handled much more coercively in black neighborhoods than in white neighborhoods and appear to benefit from a "halo effect" if confronted in white neighborhoods. Black victims by contrast are much less likely to have their victimizations reported by police in both white and black neighborhoods. Thus, crime against blacks appears to be discounted by police in certain contexts. Additionally, any offender confronted by police in lower-status neighborhoods has a higher probability of being arrested than a similarly situated offender encountered in higher-status neighborhoods. These variations in police behavior appear to contradict norms of equity on which the American criminal justice system is based.

Collectively, the results reported here suggest that any complete understanding of discretionary police behavior must address the contexts in which such behavior occurs. In addition to characteristics of individual police-citizen encounters, certain aspects of neighborhoods appear to influence police behavior. This analysis represents only a small and tentative first step toward understanding the ways in which neighborhood characteristics influence police behavior. The results raise more issues than they resolve. For example, some recent research has noted that police behavior can vary across organizational as well as geographic units. Smith (1984), for example, argued that organizational and supervisory structures of police agencies influence police decision making in encounters with offenders. To some extent, aggregating police behavior within neighborhoods may be measuring processes that operate at a higher level of aggregation (i.e., police departments). But it is equally likely that previous work on organizational variability in police behavior has failed to control for differential neighborhood composition. Neighborhood characteristics and departmental structure and policies may interact to produce systematic patterns of police behavior. Future replication and refinement of issues may move us closer to a general theory of discretionary police behavior.

## REFERENCES

Banton, Michael. 1964. *The Police in the Community*. New York: Basic.

Bayley, David H., and Harold Mendelsohn. 1969. *Minorities and the Police: Confrontation in America*. New York: Free Press.

Bittner, Egon. 1967. "The Social Distribution of Social Labels." *British Journal of Criminology* 19:134–45.

———. 1970. *The Function of Police in Modern Society*. Washington, D.C.: National Institute of Mental Health.

Black, Donald. 1971. "The Social Organization of Arrest." *Stanford Law Review* 23:63–77.

———. 1976. *The Behavior of Law*. New York: Academic Press.

Black, Donald, and Albert J. Reiss, Jr. 1970. "Police Control of Juveniles." *American Sociological Review* 35:63–77.

Blau, Peter M. 1964. *Exchange and Power in Social Life*. New York: Wiley.

Brown, Michael K. 1981. *Working the Street*. New York: Russell Sage.
Caldwell, Eddie. 1977. *Methods Report 02: Patrol Observation*. Chapel Hill, N.C.: Center for Urban and Regional Studies.
Dean, Deborah, and Roger Parks. 1977. *Methods Report 01: Citizen Interviews*. Bloomington, Ind.: Workshop for Political Theory and Policy Analysis.
Friedrich, Robert J. 1977. "The Impact of Organizational, Individual, and Situational Factors on Police Behavior." Ph.D. dissertation, University of Michigan.
Judge, George, William Griffith, R. Carter Hill, and Tsoung-Chao Lee. 1980. *The Theory and Practice of Econometrics*. New York: Wiley.
Lundman, Richard. 1974. "Routine Arrest Practices: A Commonweal Perspective." *Social Problems* 22:127–41.
Lundman, Richard, Richard Sykes, and John P. Clark. 1978. "Police Control of Juveniles." *Journal of Research in Crime and Delinquency* 15:74–91.
Manning, Peter K. 1977. *Police Work: The Social Organization of Policing*. Cambridge, Mass.: MIT Press.
Merton, Robert K. 1968. *Social Theory and Social Structure*. New York: Free Press.
Quinney, Richard. 1970. *The Social Reality of Crime*. Boston: Little, Brown.
Reiss, Albert J., Jr., and David Bordua. 1967. "Environment and Organization: A Perspective on the Police." In *The Police: Six Sociological Essays*, edited by David Bordua. New York: Wiley.
Robison, Sophia. 1936. *Can Delinquency Be Measured?* New York: Columbia University Press.
Rubenstein, Jonathan. 1973. *City Police*. New York: Farrar, Straus & Giroux.
Rumbaut, Ruben G., and Egon Bittner. 1979. "Changing Conceptions of the Police Role: A Sociological Review." In *Crime and Justice: An Annual Review of Research*, vol. 1, edited by Norval Morris and Michael Tonry. Chicago: University of Chicago Press.
Smith, Douglas A. 1984. "The Organizational Context of Legal Control." *Criminology* 22:19–38.
Smith, Douglas A., and Christy A. Visher. 1981. "Street-Level Justice: Situational Determinants of Police Arrest Decisions." *Social Problems* 29:167–78.
Sykes, Richard, and John Clark. 1975. "A Theory of Deference Exchange in Police-Civilian Encounters." *American Journal of Sociology* 81:584–600.
Werthman, C., and I. Piliavin. 1967. "Gang Members and the Police." In *The Police: Six Sociological Essays*, edited by David Bordua. New York: Wiley.
Whyte, William F. 1943. *Street Corner Society*. Chicago: University of Chicago Press.
Wilson, James Q. 1967. "The Police and the Delinquent in Two Cities." In *Controlling Delinquents*, edited by Stanton Wheeler and H. M. Hughes. New York: Wiley.
———. 1968. *Varieties of Police Behavior*. Cambridge, Mass.: Harvard University Press.

*Lawrence W. Sherman*

# Policing Communities: What Works?

ABSTRACT

Communities vary widely in the ways in which police exercise discretion; in their resources; in their mixtures of public police, private police, and voluntary citizen policing; in the nature and severity of problems requiring policing; and in the physical geography that shapes options for policing. Yet communities vary relatively little in basic police strategy. Residential neighborhoods in American metropolitan areas are policed primarily by officers driving around in unfocused patrol, largely waiting for calls for service. Public police should probably supplement the single-complaint strategy in most communities with a variety of mixed-strategy models. The specific strategies employed in any particular community should be based on the community's unique characteristics. Recent research suggests some conclusions about the relative effectiveness of various policing strategies in general, but it says little about interaction effects between strategies and neighborhoods. Informal experimentation may provide guidance for fitting strategies to the characteristics and problems of specific communities.

Policing varies substantially across communities. This variation is best documented at the citywide level of analysis by systematically observed police discretion (Black and Reiss 1967; Friedrich 1977; Smith 1984) and officially recorded rates of arrests per reported offense (Wilson 1968; Swanson 1978); of arrests per capita (Gardiner 1969; Wilson and Boland 1978); and of citizens killed by police (Robin 1963; Matulia 1982; Blumberg 1983; Sherman and Cohn 1986*a*). Such variation has also

Lawrence W. Sherman is Professor of Criminology and Director of the Center for Crime Control at the University of Maryland. Albert J. Reiss, Jr., Franklin Zimring, and Ronald V. Clarke provided helpful comments on earlier drafts.


0-226-80802-5/86/0008-0010$01.00

been documented in neighborhoods within cities. Fyfe (1978) has shown enormous variation across New York City precincts in the rates at which police use deadly force. Croft (1985) has suggested substantial variation across Rochester, New York, patrol divisions in the use of nonlethal force. And Smith (in this volume) has presented systematic observation evidence on variation in arrests, use of force, and crime reporting across neighborhoods.

This essay addresses the consequences of variations in police practice that result from planned and purposive efforts of policymakers. The question of which policing strategies work best to control crime (or to improve the quality of life, or to improve police-community relations, or to reduce public fear of crime) has received increased attention over the past two decades, especially at the community level of analysis. But the question has never been formulated in terms of the difference that community context makes in police effectiveness. Do different types of policing produce different gains and costs in different types of communities? What interaction effects, if any, exist between community characteristics and policing in shaping police effectiveness?

Unfortunately, little systematic evidence can be brought to bear on these questions. The measurement of interaction effects requires adequate sample sizes, and community-level evaluations of policing practices are woefully short on sample size even for main effects. Alternatively, it requires replication of experiments that test virtually identical policing strategies in many different types of communities. These questions can be approached through a review of the literature on police effectiveness in general, focusing on the implications it may hold for interaction effects of policing and community.

This essay defines "policing" in the means-oriented approach of Egon Bittner (1970) and Carl Klockars (1985). Policing clearly encompasses "institutions or individuals given the general right to use coercive force by the state within the state's domestic territory" (Klockars 1985, p. 12). But it should also encompass persons or institutions watching for crime, threatening to act if crime is committed, or mobilizing others to act. This definition allows this essay to focus on the question of which approaches to policing communities work best in controlling crime.

There is both more and less variation in the policing of communities than the existing literature describes. There is more variation in the mix of organizational structures of policing arrangements than the literature suggests, which implies much greater variation across communities in resources for policing than is apparent in the literature's concentration on the number of public police officers or the size of the public police budget. There is arguably less contemporary variation across communities in basic police strategies than the literature on discretion seems to imply.

Section I of this essay presents a model of the interaction between community characteristics and policing. Section II develops the model with an inventory of the basic choices of organizational structure, resources, and strategy in policing communities. Section III reviews the recent research critique of the prevailing "single-complaint" policing strategy found in the majority of metropolitan residential communities. Some possible alternatives to that strategy are examined from the perspective of public police, citizens, and private police. This essay concludes with some hypotheses and tentative policy recommendations on how police should take community characteristics into account.

The essay excludes many of the strategies that public police departments employ—including detective units, vice squads, hostage negotiation units, tactical units, and harbor police—for two reasons. First, there is almost no published evidence on the effectiveness of these units (but see Eck 1986). Second, these units are not usually designed to operate at a neighborhood level. The value in considering the difference that community context can make to policing is found largely in the "patrol" function, whether performed by citizens, public police, or private police.

## I. Varieties of Community Policing

This essay assumes that there is substantial interaction between the characteristics of each community and the way it is policed. There is enormous variation in policing across cities and within cities across neighborhoods. There is variation in the "natural" characteristics of the community, ranging from physical geography and demographics to political power. There is also variation in the decisions made by police executives and others constrained by community characteristics about policing in each community. Those decisions largely determine the structures, resources, and strategies of policing each community.

The consequences that strategic decision makers expect from policing a specific community in a given manner may vary. The selection of options for community policing may depend heavily on the theories or research that decision makers rely on in predicting the effects of various police actions. These anticipated consequences include both costs and benefits, such as judgments about how harsh a crackdown on crime is feasible without adverse effects on community relations or pressures from specific interest groups.

A third interaction is the feedback of actual and perceived consequences of community policing on the specific problems it may address. What community residents and organizations may think about the effectiveness of their community's policing, or what police officials may find in tracking crime trends or citizen complaints, or what newspapers or citywide interest groups may say can all be important in changing or sustaining the policing practices of a specific community.

Some examples may help to clarify each of these points. Wilson (1968) has shown, for example, that some cities are far more likely than are others to make arrests for public intoxication. Sherman and Cohn (1986*b*) have shown that cities vary widely in their responses to minor domestic violence, from encouraging arrest to letting police officers ignore the problem. Both kinds of variation may be due to differences in political pressures or political values in different cities.

Substantial differences in police practices can be found also at the neighborhood level within cities (e.g., Westley 1970, p. 97). Such variation is a joint product of what police expect will be the consequences of their differing behaviors in different neighborhoods and of what the political power of the different neighborhoods will let them get away with. A neighborhood that objects to police behavior may or may not be able to generate sufficient political pressure to change that behavior.

Neighborhood policing strategies aimed at solving specific problems are often generated by the changing power bases of different neighborhoods. Gentrification of previously poor areas, for example, can generate substantial pressure on police to eliminate street prostitution that may have a long neighborhood history.

Neighborhood policing strategies can also change simply because an old problem seems to be getting worse. New York City police undertook a massive effort to suppress drug dealing in the Lower East Side of Manhattan in 1984–85 after the problem received renewed media attention. Washington, D.C., police in 1985 cracked down on parking in Georgetown, which was closely linked to disorder problems caused by teenagers drinking in and around parked cars on main streets.

Some would argue that these kinds of neighborhood variations in police practices are widespread in American cities, with police officials and officers constantly adjusting their practices according to changing community characteristics. Others argue, as I do, that organizational structures and resources may vary widely across neighborhoods but that the basic strategy of putting the bulk of police resources into rapid response to dispatched calls for service varies little. Few would disagree that there could be greater diversity of police strategies across neighborhoods. There is ample room for more mixing of approaches and more sensitivity to community differences.

## II. Basic Choices in Policing Communities

Basic choices are made in each community about at least three aspects of policing—the organizational structures of policing, the nature and the level of policing resources, and the strategies used to deploy those resources. These choices are obviously interrelated since organizational structure choices may limit the availability of resources, which in turn may limit strategic possibilities. The choices may vary substantially over time. Because all these choices are not made by any centralized decision-making body, it is always difficult to measure exactly which choices any given community has made.

These choices are made for each community by public police officials, private business property owners, and residents. Some communities can afford a great deal of private policing; others cannot. Some communities are public spirited enough to generate substantial volunteer labor for policing; others are too atomized. Some communities have substantial numbers of young people or others creating disorder problems on the streets; others have little visible crime or disorder. Some communities feature a great deal of commercial and business activity; others are exclusively residential. The physical geography of communities creates different needs and limitations for policing; population and automobile density, type of housing structure, presence or absence of sidewalks, and street patterns vary greatly. Some communities are highly dense, with much foot traffic and ample opportunities for surveillance of public places from private residences. Other communities are geographically spread out, with few public or private places under surveillance. These differences determine the range of choices that can be made for community policing and create different requirements for an appropriate mix of policing strategies.

### A. *Organizational Structures*

The ideal mixture of policing produced by private organizations, public organizations, or citizen volunteers has long been a central policy issue. The solution has important implications for police efficiency and effectiveness and for the accountability of police use of force and the character of a democratic society.

At the heart of the debate are the twin problems of what government should do and how much tax money it should spend. In the "taxpayers' revolt" atmosphere of the late 1970s and early 1980s, it was fashionable to call for greater voluntary citizen participation in policing (e.g., Lavrakas 1985). At the same time, privately paid policing efforts have grown rapidly (Cunningham and Taylor 1985). The reality of modern America is a mixed model of citizen volunteers, privately paid guards, and full-time publicly paid police, with substantial variation across communities.

Klockars (1985) distinguishes different organizational systems for policing according to whether policing is vocational (a paid, full-time job) or avocational (unpaid and usually not full-time), whether it is done on an obligatory basis by governmental order (such as paying taxes) or done voluntarily, and whether it is done for fixed wages or on a fee-for-service basis. Table 1 similarly distinguishes different "structures" of policing in terms of who does the work and why. Much of the table is derived from the legal distinctions among the powers and obligations of the different actors performing police services. The table omits many important differences among the models, such as the nature of their hierarchy and accountability, the organization of their intelligence about crime, and the process by which they are mobilized.

The first structure, occasional voluntary citizen policing, may vary widely among communities. Citizen's arrest is the most dramatic example and is far from rare. A study of Part I arrests in Kansas City immediately after the offense found that 20 percent were made by

TABLE 1

Typology of Police Organizational Structures

| | Who Does the Work? | | |
|---|---|---|---|
| Why? | Citizens | Private Police | Public Police |
| Voluntary: | | | |
| Occasional | Citizen's arrest | Off-duty arrest | Off-duty arrest |
| Regular | Citizen patrols | Take-home cars | Take-home cars |
| Obligatory: | | | |
| Occasional | Hue and cry | Felony in presence | Felony in presence |
| Regular | Watch | Foreseeable crime | Special request |
| Contract: | | | |
| Public funds | . . . | "Privatization" | City police |
| Private funds | . . . | Private security | Special details |
| Rewards/fees: | | | |
| Public funds | Informants | Bounty hunters | . . . |
| Private funds | Crimestoppers | Private detectives | Moonlighting |

citizen volunteers at the scene (Kansas City Police Department 1977, p. 29). Another study found that burglars in one jurisdiction have a better chance of being shot by their victims than they do of going to prison (Kleck [1979], as cited in Wright, Rossi, and Daly [1983], p. 139). Such "self-help" (cf. Black 1983) is central to political debates over gun control and "vigilantism."

The voluntary occasional policing of off-duty police and security guards can also be quite substantial. One-fourth of the 239 officers killed in the line of duty from 1844 to 1978 in New York City were off duty (Margarita 1980, p. 83). Other studies found that 12–17 percent of the citizens killed by police are killed in off-duty incidents (Milton et al. 1977, p. 27; Fyfe 1980, p. 73). A substantial regular and predictable police presence may also result when public or private police officers are permitted to take marked police cars home and use them for personal business.

Regular voluntary citizen patrols in this country date back to the colonial watch system and were revitalized by civil defense work of the two world wars. Some cities, like New York, continued those patrols in uniform for trained auxiliary police; as of 1986, 8,700 volunteers were certified and armed with nightsticks for regular patrol to supplement some 25,000 paid police officers (Bird and Dunlap 1986). New York and other cities have also encouraged untrained and uncertified citizens to patrol in plainclothes as part of the Neighborhood Watch program. These programs seem particularly strong in middle-class or lower-middle-class, ethnically transitional neighborhoods (Marx and Archer 1971). The Guardian Angels movement of young people patrolling subways and other public places in groups (Klockars 1985, pp. 33–34) seems strongest in low-income minority neighborhoods.

Obligatory policing is now virtually gone as a matter of criminal law but has recently been revived in the civil law. The obligation of private citizens and even of public police to police public places has all but disappeared, but the obligations of property owners to their invitees and of public police to those who call on them have intensified. The expansion of tort law in recent years has affected the legal obligations of both private and public policing. Since entertainer Connie Francis won over a million dollars in a lawsuit against a motel where she was raped (*Garzilli v. Howard Johnson's Motor Lodges, Inc.*, 419 F. Supp. 1210 [1976]), many more such lawsuits have been filed and won (Sherman and Klein 1984). State supreme courts have upheld and expanded the duty of landlords to police their property adequately against foreseeable crimes committed by third parties (e.g., *Isaacs v. Huntington Memo-*

*rial Hospital*, 695 P.2d 653 [Cal. 1985]) and have upheld the duty of public police departments to respond effectively to requests for assistance. Failure to meet these legal obligations to provide police protection has, in recent years, produced a $2 million award against the New York police for failing to investigate a complaint of possible child abuse ("Court of Appeals Tells City to Pay $2 Million to Girl Father Stabbed" 1985); a $2.3 million verdict against a Connecticut police department for failing to arrest a wife beater ("Officers Must Pay $2.3 Million to Wife Maimed by Husband" 1985); and a decision against a Washington state police department that did not respond quickly enough to a 911 call to keep the callers from being attacked (*Chambers-Castanes v. King County*, 669 P.2d 451[1983]). The extent of these new obligations varies from state to state and practically across communities.

"Contract" policing denotes policing as a full-time job, generally, in a bureaucratic organization. The most common version is publicly funded and publicly operated in municipal and county police agencies.

The latest and still quite rare innovation in police structure is publicly funded and privately contracted policing in which public tax levies are used to retain a private, for-profit firm to provide basic police services. Reminderville, Ohio, became one of the first communities to employ this "privatization" arrangement with its small ($90,000 per year) police budget when the county sheriff raised the fee it would charge the city to twice that amount (Gage 1982). Although the arrangement was later discontinued because of persisting questions about the legal authority of private employees acting as city police officers (Tolchin 1985*a*), it has been employed in several small cities in Florida (George Zoley, personal communication, 1985). In a more common variant, communities contract with other public police agencies, which often creates competition among the candidate agencies and permits a community to change its police force almost overnight.

Privately funded and operated contract policing personnel now outnumber publicly funded personnel by over two to one (Cunningham and Taylor 1984, p. 3). Many work behind factory walls and apart from the community, but many are employed to protect public places such as parking lots, hospitals, and hotels. Many upper-middle-class and upper-class residential communities retain such patrol services on a collective basis, and the millions of individual home owners purchasing "central station" burglar alarms are paying, in effect, for a rapid response by private police to a signal from their home.

Less attention has been given to the privately funded public police activities, ranging from downtown Oakland property owners committing $300,000–$400,000 annually to the police department for extra downtown patrols (Reiss 1985, p. 18) to private interests in old northeastern cities hiring police to work overtime at construction sites, entertainment events, and late-night commercial establishments (Tolchin 1985*b*). In some cities, the number of public police on duty at any given time performing private tasks may be greater than the number performing public tasks.

Although Anglo-American policing once relied heavily on publicly funded rewards and fees to support apprehension of criminals (Radzinowicz 1956, p. 33), the role of such incentives is greatly restricted today. The "thief taker" has been replaced with the informant, who is generally rewarded with leniency more often than with money.

Privately funded reward policing is probably stronger now than it has been since the nineteenth century. The most visible example is the "Crimestoppers" program organized by business people in 443 cities to offer rewards for the solution of highly publicized crimes (Rosenbaum, Lurigio, and Lavrakas 1985). The Crimestoppers program uses free television or radio time to describe the facts of a crime shortly after it occurs and announces a telephone number that informants can call to arrange to provide information leading to the arrest of the guilty parties; if a conviction (or, in some cases, an arrest or even just recovery of property) results, the informant will be rewarded, with anonymity guaranteed (Rosenbaum et al. 1985). Such activity is more visible but probably smaller than the privately funded rewards or fees paid on a case-by-case basis to professional detectives.

Many of these structural choices are made at the city rather than at the neighborhood level. But even such citywide structures as a Crimestoppers program may be used more by citizens in some communities than in others. A citywide policy of allowing police to take cars home would create more policing in some communities (where police live) than in others (where they do not). Other structural choices are made by many individual decision makers, ranging from the operators of a shopping center who decide to hire private guards to citizens who chase a purse snatcher.

The possible combinations of policing structures present in any community are numerous and complex. The combinations may also be highly transitory, although some structures are clearly more stable than are others. There are limitations to the possible combinations set by both community resources and the public interest. Too much reliance on privately funded policing would leave poor areas greatly disadvantaged and could make people "prisoners" of well-guarded private places. As Reiss (1985, p. 17) points out, it may be more important to put our social resources into creating a safer public environment than into creating private "fortresses." Similarly, we cannot rely too much on voluntary citizen "self-help," given the difficulty of controlling citizen use of force and the virtual absence of residents from many neighborhoods during working hours. Whatever the combination of organizational structures, however, it will influence the level of resources allocated to policing and the probability that crime in the community will be deterred or intercepted.

None of this touches on the variation within public police organization. Cities vary widely in how their patrol forces are organized; some use a primarily temporal structure, with citywide command changing every eight hours. Others use community-oriented structures of command, with area commanders given twenty-four-hour, seven-day responsibility for all patrol work in their community. Both cities and communities also vary in their levels of police corruption and theft of time (loafing or doing personal errands while on duty), which also affect the actual level of resources brought to bear on community problems.

### *B. Resources*

Perhaps the most important policy question about police in any city is the number of police officers the department should have. On a per capita basis, cities vary by as much as 300 percent: big cities range roughly from one to three police officers per 1,000 citizens (Federal Bureau of Investigation 1985). At the community level, however, the variation can be much greater. Harlem, for example, at one point had ten times as many officers per 1,000 citizens as had Bay Ridge, a white, middle-class section of Brooklyn. Yet Bay Ridge had many more police officers per reported crime than had Harlem (Ruth 1971).

Police managers in the 1950s developed mathematical formulas for determining how many police each community "needed" based on reported crime, calls for service, and other quantifiable factors (Levine and McEwen 1985). In the 1970s, more sophisticated models of patrol allocation were developed that used queuing theory to maximize the efficiency of patrol car responses to emergency calls for service (Larson 1972; Chaiken 1975). But the structures of policing presented above should also be taken into account in measuring the level of public resources allocated to policing in any given community. The presence of other structures may reduce the need for public police officers.

Resource levels vary by factors other than the number of police officers. The number of private police assigned to work in a community either for commercial establishments or under a contract from the home owners is an obviously important factor. So is the number of public and private police who reside in a community, whether they bring their cars home, and whether they are employed after hours on special details in the community. The relative involvement of citizens in making arrests, conducting patrols, and providing police with information also affects the resource levels of community policing.

Some of these alternative structures may be strongest in communities where the public police are present in strength. The same social factors that enhance citizen policing may also enhance community effectiveness in lobbying for a larger number of officers. In the Hasidic community of Borough Park in Brooklyn, for example, the citizens often mount a hue and cry to apprehend muggers or purse snatchers. At the same time, community leaders work hard at election time to earn political capital, much of which is spent on obtaining more police presence. In the heavily Polish-American northeastern section of Minneapolis, there is substantial volunteer citizen surveillance and little reported crime. But the police chief's 1985 reduction in the number of officers assigned there touched off a bloody political battle that resulted, among other things, in the chief's temporary suspension by the mayor.

Nonetheless, the strong trend of recent years is toward increased resources for the organizational structures other than public police departments. Private police have tripled in strength since 1950 (Cunningham and Taylor 1984, p. 3). A 1982 Gallup poll reported that 17 percent of a national sample said they were aware of some sort of volunteer crime prevention effort in their neighborhood (Sherman 1983, p. 145), which seems likely to be a large rise over recent years.

The rise of the alternative structures accompanies a decline in the resources allocated to public police. This decline contrasts sharply with the steady growth in prestige and budgets throughout much of the twentieth century, especially the years after the riots of the late 1960s, when both salary levels and numbers of police officers increased dramatically. The growth curve of public police has been flat and has even declined slightly since the late 1970s (Bureau of Justice Statistics 1986).

Massive layoffs in New York, Detroit, and other cities, once inconceivable under any circumstances, were accomplished in the face of rising crime. This may help explain the rise of alternative structures.

### *C. Strategies*

Policing strategies consist of four basic elements: information gathering, mobilization of action, the nature of the action, and the target, or focus, of the action. Unlike the structures and resources of policing, which vary widely across communities, these strategic elements of policing have become remarkably similar in the public police agencies in urban communities around the country. Any progress in making policing more effective may depend heavily on our ability to diversify these strategies and to make them more sensitive to the characteristics of local communities.

1. *Information.* Policing is essentially an information-processing enterprise, which produces a relatively small amount of people processing. Most police work consists of seeking out information about potential trouble and troublemakers, communicating information about the potential consequences of troublemaking, recording and analyzing information about trouble that has already occurred, and presenting information about accused and apprehended troublemakers to judicial authorities. The technology and organization of these information systems are important factors shaping the effectiveness of the police.

The first public police departments at Scotland Yard and in New York had little technology for communicating crime reports rapidly. The geographic dispersion of large numbers of officers throughout a dense city encouraged citizens to report crimes to the police by creating a virtual "wall-to-wall-cops" system (Reiss 1971) in which it was possible to run into the street, shout "police," and have a foot-patrol officer respond fairly quickly. The officer could then use a whistle to summon his colleagues. The invention of the telegraph made it possible for police stations to communicate rapidly with each other, but it did little to help citizens notify police of crimes. Even the invention of the telephone, in itself, failed to alter the situation much because police on patrol could not be reached by phone except at regularly appointed times when they called into the station from a police telephone box; the actual uses of that system were more for controlling police loafing on duty than for directing their work (Rubinstein 1973, chap. 1).

It was only the invention of the radio and its reduction in size to fit into an automobile that made it possible to connect crime victims almost instantly to an officer who could respond quickly enough to make an apprehension. The rapid availability of that information transformed the way that police thought about information, changing their focus from information with long-term payoff potential to information with very short term payoff. The short term, of course, was the opportunity to apprehend an offender red-handed. The long-term payoff was in solving crimes where the offender gets away as well as deterring crimes by criminals who know the police are "on to them."

This technological change did not necessitate the change in informational focus, but it clearly facilitated it. With the rise of low-density communities relying primarily on automobile transportation, the information system of wall-to-wall police gave way to the "dial-a-cop." This change reduced the amount of "nonemergency" information that police received as well as limiting personal relationships with local community members. Once officers were put at the other end of requests for emergency response, everything else—including preventive patrol—became secondary to waiting for that exciting call.

What exactly was that "everything else" of information gathering besides responding to emergency calls? That is a matter of some debate. As Lane (1980, p. 13) observes, we can learn relatively little through historical research about ordinary patrol work or routine interactions with the public. Some scholars (Fogelson 1977; Walker 1977) are skeptical that police did much at all, at least by way of police work. But other sources, such as novelists who lived in turn-of-the-century urban communities (e.g., Smith 1943), describe police as fairly well integrated into the life of the neighborhood. The information that police acquired through informal contacts with local residents was often essential to solving crimes or even to preventing crimes by helping to solve family or youth problems (Murphy and Plate 1977).

Whether police actually spend less time talking to neighborhood residents today than they did two decades or half a century ago is unclear. But a number of developments have clearly encouraged them to move in that direction. One is air conditioning, which led police to drive through the streets with their car windows rolled up, maintaining a splendid and sanitary isolation from the sounds and smells of the streets. More important, perhaps, and clearly more variable across communities within cities is the availability of residential air conditioning. Air conditioning keeps people inside more months of the year, discouraging the sidewalk community dialogues on summer evenings that police can join in so easily. Air conditioning in communities of detached homes also led to the architectural decline of the front porch, that facilitator of informal, avocational surveillance of all aspects of public neighborhood social life. Neighborhood residents in many communities became less knowledgeable about each other and less able to share their insights with the police. The possibility that there may be much more contextual knowledge to obtain in communities without air conditioning has been lost in the process of developing a relatively uniform information-gathering strategy for all kinds of communities.

Police administrators have long been aware of these problems. As early as the 1960s, the Chicago police attempted to combine walking and riding on patrol so that police would have more informal contacts. Police in other cities employed motorcycles, scooters, motorbikes, bicycles, and horses as forms of transportation that posed less of a barrier to police-citizen contacts. In theory, all these programs show how there is no necessary conflict between rapid police mobility and informal intelligence gathering. But virtually every evaluation of such programs shows that they encounter enormous resistance from police officers, who find it much easier to stay with their vehicles and talk with other police than to park, walk, and talk with the citizenry (e.g., Sherman, Milton, and Kelley 1973; Sherman 1983). Police isolation may not be an inherent characteristic of mobile patrol, but it is a consequence that is difficult to reverse.

Information exchange among police officers is also important for contextual knowledge and may vary widely across communities. Communities with local precinct stations may have better exchange among officers than do communities whose officers report to work in a downtown headquarters. But even precinct stations may have minimal formal exchange. Despite the television image of police roll call as an announcement session (as in "Hill Street Blues"), most actual roll calls are confined to announcements of bureaucratic imperatives such as training sessions and pension forms. A detailed picture of recent crime events throughout an entire precinct would take too long to relate in a brief roll call. Written handouts are also discouraged because the mass of crime information changes so quickly.

The consequence of these changes in the technology and organization of police information is that police work has become ahistorical. Each police task is approached without information on the past or on the likely future of the parties involved. The primary unit of analysis is the single complaint, the telephone call to which a patrol car responds. Urban police must usually enter a situation stripped of any contextual knowledge about its causes or likely consequences. They often spend a great deal of time trying to elicit that information, although they are frequently plagued by suspicions that the information may not be reliable. The same people may have encountered other police officers a few hours ago, yet most urban police officers would have little chance of knowing that fact. The typical car-patrol officers are as unknown a quantity to the people they police as the people are to them.

2. *Mobilization.* The most controversial aspect of community policing is the manner in which police efforts are mobilized (Reiss and Bordua 1967). The mobilization of police at their own initiative, or proactive policing, is often associated with restriction of individual freedom and privacy. The mobilization of the police at the initiative of citizens is often viewed as the most democratic and fair method of policing a free society (Black 1973). The choice is not mutually exclusive, of course, since almost all societies feature both systems of mobilizing police, and totalitarian societies have a frightening capacity to induce citizens to volunteer information to the police.

Modern American urban communities may differ very little in the way that police are mobilized except to the extent that they are policed by foot-patrol officers. Foot-patrol officers, historically, have been especially proactive in the maintenance of public order. Early American police bureaucracies generated phenomenal numbers of public order arrests per officer per day (Levett 1975), which is hardly likely to have been a result of reacting to specific citizen requests. Even as late as 1966 in three inner-city communities, police in patrol cars initiated some 13 percent of all their mobilizations (Reiss 1971, p. 11).

But the rise of the modern police information system described above substantially changed the nature of proactive policing. The bulk of police patrol time and of police resources in general were drawn into single-complaint, rapid-response, reactive mobilization. Just as they rarely stop to chat with neighborhood residents, the police driving by in air-conditioned cars may rarely keep an eye on any known suspicious people.

The evidence of variation in proactivity is substantial at the intercity level. Friedrich (1977, p. 251) found that Boston police stopped one-tenth as many motorists per tour of duty as did Chicago police. Whether it varies as much across communities within cities is unclear. But even substantial variation would probably leave reactive mobilization with the vast majority of all contacts in all communities.

Moreover, modern proactive patrolling is based less on direct knowledge and observation of community residents and more on the use of computerized information systems. Proactive patrol is now less a matter of stopping local drunks or breaking up visible fights than it is a matter of checking license plates against a computerized list of stolen cars or stopping suspicious people to check their identification against a computerized list of persons wanted on arrest warrants. These modern "stranger" policing methods are often criticized for hurting police-community relations (National Advisory Commission on Civil Disorders 1968) and may further undermine the flow of intelligence through informal citizen contacts.

3. *Action and Targets.* Once police are mobilized to deal with certain information, they can take a variety of actions. These could theoretically vary across communities, but they rarely seem to in practice. Targets include locations, perpetrators, complainants, victims, relationships, generic problems (such as the mentally ill), suspected classes (such as young men in groups), and, of course, neighborhoods. Methods include surveillance—either visible or covert, roving or stationary—and street stops, roadblocks, interviews, community meetings, informants, traps or "stings," raids, warnings or threats to arrest, arrest, mediation and negotiation, referral to social or health agencies, and a myriad of other options (Goldstein 1977). But most policing in most communities is confined to the complainant as target and is limited to the actions of interviews, warnings, negotiations, and arrests. The roving, visible surveillance is relatively unfocused as to target; patrol is rarely addressed to specific communities as distinct from the city in general. Private police probably differ from public police in their greater focus on the properties of their clients, just as citizen patrols are more focused on the citizens' own communities.

Other combinations of targets and methods produce familiar police strategies. A highly crime-prone physical location target approached with fixed, covert surveillance constitutes a "stakeout," for example. Traps and stings used to catch highly crime-prone perpetrators are the common strategy of at least one police department's "Repeat Offender Project" (Martin and Sherman 1986). Street stops of the suspicious class of young, poor males constitute a large part of the "aggressive patrol," or field interrogation, strategy. But all these strategies are relatively rare. Moreover, their selection is rarely linked to community characteristics that may make them more or less effective. They are usually adopted at the citywide level to supplement the basic single-complaint, reactive strategy common to most communities.

## III. Critique of Single-Complaint Policing

Recent research has suggested that single-complaint policing is wasteful and possibly ineffective. The critique began early (Wilson 1963, p. 237). As crime grew rapidly in the 1960s, some observers began to blame the increase on the shift in police strategy (President's Commission on Law Enforcement and Administration of Justice 1967, p. 54). The National Advisory Commission on Civil Disorders (1968, pp. 304–5) blamed poor police-community relations on the motorization of patrol and the attendant loss of contact with the community, which adversely affects law enforcement. The commission blamed proactive policing in the absence of this contextual knowledge for causing minority perceptions of police harassment and attacked the aggressive style of proactive "stranger" patrol.

Ironically, the justification for moving to single-complaint policing was to focus the police role on crime fighting. The abandonment of proactive order maintenance and intelligence gathering was the price of this emphasis on crime control. But recent research has supported the theory that single-complaint policing is less effective in controlling crime than was community policing.

1. *Preventive Patrol in Cars.* The Kansas City Preventive Patrol Experiment (Kelling et al. 1974*a*) tested the assumption that police driving around streets in cars create a visible presence that prevents crime in public places through general deterrence. The experiment varied the level of patrol presence in three groups of five beats each and compared the before and the after differences in literally hundreds of measures of crime. The Kansas City police chief (McNamara 1974, p. vi) concluded that the lack of significant differences in the three types of beats showed "that routine preventive patrol in marked police cars has little value in preventing crime or making citizens feel safe." Others were more reserved in their judgment, especially given some question about the actual extent of the differences in patrol presence across the three types of beats (Larson 1975) and the manner in which levels of patrol were assigned to the different beats (Farrington 1982). A more basic research-design problem of small sample sizes used in evaluating community policing efforts also limits scientific confidence in the findings.

Despite these questions, the Kansas City findings have been widely accepted among police executives as showing that modest increases in the number of patrol cars are unlikely to reduce crime. One reason for this gradual acceptance may be the suspicion that police managers have that the officers are not using their patrol time very productively but are just waiting for calls for service to come in. Since the experiment found that this waiting encompassed about 60 percent of on-duty patrol time, it raised the question of what better use police might make of that time. But many plans to develop new tasks have run afoul of police union opposition (since the plans mean more work for police), cloaked in the argument that such tasks would increase police response time to calls for service.

2. *Rapid Response Time.* Arguments are made that ready availability of officers in cars, geographically dispersed throughout the community, is imperative if rapid responses are to be logistically feasible. Rapid response has been justified as necessary to increase the deterrent threat of apprehension for criminals.

A second research project in Kansas City (Kansas City Police Department 1977), however, undermined those arguments. It began by systematically analyzing the components of "response" time, including time of crime occurrence, time involved in reporting (by telephone) to a police operator, time involved in sending a radio dispatch to a police car, and travel time of that car to the scene of the crime. Response time is important, even in theory, only for "involvement" crimes, in which the victim confronted the offender who escaped immediately thereafter. Response time is clearly not an issue for "discovery" crimes, in which the offender may have fled hours earlier. So the study examined departmental records and other data on 352 involvement crimes.

The findings showed that, by the time a police car begins its travel to the scene of most involvement crimes, so much time has elapsed that the chances of apprehending an offender are extremely small. Of the average fifty-minute total response time, only four and a half minutes consisted of police travel time. On average, it took crime victims and witnesses almost forty-one minutes to report the crimes (Kansas City Police Department 1977, p. 19). Since the availability of police waiting in cars can only reduce travel time, the citizen delay in reporting poses a major obstacle to apprehension of fleeing criminals. Only 12 percent of 949 Part I crime calls analyzed resulted in arrests at the scene. Of these, only one-third—3 percent of all calls to police for Part I crimes—could reasonably be attributed to the rapid police response (p. 29).

Police chiefs who were skeptical that these findings applied to their cities volunteered to have the Police Executive Research Forum replicate the citizen-delay study. The National Institute of Justice–funded study in San Diego, California; Peoria, Illinois; Jacksonville, Florida; and Rochester, New York, found similarly long delays and confirmed the need for police to rethink the rapid-response, single-complaint strategy (Spelman and Brown 1981). Some chiefs said that the solution lay in public education to stimulate more rapid reporting. But others saw a need for alternative strategies to supplement—not replace—the rapid-response strategy.

3. *Public Demands for Rapid Response.* Many chiefs believed that, regardless of the ideal mix of strategies, their hands were tied because of citizen demands for rapid response. But further research sponsored by the National Institute of Justice falsified that argument as well.

In a field test in Toledo, Ohio; Garden Grove, California; and Greensboro, North Carolina, a differential police response (DPR) strategy was implemented on a random-assignment basis. The control group received the standard rapid response for most kinds of calls for service. The experimental groups received a variety of responses, depending on the nature of the call: rapid response, referral to a telephone report unit for taking reports over the phone, a delayed mobile response (in which callers would be told that police would not be there for thirty to sixty minutes), referral of the call to another agency, scheduled appointments with police, walk in, or mail in (McEwen, Connors, and Cohen 1984, p. 8). The results in all three sites showed that the number of nonemergency calls handled with a rapid response could be reduced significantly without any reduction in citizen satisfaction (p. 17). Citizens seemed willing to accept both delayed responses and alternative responses as long as the dispatchers clearly told them what to expect.

The DPR experiments suggest that it may be politically feasible to abandon rapid responses to most incidents and even any personal response to some kinds of incidents. More research is needed to be certain about the costs and benefits of different kinds of response to the different kinds of calls. Much will depend on the kind of information that police seek to obtain and are able to use. But the experiments provide added evidence against the use of rapid, single-complaint policing as the nearly exclusive strategy for policing residential communities. All communities will continue to demand, and police must continue to provide, a rapid-response capacity for some calls. Depending on the nature of the community, however, much of the time now devoted to rapid response could more usefully be devoted to other strategies.

There are many examples of mixed-strategy policing tailored to the needs of specific communities. Many of the decisions to employ such mixed strategies are politically determined responses to demands for police action on specific and highly newsworthy community problems (e.g., crackdowns on prostitution in newly gentrified red-light areas). But in the absence of such political pressures, most communities still feature little mixing of policing strategies, relying primarily on single-complaint responses.

Assuming that it is politically feasible to reallocate some of the police resources currently devoted to rapid response, the question then becomes, What alternatives can be pursued most productively? What strategies can public police, private police, and private citizens employ to supplement the single-complaint model in ways sensitive to the unique characteristics of each community?

## IV. What Can Public Police Do?

Many alternatives to single-complaint policing have recently been tried or experimented with. Some are widely used. These strategies have been evaluated only to a limited extent, and the evaluations all suffer from a major problem of interpretation.

### A. *The Evaluation Problem*

The problem is sample size, in two respects: the number of citizens that researchers must survey to estimate criminal victimization rates in any given community and the number of communities that must be included in any test of policing strategy at the community level. Most kinds of crime are relatively rare, in absolute numbers, within the boundaries of most patrol beats or neighborhoods. That rarity biases most statistical tests. Given the small numbers involved, even large percentage differences in crime across beats can fail to achieve statistical significance at conventional levels, and justifiably so since such small absolute differences can be obtained by chance.

In the original Kansas City experiment, a 300 percent difference in the average before-after change in reported outside robberies each month was not statistically significant, although it came close (Kelling et al. 1974*b*, p. 96). The enormous percentage difference reflected the absolute difference between an increase of .936 outside robberies per month in the beats with reduced patrol and an increase of only .003 outside robberies per month in the beats with a doubled level of patrol (the beats with unchanged patrol intensity were close to the doubled beats, at .269). This pattern is all the more important because it is consistent with the hypothesis that patrol can deter and with what is arguably the most suppressible kind of crime. Whether a larger sample size, or higher absolute levels of crime, would have produced significant differences is impossible to say. But the problem clearly complicates interpretation of the study.

In their redesign of the Kansas City experiment, Fienberg, Larntz, and Reiss (1976) suggest abandoning public surveys as the principal method for measuring community policing effectiveness. Concluding that the sample sizes in the Kansas City experiment were much too small, they recommend using a variety of official police records to measure deterrent effects in more creative ways than simply counting the number of recorded crimes, including data on offender modus operandi, rearrest rates and place of occurrence of rearrest, demographic characteristics of arrested street criminals, ratio of property to person crimes, ratio of first to repeat offenders arrested, and distance from the place of arrest to the arrestee's residence. While these indicators would not yield estimates of prevalence of victimization in the community, they would yield more reliable estimates of indirect measures of that concept than victimization surveys are ever likely to produce—and at far less cost.

The largely unheeded Fienberg et al. (1976) paper also solves the second sample-size problem. The bias toward finding no effect from an innovation is related to the small number of patrol beats (fifteen) used in the Kansas City study and to the even smaller numbers used in other studies. Because expensive victimization surveys would not be used, much larger numbers of communities or patrol beats can be included in experiments. The authors recommend a minimum of at least twenty-eight patrol beats for their sophisticated three-year, three-treatment design, in which crossovers make each beat act as its own control, and each "primary treatment" beat is cushioned from the others by a layer of secondary beats that surround each primary beat with a common treatment.

This design is not without its drawbacks. It would, for example, be almost impossible to use with citizen participation strategies, given the need to change strategies each year in each community—something to which few communities would be likely to agree. The three-year time frame is also troublesome, given the political instability surrounding both police and (some) research organizations. In a three-year experiment in citizen-police action in Minneapolis, for example, the action program director resigned in a dispute with the city council in the first year, and the evaluation project director was replaced in the third year. Maintaining experimental conditions and analyzing data with full contextual knowledge of the project are difficult with such turnover. Finally, the large number of communities in the proposed design would create substantial practical problems of experimental control, with ample opportunities for officers or others to sabotage the design by altering the designed treatment in an area.

Nonetheless, the Fienberg et al. design appears to be the only feasible way of removing the bias toward the null hypothesis in reliably estimating the effect of community policing strategies. There may be no better alternative design for testing for interaction between policing strategy and community characteristics, which requires even larger sample sizes. Whether any of these designs have much future in an era of research-funding austerity seems doubtful.

In the absence of research results from such designs, we can only accept the premise that knowledge derived from less rigorous sources still has validity for policy-making purposes (Lindblom and Cohen 1979). Both limited evaluations and practitioner intuition may thus be usable data (until proven otherwise by more systematic tests) for assessing which strategies are most promising in general and in specific kinds of communities.

Wilson (1983) has offered a useful distinction in theories of how these various approaches can reduce crime. He defines the community-service approach as any means of making officers more familiar with their neighborhoods in order to win the confidence and cooperation of local residents as well as better intelligence about criminal activities. The crime-attack approach, in contrast, while not logically incompatible with community service, places officers as close as possible to likely locations or perpetrators of crimes "in ways that will enable them to apprehend the criminal in the act, or at least cut short his crime almost as soon as it begins" (Wilson 1983, p. 68). One might add efforts to deter crime by visible surveillance of potential targets (e.g., bodyguards and off-duty police at late-night commercial establishments) as an additional element of the crime-attack approach. The evidence for both strategies is mixed, although the evidence against at least one of the crime-attack strategies ("tailing" suspects) is quite strong.

### *B. Community Service*

The 1967 Crime Commission report stimulated many police departments to undertake neighborhood team policing, one of the earliest versions of the community-service approach. These programs varied, but they generally fostered greater police knowledge of their communities through greater geographic focus and stability of patrol assignments, increased communication with the community, and increased communication among the officers working in the small beat area (Sherman et al. 1973). The beat teams were led generally by sergeants, who were given unusual flexibility to schedule their officers and assign them to various tasks. Like many organizational innovations, however, a variety of organizational constraints generally blocked this one from being implemented and ultimately discredited both the idea and its name.

One leading constraint was the unrelieved imperative to answer the calls for service on the beat. To the extent that the beat-team officers spent time in neighborhood meetings, playing basketball with marginally delinquent kids, staking out the welfare office, or doing other innovative, proactive things, the other officers in the precinct would have to come into their beat to answer the radio calls they could not handle. This created rivalry and tension across beats.

More important was the power balance between the team-leader sergeants and the middle managers above them (Sherman 1975). The demonstration projects often gave sergeants more power than lieutenants and captains, whose jealousy led them to countermand and sabotage the orders of the team leader. While the sergeant's unusual authority made programmatic sense, it made little sense from the standpoint of the larger bureaucratic turf concerns. Thus what could have been a substantive innovation never went beyond the problems of structural reorganization.

One consequence of all these implementation problems was that, even when the innovation was carefully evaluated, as in the Police Foundation experiment in Cincinnati (Schwartz and Clarren 1977), it was impossible to tell whether the theory of the program was successful in controlling crime. The program failure meant that the theory was not properly tested. Perhaps in the wake of DPR (McEwen et al. 1984) it will be possible to try again to use the beat-team approach to gathering information. Failing that, the idea could still be pursued at the level of the individual officer. For example, a demonstration project in San Diego showed the feasibility (but not the effects on crime) of having individual police officers, working in the normal chain of command, develop detailed profiles of the communities they policed (Boydstun and Sherry 1975).

Other community-service strategies have been evaluated in recent years. Foot patrol, which is feasible only in dense areas (and desirable for police only in good weather), has been evaluated in several experiments. All suffered from a small number of beats available for evaluation and the small numbers of crimes within each beat. Not surprisingly, then, a major experiment in Newark (Police Foundation 1981) found that foot patrol had no effect on crime as measured through victimization surveys. A Northeastern University project is now examining a much larger data set on changes in reported crime on beats in Boston over the course of several introductions and withdrawals of foot-patrol officers (Bowers 1985).

Perhaps more important was the Newark finding concerning fear of crime, which was lower in the beats receiving foot patrol. Wilson and Kelling (1982) explained this finding as a result of the proactive order-maintenance efforts of the foot-patrol officers. Given research findings that fear of crime is generated by such "signs of crime" as disorderly youths, panhandlers, garbage-strewn streets, and broken windows (Skogan and Maxfield 1981), it makes sense that foot patrol aimed at controlling pedestrian disorder could reduce the fear of crime. Fear reduction is legitimately an explicit goal for neighborhood policing, and the Newark experiment showed that it could be accomplished.

The recent experiments in police fear-reduction strategies conducted by the Police Foundation in Houston and Newark also included a community-service strategy (Wycoff et al. 1985*a*). In one of the Houston experiments, officers were trained to focus on one beat and to attempt to make as many contacts as possible with people who lived and worked on that beat. They ultimately visited one-third of all the households on the beat, introducing themselves and asking residents to tell them of any concerns or neighborhood problems they could identify. The outreach effort was combined with an increased presence of police cars in the beat, although surveys showed no difference in citizen awareness of police presence. The outcome was not only a substantial reduction in the fear of crime but also a statistically significant reduction in the percentage of households reporting that someone in the household had been victimized by crime—almost all of which was property crime (Wycoff et al. 1985*a*). The experiment was limited by a sample of two: the demonstration beat and an unchanged, matched-comparison beat. But it was also limited by the usual bias toward the null hypothesis, which is not what was found.

The Houston findings may conceivably result from some unique event such as the incarceration of an active neighborhood delinquent, or the neighborhood crime may simply have been displaced to other areas where police were not quite so active. But it is also possible that the community-service approach—when done with enthusiasm by officers enjoying a Hawthorne effect and in a racially mixed but predominantly white lower-middle-class neighborhood of single-family detached houses—might just work to reduce crime.

### *C. Crime Attack*

Somewhat less evidence is available about the effectiveness of proactive crime-attack strategies. That evidence suggests that some such strategies are clearly ineffective but that others can be used to increase arrests of serious criminals and perhaps to decrease crime. Perhaps even more than with the community-service strategies, success may depend on very subtle aspects of how an approach is implemented and how well it fits within a particular community.

1. *Decoys.* Wycoff, Susmilch, and Brown's (1981) evaluation of a Police Foundation–funded experiment in Birmingham, Alabama, demonstrated that crime-attack strategies cannot always be transported easily from one police department to another. The plan to test the crime-control effectiveness of an antirobbery unit using decoy methods ran into a number of snags, not the least of which was the police officers' relative disinterest in dealing with crime. For example, they decided to run their decoy operation during the "high robbery hours" of Monday through Friday, 8:00 A.M. to 4:00 P.M. They were also reluctant to engage in any dirty or dangerous methods of decoy operation. Thus an idea that had received much prominence in New York and elsewhere failed to work in Birmingham because it did not fit the local culture of policing.

The effectiveness of decoy operations—a classic crime-attack strategy—remains unclear. Some critics argue that decoys often attract people to commit crimes who otherwise might not have committed them. Given the high risk of danger to both police and citizens, a careful evaluation of this strategy merits high priority and should consider whether effects depend on the kind of neighborhood in which a decoy operation is attempted. For example, decoys in center-city vice areas may attract predisposed assailants, while decoys in residential areas may entice people to commit crimes who otherwise would not have.

2. *Covert Patrol.* Patrol in disguise is another common crime-attack strategy that remains unevaluated. This strategy obviously requires a community with a high-enough street-crime rate per square foot so that it is feasible for anyone to intercept crimes in progress. New York City,

or parts of it, clearly qualifies. The 5 percent (or less) of the patrol force assigned to this strategy in the early 1970s accounted for over 18 percent of all felony arrests, including over half the robbery arrests and 40 percent of the burglary and robbery arrests (Wilson 1983, p. 70). But the effect of these efforts on crime remains unclear.

3. *Field Interrogations.* The National Advisory Commission on Civil Disorders (1968) attacked field interrogations for breeding poor police-community relations. It is a crime-attack strategy in which many police have a good deal of confidence as a way to deter crime. The anecdotal evidence that this strategy can cause race riots is substantial. But such accounts are counterbalanced by the results of a careful evaluation of an experiment in the San Diego Police Department.

In a context in which police had a long history of active use of field interrogations, the experiment compared three patrol beats: in one, field interrogations were stopped altogether; in a second, they remained unchanged; and in a third, police were given special training in how to conduct the street stops in a sensitive and nonabrasive fashion. The evaluation found little difference in the crime rates between the special training and the normal areas. But it did find that, where field interrogations were withdrawn compared with the other areas, there was a statistically significant increase over a nine-month period in the average monthly number of reported total crimes, total Part I crimes, and burglaries. Moreover, there was no difference in the results of before-and-after surveys of community attitudes toward the police (Boydstun 1975). These results were obtained despite the bias in favor of the null hypothesis about crime rates and despite no bias about community attitudes (which, unlike crime, are not exactly rare and more easily lead to significant differences). The small sample size (three patrol areas) again means that some unique phenomenon may have affected the crime-rate differences. But barring that, the experiment suggests that field interrogations can deter certain kinds of crime without annoying the community—at least in a community that is already accustomed to having an intrusive, proactive police department.

Such departments can generally deter robberies more effectively than can their more reactive counterparts in other cities. In a cross-sectional analysis of cities with high and low traffic-enforcement rates, Wilson and Boland (1978) concluded that the high-traffic-enforcement departments produced lower robbery rates. They acknowledge the difficulties in interpreting such cross-sectional data but suggest the importance of further experimentation along those lines.

One of the Newark fear-reduction experiments (Pate et al. 1985*a*) addressed the question of what effect intensified field interrogations can have in the context of generally intensified proactive enforcement. The "signs of crime" strategy in one Newark patrol beat was designed in part to test the Wilson-Kelling (1982) argument about controlling crime through control of disorder. The program consisted of a twenty-four-officer, specially trained task force that performed a variety of tasks within the experimental area at least three times a week. The task force spent over 2,500 hours in the program area over the course of nine months. Seventy percent was devoted to foot patrol, 15 percent to radar speed checks, 7.5 percent to bus checks, 4 percent to enforcement of disorderly conduct laws, and 3 percent to conducting road checks. The disorderly conduct enforcement was particularly aggressive, consisting of an order to clear the sidewalk (if four or more people were congregating) and arresting anyone who failed to comply.

The results were mixed and hard to interpret. Before-and-after survey data were largely negative: area residents were less satisfied with the area and reported significantly higher levels of crime victimization than did residents of a matched comparison area. Yet the residents perceived the police as becoming less aggressive. The recorded crime data showed statistically significant reductions in total Part I crimes, burglary, and personal crimes, while no significant reductions were found in the comparison area. It is possible that both measures of crime may be correct since the survey measured the prevalence of crime (the percentage of households suffering one or more crimes during the experimental period) while the recorded crime data measured the incidence of crime (the total number of crimes recorded, including repeated victimizations of the same people or households). It is also possible that the recorded crime data were manipulated to produce an apparent program effect. But the findings are at least as strong as the San Diego experiment in showing that recorded crime is lower under conditions of aggressive field interrogation and proactive citizen street contacts.

4. *Repeat Offenders.* The increasing policy attention to repeat offenders has spilled over from prosecution and sentencing into police. The first evaluation of this strategy was done in Kansas City by Pate, Bowers, and Parks (1976), who found more of a program failure than a theory failure. The Kansas City police at that time insisted that all its tactical officers, including those assigned to covert surveillance of suspected active criminals, drive official (if unmarked) police cars and remain clean shaven and close cropped. Their identity was frequently recognized, and much of the surveillance was unproductive.

A similar unit, devoted to apprehending highly active offenders, was implemented in Washington, D.C., a decade later, with much greater sophistication. What they found, however, was that covert surveillance of individual suspects was an extremely inefficient and frustrating way for police to spend their time. The strategy produced more "serendipitous" arrests of nontargets committing crimes in the presence of the covert officers than it did of the intended targets (Martin and Sherman 1986). Other methods of the Repeat Offender Project (ROP) paid off, however, such as searching out the whereabouts of reportedly active offenders who were already wanted on warrants, using sting-type decoys, and responding to hot tips from informants about the immediate whereabouts of an active offender who had incriminating evidence on him.

The effects of these efforts on crime is unclear, but a randomized experiment (Martin and Sherman 1986) found, predictably, that the ROP unit was five times more likely to apprehend someone they targeted than was the rest of the department in the course of its normal operations (not knowing that such persons were designated as targets). Moreover, the average length of the criminal history of persons arrested by ROP officers increased substantially over those of the persons they had been arresting in other units prior to their assignment to ROP. The number of arrests per officer declined after their transfer to ROP, but that is a predictable result of working in four- to six-officer teams. Such a program, then, only makes sense to the extent that the longer records of those apprehended indicate a higher current rate of offending than the suspects who would have been arrested by the same officers producing a greater quantity of arrests in patrol.

Overall, ROP succeeded in focusing scarce police resources on persons for whom there was probable cause to believe were highly active criminals. At the same time, ROP suffered relatively little controversy or questions about the constitutionality of their methods. Since ROP is a citywide venture, however, it is not clear that it is the kind of program that can be varied in its administration across communities.

5. *Saturation Patrol.* What most communities dream of, of course, is having lots of police patrolling the neighborhood. Several tests of this idea all show the same result, although with varying degrees of rigor. The first was the "Operation 25" pretest/posttest design in New York City in 1954, in which the presence of foot-patrol officers in a Manhattan precinct was about tripled and street crime fell dramatically (Wilson 1983, p. 62). A later analysis of a similar change in personnel resources, with two comparison precincts, showed similar if less dramatic results

(Press 1971). The most rigorous test was an experiment in four high-crime residential areas of Nashville, Tennessee, which increased patrol presence by 400 percent and increased slow patrol movement (under twenty miles per hour) by 3,000 percent for ten days (Schnelle et al. 1977). Time-series analysis showed statistically reliable reductions in nighttime, but not daytime, Part I offenses. These levels of patrol presence may be too costly to implement on a widespread basis, but the tests do support police executives' views that saturation patrol can indeed reduce crime.

6. *Repeat Complaint Address Policing.* Many crime-attack strategies remain unevaluated. One possible approach, for example, is to focus police efforts on those addresses that account for the highest proportions of calls for police service. According to an analysis of Boston citizen call data (Pierce, Spaar, and Briggs 1984), as few as 10 percent of the addresses that police are ever dispatched to may account for up to 40 percent of all dispatches, for some types of calls. It follows that solving the underlying problems producing those repeat calls at those most active locations would theoretically reduce the total call load by up to 40 percent.

Such problems can be addressed through a strategy of repeat complaint address policing (RECAP) (Sherman 1985). The strategy would consist of four steps: (1) analysis, in which the police-dispatching computer would rank all addresses responded to by frequency of responses over a fixed period; (2) diagnosis, in which the most highly ranked addresses would be studied through written reports and site visits; (3) action, in which police officers would implement an action plan reviewed with their supervisors, encompassing anything from threatening to arrest a repeat wife beater to assisting a bank manager in having the alarm system rewired to reduce false burglary alarms; and (4) follow-up, in which the officers who implemented the action plan monitor the address regularly for the next several months to determine how well the plan is working and whether another plan is needed.

The RECAP strategy would require highly creative officers who can imagine how best to use their unique position as dispensers of coercive threats to cope with the problems underlying the repeat calls. It would also require a substantial reorganization of most police departments to allow some patrol officers to devote full time to such problem solving and remain free of the need to answer radio calls. But it would be easy to test the RECAP strategy on a limited scale prior to any broader implementation (Sherman 1985). Simply by dividing the most active addresses in half on a lottery basis, RECAP officers could work on one-half and leave the other half alone, thus creating a controlled experiment. Any differences between the groups over the follow-up period in the number of repeat calls or the seriousness of subsequent problems could then be attributed to the difference in police strategy.

Like several of the crime-attack strategies, RECAP is not especially neighborhood sensitive. The basic strategy could be pursued in almost any neighborhood. But the creative search for solving the unique problem generating each set of repeat calls could be done much better by officers familiar with the neighborhood context and resources.

## V. What Can Private Police Do?

Many, if not all, things the public police do could be done by private police. More important, private police perform many functions that public police and citizens would rarely perform because of the labor cost involved, such as controlling access to parking garages or to lobbies of apartment buildings. The contribution of private policing to community crime control is probably substantially underestimated.

1. *Routine Patrol.* The use of private guards for routine patrol in wealthier neighborhoods grew substantially in the 1970s. Residents who were dissatisfied with public police patrol banded together or worked through existing homeowners' associations to raise funding for private uniformed patrols in marked cars. In dense cities like New York, some blocks hired private foot-patrol officers. And in the growing realm of quasi-public spaces, such as shopping centers, all kinds of parking lots, and other private property open to the public, private police often conduct routine patrol at the expense of the property owner. Much of this patrol is performed indoors, which is generally defined by public police as beyond their scope of responsibility. While few guards are armed with guns, they usually wear enough other armament (like nightsticks) to communicate a threat that they will use force if necessary.

2. *Order Maintenance.* Whatever deterrent value these patrols may have, their order maintenance value is demonstrably substantial. Private police keep people from drinking from bottles, arguing loudly, running around recklessly, or playing loud music. Nonuniformed private employees such as bouncers and doormen also maintain order on the streets immediately off the premises where they are employed. And because their job is tied to a specific location, they perform such tasks far more thoroughly and intensively than public police usually do. If,

as Wilson and Kelling (1982) suggest, the failure to maintain order can lead to serious crime, the order-maintenance efforts of private police may help control crime as much or more than their deterrent value. At the very least, as the Newark foot-patrol experiment suggests (Police Foundation 1981), such private policing should help reduce public fear of crime.

3. *Saturation Patrol.* Many operators of quasi-public places have adopted saturation patrol techniques. The defendant hospital in a landmark California Supreme Court case on landlord liability for third-party crime (*Isaacs v. Huntington Memorial Hospital*, 695 P.2d 653 [Cal. 1985]) provides a good example. After a doctor was shot in 1978 in an apparent robbery attempt in a parking lot right across the street from the emergency room, the hospital increased its outside nighttime security patrols so that the lot would almost always be in view of a guard (during selected high-risk hours). The hospital also constructed a guard kiosk in a central location and added a surveillance camera to monitor the doctors' parking lot at all times. If the intensity of private policing has increased as much at many other locations where crimes occurred during the 1970s, it could be one factor in the slight decline of stranger crime in the 1980s.

4. *Access Control.* One function public police perform only for officials and for virtually no one else is controlling access to secured places. Private police control access to parking garages, apartment and office buildings, and entire residential developments. These services are more common in rich neighborhoods than in poor ones. Their role in reducing the crime risk of those they protect is nonetheless hard to dispute.

5. *Location Defense.* More ubiquitous are the private police who defend specific locations from armed robbery. These guards, usually armed, can be found in banks and late-night retail operations from supermarkets to fast-food stores. There is a substantial debate among practitioners about whether these guards attract more violence (from criminals looking for a challenge) than they deter (Johnson 1984). They may also displace crime from one kind of target to another—from commercial establishments to more vulnerable individuals. But their presence also adds to the order-maintenance aspects of local policing.

## VI. What Can Private Citizens Do?

One limitation of all the strategies discussed above is that none of them involve citizens in any major way. Some proponents of such involvement seem committed to the idea for ideological reasons, while others have theoretical justifications (Curtis 1985). One motivation for citizen involvement in policing, for example, may be an agenda for dismantling the public sector in favor of a philosophically preferable voluntarism in many spheres (Currie 1985). It is therefore no surprise that many police unions are suspicious of citizen-involvement programs.

As much as police might like to keep such programs under their control, community policing is increasingly done outside the auspices of the public vocational police. Foundation and even federal grants are often made directly to community groups, many of which operate without any funding to provide patrol and other forms of surveillance. Unfortunately, it is almost impossible to compare the relative effectiveness of police-directed and other programs since very little research has been done on the nonpolice programs.

### A. *Police Programs for Citizens*

Police programs for fostering citizen involvement consist generally of efforts to organize voluntary efforts to watch the neighborhood for anything suspicious and to call the police when appropriate. Such programs have been hard to sustain since one meeting with a police officer can cover the basic point of the program. What they usually lack is continuing neighborhood leadership to keep people watching the streets and a systematic plan for insuring that the neighborhood is watched at all vulnerable times—especially during business hours.

More recently, some police projects have taken a broader approach to organizing citizen and private efforts. They have also tested some strategies of communication, as distinct from organizing, to establish more of a direct link to individual citizens. Recent research sheds some insight on several of these efforts.

1. *Police Organizing.* From 1983 to 1985, the Minneapolis Police Department made a sustained effort to involve some twenty-five police officers in a community-organizing effort led by the city's independent community crime prevention agency. Their planned role was to serve as the "cop of the block" for several blocks each, combining the community-service model of stimulating grass-roots voluntarism. The block cop's responsibilities were to include daily visits to the block to stop and talk with residents, assistance to the block club in drawing up a plan for identifying and dealing with local quality-of-life problems (not necessarily criminal in nature), and communication to block residents about recent crime developments on and around their block.

The problem was that the plan called for the officers to perform these new tasks in addition to their regular duties of answering calls. The preliminary indications were that few police officers actually played the kind of role the program called for. No matter what the impact evaluation may show about the overall program (including the independent agency's efforts to organize citizen policing), it is unlikely that the cop-of-the-block element will contribute much to that impact. Moreover, the police resistance may have been related to citizen resistance that was more prevalent in lower-class, transient, single-occupant, and minority neighborhoods, the areas with highest crime that needed the program most.

A more successful organizing project was included in the Houston fear-reduction experiments. In one middle-class patrol beat, a specialist group of officers (who were not obliged to answer radio calls while working on this task) worked for nine months to create a community organization in a neighborhood where none had existed. They began by conducting a door-to-door survey of neighborhood residents (as distinct from the evaluation survey done by Police Foundation researchers) to ask them to identify neighborhood problems and potential interest in voluntary efforts. The survey was followed by thirteen neighborhood meetings attended by twenty to sixty people each, which in turn were followed by police asking twelve residents to meet each month with the precinct captain to identify community problems and solutions. The twelve-member task force was then encouraged to turn itself into a community organization, which took responsibility for carrying out such programs as "safe houses" for children, a drug information seminar, and identification of household goods with marked numbers.

The evaluation of the Houston Community Organizing Response Team program (Wycoff et al. 1985*c*) showed no effect on the prevalence of victimization (which was not its goal) or on the fear of crime (which was), but it did reduce perceptions (compared with a matched comparison area) of the level of social disorder and crime in the area. And like other fear-reduction experiments in Houston, the evaluation suggested that the program had relatively less beneficial effect on, and was less successful in reaching, blacks and Hispanics.

A related fear-reduction experiment in Newark (Pate et al. 1985*b*) examined the effect of police-organizing efforts in the context of a program of multiple strategies in one neighborhood. The program included a community police storefront center, a door-to-door police contact program, a neighborhood police newsletter, intensified law-enforcement and order-maintenance efforts, and neighborhood cleanups. Given the multiple treatments, it is impossible to draw any conclusions about the effect of any single element on the community problems of crime and fear. But this highly intensive effort, according to the results of before and after panel surveys, did produce these statistically significant findings in relation to the comparison area: a reduction in fear of crime and dissatisfaction with the quality of life in the area at the same time as an increase in the prevalence of households victimized by crime.

A similar problem of multiple simultaneous treatments limits our ability to draw conclusions about the effect of police organizing efforts in the Hartford Asylum Hill project in the early 1970s (Murray 1983). The program was an ambitious combination of redesigning the physical environment and of building neighborhood organizations with the involvement of a local neighborhood police team. The program was not focused on particular crime-prevention activities but rather on creating an environment for neighborhood self-control. After three years, the evaluation showed an increase in such control, including residents' ability to recognize strangers and willingness to take action in suspicious circumstances. But it also found that, despite a first-year decline in burglary and robbery, crime rose thereafter and returned to the levels predicted from citywide trends.

2. *Police Communicating.* The idea of informing the public about crimes has great appeal not only as news but also as practical information that people can use to protect themselves. It is consistent with the American commitment to an informed public. It is not consistent, however, with the modern information glut. Two of the fear-reduction experiments, one each in Houston and Newark, probably encountered this problem in attempting to use a police newsletter to address crime and fear problems. The newsletter in both cities was tested through a randomized experimental design with three comparison groups: households mailed no newsletter, a newsletter with only general area news about police and crime, and the same newsletter with an insert giving detailed information about all recently reported crimes in the beat area. The Newark and Houston newsletters differed only slightly in content, format, and frequency. Before-and-after personal interviews of household members in the three conditions showed relatively low levels of recall of having seen or read the newsletter although very high levels of appreciation for the police effort in producing the newsletter.

The evaluation (Pate et al. 1985*c*) showed no effect of either version of the newsletter (with or without crime information) on a wide range of fear- and crime-related behavior measures. It is possible that the experiment measured the wrong things and that, at least among those who read it, the information had some beneficial effects. But it is also possible that such a communication strategy needs to be reconceptualized in a more tightly theoretical fashion, such as tying crime information to crime analysis on which citizens can act. For example, such analysis might advise citizens to stay away from certain street corners or parts of streets during certain hours.

Encouraging communication to flow the other way (from citizens to police) is also an old idea, with a few modern twists. In Oakland, California, for example, the special central business district police project distributed thousands of report forms on which citizens could write up their description of a problem or an incident that made local quality of life suffer, for example, a drunken panhandler or a prostitute accosting them, witnessing an openly visible narcotics transaction, or teenagers running wild. Citizens were encouraged to give these completed report-it-directly forms to police or to security guards, who would pass them on to police. In theory, police would then analyze the information and use it to direct police attention to those problems, and that is how the program worked initially. But, like many of the programs reviewed here, it encountered difficulty in keeping going. For example, many of the reports given to security guards were not passed on to the police until long after they were received, which made it unlikely that the forms had much more value than as a catharsis for citizen anger. Fewer cards were turned in over time, although that may have been because foot-patrol officers obtained much of the same information through word of mouth (Reiss 1985, pp. 22–23).

A more common means of fostering two-way communication flow is the police storefront idea. Its starting point is that police precinct stations have become backstage areas for police use rather than an on-stage scene for relaxed and cordial citizen-police communication. The storefront provides a setting that is free of the symbolic overtones of coercion and administrative pressures. Depending on their location, staffing, and hours of operation, they may be more or less successful in gathering information; depending on how the mission of the storefront is conceived, they may be more or less successful in communicating crime-related information. Most of them appear to be largely reactive in this respect.

The Houston and Newark storefronts that were created for the fear-reduction experiments, however, took a proactive stance toward communication. It is again hard to assess the effect of the Newark storefront in the context of the multiple programs in that area. But the Houston storefront stood alone, reaching out to tell the community about the storefront's activities: monthly neighborhood meetings, a truancy program, fingerprinting of children for parents' records, a monthly blood-pressure screening test, a ride-along program, and a program for increasing use of and reducing vandalism at a local park. The evaluation (Wycoff et al. 1985*b*) found that the area served by the Houston storefront experienced significant reductions in fear of crime and in perceptions of the level of crime against persons. The evaluation did not detect any effect on the prevalence of household victimization.

3. *Citizens Acting Alone.* One of the first evaluations of a non-police-coordinated community policing program was done in Seattle (Cirel et al. 1977). The program consisted of governmentally funded project personnel helping residents do three things: mark their property through operation identification, improve the physical security of their homes by implementing the recommendations of a security inspection, and increase their surveillance of neighborhood activities. A before-and-after survey of this program over a one-year period suggested substantial reductions in burglary rates for citizens within experimental areas who cooperated with the program as compared with citizens who did not and marginally significant burglary reductions in the experimental areas compared with the comparison areas. While it is not clear whether such effects can be sustained over the long term, they are nonetheless impressive.

Such a program is not strictly citizens acting alone since they were assisted by tax-supported professionals. Nor is the Chicago program (recently evaluated by Rosenbaum, Lewis, and Grant [1985]), which was funded by the Ford Foundation to continue efforts initiated under federal grants and without police involvement. Yet the results of that evaluation are important and disturbing. The evaluation found that the program succeeded in implementing its strategy of organizing residents of selected neighborhoods through door-to-door canvassing, block meetings, and neighborhood meetings, all aimed at increasing citizen surveillance of the neighborhood. The experimental areas showed substantial awareness of these efforts, but the efforts did not work. Instead they may have backfired.

Using pretest/posttest interviews of over 3,000 respondents, the evaluation found that the large majority of comparisons revealed no significant differential change over time between the treated and the untreated areas. But in the three treatment areas with the strongest program implementation, there were statistically significant increases in such measured problems as fear of crime, perceptions of the severity of the crime problem, vicarious victimization, and concern about the future of the neighborhood. The authors conclude (p. iii) that "crime prevention meetings may have exacerbated preexisting concerns about neighborhood decline. In any event, the interventions were unable to retard these negative processes." The findings show (p. iv) "a pressing need to rethink our expectations for these popular programs," just as there is a need for rethinking community policing in general.

## VII. Fitting Policing to Communities

The best answer to the question of what works in policing different kinds of communities is that we do not know. Beyond the basic minimum of having tax-supported police, the optimal combination of public and private and vocational and avocational structures, of their information systems, and of their strategies is unclear. Yet, for all that we do not know, the research of the past fifteen years has put us light-years ahead of our knowledge for most of the past two centuries. Further research may contradict the current state of that knowledge, but at this point these tentative conclusions about community policing in general seem to be warranted:

1. The allocation of patrol cars for rapid response should be systematically varied by neighborhood according to the expected rate of calls truly requiring such a response.
2. A system of differential police response could satisfy most citizens and free enormous amounts of police time for alternative strategies of crime control.
3. Saturation patrol and field interrogations may be useful in suppressing street crimes and disorder, especially in dense high-crime areas.
4. Done properly, proactive strategies need not abuse minority rights or constitutional due process nor hinder community relations. But the difficulties of implementing such strategies are substantial, and great care is required to succeed at implementation.
5. Police efforts to involve citizens in policing may have positive effects on community quality of life, which may have long-term

benefits for crime control, but they have shown little evidence of short-term crime-control benefits.
6. In general, policing will probably be more effective to the extent that it relies on a mix of strategies appropriate to each neighborhood rather than relying on the single complaint strategy as the primary approach for all neighborhoods.

As for the question of what works best in different kinds of communities, the research suggests these meager policy considerations:

1. Police efforts to involve citizens in policing will be more successful in stable middle-class and lower-middle-class family neighborhoods than in transient, singles, apartment-building, or poverty-stricken neighborhoods.
2. In analyzing and planning community-level policing strategies, public police should consider the residence of police officers, the employment of private police, and the propensity of citizens to render voluntary policing services as factors enhancing the possibilities of strategies available.
3. Foot patrol is obviously more efficient in high-density, pedestrian communities than in low-density, automobile communities, but door-to-door policing visits in the latter type may produce the same effects as does foot patrol in the former.
4. Community police commanders should be given the authority to conduct informal experiments with different strategies to determine the optimal fit between the unique characteristics of the community and the mixture of policing strategies.

The last recommendation could be undertaken in a quasi-experimental, trial-and-error fashion. For example, Washington, D.C., police in Georgetown noticed in 1985 that teenagers were causing increased disorder problems on the streets and were drinking in their cars. They launched an order-maintenance crackdown of intense foot-patrol and parking enforcement, which was followed by an immediate, though not statistically significant, reduction in police-recorded crime (Sherman 1986). This kind of analysis is obviously limited for purposes of broad generalizations (Campbell and Ross 1968), but it is well suited for guiding specific policy decisions about specific communities.

The basic question underlying all these issues is whether the community is the most appropriate unit of analysis for policing structures and strategy. While nostalgia for small-town community life may lead our thinking in that direction, it is possible that policing may be equally or more effective when focused on other units of analysis or on other targets for proactive efforts. Offenders, addresses, problems, relationships, and social networks may be as important targets as are communities, especially with modern revolutions in life-style that make many residential neighborhoods largely empty for most of the business day. The optimum balance between focusing on communities and on other targets should be recognized as an empirical question. But, whatever the focus, police effectiveness will probably be enhanced by paying more attention to community context and how it interacts with police strategies.

## REFERENCES


Bird, David, and David Dunlap. 1986. "Day by Day: Volunteers Again." *New York Times* (February 22).

Bittner, Egon. 1970. *The Functions of the Police in Modern Society*. Chevy Chase, Md.: National Institute of Mental Health.

Black, Donald. 1973. "The Mobilization of Law." *Journal of Legal Studies* 2:125–49.

———. 1983. *The Manners and Customs of the Police*. New York: Academic Press.

Black, Donald, and Albert J. Reiss, Jr. 1967. "Patterns of Behavior in Police and Citizen Transactions." *Studies of Crime and Law Enforcement in Major Metropolitan Areas*, vol. 2, Field Surveys III, Sec. I. Washington, D.C.: President's Commission on Law Enforcement and Administration of Justice.

Blumberg, Mark. 1983. "The Use of Firearms by Police Officers." Ph.D. dissertation, State University of New York at Albany.

Bowers, William. 1985. Presentation to the Fifth Annual Crime Control Theory Conference, National Institute of Justice, University of Maryland, Donaldson Brown Conference Center.

Boydstun, John E. 1975. *San Diego Field Interrogation: Final Report*. Washington, D.C.: Police Foundation.

Boydstun, John E., and Michael Sherry. 1975. *San Diego Community Profile: Final Report*. Washington, D.C.: Police Foundation.

Bureau of Justice Statistics. 1986. *Police Employment and Expenditure Trends*. Washington, D.C.: U.S. Department of Justice.

Campbell, Donald T., and H. Laurence Ross. 1968. "The Connecticut Crackdown on Speeding: Time-Series Data in Quasi-experimental Analysis." *Law and Society Review* 3:33–53.

Chaiken, Jan. 1975. *Patrol Allocation Methodology for Police Departments*. Santa Monica, Calif.: Rand.

Cirel, Paul, Patricia Evans, Daniel McGillis, and Debra Whitcomb. 1977. *An Exemplary Project: Community Crime Prevention Program, Seattle, Washington.* Washington, D.C.: U.S. Government Printing Office.

"Court of Appeals Tells City to Pay $2 Million to Girl Father Stabbed." 1985. *New York Times* (July 10).

Croft, Elizabeth. 1985. "Police Use of Force: An Empirical Analysis." Ph.D. dissertation, State University of New York at Albany.

Cunningham, William C., and Todd H. Taylor. 1984. *The Growing Role of Private Security.* Washington, D.C.: U.S. Government Printing Office.

———. 1985. *Private Security and Police in America.* Portland, Oreg.: Chancellor.

Currie, Elliott. 1985. "Crimes of Violence and Public Policy: Changing Directions." In *American Violence and Public Policy*, edited by Lynn A. Curtis. New Haven, Conn.: Yale University Press.

Curtis, Lynn A. 1985. "Neighborhood, Family and Employment: Toward a New Public Policy against Violence." In *American Violence and Public Policy*, edited by Lynn A. Curtis. New Haven, Conn.: Yale University Press.

Eck, John. 1986. "The Role and Management of Criminal Investigation in Neighborhood Policing." Paper presented at the Canadian Police College Conference on Community Policing in the 1980s, Ottawa, March 18.

Farrington, David P. 1982. "Randomized Experiments on Crime and Justice." In *Crime and Justice: An Annual Review of Research*, vol. 4, edited by Michael Tonry and Norval Morris. Chicago: University of Chicago Press.

Federal Bureau of Investigation. 1985. *Crime in the United States–1984.* Washington, D.C.: U.S. Government Printing Office.

Fienberg, Stephen, Kinley Larntz, and Albert J. Reiss, Jr. 1976. "Redesigning the Kansas City Preventive Patrol Experiment." *Evaluation* 3:124–31.

Fogelson, Robert. 1977. *Big City Police.* Cambridge, Mass.: Harvard University Press.

Friedrich, Robert J. 1977. "The Impact of Organizational, Individual, and Situational Factors on Police Behavior." Ph.D. dissertation, University of Michigan.

Fyfe, James. 1978. "Shots Fired: An Examination of New York City Police Firearms Discharges." Ph.D. dissertation, State University of New York at Albany.

———. 1980. "Always Prepared: Police Off-Duty Guns." *Annals of the American Academy of Political and Social Sciences* 452:72–81.

Gage, Theodore. 1982. "Cops, Inc." *Reason* (November) pp. 23–28.

Gardiner, John A. 1969. *Traffic and the Police.* Cambridge, Mass.: Harvard University Press.

Goldstein, Herman. 1977. *Policing a Free Society.* Cambridge, Mass.: Ballinger.

Johnson, Elaine. 1984. "Fast Food Chains Act to Hold Down Crime and Prevent Lawsuits." *Wall Street Journal* (November 8).

Kansas City Police Department. 1977. "Response Time Analysis." Unpublished manuscript, Kansas City, Mo., Police Department.

Kelling, George, Antony M. Pate, Duane Dieckman, and Charles Brown.

1974*a*. *The Kansas City Preventive Patrol Experiment: Summary Report*. Washington, D.C.: Police Foundation.

———. 1974*b*. *The Kansas City Preventive Patrol Experiment: Technical Report*. Washington, D.C.: Police Foundation.

Kleck, Gary. 1979. "Guns, Homicide, and Gun Control: Some Assumptions and Some Evidence." Paper presented at the annual meeting of the Midwest Sociological Society, Minneapolis.

Klockars, Carl. 1985. *The Idea of Police*. Beverly Hills, Calif.: Sage.

Lane, Roger. 1980. "Urban Police and Crime in Nineteenth-Century America." In *Crime and Justice: An Annual Review of Research*, vol. 2, edited by Norval Morris and Michael Tonry. Chicago: University of Chicago Press.

Larson, Richard C. 1972. *Urban Police Patrol Analysis*. Cambridge, Mass.: MIT Press.

———. 1975. "What Happened to Patrol Operations in Kansas City?" *Evaluation* 3:117–23.

Lavrakas, Paul J. 1985. "Citizen Self-Help and Neighborhood Crime Prevention Policy." In *American Violence and Public Policy*, edited by Lynn A. Curtis. New Haven, Conn.: Yale University Press.

Levett, Alan. 1975. "Centralization of City Police in the Nineteenth Century United States." Ph.D. dissertation, University of Michigan.

Levine, Margaret J., and J. Thomas McEwen. 1985. *Patrol Deployment*. Washington, D.C.: U.S. Government Printing Office.

Lindblom, Charles E., and David K. Cohen. 1979. *Usable Knowledge: Social Science and Social Problem Solving*. New Haven, Conn.: Yale University Press.

McEwen, J. Thomas, Edward F. Connors III, and Marcia I. Cohen. 1984. *Evaluation of the Differential Police Response Field Test: Executive Summary*. Alexandria, Va.: Research Management Associates.

McNamara, Joseph. 1974. "Foreword." In Kelling, Pate, Dieckman, and Brown (1974*a*).

Margarita, Mona. 1980. "Criminal Violence against Police." Ph.D. dissertation, State University of New York at Albany.

Martin, Susan E., and Lawrence W. Sherman. 1986. "Selective Apprehension: A Police Strategy for Repeat Offenders." *Criminology* (in press).

Marx, Gary T., and Dane Archer. 1971. "Citizen Involvement in the Law Enforcement Process: The Case of Community Police Patrols." *American Behavioral Scientist* 15:52–72.

Matulia, Kenneth. 1982. *A Balance of Forces*. Gaithersburg, Md.: International Association of Chiefs of Police.

Milton, Catherine H., Jeanne W. Halleck, James Lardner, and Gary L. Abrecht. 1977. *Police Use of Deadly Force*. Washington, D.C.: Police Foundation.

Murphy, Patrick V., and Thomas Plate. 1977. *Commissioner: A View from the Top of American Law Enforcement*. New York: Simon & Schuster.

Murray, Charles A. 1983. "The Physical Environment and Community Control of Crime." In *Crime and Public Policy*, edited by James Q. Wilson. San Francisco: Institute for Contemporary Studies Press.

National Advisory Commission on Civil Disorders. 1968. *Report*. New York: Bantam.

"Officers Must Pay $2.3 Million to Wife Maimed by Husband." *New York Times* (June 26).

Pate, Antony M., Robert A. Bowers, and Ron A. Parks. 1976. *Three Approaches to Criminal Apprehension in Kansas City: An Evaluation Report*. Washington, D.C.: Police Foundation.

Pate, Antony M., Wesley Skogan, Mary Ann Wycoff, and Lawrence W. Sherman. 1985*a*. *Reducing the Signs of Crime: Executive Summary*. Washington, D.C.: Police Foundation.

———. 1985*b*. *Coordinated Community Policing: Executive Summary*. Washington, D.C.: Police Foundation.

———. 1985*c*. *Neighborhood Police Newsletters: Executive Summary*. Washington, D.C.: Police Foundation.

Pierce, Glen L., Susan A. Spaar, and LeBaron R. Briggs IV. 1984. "The Character of Police Work: Implications for the Delivery of Services." Mimeographed. Boston: Northeastern University, Center for Applied Social Research.

Police Foundation. 1981. *The Newark Foot Patrol Experiment*. Washington, D.C.: Police Foundation.

President's Commission on Law Enforcement and Administration of Justice. 1967. *Task Force Report: The Police*. Washington, D.C.: U.S. Government Printing Office.

Press, S. J. 1971. *Some Effects of an Increase in Police Manpower in the 20th Precinct of New York*. New York: Rand.

Radzinowicz, Leon. 1956. *A History of English Criminal Law and Its Administration from 1750*, vol. 2. London: Stevens.

Reiss, Albert J., Jr. 1971. *The Police and the Public*. New Haven, Conn.: Yale University Press.

———. 1985. *Policing a City's Central District: The Oakland Story*. Washington, D.C.: U.S. Government Printing Office.

Reiss, Albert J., Jr., and David Bordua. 1967. "Environment and Organization: A Perspective on the Police." In *The Police: Six Sociological Essays*, edited by David Bordua. New York: Wiley.

Robin, Gerald D. 1963. "Justifiable Homicide by Police." *Journal of Criminal Law, Criminology, and Police Science* 54:225–31.

Rosenbaum, Dennis P., Dan A. Lewis, and James A. Grant. 1985. "The Impact of Community Crime Prevention Programs in Chicago: Can Neighborhood Organizations Make a Difference?" Mimeographed. Evanston, Ill.: Northwestern University, Center for Urban Affairs.

Rosenbaum, Dennis P., Arthur J. Lurigio, and Paul J. Lavrakas. 1985. *Crime Stoppers: A National Evaluation of Program Operations and Effects*. Draft final report. Washington, D.C.: U.S. Government Printing Office.

Rubinstein, Jonathan. 1973. *City Police*. New York: Farrar, Straus & Giroux.

Ruth, Henry S. 1971. *Criminal Justice Plan*. New York: City of New York.

Schnelle, John F., Robert E. Kirchner, Jr., Joe D. Casey, Paul H. Uselton, Jr., and M. Patrick Mcnees. 1977. "Patrol Evaluation Research: A Multiple-Baseline Analysis of Saturation Police Patrolling during Day and Night Hours." *Journal of Applied Behavior Analysis* 10:33–40.

Schwartz, Alfred I., and Sumner N. Clarren. 1977. *The Cincinnati Team Policing Experiment: Summary Report*. Washington, D.C.: Police Foundation.

Sherman, Lawrence W. 1975. "Middle Management and Police Democratization: A Reply to John E. Angell." *Criminology* 12:363–77.

———. 1983. "Patrol Strategies for Police." In *Crime and Public Policy*, edited by James Q. Wilson. San Francisco: Institute for Contemporary Studies Press.

———. 1985. "Repeat Complaint Analysis Policing (RECAP)." Proposal submitted to the National Institute of Justice. Washington, D.C.: Crime Control Institute.

———. 1986. "Uncertain Punishment: Crackdown and Backoff in Crime Control." Report submitted to the National Institute of Justice by the Center for Crime Control, University of Maryland Research Foundation.

Sherman, Lawrence, and Ellen G. Cohn. 1986*a*. "Citizens Killed by Big-City Police, 1970–84." *Crime Control Reports*, no. 2. Washington, D.C.: Crime Control Institute.

———. 1986*b*. "Police Policy on Domestic Violence: A National Survey." *Crime Control Reports*, no. 1. Washington, D.C.: Crime Control Institute.

Sherman, Lawrence, and Jody Klein. 1984. "Major Lawsuits over Crime and Security: Trends and Patterns, 1958–82." Mimeographed. College Park: University of Maryland, Institute of Criminal Justice and Criminology.

Sherman, Lawrence W., Catherine H. Milton, and Thomas Kelly. 1973. *Team Policing: Seven Case Studies*. Washington, D.C.: Police Foundation.

Skogan, Wesley, and Maxfield, Michael. 1981. *Coping with Crime*. Beverly Hills, Calif.: Sage.

Smith, Betty. 1943. *A Tree Grows in Brooklyn*. New York: Harper.

Smith, Douglas. 1984. "The Organizational Context of Legal Control." *Criminology* 22:19–38.

———. In this volume. "The Neighborhood Context of Police Behavior."

Spelman, William, and Dale K. Brown. 1981. *Calling the Police: Citizen Reporting of Serious Crime*. Washington, D.C.: Police Executive Research Forum.

Swanson, Cheryl. 1978. "The Influence of Organization and Environment on Arrest Policies in Major U.S. Cities." *Policy Studies Journal* 7:390–98.

Tolchin, Martin, 1985*a*. "Private Guards Get New Role in Public Law Enforcement." *New York Times* (November 29).

———. 1985*b*. "Off-Duty Officers Doubling as Private Guards, but System Draws Criticism." *New York Times* (December 1).

Walker, Samuel. 1977. *A Critical History of Police Reform*. Lexington, Mass.: Heath.

Westley, William. 1970. *Violence and the Police*. Cambridge, Mass.: MIT Press.

Wilson, James Q. 1968. *Varieties of Police Behavior*. Cambridge, Mass.: Harvard University Press.

———. 1983. *Thinking about Crime.* New York: Basic.

Wilson, James Q., and Barbara Boland. 1978. "The Effect of the Police on Crime." *Law and Society Review* 12:367–90.

Wilson, James Q., and George L. Kelling. 1982. "Broken Windows: The Police and Neighborhood Safety." *Atlantic* (March), pp. 29–38.

Wilson, Orlando W. 1963. *Police Administration.* New York: McGraw-Hill.

Wright, James D., Peter H. Rossi, and Kathleen Daly. 1983. *Under the Gun: Weapons, Crime and Violence in American Life.* New York: Aldine.

Wycoff, Mary Ann, Wesley Skogan, Antony Pate, and Lawrence W. Sherman. 1985*a*. *Citizen Contact Patrol: Executive Summary.* Washington, D.C.: Police Foundation.

———. 1985*b*. *Police Community Stations: Executive Summary.* Washington, D.C.: Police Foundation.

———. 1985*c*. *Police as Community Organizers: Executive Summary.* Washington, D.C.: Police Foundation.

Wycoff, Mary Ann, Charles Susmilch, and Charles Brown. 1981. *The Birmingham Anti-Robbery Experiment.* Draft report. Washington, D.C.: Police Foundation.

*Ralph B. Taylor and Stephen Gottfredson*

# Environmental Design, Crime, and Prevention: An Examination of Community Dynamics

ABSTRACT

Property offenders construct cognitive images of the physical environment to decide where to commit crimes. At least three levels of target selection occur—neighborhoods, or regions; street blocks; and specific sites. Information on the physical characteristics of neighborhoods, such as ease of entry and exit, the number of internal boundaries limiting ease of circulation, and signs of guardianship or of incivilities, are weighed by the offender to determine risks, opportunities, and conveniences. This framework for understanding links between offenders and the physical environment provides a typology for evaluating research on environmental design and crime prevention, especially research on defensible-space theory, territorial perspectives, and the incivilities thesis. The incivilities thesis suggests that offenders take into account social and physical incivilities when deciding which neighborhood to choose as crime targets. Three recent studies involving neighborhoods in Atlanta, Georgia, Baltimore, Maryland, and Hartford, Connecticut, show that the effects of environmental design on crime range from small to moderate. Available research suggests that crime prevention efforts should be directed at the street-block rather than at the neighborhood level of analysis.

Ralph B. Taylor is Professor, Department of Criminal Justice, Temple University, Philadelphia, Pennsylvania. Stephen D. Gottfredson is Executive Director of the Maryland Criminal Justice Coordinating Council, Baltimore, Maryland. The authors are indebted to Ronald V. G. Clarke and an anonymous reviewer for helpful comments on an earlier draft of this essay.


0-226-80802-5/86/0008-0011$01.00.

During the last quarter of a century, stimulated by the publication in 1961 of Jane Jacobs's classic book, *The Death and Life of Great American Cities*, a sizable body of research has accumulated on links between crime, crime prevention, and the built environment. Crime prevention hypotheses have been developed at neighborhood, community, street, and site levels, and some of these have been tested. This essay summarizes the resulting literature and sets out a conceptual framework for understanding links between crime and the physical environment. Section I of this essay presents a conceptual framework for specifying how the physical environment is relevant to offender decisions and behaviors and for classifying work on design and crime at neighborhood and subneighborhood levels. Section II considers work carried out at the subneighborhood, or street-block, level, using defensible-space, or, more recently, territorial approaches. Sections III and IV discuss recent investigations of crime and physical environment at the neighborhood level. These studies indicate that physical environment does not have "stand alone" crime prevention effectiveness but rather can play a role in preventing or displacing crime, that theories appropriate to neighborhood-level dynamics have not yet been adequately developed, and that the specific ways that environmental alterations can prevent crime have yet to be disentangled. Section IV shows how the conceptual framework set out in the first section can be used as a guide for elaborating and linking crime-environment theories currently in use.

## I. Potential Offenders, Physical Environment, and Selection: A Framework

This section proposes a framework that links offenders, target regions, and target sites. Factors connecting potential offenders, site, and victim, or target, are mapped out. Assumptions and theoretical origins are clarified, and key concepts are introduced.

People who consider committing crimes take a variety of factors into account in deciding whether to commit an offense, where and when to commit it, and against whom or what. Figure 1 sets out a model of how prospective offenders might process information in deciding whether neighborhoods and communities offer attractive crime targets.

The proposed framework makes a number of assumptions.[1] First,

[1] The framework has three primary conceptual roots: the concept of *environmental images* from environmental cognition (Lynch 1960; Downs and Stea 1977; Kaplan and Kaplan 1982); the concept of *project* from environmental geography; and the concept of *template* from environmental criminology (Brantingham and Brantingham 1981). "From a

offenders are rational (Clarke and Cornish 1985), but their rationality is limited and tempered by preferences, habits, social influence, and experience (Rengert and Wasilchick 1985; Weaver and Carroll 1985). Second, as perceived by the offender, physical and social elements in a target region or at a target site are intertwined. Third, target selection is a multilevel, sequential process. Particular areas are identified as affording an abundance of targets, and particular blocks or houses within those areas are then selected as targets. Fourth, in selecting targets and timing, offenders are influenced by the "norms" and preferences of other offenders with whom they interact. Some are more influenced than others. Fifth, target areas and particular target sites are perceived as a whole. Particular elements seldom stand out but rather are assessed in combination with other available cues and filtered through expectations and experience.

The framework developed concentrates largely on residential environments and does not address crime in commercial areas. Nor does it touch on fear of crime (see Skogan, in this volume; Taylor and Hale 1986). It is concerned mainly with offense rates, not with offender rates, and it applies most clearly in cases of planned, or premeditated, offenses.

The conceptual goals are to illuminate factors in target-region selection, to indicate links between sequential selections at progressively lower levels (Brantingham, Dyreson, and Brantingham 1976), and to clarify the role of physical environment factors relative to other factors, allowing a realistic view of the relative effect of physical environment features on crime prevention. The occurrence of a crime represents a unique conjunction of potential offender, potential victim or target site, and surrounding circumstances conducive to the commission of the crime.

Three levels of target selection are discussed below, namely, neighborhoods, street blocks, and sites. For offenders coming into a neighborhood or community from "outside," these represent successive levels of selection.

### A. *Region Selection*

The first level at which physical environment comes into play is the selection of a neighborhood or community where an offense may be

time-geographic perspective, a project consists of the entire series of tasks necessary to the completion of any goal-oriented behavior" (Pred 1981, p. 236). A template represents a goal-oriented schema that is internalized by the offender and based on past experience, against which the viability of locations as potential crime sites can be assessed.

carried out. Offenders who reside outside of the community or neighborhood where they will carry out an offense select one particular locale over another. What determines why one region is chosen, and what roles does the physical environment play in this choice?

We postulate that the selection turns on neighborhood image. That is, over time, potential offenders build up cognitive images of particular neighborhoods or communities. These images are compared to determine the most potentially fruitful target area, and selections are made accordingly.

Five classes of factors are likely to influence the content and clarity of the neighborhood image held by a particular offender, namely, physical environment features, resident sociodemographic characteristics and behavior patterns, policing patterns, offenders' collective social knowledge of locale, and the knowledge and disposition of the individual offender (see fig. 1). Space limits preclude discussion of each class of factors. In keeping with the central focus of this essay, we elaborate below the roles played by physical environment features in shaping neighborhood images held by offenders.

The neighborhood image may include specific landmarks, paths and edges (Lynch 1960; Kaplan and Kaplan 1982), and specific qualities of the locale relevant to the potential offender's intentions. It is not, however, static. It may shift, depending on long-term changes such as neighborhood decline or revitalization, the time of day, seasonal factors, or external changes (e.g., increased levels of police patrolling). The images are both relative and absolute, indicating both qualities of the locale per se and qualities of the locale compared with other potential target areas. Although neighborhood images are interpreted variously by different individuals, they are social constructions (Berger and Luckmann 1963; Triandis 1977).

Physical environment and land-use features influence the ease of entry and movement in the target neighborhood. Objective characteristics of the resident population such as social status determine the relative attractiveness of targets. Stability of the population influences the likelihood that residents will exercise guardianship (Cohen and Felson 1979) and surveillance. The race of the resident population also influences the effectiveness of surveillance. The potential offender may be similar or dissimilar to the resident population and will be more or less likely to stand out. Policing patterns influence potential risks of detection and apprehension.

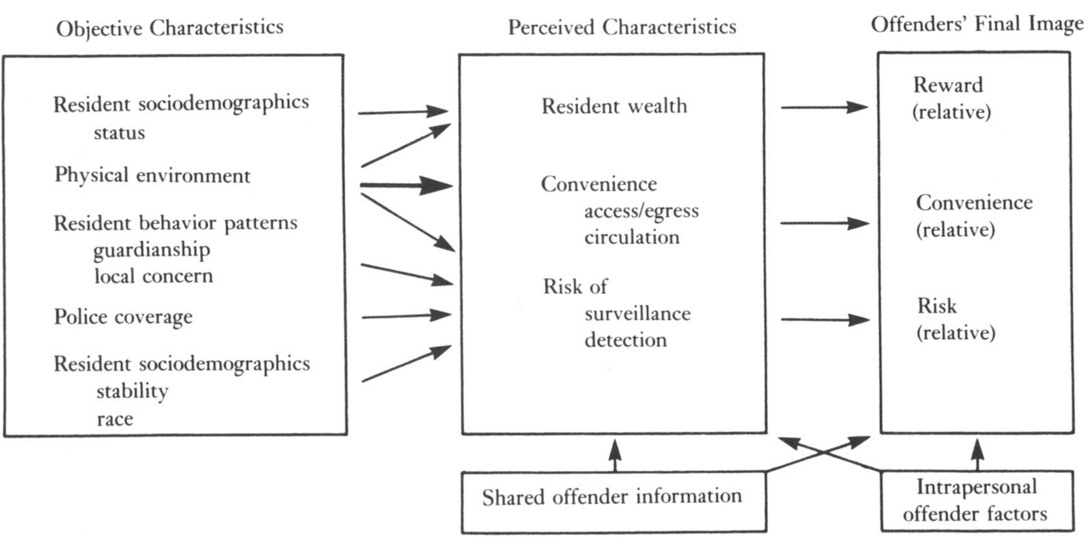


FIG. 1.—Development of offenders' neighborhood level images

The physical characteristics of the locale can influence neighborhood images in three ways: by shaping offenders' perceptions of the characteristics of residents (e.g., unkempt properties suggest that residents do not look out for one another, or affluent settings suggest high target attractiveness); by influencing the characteristics of the resident population (e.g., higher-quality housing stock is accessible only to up-scale households); and by setting the salient features of the crime activity space. This third class of physical environment effects is more important than the other two and is elaborated below.

Several physical features make neighborhoods more or less easy to enter and determine the permeability of the neighborhood boundary. A neighborhood is more permeable if it has more streets leading into it, if it directly adjoins a main artery (e.g., four-lane vs. two-lane roads), or if it is close to an exit off a major highway. Permeability is important to potential offenders for several reasons. It decreases entry and exit time, thereby reducing chances of detection and possible apprehension. Multiple available exits lessen chances of apprehension even if one is detected.

Ease of internal circulation is determined by patterns of traffic circulation and street design. It will be higher if streets are two-way rather than one-way and if there are fewer cul-de-sacs or "T" intersections. Neighborhoods where internal circulation is easier provide a lower risk because time for entering and leaving the particular site within the neighborhood is shortened. Thus chances of detection are lowered, and, even if detected, multiple, easily available routes to the neighborhood perimeter make chances of apprehension lower.

The relation between the neighborhood and adjoining or internal land uses is captured with the concept of enclavization, or insularity. Enclavization decreases as land-use factors result in higher levels of outsider pedestrian traffic in the neighborhood itself. Physical factors within, around, and outside the neighborhood influence the volume of outsider pedestrians in the neighborhood. For example, if the neighborhood is adjacent to a commercial center, pedestrian traffic that is drawn to the center will move through the neighborhood. The larger the center, or the closer it is to the neighborhood, the more outsider through traffic there will be. Commercial and institutional locations inside the neighborhood and at its boundaries are important to the extent that they draw outsider pedestrians into the neighborhood and reduce enclavization. Pedestrian through traffic will be lower if the adjoining locations are residential rather than commercial or institutional and lower still if adjoining land uses are industrial (e.g., factories, warehouses, railroads, and tank farms), presenting a "barrier" to through-pedestrian circulation.

The degree of pedestrian insularity is important to the potential offender for several reasons. If the potential target area is an enclave and through-pedestrian traffic is low, the potential offender as an outsider is more easily identified. Also a neighborhood that is low on insularity is likely to be within or near the activity space (Brantingham and Brantingham 1981) of a larger number of potential offenders, making it more likely to be chosen as a crime activity site.

Physical incivilities encompass another set of physical features relevant to offenders' perceptions of neighborhoods. They indirectly influence perceptions of risk by influencing offenders' perceptions of residents' attitudes and behaviors. Physical incivilities are signs of community breakdown and lack of caring, such as vacant houses and lots, littered playgrounds, abandoned cars, and graffiti. Wilson and Kelling (1982) suggested that offenders from adjoining areas will move into a neighborhood if they see physical cues suggesting residents' lack of caring for their environment, co-residents, and street activities. Physical incivilities act as such cues. Hunter (1978) has also suggested that such cues also elevate residents' fear levels. To date, links between actually assessed incivilities and crime remain, with one exception, unexamined.[2]

An important issue yet to be addressed concerns the relative effect of physical environment features compared with other objective characteristics in shaping offenders' neighborhood images. If physical features play only a minor role, physical changes will not substantially reduce the attractiveness of the target area. But, if the physical features play a larger role, physical changes can effectively reduce a neighborhood's relative attractiveness.

*Other Issues.* Groups of offenders who are engaged in similar types of crime and who live close to one another or who converse frequently build up partially shared images regarding the attractiveness of various neighborhoods as crime sites. These images are ranked in a relative ordering. Given the relative nature of this ranking, the subjective distance between neighborhoods in the preference hierarchy determines the displacement of crime across neighborhoods. The amount and di-

[2] The incivilities perspective touches on issues beyond the scope of this essay. For a fuller discussion, see Green and Taylor (1986).

rection of displacement can be predicted by knowing the perceived similarity between different neighborhood images. Changes occurring in the neighborhood, after a lag, are reflected in offenders' images. Longer-term changes are reflected more accurately than are shorter-term ones.

*Salient Dimensions in the Target Region Image.* Information about the neighborhood is used by potential offenders to estimate the potential reward, the potential return for the contemplated crime; convenience, the amount of difficulty getting to and circulating about the neighborhood; and potential risks, the potential hazards of being detected, obstructed, or apprehended while carrying out the crime or soon thereafter.[3]

*B. Street-Block Selection*

The selection of blocks as crime sites is similar to the selection of neighborhoods as crime sites. As with the neighborhood image, a range of factors determines block images. The characteristics of residents, as indicated by features such as housing quality, suggest the relative amount of available opportunities on a block. Routine activity patterns of residents and the degree of observable social cohesion among neighbors give rise to particular levels of offender-perceived guardianship.

Physical factors are relevant to block-level target selection in several ways. Features may shape offenders' perceptions of guardianship. Street blocks with clear demarcations between public and private areas by means of real or symbolic barriers, or those with clear signs of resident investment and involvement such as extensive signs of beautification and physical upkeep, would underscore the message obtained from observing behavior patterns on the block that block residents care and are vigilant.

Physical factors shape ease of access. Blocks farther from major roads or on one-way streets are less easily entered and exited. Physical factors make the potential offender more or less likely to stand out. A corner store on the block or nearby that draws a substantial amount of pedestrian foot traffic makes the potential offender less conspicuous as he circulates the block.

Physical factors also determine the extent to which the potential offender is subject to surveillance. Blind alleys or gaps between houses,

[3] This is not to deny that particular potential offenders also use idiosyncratic dimensions. This is probably also the case. Rather, major dimensions of the target-region image are commonly used or "shared" among different offenders or groups of offenders.

extensive shrubbery, wider streets, a lack of good street lighting, and a lack of clear lines of sight from the houses to the streets and sidewalks make it less likely that a crime in progress would be detected or that an offender-in-waiting would be spotted.

Socially generated information obtained from other offenders or potential offenders may play a role in shaping target-block images. Idiosyncratic or personal factors (personal preferences, levels of familiarity, and experience with similar types of blocks) probably also play a role in shaping target-block images. Again, as with neighborhood images, images of blocks within a neighborhood are categorized relative to one another.

There is little solid empirical evidence that potential offenders select and "work" particular blocks. Nonetheless, burglars and police personnel do report burglars who "work up and down a block" as long as it remains profitable (George Rengert, personal communication, 1985). In addition it appears that property offenders do perceive some blocks as more viable than others (see Bennett and Wright 1984, table A6). Whether perpetrators of street crimes proceed similarly is not clear.

### C. *Site Selection*

After a property offender selects a neighborhood and a block, the next choice is the target site. We know much about site selection from various studies with burglars (Letkemann 1973; David 1974; Bennett and Wright 1984; Rengert and Wasilchick 1985). Given the community and ecological focus of this essay, research on selection of particular sites is not examined here.

### D. *The Framework and the "Reasoning" Offender*

The multilevel selection framework presented here extends earlier work on the "reasoning" offender (Clarke and Cornish 1985; Carroll and Weaver 1986) that indicates that offenders are sensitive to the relative risks and rewards present in various criminal opportunities. The present framework, like this earlier work, assumes that limited rationality is operating and that individual differences, preferences, and idiosyncratic factors influence offenders' decision processes.

Our framework goes beyond earlier work by injecting an explicitly spatial dimension, viewing site selection as a series of spatially nested choices; by interposing cognitive maps or images between the potential offenders and target regions, blocks, and sites; by highlighting the multilevel nature of the target selection process; and by predicting the direction of displacement of offenses based on relative perceived attributes of different neighborhood and block images. The framework provides an organizing schematic that can be used to classify prior research, to indicate the types of preventive capabilities of different physical features at neighborhood and at subneighborhood levels, and to clarify how physical environment effects operate within the context of other, nonphysical features. This perspective emphasizes how physical features mesh with other characteristics of locale to provide overall impressions of risk, convenience, and opportunity for various potential offenders.

As analysis shifts from the neighborhood to the block to the site, two important practical consequences ensue. It becomes more likely that crime prevention efforts will result in immediate displacement because of the closer proximity of alternative sites, and costs involved in making physical environment changes decrease dramatically.

Two important changes in the cognitive images themselves occur. Individual differences between offenders play a larger role in the images formed at the lower levels of analysis, and images become less stable over time. Site-level images of the opportunities, risk, and convenience are subject to more short-term temporal variation than are block or neighborhood images.

### E. *Using the Framework to Generate a Preventive Typology*

Figure 2 shows a typology of crime prevention efforts that derives from the analytical framework described in this essay. The premise of the figure is that crime prevention efforts should take account of interaction between the level of analysis and prospective offenders' perceptions of areas. The "level of analysis" refers to sites, street blocks, and neighborhoods.

| | Dimension of Offenders' Image Influenced | | |
|---|---|---|---|
| Level of Analysis | Opportunity | Risk | Convenience |
| Site | | | |
| Street block | | | |
| Neighborhood | | | |

FIG. 2.—Typology of preventive efforts

1. *Level of Analysis.* Physical environment may dissuade potential offenders at the neighborhood, street-block, or site levels. Of most interest from the perspective of this volume are links between physical design, crime, and prevention at the community or neighborhood level. Several factors are relevant. Neighborhood-level dissuasion of potential offenders is more limited than are prevention efforts at the street-block or the site level. The level of analysis changes the demarcation between insiders and outsiders. At the street-block level a much higher proportion of offenses is likely to be committed by outsiders than at the neighborhood level. We assume that "outsiders" are the prime focus of crime prevention efforts or are the class of persons for whom such efforts are likely to be most effective. "Insiders," with their superior knowledge of locale, are probably much more difficult to dissuade. Preventive efforts at the street-block level probably result in more immediate displacement of offenses than do preventive efforts at the neighborhood level, although there is no empirical evidence on this point.

2. *Offenders' Images.* The three dimensions of potential offenders' images in figure 2 are opportunity, risk, and convenience. The most salient opportunities are, for street crimes, the relative abundance of appropriate victims, and, for burglaries, the relative abundance of property worth stealing. "Risk" describes the relative chances of being detected, acted against, chased, apprehended, and arrested at or near the site of the crime. "Convenience" refers to ease of ingress and egress with minimal time delay and fuss.

Research on physical environment and crime at the neighborhood and the street-block level can be organized using the preventive typology in figure 2. Although the research does not directly assess offender decisions and behaviors, links between crime and environment point toward these offender-based processes. These relations suggest the potential preventive capability of manipulations of the physical environment at different levels on different aspects of offender images.

## II. Physical Environment and Crime: Subneighborhood Dynamics

This section considers the crime prevention orientation inherent in defensible-space theory. Research conducted after 1979 is reviewed. For a detailed discussion of earlier work, see Taylor, Gottfredson, and Brower (1980). For more critical comments on the theory and the research, see Hillier (1973), Mawby (1977), or Mayhew (1979). The related area of crime prevention through environmental design, in many ways a "stepchild" of defensible-space theory, is reviewed by Taylor, Gottfredson, and Brower (1980) and is not pursued here.

### A. *Defensible Space*

Jane Jacobs (1961) proposed the theoretical nucleus of defensible-space theory. On the basis of her observations in Greenwich Village in the late 1950s, she concluded that certain design principles could reduce crime in urban residential areas: principle 1—orient buildings to encourage surveillance by residents; principle 2—separate public and private spaces into clearly differentiated domains; principle 3—situate public places in proximity to intensively used areas. Principles 1 and 3 seek to make the street safer by having more people on the street or watching it. It is assumed that potential offenders will be aware of these higher levels of "natural" surveillance and will be more hesitant about offending. More generally in defensible-space theory, design influences residents' behavior, and residents' behavior influences potential offenders. These two principles fit into the street-block-risk cell of our crime prevention typology. Principle 2, by contrast, hypothesizes that design modifications can directly influence potential offenders' perceptions of an area and their behaviors. It fits into the street-block-convenience cell of the preventive typology.

These ideas were later elaborated and labeled "defensible space" by Oscar Newman (1973*a*, 1973*b*). The design ingredients in Newman's work include (1) the use of real and symbolic barriers to separate residential neighborhoods into manageable units; (2) the creation of opportunities for residential surveillance; (3) the creation of nonstigmatizing exterior designs in low-income housing projects; and (4) the placement of residential areas near safe or nonthreatening areas. The various design features are directed at different targets. Barriers and surveillance opportunities are aimed at influencing residents' behavior, encouraging them to be more "territorial." These principles belong in the street-block-risk cell of the preventive typology. By contrast, the design principles for nonstigmatizing designs and distances from unsafe areas appear geared toward directly influencing the potential offender, by not attracting his interest, and by making entry to the site difficult. They belong in the street-block-convenience cell of the preventive typology.

Later defensible-space theory (Newman 1975, 1979) introduced new design "principles," such as having a low number of persons or households sharing an entranceway.

A study of the revised version of defensible-space theory at the site level (Newman and Franck 1980, 1982) found that physical features such as building height and accessibility had the expected effects on residents' attitudes and behaviors and that these in turn had the expected effects on personal crime and fear. For example, greater building size was associated with less use of adjoining spaces, less social interaction, and lower feelings of control over space. All these were in turn associated with higher levels of personal crime. Thus Newman and Franck confirmed the essential logic of defensible-space theory: physical factors, controlling for sociocultural background, may facilitate certain attitudes toward, and activities in, exterior spaces, and these in turn may make crime less likely.

In terms of our preventive typology, defensible space, particularly, in its latest incarnation, is most clearly relevant to the street-block-risk cell. Newman's consideration of real and symbolic barriers, surveillance opportunities, accessibility, and the anticipated effects of these features on residents' behaviors seem relevant to the risk dimension of offenders' perceptions of a locale. Perceived risk would be heightened because residents would act in a more proprietary and vigilant manner. And, as the theory implies, potential offenders would be aware of these changes. Thus increased risk for potential offenders is achieved by means of the effects of physical environment on residents' attitudes and behaviors.

The key roles played by resident attitudes and behaviors were highlighted in Merry's (1981*a*, 1981*b*) study of a multiethnic housing project. Even though the housing project contained numerous design features consistent with defensible-space principles, crimes and antisocial behaviors were frequent. Merry argued that the cultural diversity of the resident population and the resulting distrust between co-residents prevented accurate characterizations of insiders and outsiders, thereby blocking the emergence of effective informal social control.

Physical features may also influence potential offenders' images of locales even though the features have no effect on resident behavior. Symbolic barriers, or signs of beautification or upkeep, for example, may communicate to the offender the increased likelihood that residents who witness antisocial or criminal activity within their domain will take action of some sort. This suggests that offenders base environmental inferences largely on physical elements in the locale (cf. Craik and Appleyard 1980). Such possibilities are not addressed by defensible-space theory but are addressed by territorial approaches to understanding crime and its prevention.

*B. Territorial Perspectives*

Two models of territorial functioning relevant to crime prevention at the street-block level have been proposed. One, developed by Altman and his colleagues, focuses on offender perceptions and actions. The other, developed by the present writers, focuses on residents' attitudes and behaviors.

1. *Territoriality and Burglary Prevention.* Brown and Altman's (1981) model is based on Altman's (1975) threefold classification of territories. Going from primary to secondary to public territories, one progresses from territories that are more central to occupants to those that are less central and from territories where residents spend more time and are more likely to see people they know to territories where they spend less time and are more likely to see strangers. Primary territories are places like a living room at home, a dorm room, or an office. Secondary territories, where one spends some time and may see acquaintances, are places like a fraternity or sorority house, neighborhood bar, or club. Sidewalks in front of the home and yard may be secondary territories. Public territories are temporary, like a seat on a bus or a seat in a theater.

Brown and Altman (1981, pp. 64–65) argue that burglars cross a series of territorial boundaries from public to primary as they proceed from neighborhood, to street, to site, and, finally, to the home. It is proposed that the burglar assesses territorial signs or markers as he passes through different territories. The stronger or more salient are the boundaries, the more likely is the burglar to be dissuaded from crossing the territorial boundary. This decision-making process is hypothesized as especially relevant to experienced burglars.

Two studies provided some support for this theoretical perspective (Brown 1982; Brown and Altman 1983). The features assessed include fixed environmental features, such as surveillance opportunities; semifixed features, such as fences and shrubbery; decoration, such as name plates on the side of the house; and behavioral traces, such as toys or garbage cans left out. Territorial signage, broadly interpreted, varies with the probability of burglarization at the street-block, but not at the site, level. This suggests that offenders "read" the signage at the block level and use other clues to pick particular targets on that block. It seems likely that temporary attributes of and around the site—no one home, neighbors across the street not at home, and other factors reflecting the probable location of nearby residents—determine site selection. The results of these studies are limited, in that they do not substantiate the hypothesized effect of the signage on potential or actual offenders, nor do the results confirm the hypothesized sequence of boundary transitions. The conceptual model is offender centered and dynamic, but the research to date has not captured these features of the theoretical framework.

Nonetheless, the Brown and Altman (1981) model provides an interesting framework for investigating the possibility that offenders directly "decode" various physical cues in the environment and then use that information to determine target location. This theme fits well with the proposed framework in this essay and with Rapoport's (1982) discussion of how the environment can send "nonverbal messages."

The linkages discussed between physical environment features and burglary seem most appropriately placed in the "street-block-risk" cell. Most of the physical elements pinpointed make the potential offenders' work more risky. Surveillance factors and boundaries that lengthen entry and exit time make detection more likely. Behavioral traces likewise suggest more guardians and more chances of detection.

Unfortunately, the Brown and Altman perspective and other territorial approaches have little application at the neighborhood level. Territorial functioning is concerned with control over delimited, bounded spaces (Sundstrom 1977; Taylor 1978). Groups can appropriate and control territories, but it appears that these groups must be fairly small (Brower 1980), particularly in high-crime, lower-income areas. Groups that do not function face-to-face, such as the residents of a sizable neighborhood, do not know enough about one another and cannot rely enough on one another to be able to control a territory as large as a neighborhood or community unless there are very clear-cut differences such as race between the potential offender population and the resident population. Barring such cases, jurisdiction over a territory as large as a neighborhood and usage of territorial signage to communicate that control to potential offenders are simply not feasible.

2. *Territoriality and Street Crime.* The territorial model developed by Taylor and various colleagues is resident centered (Brower 1980; Tay-

lor et al. 1980; Taylor, Gottfredson and Brower 1981, 1984, 1985; Brower, Dockett, and Taylor 1983; Taylor and Brower 1985; Taylor 1986). The central construct is residents' territorial functioning, that is, the attitudes that residents have toward adjoining and nearby outdoor spaces, the behaviors they exhibit in those territories or expect co-residents to exhibit in those territories, and territorial markers such as upkeep, gardening, and ornamentation. The focus is on street blocks; the assumption is that the street-block population can function as a small group (cf. Unger and Wandersman 1983). It is further expected that social bonds between co-residents on the street, whether they are superficial or more substantial, support and encourage the group to exercise territorial control over their street.

The main types of crime to which this model is relevant are street crimes such as assaults, robbery, and muggings. The model suggests that a primary orientation of the territorial system is toward maintaining local order in public spaces. Crimes such as burglary, which are carried out at times and places where the probability of detection is low, escape the purview of this model.

The conceptual model is relevant to fear of crime. It is hypothesized that, on blocks where local social ties and territorial functioning are "strong," residents' fear levels will be lower. Thus this model is distinct from the Brown and Altman (1981) model in its resident-centered focus, group orientation, focus on street crime, and inclusion of fear.

In a Baltimore study of sixty-three street blocks, the proposed model received strong support. At this level, territorial functioning and, to a lesser extent, physical environment features are linked with street-crime rates and fear levels. Thus territorial dynamics at the street-block or face-to-face group level can be modeled.

This territorial framework, like Brown and Altman's, probably cannot be applied at the neighborhood or community level. This is because the drastic enlargement of the outside spaces under consideration at the community level changes the nature of the peoples' bonds to places. Territoriality does not apply to such a large scale as a neighborhood. Further, neighborhood populations, in contrast to street-block groupings, are not face-to-face groups. Therefore, the interpersonal dynamics necessary to undergird stronger territorial attitudes and behaviors are not available. Theoretical frameworks at the community or neighborhood level that incorporate physical environment features cannot include territoriality as a construct.

## III. Incivilities and Crime: Neighborhood Dynamics

An incivilities theory concerned with crime, fear, and physical environment and explicitly couched at the neighborhood level has been developed by Hunter (1978), Wilson and Kelling (1982), and others. It is concerned with links between physical deterioration, crime, and fear. Other perspectives linking crime and physical environment at the neighborhood level have either been loose, open-ended models rather than articulated theories or have attempted to transplant block-level theories to the neighborhood level. Studies that have dealt with offender rather than offense rates (e.g., Kobrin and Schuerman 1982) are not covered.

Hunter (1978) focused on the environment-fear links. Drawing on a symbolic interactionist perspective, he argued that residents want to see other residents behaving in public places in ways that are supportive of public norms. These norms may vary from area to area, but each community is said to have its own set of shared, subcultural norms (Fischer 1975). These public norms are not entirely subject to local whim or preference but are circumscribed by the larger concept of "citizenship," which links residents to one another and to the state.

Hunter suggested that there can be social or physical signs of civility or observance of the public order. Social signs of civility include politeness in public space encounters or provision of assistance in critical situations. Social signs of incivility include public drinking or drunkenness, public drug abuse or drug sale, "hey, honey" hassles, and children out of control. Physical signs of civility include well-trimmed lawns, bushes, and yards; clean steps, sidewalks, and alleys; well-painted houses; clean windows; and unlittered playgrounds with intact equipment. Physical signs of incivility include vacant or abandoned or run-down housing, vacant lots that are overgrown or littered, graffiti, autos in disrepair, littered alleys, and scattered bulk trash such as refrigerators.

Hunter links the spatial patterning of social and physical incivilities with neighborhood change. According to this perspective, it is natural to expect social and physical incivilities at the boundaries of communities, but residents perceive a breakdown in the local social order when incivilities become commonplace throughout a community. This awareness of social and physical incivilities creates fear among residents.

Whereas Hunter focused on fear as an outcome of incivilities, Wilson and Kelling (1982) focused on criminal invasion. They argue that residents will then be less likely to get involved in situations in which help is needed if social and physical incivilities make residents fearful. If residents become less vigilant and less action oriented, capacities for local social control will erode. As a result, the area will become "vulnerable to criminal invasion."

Graphically, Wilson and Kelling propose the following causal sequence:

| | | | | | | | | | | |
|---|---|---|---|---|---|---|---|---|---|---|
| Disorder | → | Physical and Social Incivilities | → | Fear | → | Less Informal Social Control | → | More Crime | → | More Fear |

Physical changes in environment such as increased dilapidation—through cognitive effects on fear levels and behavioral effects on informal social control—will lead to criminal invasion and higher crime levels. This suggests, as a crime prevention strategy, that major physical improvements—renovating rundown housing, razing or restoring abandoned housing, cleaning up of playgrounds and public areas, and strict enforcement of housing codes—will lower fear levels, thereby increasing levels of informal social control and decreasing the chance of invasion from outside offenders.

The incivilities perspective addresses the issue of offender perceptions and behaviors. Wilson and Kelling argue that potential offenders "read" the physical and social signs of civility or incivility in an area and use this information in deciding whether to "move into" an area. Wilson and Kelling discuss mostly potential street criminals, but the same logic would apply to potential property offenders. The incivilities thesis can be placed in the neighborhood-risk cell of the preventive typology developed in Section I.

An argument concerning prevention can be developed from the incivilities thesis. Crime prevention can be mounted at the neighborhood level by decreasing social and physical incivilities and thereby increasing potential offenders' perceptions of risk. When potential offenders see signs of social and physical incivilities in a locale, they assume there is a low level of informal social control in the locale and that municipal authority is also weak. The potential offender therefore concludes that the area is "ripe" for criminal invasion. By implication, then, potential offenders can be dissuaded from invading an area by a removal or diminution of signs of incivility. The diminution of such signs would lead offenders to reevaluate the amount of resident vigilance in the locale and therefore the risks of carrying out an offense. This should lead ultimately to less crime by outsiders.

The incivilities thesis proposes a process that links resident and offender perceptions with residents making inferences about potential offenders and offenders making inferences about potential interventions by residents. Physical environment serves as a complex cluster of cues about the locale and likely resident behaviors, cues that are interpreted by residents and potential offenders alike.

The incivilities thesis thus offers a comprehensive perspective that links offenders and residents, an explicitly longitudinal argument that allows further elaboration through articulation with theories of neighborhood change (e.g., Taub, Taylor, and Dunham 1984) and plausible application in a cross-sectional perspective. The incivilities argument suggests that potential offenders, when deciding which of several possible neighborhoods to "choose" as a site for crimes, will take into account the comparative amounts of incivilities in the various neighborhoods.

Problems with the incivilities thesis that are pertinent to the focus of this essay include its insensitivity to local context and the assumption that incivilities are interpreted similarly regardless of the particular situation as well as a dramatically oversimplified treatment of the dynamics of informal social control (cf. Greenberg and Rohe 1986).

Notwithstanding its appeal, little evidence on the incivilities thesis is available. Much of the evidence to date (Lewis and Maxfield 1980; Skogan and Maxfield 1981) has focused on links between incivilities and residents and has used questionable measures of incivilities. Links between incivilities and offender perceptions remain uninvestigated.

## IV. Physical Environment and Crime: Neighborhood-Level Findings

This section considers several recent studies that have addressed the relation between physical environment and crime, using neighborhoods or comparably sized areas as the unit of analysis. We review the theoretical orientation and method of each study, major relevant findings, and, where appropriate, we comment on the limitations.

### A. *Atlanta: Six Neighborhoods*

Greenberg, Rohe, and Williams (1982) and Greenberg and Rohe (1984) assessed the physical design differences between six different neighborhoods in Atlanta. The six neighborhoods consisted of three pairs matched for race and income.

Using an "opportunity" perspective on crime, the authors hypothesized that higher-crime neighborhoods should have more potential crime targets, such as commercial locations, and should be more accessible, for example, have wider, more heavily used thoroughfares. They proposed to contrast this purely physical model with a defensible-space/informal social control model. The latter would suggest, the authors maintained, that high- and low-crime neighborhoods would not only have different design characteristics but that territorial attitudes, expectations about informal social control, and local social networks would be stronger in the lower-crime neighborhoods.

The findings tended to support the opportunity perspective but not the defensible-space/informal social control perspective. The physical differences observed were by and large in the direction predicted by an opportunity approach. Both boundary characteristics and internal features appeared important.

Internal layouts differed in several ways. In lower-crime neighborhoods there were fewer major streets and more small, one-way and two-lane streets; smaller proportions of nonresidential land use; more "private" parking arrangements such as driveways instead of lots or on-street parking; and a greater preponderance of single-family dwellings. These findings suggest that neighborhoods where the boundary and internal arrangements were more "private" had lower crime rates. From the offender perspective, the physical arrangements made entry and movement more difficult (neighborhood-risk and neighborhood-convenience cells of our preventive typology), perhaps thereby increasing perceived risks of detection or apprehension and impeding convenient access to crime sites.

Attitudinal and behavioral self-report differences, however, were not so clear-cut. No consistent differences between high- and low-crime neighborhoods were observed on informal surveillance, informal social control, and local social ties. The authors concluded that "the results of this study lend far more support to the opportunity model of crime in residential areas than to the defensible space model" (Greenberg and Rohe 1984, p. 57).

As we have pointed out above, however, defensible space is not a neighborhood-level theory. It does not make predictions about differences between neighborhoods. It does make predictions about differences between public housing sites. Related territorial perspectives make predictions about differences between street blocks. Thus the Atlanta study could not serve as a test of defensible-space or territorial perspectives because it was carried out at the wrong level of analysis for making such tests. Defensible-space and territorial functioning are both clearly tied to small-group dynamics.

The most important point about the Atlanta study may be the suggestion that physical differences in boundary and interior characteristics are associated with more or less crime at the neighborhood level.

### B. *Baltimore: Sixty-six Neighborhoods*

Taylor and his colleagues examined neighborhood-level responses to crime in a random sample of sixty-six neighborhoods in Baltimore, Maryland (Taylor, Gottfredson, and Shumaker 1984; Taylor, Shumaker, and Gottfredson 1985). The purpose of the study was to determine why some neighborhoods responded more vigorously when confronted with the threat of crime. The key hypothesis was that, in neighborhoods where the social, affective, and attitudinal bonds between the residents and the neighborhood were stronger, the resident population would be more likely to respond informally and organizationally to crime and related problems. These bonds included local social ties, attachment to place (Shumaker and Taylor 1983), sense of community, and neighborhood confidence. It was expected that crime and incivilities would be positively linked and that more extensive incivilities would be associated with weaker formal and informal responses to crime.

The zero-order correlations between physical environment and crime rates were substantial and significant. The incivilities factor correlated .63 with crime rates, and the land-use factor correlated .38. But these two physical dimensions also correlated strongly with sociodemographic characteristics of the neighborhood—both correlated −.64 with the sociodemographic composite. When sociodemographic composition of the neighborhood was controlled for, the environment-crime link was reduced to nonsignificant levels. This analysis suggested that the design-crime link was "spurious," in that both design and crime were influenced by the relative position of the neighborhood in the urban stratification.

The Baltimore results raise serious questions about the causal sequence proposed by the incivilities thesis. Once social class was taken into account, the deterioration-fear-crime links did not hold up; however, they do not contradict the Atlanta results. Very different types of environmental features were measured in the two studies. The Atlanta measures focused on issues of accessibility versus privacy, or openness versus closedness. The Baltimore assessments, although containing some comparable measures such as type of street layout and lanes of traffic, concentrated mostly on matters of upkeep versus deterioration. The two studies together suggest that physical environment features, reflective of privacy versus accessibility, are more relevant to crime than are physical measures of upkeep versus deterioration.

### C. *Hartford: Asylum Hill Demonstration Project*

During the 1970s a demonstration project was carried out in one lower-income neighborhood in Hartford, Connecticut (Gardiner 1978; Fowler 1981; Fowler and Mangione 1981). Organizational, policing, and physical changes were sequentially phased in over a period of several months. Physical changes consisted of closing off some entrances to the neighborhood, embellishing other entranceways and thereby making them into more "symbolic" entrances, and changing traffic patterns so that most through traffic was funneled onto a few streets.

The theoretical framework used was a loose informal social control perspective. Three rough hypotheses were generated. First, if resident-based control over the streets in the neighborhood could be reasserted—if the streets could be "turned back" to the residents—then street crime and burglary would go down. Second, changes in physical environment characteristics, resulting in less through traffic, would give the streets a more "residential character," increase the use of these streets by people in the neighborhood, and increase residents' control over these locations. Third, police and citizens had to work together to achieve these goals.

The demonstration was evaluated twice, once in 1977 after the changes had been in place for at least a year and once in 1979 after the changes had been in place for at least three years. Attitude surveys of residents in both the study neighborhood and the city as a whole were carried out in 1973, 1976, 1977, and 1979. Police data were collected, and vehicle and pedestrian counts were made. Changes in the neighborhood were compared with changes overall in the city and were deemed significant if the improvement was greater than that observed citywide.

The first evaluation found changes in residents' reported attitudes and behaviors, but these were not as significant as had been hoped. Residents reported walking more, increased ease of stranger recognition, and increased watching of others' houses but reported no general attitude or perception changes such as a decrease in fear levels, or increased levels of neighborhood confidence, or increases in informal social control. In terms of crime there appeared to be a shift in street crime from the smaller streets to the main streets to which through traffic had been diverted. There were increases in burglary and robbery arrests.

There were several changes in the neighborhood between the first and the second assessments. Many community organizations became quiescent. Block-watch activities in the area slackened considerably. There was housing rehabilitation going on in some parts of the neighborhood. In several locations there had been an increase in social incivilities. The planters at the symbolic entranceways were no longer cared for. Localized team policing eroded in part because of citywide manpower shortages. In short, there had been a general wearing away of the "treatments" that had been implemented earlier.

At the second assessment in 1979, positive perceptual and attitudinal changes were observed, but improvements in crime were not. Many of the expected resident-based changes were noted. For example, residents reported being more attached to, and reported increased use of, the neighborhood. Fear of robbery and of burglary were lower than expected. The authors interpret these as indicators of increased informal social control; however, crime levels did not decline. Neither burglary nor robbery were below the level expected given changes in crime rates elsewhere in the city. There had also been a return of serious crime, spreading back from the major arteries to the side streets. The authors concluded that the design changes had increased informal social controls but not sufficiently to affect crime rates.

An alternative explanation is that the more positive attitudes reported in 1979 were a function of the decreases in crime that had been observed earlier from 1976 to 1977. In other words, there may have been a "lag" between changes in crime levels and changes in attitudes toward, and perceptions of, neighborhoods.

The Hartford results are intriguing and suggestive, but it is difficult to generalize from the results. The overall pattern suggests the following interpretation. When the physical changes were first implemented and were complemented by changes in police practices and local organizational activity, less criminal activity was observed. That is, when physical changes enhancing the "privacy" and lowering the accessibility of the neighborhood were supported by other types of changes, a dampening effect on crime was observed. But when these organizational and policing changes weakened, the physical features alone were not capable of preventing crime.

In the context of the prevention typology being used in this essay, the physical design changes in Hartford were designed to reduce the level of convenient access experienced by the offenders and to increase offenders' perceptions of risk. The latter was to be accomplished by "privatizing" the streets, thereby stimulating residents' use of and watch over them. Thus the prevention efforts were aimed at the neighborhood-risk and the neighborhood-convenience cells of our preventive typology.

## V. Conclusions

The bulk of empirical evidence linking crime and physical environment has emerged from analyses at the subneighborhood level that focused on housing projects or street blocks. The guiding theories, primarily defensible-space or territorial approaches, are dominantly resident centered, however, and do not clearly articulate linkages between environment and potential offenders. (Brown and Altman's territorial theory explicitly addresses offender perceptions but is geared toward site-level dynamics.) At the street-block level, future researchers need to make empirical connections between resident dynamics, physical features, and offender perceptions and actions.

Researchers have attempted to extrapolate street-block level theories to the neighborhood level. Greenberg et al. (1982) attempted to test defensible space at the neighborhood level, and Fowler (1981) and Fowler and Mangione (1981) attempted to apply a variant of territorial theory at the same level. These extrapolations are inappropriate because the theories are inextricably linked to small, functioning face-to-face groups. Such groups do not exist at the neighborhood level. Making such extrapolations loses sight of the key processes that drive the theory.

The incivilities thesis is explicitly couched at the neighborhood or community level. It incorporates linkages between residents' attitudes and behaviors, physical and social environment, and offender perceptions and actions. Thus it brings together the critical elements needed for understanding crime-design-prevention links and can be useful in a longitudinal or cross-sectional framework. However, it is also flawed in its treatment of several aspects of community. Empirically, the thesis remains untested, although initial fragmentary evidence suggests that physical environment effects may be more modest than anticipated. Clearly, an important task for future research in this area is to further articulate the incivilities perspective by bringing into closer concordance findings from urban sociology about neighborhood dynamics and by conducting a complete, careful test of the model.

The studies at the street-block and the neighborhood level agree on one important point: simple effects of physical environment on crime range from small to moderate. Direct effects of physical environment, in both the Newman and Franck (1980) and the Taylor et al. studies (Taylor, Gottfredson, and Shumaker 1984; Taylor, Shumaker, and Gottfredson 1985) were modest. At the neighborhood level the Atlanta study indicated a moderate-sized "stand-alone" linkage between design and crime (Greenberg et al. 1982; Greenberg and Rohe 1984). Other studies, however, have been more disappointing. The Baltimore study (Taylor, Gottfredson, and Shumaker 1984; Taylor, Shumaker, and Gottfredson 1985) found that zero-order links between design and crime were "explained away" by relative social status of the neighborhood and by residents' involvement in locale and with one another. The Hartford case study found that physical features were linked to crime only when other conditions were also present, such as community policing and active local organizations (Gardiner 1978; Fowler 1981; Fowler and Mangione 1981). Consequently, it appears that alteration of physical environment features cannot have stand-alone crime prevention effectiveness. Resident dynamics are key mediators of the environment-crime linkage.

The results do suggest some points about offenders' perceptions of physical environment. Physical features that make the neighborhood boundaries and interior more or less private, raising or lowering the perceived risk and convenience of operating in the neighborhood, probably have a low-to-moderate effect on potential offenders' images of communities. But the effect of these features is probably outweighed by other factors such as residents' behavior patterns and the neighborhood's social class. Physical factors indicative of "deterioration," net of neighborhood social class and resident attitudes and behaviors, probably have a negligible effect on offenders' images.

The Hartford results suggest that the crime-preventive or crime-supportive effects of physical environment features at the neighborhood level may be more substantial than the "stand-alone" effects when particular nonphysical conditions are present.

These conclusions have a number of implications. The main practical implication is that, for now, crime prevention efforts should focus on street blocks rather than on neighborhoods. Block-level theories have advanced substantially in recent years. Models describing both the resident-based and the offender-based processes linking design and crime have been specified and tested in several cases. How these processes work in different sociocultural contexts is beginning to be understood. In short, at the subneighborhood level, there have been gains in understanding the how, where, and why of design-crime links.

That these theoretical gains can be implemented in a practical way is currently being demonstrated in an action research project ongoing in Brooklyn (Wandersman et al. 1985). Researchers are collaborating with block organizations to make physical and other changes that will reduce crime and fear.

Design-crime links of weak to moderate strength probably do exist at the neighborhood level. Stronger linkages are dependent on other, nonphysical setting conditions, but we have little evidence about the processes mediating such connections. Physical environments do not directly cause or prevent crime except in the case of security hardware. They influence crime by way of their influence on residents' and offenders' perceptions and behavior. Given what we know from neighborhood studies about local organizations, local social networks, senses of community, and intergroup relations, a number of processes could be examined as possible resident-based mediators of the design-crime link. The framework we developed in Section I is an attempt to identify some of the factors that shape the offender-based design-crime linkages.

The best model will probably be the one that assesses both resident-based processes and offender-based processes and that indicates how the two interrelate. Up to now, most of the empirical data gained has been from residents, using survey and behavioral instruments.

In these future neighborhood-level models, linkages with the other aspects of neighborhood life that are connected with crime—sociocultural, social, political, organizational, and historical contexts—need to be systematically examined and incorporated. A comprehensive, multifaceted approach to understanding crime-design-prevention-resident-offender links in communities, part of which is the crime-design link, seems a far way off.

REFERENCES

Altman, I. 1975. *The Environment and Social Behavior.* New York: Columbia University Press.

Bennett, T., and R. Wright. 1984. *Burglars on Burglary: Prevention and the Offender.* Hampshire, England: Gower.

Berger, P., and M. Luckmann. 1963. *The Social Construction of Reality.* New York: Anchor/Doubleday.

Brantingham, P. J., and P. L. Brantingham, eds. 1981. *Environmental Criminology.* Beverly Hills, Calif.: Sage.

Brantingham, P. J., D. A. Dyreson, and P. L. Brantingham. 1976. "Crime as Seen through a Cone of Resolution." *American Behavioral Scientist* 20:201–73.

Brower, S. 1980. "Territory in Urban Settings." In *Culture and Environment,* vol. 4, *Human Behavior and Environments: Advances in Theory and Research,* edited by I. Altman, A. Rapoport, and J. Wohlwill. New York: Plenum.

Brower, S., K. Dockett, and R. B. Taylor. 1983. "Residents' Perceptions of Site-Level Features." *Environment and Behavior* 15:419–37.

Brown, B. B. 1982. "House and Block as Territory." Paper presented at the annual meeting of the American Psychological Association, Washington, D.C., August.

Brown, B. B., and I. Altman. 1981. "Territoriality and Residential Crime: A Conceptual Framework." In *Environmental Criminology,* edited by P. J. Brantingham and P. L. Brantingham. Beverly Hills, Calif.: Sage.

———. 1983. "Territoriality, Defensible Space and Residential Burglary: An Environmental Analysis." *Journal of Environmental Psychology* 3:203–20.

Clarke, R. V., and D. B. Cornish. 1985. "Modeling Offenders' Decisions: A Framework for Research and Policy." In *Crime and Justice: An Annual Review of Research,* vol. 6, edited by Michael Tonry and Norval Morris. Chicago: University of Chicago Press.

Cohen, L. E. and M. Felson. 1979. "Social Change and Crime Rate Trends: A Routine Activity Approach." *American Sociological Review* 44:588–608.

Craik, K., and D. Appleyard. 1980. "Streets of San Francisco: Brunswik's Lens Model Applied to Urban Inference and Assessment." *Journal of Social Issues* 36:72–85.

David, P. R. 1974. *The World of the Burglar.* Albuquerque: University of New Mexico Press.

Downs, R., and D. Stea. 1977. *Maps and Minds.* New York: Holt, Rinehart & Winston.

Fischer, C. S. 1975. "Toward a Subcultural Theory of Urbanism." *American Journal of Sociology* 80:1319–41.

Fowler, F. G. 1981. "Evaluating a Complex Crime Control Experience." In *Applied Social Psychology Annual,* vol. 2, edited by L. Bickman. Hillsdale, N.J.: Erlbaum.

Fowler, F. G., and T. W. Mangione. 1981. *An Experimental Effort to Reduce Crime and Fear of Crime in an Urban Residential Neighborhood: Reevaluation of the Hartford Neighborhood Crime Prevention Program.* Draft executive summary. Cambridge: Harvard/Massachusetts Institute of Technology, Center for Survey Research.

Gardiner, R. A. 1978. *Design for Safe Neighborhoods*. Washington, D.C.: U.S. Government Printing Office.

Green J., and R. Taylor. 1986. "The Theory of Community Policing." Paper presented at the annual meeting of the Academy of Criminal Justice Sciences, Orlando, Fla., March.

Greenberg, S., and W. Rohe. 1984. "Neighborhood Design and Crime: A Test of Two Perspectives." *Journal of the American Planning Association* 49:48–61.

Greenberg, S., and W. Rohe. 1986. "Informal Social Control." In *Urban Neighborhoods*, edited by R. B. Taylor. New York: Praeger.

Greenberg, S., W. Rohe, and J. Williams. 1982. "Safety in Urban Neighborhoods." *Population and Environment* 5:141–65.

Hillier, B. 1973. "In Defense of Space." *RIBA Journal*, pp. 539–44.

Hunter, A. 1978. "Symbols of Incivility." Paper presented at the annual meeting of the American Society of Criminology, Dallas, November.

Jacobs, J. 1961. *The Death and Life of Great American Cities*. New York: Vintage.

Kaplan, S., and R. Kaplan. 1982. *Cognition and Environment: Functioning in an Uncertain World*. New York: Praeger.

Kobrin, J., and L. A. Schuerman. 1982. "Interaction between Neighborhood Change and Criminal Activity." Draft final report. Los Angeles: University of Southern California, Social Science Research Institute.

Letkemann, P. 1973. *Crime as Work*. Englewood Cliffs, N.J.: Prentice-Hall.

Lewis, D. A., and M. G. Maxfield. 1980. "Fear in the Neighborhoods: An Investigation of the Impact of Crime." *Journal of Research in Crime and Delinquency* 17:160–89.

Lynch, K. 1960. *The Image of the City*. Cambridge, Mass.: MIT Press.

Mawby, R. I. 1977. "Defensible Space: A Theoretical and Empirical Appraisal." *Urban Studies* 14:169–79.

Mayhew, P. 1979. "Defensible Space: The Current Status of a Crime Prevention Theory." *Howard Journal of Penology and Crime Prevention* 18:150–59.

Merry, S. E. 1981*a*. "Defensible Space Undefended: Social Factors in Crime Prevention through Environmental Design." *Urban Affairs Quarterly* 16:397–422.

———. 1981*b*. *Urban Danger: Life in a Neighborhood of Strangers*. Philadelphia: Temple University Press.

Newman, O. 1973*a*. *Architectural Design for Crime Prevention*. Washington, D.C.: U.S. Government Printing Office.

———. 1973*b*. *Defensible Space: Crime Prevention through Urban Design*. New York: Macmillan.

———. 1975. *Design Guidelines for Creating Defensible Space*. Washington, D.C.: U.S. Government Printing Office.

———. 1979. *Community of Interest*. New York: Doubleday.

Newman, O., and K. A. Franck. 1980. *Factors Influencing Crime and Instability in Urban Housing Developments*. Washington, D.C.: U.S. Government Printing Office.

———. 1982. "The Effects of Building Size on Personal Crime and Fear of Crime." *Population and Environment* 5:203–20.

Pred, A. 1981. "Of Paths and Projects: Individual Behavior and Its Societal

Context." In *Behavioral Problems in Geography Revisited*, edited by K. R. Cox and R. G. Golledge. New York: Methuen.

Rapoport, A. 1982. *The Meaning of the Built Environment*. Beverly Hills, Calif.: Sage.

Rengert, G., and J. Wasilchick. 1985. *Suburban Burglary: A Time and Place for Everything*. Springfield, Ill.: Thomas.

Shumaker, S. A., and R. B. Taylor. 1983. "Toward a Clarification of People-Place Relationships: A Model of Attachment to Place." In *Environmental Psychology: New Directions and Perspectives*, edited by N. R. Feimer and E. S. Geller. New York: Praeger.

Skogan, W. In this volume. "Fear of Crime and Neighborhood Change."

Skogan, W., and M. G. Maxfield. 1981. *Coping With Crime*. Beverly Hills, Calif.: Sage.

Sundstrom, E. 1977. "The Physical Environment and Social Behavior." In *Social Psychology*, edited by L. Wrightsman. Monterey, Calif.: Brooks/Cole.

Taub, R. P., D. G. Taylor, and J. D. Dunham. 1984. *Paths of Neighborhood Change: Race and Crime in Urban America*. Chicago: University of Chicago Press.

Taylor, R. B. 1978. "Human Territoriality: A Review and a Model for Future Research." *Cornell Journal of Social Relations* 13:125–51.

Taylor, R. B. 1986. "Toward an Environmental Psychology of Disorder." In *Handbook of Environmental Psychology*, edited by D. Stokols and I. Altman. New York: Wiley.

Taylor, R. B., and S. Brower. 1985. "Home and Near Home Territories." In *Home Environments*, vol. 8, *Human Behavior and Environment: Current Theory and Research*, edited by I. Altman and C. Werner. New York: Plenum.

Taylor, R., S. Brower, W. Drain, and K. Dockett. 1980. "Toward a Residential-based Model of Community Crime Prevention: Urban Territoriality, Social Networks, and Design." Manuscript 2044. *JSAS: Catalogue of Selected Documents in Psychology* 10:29–30.

Taylor, R. B., S. D. Gottfredson, and S. Brower. 1980. "The Defensibility of Defensible Space." In *Understanding Crime*, edited by T. Hirschi and M. Gottfredson. Beverly Hills, Calif.: Sage.

———. 1981. "Territorial Cognitions and Social Climate in Urban Neighborhoods." *Basic and Applied Social Psychology* 2:289–303.

———. 1984. "Block Crime and Fear: Defensible Space, Local Social Ties, and Territorial Functioning." *Journal of Research in Crime and Delinquency* 21:303–31.

———. 1985. "Attachment to Place: Discriminant Validity and Impacts on Disorder and Diversity." *American Journal of Community Psychology* 13:525–42.

Taylor, R. B., S. D. Gottfredson, and S. A. Shumaker. 1984. "Neighborhood Responses to Disorder." Unpublished final report. Baltimore: Johns Hopkins University, Center for Metropolitan Planning and Research.

Taylor, R. B., and M. M. Hale. 1986. "Testing Alternative Models of Fear of Crime." *Journal of Criminology and Criminal Law* (in press).

Taylor, R. B., S. A. Schumaker, and S. D. Gottfredson. 1985. "Neighborhood-Level Link between Physical Features and Local Sentiments: Deterioration, Fear of Crime, and Confidence." *Journal of Architectural Planning and Research* 2:261–75.

Triandis, H. 1977. *Interpersonal Behavior.* Monterey, Calif.: Brooks/Cole.

Unger, D., and A. Wandersman. 1983. "Neighboring and Its Role in Block Organizations: An Exploratory Report." *American Journal of Community Psychology* 11:291–300.

Wandersman, A., P. Florin, D. Chavis, R. Rich, and J. Prestby. 1985. "Getting Together and Getting Things Done." *Psychology Today* 19(11):64–71.

Weaver, R., and Carroll J. 1985. "Crime Perceptions in a Natural Setting by Expert and Novice Shoplifters." *Social Psychology Quarterly* 48:349–59.

Wilson, J. Q., and G. L. Kelling. 1982. "Broken Windows: The Police and Neighborhood Safety." *Atlantic* 249(3):29–38.

# Index